PENGUIN BOOKS

WITHOUT A DOUBT

Marcia Clark was a prosecutor in the Office of the Los Angeles District Attorney, trying cases for more than thirteen years before becoming the lead prosecutor in the criminal trial of O.J. Simpson, the "Trial of the Century." She lives on the West Coast with her sons.

Teresa Carpenter is a Pulitzer Prize–winning journalist and the bestselling author of *Missing Beauty* and *Mob Girl*. She lives in New York City with her husband, the writer Steven Levy, and their son.

Without a Doubt

Marcia Clark

with Teresa Carpenter

With a new Afterword

PENGUIN BOOKS

To my sons

PENGUIN BOOKS
Published by the Penguin Group
Penguin Putnam Inc., 375 Hudson Street,
New York, New York 10014, U.S.A.
Penguin Books Ltd, 27 Wrights Lane,
London W8 5TZ, England
Penguin Books Australia Ltd, Ringwood,
Victoria, Australia
Penguin Books Canada Ltd, 10 Alcorn Avenue,
Toronto, Ontario, Canada M4V 3B2
Penguin Books (N.Z.) Ltd, 182–190 Wairau Road,
Auckland 10, New Zealand

Penguin Books Ltd, Registered Offices:
Harmondsworth, Middlesex, England

First published in the United States of America by Viking Penguin,
a member of Penguin Putnam Inc. 1997
This edition with a new afterword by Marcia Clark
published in Penguin Books 1998

10 9 8 7 6 5 4 3 2 1

The names of Ms. Clark's two children have been changed
to protect their privacy.

ISBN 0-670-87089-7 (hc.)
ISBN 0 14 02.5977 5 (pbk.)
(CIP data available)

Printed in the United States of America
Set in Adobe Garamond
Designed by Jaye Zimet

Contents

Prologue

April 30, 1996

This is painful. I don't even know where to begin. When I try to find a starting place, headaches, backaches, this damned cough that won't go away, all pull me down. My confidence collapses out from under me and I have to curl up on the couch until I feel better. I hope for sleep. But sleep won't come.

I drink Glenlivet, but then you probably know that. And you know that I smoke Dunhills. And you know, or at least you think you do, that my "addictions" include crossword puzzles and detective novels, and that I have "unpredictable" taste in men. I am reading now from *People* magazine. I've never talked to anyone from *People*, but they seem to like me. Funny—when the media likes you, they can take scraps that your friends toss out, and spin them into flattering fairy tales. (But when they don't like you, they take the scraps from ex-husbands.) God, don't get me started. I look at myself in the *Globe* and see a man-crazy lush. And then I look at *Ladies' Home Journal* and see a serene professional woman at the top of her game. And I look and look and look and don't see myself at all.

All the attention I've gotten—it's something I still cannot wrap my mind around. There was a time when I would have been thrilled by it. Back in high school, I wanted to be an actress. No fifteen-year-old wants to be an actress without wanting to be famous. Somewhere along the line, I outgrew wanting to be famous. I wanted to do something truly useful with my life. I wanted to make a real contribution. The irony, of course, is that the most serious job I ever undertook turned into a damned circus.

During the fourteen years I spent as a deputy D.A. for Los Angeles County, I believed in justice. To me it wasn't an abstract idea. Before the Simpson case, I'd prosecuted twenty homicides. I'd brought cases against twenty defendants who I believed in my heart were guilty. And all but one jury agreed. I felt The Force was with me, if you know what I mean. Even in the difficult cases, it had been my experience that when people got onto juries they usually acted in better conscience than they did in their private lives. I had faith they'd rise to the occasion.

On the morning of June 13, 1994, when Nicole Brown Simpson and Ronald Goldman were found—their bodies butchered and discarded like grass clippings—all of that changed. Their murderer, O. J. Simpson, would turn justice on its head. By virtue of his celebrity, he would be coddled by worshipful cops, pumped up by star-fucking attorneys, indulged by a spineless judge, and adored by jurors every bit as addled by racial hatred as their counterparts on the Rodney King jury. O. J. Simpson slaughtered two innocent people, and he walked free—right past the most massive and compelling body of physical evidence ever assembled against a criminal defendant.

I am not bitter. I am angry. And I ask myself over and over again, *How could this jury fail to see? Was there something else we could have done? Something more we could have said?* How many times did I lead that jury along the blood trail? Following the bloody prints of that rare and expensive Bruno Magli loafer—size 12, the same as Simpson wears—leading away from the bodies, up the front steps to the rear gate of Nicole Brown's condo. A blood trail leading right to the foot of O. J. Simpson's bed, for God's sake! On Ronald Goldman's shirt, a head hair that matched those of the defendant. Simpson's hair. On the navy-blue cap dropped at the crime scene, the same black hairs, as well as a carpet fiber matching those found in the defendant's Bronco. Stop and think for a moment. How did all this stuff get there? The defendant's blood is found where there shouldn't be blood. The defendant's hair where there shouldn't be hair. There was enough physical evidence in this case to convict O. J. Simpson twenty times over.

Defendant "not guilty" on all counts.

I feel bad about a lot of things. I feel bad for the Browns and the Goldmans, for the way the system failed them. I feel bad for my fellow deputies, who so often stayed at the courthouse until two or three A.M., working themselves into a stupor of fatigue. I feel bad for all the *good* cops at LAPD who got a bum rap because of the transgressions of a few. I feel bad for the D.A. investigators who pulled off some truly extraordinary feats of behind-the-scenes investigation. I feel especially bad for our young law clerks, who poured their hearts into this case for fourteen months—only to have them broken by that unthinkable verdict. For many, it was their first case. How could anyone explain to them what an anomaly it was? No other criminal case in American history has generated such massive publicity. No other criminal defendant has entered the dock so perfectly insulated by personal wealth and public sympathy. What those fresh, idealistic young clerks saw, to their dismay, was a defendant who was virtually unconvictable. And that, quite understandably, shook their faith in American justice.

I'm ready now to do this. I'm upright at my laptop, ready to begin this story. Every time I feel overwhelmed by the desire to curl up on the couch and pull an afghan over my head, I'll fight that urge down, because this is important. I just ask you to understand how hard this is. The event is so huge, it's difficult to figure out how to shrink it into words, or even to make a start. The definitive account, I cannot give you. No one can. But I can tell you what the case meant to me. I can tell you about the strategies and the courtroom skirmishes. About moments of exultation and days of heartache. I can give you my private reflections. Particularly those. Because that's what it all comes down to. Just as all politics is local, all good history is personal.

The Has-been

About the best thing you could say about my life before Monday, June 13, 1994, is that my problems were *my* problems. Nobody else was interested in them. No one except a handful of intimates, including my friend Lynn Reed, another deputy D.A. in the L.A. County District Attorney's office. For weeks, she'd been urging me to file for divorce.

"Do it! Just do it!" she would tell me. I knew she was right. I'd been separated from my husband, Gordon, for about six months. In January he had moved out of our dilapidated tract house in Glendale, a suburb of Los Angeles. He was not deserting me; I'd asked him to leave. Our marriage had degenerated into the gray misery that appears vivid only in retrospect. I will not go into particulars because they are no one's business but our own.

Suffice it to say that the previous year had been hell. I'd just left the D.A.'s Special Trials Unit for a management job in Central Operations. That allowed me to spend evenings with my sons. Tyler was just a baby; Matthew was then a toddler. I enjoyed better prospects as a pencil pusher, but the work left me in a state of chronic discontent. The trade-off for a carpeted office and a shot at six figures, I discovered, is boredom. Absolute, brain-numbing boredom. Old line lawyers like me are adrenaline junkies. We like getting out on the streets with the police and arguing before juries. Scheduling cases for other attorneys to try is a drag.

So I was unhappy with my job and unhappy in my marriage. I knew I could limp along like this, or I could take some decisive action to turn my life around. In December 1993, I asked for my old job back. And I asked Gordon to leave.

I'd spent most of my adult life with a man under the same roof, and now, trying to cope with plumbing problems, cable bills, and the furious demands of being a working mother, I was constantly terrified. It was, I knew, a hell of my own devising—I had no grounds to complain about it. At times I was ready to break down and ask my husband to come back. Yet I resisted the temptation to return to a lousy marriage just for the sake of expediency. Even so, I let the separation drag on for six months before I took Lynn's advice: "Let him know it's over." So I went out and bought myself one of those do-it-yourself divorce kits. Money was tight; it seemed like a good idea at the time. But the lawyer who represents herself has a fool for a client.

There were no reporters in the bushes, no paparazzi peeping through the windows, when I filed the divorce papers on June 10. Three days later, O. J. Simpson crashed into my life like a meteor.

On Monday morning, June 13, 1994, I was struggling to get out of the house. Any parent with a preschooler knows the drill.

Honey, we're late.

I don't want to go!

Shoe!

By the time he reaches nursery school, that same child will run off happily to play with his pals.

I had a parking space in the lot behind the Criminal Courts Building, and that morning when I pulled in I waved to one of the attendants, Arturo.

"Mucho trabajo hoy?" he called out to me.

"Sí, como siempre."

In fact, that morning, I had no court appearances, no witness interviews. There was nothing on my calendar to indicate that this would be anything other than a short-skirt day. No need for a "believe me" suit.

It was 9:30, and I was late—as I usually am when I don't have to make it in under the gavel. Well, the truth is, I am just chronically late. It's a character flaw, but one I can't seem to rectify. My friends even have a term for it: Marcia Standard Time.

I'm not proud of being late, but it does afford a slight advantage at the CCB. It allows one to avoid the crush at the elevators, which are, by far, the slowest in L.A. County. During rush hours, attorneys who are headed for Special Trials on the eighteenth floor and imprudent enough to arrive on time often find themselves fifteen to twenty minutes behind schedule for court, because the "express" elevator—specially designed by outside consultants—inevitably stops mid-route. Latecomers, however, running on Marcia Standard Time, often enjoy a clear shot.

At the eighteenth floor, the elevator doors open upon Mordor, Land of Darkness: my private name for the courthouse's dreary labyrinth of smog-soiled cement hallways. On some mornings a touch of claustrophobia leaves me breathless until I open the door of my high-ceilinged office, where I find sunlight streaming through the window. For seconds afterward, motes of dust swirl like snowflakes in that strong, welcome light.

No civil servant takes a window for granted. Certainly not me. During my early years on the job, I toiled away in sunless, airless cubicles in a series of far-flung outposts of the L.A. District Attorney's dominion. West L.A., Beverly Hills, Culver City. In my early days as a baby D.A., I caught mainly deuces—drunk driving charges. Every once in a while I'd get to do the preliminary hearings on a homicide. That was what made the overtime worthwhile. Murder is so much more compelling than other crimes. There's more complexity, more sophisticated forms of evidence. You get tool marks. You get blood markers. There's stuff to play with.

I was always itching to get beyond the preliminaries to trials. Real trials. Criminal trials where you have to think quickly, react quickly. I wanted to be drawn into an experience that was totally absorbing. Trial work is especially appealing to the workaholic. I'd go through the docket like Pac-Man, grabbing cases no one else would touch, putting in ten- to twelve-hour days in the process. What gave rise to this fervor is hard for me to explain. Work offers a defensible escape from a private life on the skids. Working myself to the point of exhaustion left me feeling purified. Exhilarated. I think it also gave me a sense that I was cheating mortality. Ever since I was small, I've been dogged by the premonition that I would die young. I couldn't imagine living past forty. Forty-five, tops. That kind of deadline adds a sense of urgency to everything. It's like—I can keep on living if I run fast enough.

Beyond that, the courtroom is the ideal venue for someone who likes to argue. For most of my life I've been contentious, and it's gotten me into a lot of trouble. But verbal dexterity and strong opinions are welcomed at the bar. There are clearly delineated rules of combat, rules that favor reason. Humans may be capricious—but, to my naive way of thinking, justice was not.

I was assigned to the Juvenile Division, where, early on, I volunteered for the "county run." That meant traveling an exhausting circuit of county juvenile court offices, some of them in neighborhoods so dangerous no one even went out for lunch. The advantage of the "run," however, was that it allowed me to try one juvy case after another. In juvenile cases, unlike regular trials, the defendant almost always testifies. For the most part the defendants are kids pumped up on ego. They love the attention they get by simply taking the witness stand. It would have been sad, except that the juvy penalties aren't terribly severe. Generally the kids get HOP, home on probation. So I logged in a lot of time cross-examining the accused. By the time I was finally transferred Downtown to Central Trials in 1984, I had a reputation as a hard charger.

Anyway, in 1984, the year I turned thirty, the district attorney, Ira Reiner, made it a policy to scout out the rising stars and apprentice them to veteran prosecutors. I was one of those who came to his attention. Reiner brought me over to the CCB and assigned me to a man I revered: Harvey Giss. Harvey was a courthouse legend. He was so handsome that women jurors swooned during his final arguments. He was also brilliant, irreverent, and one great trial attorney. To this day Harvey Giss remains the only prosecutor in L.A. County who has ever gotten a death-penalty conviction against a client of Leslie Abramson, the lawyer who would later mount the successful, if unorthodox, defense of Erik Menendez.

But a trial lawyer has only so many of those big cases in him. By the time I moved my files into the windowless office, hardly bigger than a utility closet, across from Harvey's, he confessed to me that these cases were wearing him out. Harvey had been going through the wringer with a defendant named James Hawkins, a tough man to prosecute because his neighbors considered him a good Samaritan. One day, outside his father's grocery store, Hawkins had shot a man who was supposedly trying to rob a local woman. Upon closer investigation, it turned out that our "hero" had gunned down his victim long after the woman had left the scene. That wasn't all. Detectives looking into the murders of two drug dealers developed evidence that led to none other than James Hawkins. Harvey had fought like hell and won a conviction on the grocery store shooting; he'd just received that second case for filing. By the time I moved my files and scrawny potted philodendron into the CCB, the double homicide was nearing its trial date.

Harvey assigned me the ballistics part of the case. Every night I hauled home volumes of arcane texts on firearms, studying them until my eyes blurred. Eventually I gained such expertise that I could have passed the qualifying tests given to police firearms experts. As far as the Hawkins case was concerned, however, this was academic: we hadn't found a murder weapon. A search warrant served on Hawkins's home had turned up several different guns, but none capable of firing the bullets found in the bodies of our victims. Then, in one of several bizarre turns in this case, Hawkins escaped from a holding cell in the CCB and went on the lam.

In the wake of that escape, both Harvey and I were assigned around-the-clock security. For myself, I frankly thought this was overkill; the defendant had always been rather cordial to me. But Harvey, I knew, might well have been in danger. Hawkins blamed him personally for destroying his local-hero rep. Several weeks later, during a wild shoot-out, the fugitive was finally caught. The search of his car turned up two more guns—and they were the same make and caliber as the weapons used in the double homicide.

Hawkins had taken a metal file to the inside of both barrels, trying to obliterate the fine stria that leave their imprint on bullets. It wasn't easy to tell if the guns had fired any rounds, let alone the ones that killed those drug dealers. But I finally got to put all my ballistics knowledge to use. Working with Sergeant Lou Barry of the Sheriff's Department, I was able to match the bullet from one of the victims' bodies with the bullet Hawkins had fired into a wall during a random robbery. It was a coup, and it made me the deputy darling of the moment.

That trial was almost two years of pure hell. Hawkins's attorney was a crafty, tenacious brawler named Barry Levin who made us fight for every motion. It took eight months to pick the jury and another excruciating thirteen months to try this monster. But I watched everything Harvey did, and I learned from him. I learned how to organize a big case, one with forty or fifty witnesses. I learned where you object and where you don't. I learned how to keep my head up and take the hits.

I also learned how to hold up in the face of a difficult judge. Ours, Marsha Revel, was a former prosecutor, and like a lot of old D.A.s who've gone on to the bench, she seemed intent upon demonstrating her impartiality by favoring the defense. She lost no opportunity to discredit us. Harvey's objections were overruled so frequently that I had to count paper clips to distract myself from the pain of it all. The worst came during closing arguments, when the defense objected over and over again, intent on throwing Harvey off stride. Though this is regarded as a bush-league tactic and most judges won't tolerate it, Revel refused to intervene. The objections increased to the point that Harvey couldn't utter three consecutive words without getting cut off. The judge called for a recess and Harvey returned to his seat. He looked beaten.

"Marcia," he told me wearily, "it's time to cut my losses. I'm going to end after the break."

"But Harvey," I replied, "you can't just leave out the rest. It's important."

"You can cover it in your argument," he told me. "Barry won't want to bully you in front of the jury. This is best for the case. You can do it."

It's possible Judge Revel caught the look of panic on my face, because—in an uncharacteristic gesture of thoughtfulness—she recessed court for the weekend immediately after Harvey concluded.

If anyone was going to finish our opening arguments, it would have to be me. Yet, I found myself paralyzed. Over the months, I had been ground into the dirt by the same stresses that had gotten to Harvey. My spirits were at an all-time low. I didn't have much fight left. Above all, I was inexperienced. I'd never delivered a summation where this much was on the line.

That weekend I went to a cousin's wedding in a suburb of L.A. I shouldn't have even attempted a social ordeal like this. I knew perfectly well that I was physically and mentally exhausted, that I should have spent my two days preparing, or better yet, getting some sleep. Instead, I tried to put on a happy face in front of friends and family. I was doing all right until I caught sight of my mother standing off to one side. You remember how it was when you were a kid? You'd fall and scrape your elbow and you could hold in the tears—until you caught sight of your mom? Then the dam would burst.

"What's wrong?" she asked me. That's all it took.

I threw my arms around her, sobbing. "I can't do it, Mom. It's just too much. I'll never be able to pull it together."

This was not the kind of scene that is welcome at a wedding. And, anyway, these outbursts were not my mother's style.

She patted me on the shoulder.

"You'll pull it off, Marcia. You always do."

Her words hit me like a splash of cold water. But she was right. I wasn't a child anymore. I was an adult. A professional. I couldn't count on my mother—or anyone else—coming to my rescue. I realized, as I stood sniffling in the reception line, that if I were to be saved, I'd have to save myself. Life's hardest lesson.

The following week, I marched back into court and delivered the rest of the damned summation. I don't know that I did such a brilliant job of it. Probably not. The point is, I finished. I didn't give in to despair. The memory of that experience gave me a world of confidence during the years, and trials, to come. As Lillian Hellman once said, "Half the battle is being able to take the punishment."

We got our conviction. Harvey transferred out to a quieter post in Santa Monica. I moved into his office and became one of five deputies

at Special Trials, the unit that handles L.A. County's high-profile
cases. Over the next five years, I caught some of the cases that might
ordinarily have come to Harvey. One of these was the case of *People v.
Robert Bardo.*

The Bardo case was known more popularly as the Rebecca Schaeffer
case, after its victim, a pretty twenty-one-year-old actress who played
Pam Dawber's sister on the sitcom *My Sister Sam.* An obsessed fan
named Robert Bardo wrote Rebecca a series of letters. Unfortunately,
she wrote one back. It was just a generic thank-you-for-your-interest,
but it was enough to make the twisted son of a bitch think they had
made some kind of connection. He hired a private investigator, who
turned up Rebecca's address. Then he showed up at her apartment
with a bag containing copies of his letters to her, a paperback of *The
Catcher in the Rye,* her publicity photo, and a gun.

When he rang the bell, Rebecca answered it herself. That caught
him off guard. I guess he was expecting she had servants to sweat the
small stuff. She was gracious enough to shake his hand, but then eased
the door shut on him. Bardo, apparently offended by the rebuff,
retreated to a nearby restaurant to collect his wits. He went into a
men's rest room to load the last chamber in his handgun. Then he
went back to Rebecca's apartment. This time, when she came down to
answer the buzzer, he gestured that he wanted to give her something.
For whatever reason, she opened the door. And he shot her point-
blank through the heart.

Bardo was my first "celebrity" case. I didn't ask for it; it simply
landed on my desk. The deputies at Special Trials do not as a rule
clamor for big assignments like hounds after hush puppies. Our office
has learned from hard experience that every celebrity case carries with
it the potential for disaster. Though it can be a career-maker, as the
Manson case was for Vincent Bugliosi, it is just as likely to be a sink-
hole. And the more titanic the celebrity, the deeper the potential drop.

When Bardo landed on my desk, I'd never really had any experience with the press. To me, the attention this case attracted only created annoying complications. The trial was covered, gavel-to-gavel, by
a new cable network called Court TV. In the Bardo case, the fact that

hearings were broadcast seemed to have little impact on the proceedings. The real problems began when TV and print reporters "interviewed" witnesses, causing several to drop out of sight before _we_ could get to them. Journalists invariably wound up telling their sources things about the case, which meant that the integrity of the witnesses' memory was compromised. Only after I sat down with each of them and did a careful remedial interview was I able to get clean statements, unencumbered by hearsay.

It was my job to convict Bardo of the heinous crime of murder while "lying in wait"—one of several "special circumstances" that can put a defendant in line for the death penalty.

Bardo was claiming he suffered from a peculiar if convenient mental deficiency that precluded premeditation. Had he made this argument fly, he would have avoided the special-circumstances sanction. The defense hired Park Dietz, a psychiatrist of national renown, to examine Bardo. Then it submitted two hours of videotaped interviews between the two, offered as proof that the defendant could not have premeditated his gruesome crime.

At one point on tape Bardo reenacted his killing of Rebecca Schaeffer. As I watched that scene, something bothered me. I rewound it and watched it again. And again.

Bardo had claimed that the gun was in his bag, and that when he pulled it out to look for something else, Rebecca panicked and grabbed the weapon. In the struggle, he claimed, it discharged accidentally, killing her. But in Bardo's reenactment, he kept his right arm behind his back and drew it out as though he were holding a gun. That was the physical equivalent of a Freudian slip—something that would tip the court off to the fact that this was no accidental or impulsive shooting. It did precisely that.

I played the tape for Dino Fulgoni, the brilliant no-nonsense judge who sat on this case. (Bardo had forgone his right to a jury trial.) Fulgoni could see with his own two eyes that this was no accidental or impulsive shooting. He sentenced Bardo to life without parole.

Over the two years I worked on that case I got to know Rebecca Schaeffer's parents—particularly her mother, Danna—extremely well. If anything will remind you that the practice of law is not just an intellectual exercise, it's observing the effects of a homicide upon those who loved the victim. Misery spreads out from a murder in ripples, blighting everything it touches. Some survivors are too damaged to be helpful. Others are so driven by the desire for revenge that they can actually obstruct a prosecutor's efforts. The Schaeffers were neither. They managed their grief with patience and dignity.

I was always happy to take Danna Schaeffer's calls. Sometimes we talked about the legal aspects of the case. Sometimes she'd just want to talk about Rebecca. On a couple of occasions I sent her letters to express thoughts too painful to convey in person.

"Even as I'm writing this I'm crying again," I wrote her on one occasion. "As I feared, once you start letting yourself feel, it's an endless thing. . . . If all goes well, the miserable slimy piece of cow dung will be convicted of everything. I can offer only that I will do everything in my power to see that her loss is avenged—I cannot promise justice because to me justice would mean Rebecca is alive and her murderer is dead. The one thing I can promise you is that when this is all over I will honestly be able to tell you that I gave it my all, my very best, without reservation. Beyond that you have my love and my empathy forever."

After receiving that letter, Danna actually called to comfort *me*. She was so intelligent, so sensitive and caring—the kind of mother everyone should have. A guilty verdict was such a small thing to give that family in light of what they'd lost, but it seemed to bring them some measure of peace. It felt good to be their champion. It was the sort of feeling I'd missed during that year I spent in management: the exultation of exhausting myself for the sake of a principle, and in some small but significant way, avenging someone whose life had been stolen. The long days and late nights; my desk strewn with coffee cups, Werther's candy wrappers, notepads, and dog-eared briefs: I missed all that.

I think I was probably the only person in departmental history actually to ask for a demotion. As I carried my potted philodendron back down the hall to take my place among the grunts, I almost could hear my colleagues whispering, "What kind of woman gives up a six-figure salary? Can't she cut it?"

On June 13, 1994, after nearly six months back in Special Trials, my caseload still wasn't up to speed. Arriving in the office that morning, I

propped the door open with a wooden doorstop and confronted a desk
that was nearly clean! For a moment I studied that expanse of scuffed
cherry veneer. It struck me as a reproach. No case on my calendar was
anywhere near trial. The only thing I had going was a kidnap-murder
I'd just taken to the grand jury. My plans for the morning were to hole
up and study the "murder book," a large black binder of witness
reports compiled by the investigating officers. Later in the day, I'd
planned to go to Lynn Reed's bridal shower.

The phone rang.

"Hey, Clark, got a minute?"

"I got one or two, man; what's up?"

It was Detective Phil Vannatter of the LAPD's Robbery/
Homicide Division.

I liked Phil. We'd worked together on a murder case two years earlier. The body never turned up, but we'd managed to get a conviction
based on the DNA in a single drop of blood. Phil was crusty and hard
to push around, but somehow we got to be good friends. We'd run
into each other all the time and go out for drinks. We talked a lot
about how great it would be to work another case together. But he was
close to retirement and it didn't seem likely that we'd ever team again.

"I've got this double," Phil continued evenly. "I need to run it
by you."

Cops often do this, call a D.A. to see if the facts of a case justify a
search warrant.

"Okay," I said, pulling out a fresh yellow county-issue notepad.
"Fire away."

"O. J. Simpson. Do you know who this guy is?"

The name stirred only a vague recollection.

"Wasn't he in _Naked Gun_ or something?"

I've never been much of a sports fan. I couldn't even remember for
sure what game O. J. Simpson had played. I just had the general
impression that he was a has-been.

Phil ticked off the basics:

Two bodies—Simpson's ex-wife, Nicole Brown, and an unidentified male companion. Murdered.

Location. Brentwood. On Bundy Drive.

A lot of blood, in fact a _trail_ of blood, leading away from
the bodies, but cause of death not immediately apparent.

A beeper. A blue knit ski cap. A brown leather glove.

Phil, his partner, Tom Lange, and two other detectives from the West L.A. station had gone out to Simpson's house to notify him of his ex-wife's death. They hadn't found Simpson but they talked to his daughter, who left Phil with the impression that her father had taken an "unexpected flight."

"You know when it left or where it was going?" I asked Phil.

"Chicago," he told me. "I think it left around midnight or one."

Phil also mentioned that they'd found a bloody glove on the pathway.

"Mate to the other?" I asked, referring to the glove at Bundy.

"Someone's out there checking, but yeah," Phil said. "It sure looked that way to me."

What he wanted to know was, Would a judge approve the warrant?

Now, keep in mind that when a D.A. gives a cop advice on a warrant, that D.A. must rely solely upon the facts as represented by the officer. On the morning of June 13, all I knew about this case was what Phil had just told me. I trusted him. We were buds. I realized that Phil was doing me a favor: he was throwing business my way, and I appreciated it. This one looked promising. If there was blood, that meant lots of DNA work. Physical evidence was my specialty.

"Yeah," I told him. "Sounds like you have enough there."

I told Phil that I'd go out to Rockingham to baby-sit the cops serving the warrant if he wanted. He thought that was a good idea and said he'd call me after he got the warrant typed. About an hour or so later he phoned.

"Warrant's signed," he told me. "We're on our way."

Signed? I thought. Wasn't he going to read me the final draft? I found that a little odd, but decided not to make an issue of it.

"Oh, Phil," I caught him before he hung up. "Have you got someone really good on this?"

I meant the assignment of a criminalist, the technician from the police crime lab who bags and tags the evidence at a crime scene. A prosecutor's fortunes at trial rise and fall on the strength of the criminalist's work. If evidence is overlooked, mishandled, or destroyed, you can never recoup your loss. A great criminalist is both paranoid and anal-retentive. He's suspicious of a pebble if it looks out of place.

He seizes more rather than less. He makes sure everything is meticulously packaged, precisely labeled. He goes to Jesuitical lengths to ensure that the chain of evidence is intact. That's the ideal, anyway; unfortunately, most of the technicians at the police crime lab fell well short of it. The decent ones moved up in the department, or out of it. The bad ones, unfortunately, stuck like barnacles to the hull of the county bureaucracy.

Over the years I'd gotten into beefs with the LAPD over who should be assigned to collect and analyze evidence. In the Hawkins case, I'd peppered the brass with letters and phone calls demanding that they give me more senior firearms experts to redo some of the haphazard work already performed. Tempers ran so high that they told me to take the case to the Sheriff's Department, where, they figured, I'd be given the standard treatment for a pushy babe: the cold shoulder.

They were wrong. The Sheriff's Department came through for me in spades. It loaned me a meticulous expert who helped me salvage what would otherwise have been a disaster. I'd scrapped with the LAPD on several other cases, too, hassling them to make sure they didn't botch the fundamentals.

"How about Doreen Music?" I asked Phil. Doreen was a field criminalist who had recently been promoted to a supervisory position in the Firearms Section. Phil and I had worked with her on our no-body case, where she had been fantastic.

"We've already got someone on it," Phil replied. I thought he sounded uneasy. "I heard he was okay," he said.

"Okay" was not terribly reassuring. Typical LAPD, I thought to myself. Whoever's next up gets it. "What's his name?" I asked.

"Dennis Fung."

Brentwood was definitely not my neck of the woods. The conventional wisdom about this upscale 'hood was that it was a place where people air-kissed, compared implants, and did lunch. During my stint in Beverly Hills, I discovered that the clichés were pretty much true. The hills north of Sunset were jammed with multimillion-dollar estates hidden behind many millions more dollars' worth of landscaping. All to create the illusion of privacy. The farther north you went, and the higher you climbed into the hills, the narrower the streets became, and the more obscure the street signs were. I strained to find Rockingham Drive.

There was a cruiser parked up ahead, where a uniformed officer directed traffic. A few civilians milled around outside an iron security gate. Some of them had the nervous, unfed look of reporters. Still, the scene was not exactly bustling with activity. I got the impression that the main show had come and gone.

I slipped unnoticed past the press and through the gate, where I got my first look at the larger Tudor-style house overhung with old eucalyptus trees. The manicured grounds seemed to glow an unnatural shade of green in the midday light. In one corner of the lawn stood a child's playhouse. O. J. Simpson might be a has-been, I thought, but he must still be bringing in serious bucks to manage the upkeep on this place.

A white Ford Bronco sat nosed into the curb on Rockingham. Extending up the driveway from the rear of the vehicle was a trail of reddish-brown spots. The rust-colored droplets stopped several yards short of the house. The front door was open and in the foyer I could see more droplets. They appeared to be blood. Gingerly, careful to disturb nothing, I stepped inside.

Search warrant or no, it always felt weird to me to walk into the house of a stranger. But there's also a voyeuristic fascination: what a person chooses to surround himself with tells you a lot about him. This interior of O. J. Simpson's house was exquisitely appointed with overstuffed white furniture, Lalique glass, and Berber carpeting. And yet the place gave off a faint odor of mildew and neglect.

Beyond the living room lay the gleaming kitchen. Seated at a counter was Bert Luper, one of Phil's buddies from Robbery/ Homicide. Balding, with tufts of curly hair rimming his head and bifocals perched at the end of his nose, Bert was an old-timer in RHD. He had an offbeat sense of humor, and the two of us always clicked. It was good to see a familiar face. Bert motioned me over.

"Tom and Phil here?" I asked him.

"O.J. showed up here, back from Chicago," he told me. "Phil and Tom scooped him up and took him downtown for questioning."

The house seemed awfully quiet. No one was doing any searching that I could see.

"Where's the team?" I asked.

"They left to check out the murder site, on Bundy." The criminalists, Bert explained, had done some preliminary work here collecting blood from the driveway and foyer; they'd return later in the afternoon, when Phil and Tom could get back to oversee things. Great, I thought. No wonder things are moving at a worm's pace. Still, I couldn't fault Phil and Tom for leaving the crime scene to interview Simpson. You get your best shot before a suspect has had the chance to learn enough, or collect his wits sufficiently, to compose a convincing lie. By this point Simpson was, at the very least, a potential suspect.

I was checking my watch, wondering whether to return to the office, when I noticed a couple of guys in sports jackets approaching. They had the unmistakable swagger of detectives. I was familiar with most of the downtown guys and I knew these weren't from Robbery/Homicide. They had to be from the West L.A. station, so Brentwood was their jurisdiction. The older of the two identified himself as Detective Ron Phillips. He introduced me to his companion, Detective Brad Roberts. We shook hands and they asked me whether anyone had shown me around the house. I was about to reply when a third detective joined the party. He was a real straight-arrow, hair closely trimmed, shirt pressed a little more neatly than the others'.

"Marcia," said Ron Phillips, "this is Detective Mark Fuhrman."

So much has been said and written about Fuhrman since then that it is difficult to conjure a pure and unbiased recollection of him. He seemed calm, professional, on top of his game. He was not particularly personable. Normally in a situation like this, you lighten the morbidness with some banter. But there was none of that with Mark Fuhrman. Instead, as I think back on it, he was politely condescending.

It was Fuhrman, however, who seemed most thoroughly familiar with the facts of the case. And it was Fuhrman who ended up giving me the Grand Tour. He led me out the back door of Simpson's house, which opened onto a patio and an impressive little grotto. Off to one side, a waterfall cascaded over natural boulders into a large amoeba-shaped swimming pool. To the south of the pool lay a Jacuzzi and three adjoining guest rooms. As we strolled, Fuhrman gave me a clear, no-bullshit account of the events of the early morning.

The guest house on the left, he told me, was where Vannatter and Lange had found a young black woman named Arnelle, O. J. Simpson's daughter by an earlier marriage. I remembered Phil had said she'd been pretty shaken up when he told her Nicole was dead.

Fuhrman himself hadn't interviewed Arnelle. He'd gone to the middle guest house, where he'd found a white male named Brian Kaelin, who, for some reason, everyone called Kato. Fuhrman awakened Kaelin at around six A.M. and began to question him about the previous evening's activities. Kato told him how he had heard "a thump" on his rear wall. The sound was so loud he thought it might have been an earthquake.

Fuhrman told me how he'd parked Kato in the kitchen to wait for Phil. Then, for my benefit, he retraced his own steps through the main house. I followed him past a large pool table and through a trophy room studded thickly with awards, plaques, and photos. We left by the front door. Then Mark turned left to an alleyway that cut along the south side of the house. I hadn't even noticed it when I first walked up the drive. We went through one metal gate, then another. Even on that bright, sunny day, the overhanging trees left the path dark. The air back there felt damp. The ground was littered with leaves, dirt, and debris. When we got to the point where the back of an air conditioner overhung the path, Mark stopped.

"Here's where I found the glove," he said, pointing to the ground.

"So it was you who found it," I said.

"Yeah, it was lying right about here." He indicated a spot a foot or so in front of the air conditioner.

"You didn't pick it up?" I asked him, already worrying about the possibility that he might have carelessly contaminated the evidence.

"No," he answered scornfully. He knew what I was getting at. "I never picked it up. I left it there for the criminalist.

"I figure on his way down he must have run into this"—he indicated the air conditioner—"and he dropped the glove without knowing it."

It was past noon, and yet the pathway was so dim and isolated that I actually felt relieved to get back into the sunlight.

We checked out the pool house, which was outfitted with a kitchen and a room that could function as a bedroom. I stuck my head in and looked around.

"Sure as hell nicer than any place I've ever lived," I remarked.

Fuhrman didn't comment. During this entire walk-through he'd refrained from small talk. Once I got used to it, I kind of admired the severe simplicity of his manner.

As we walked the lawn that sloped north toward Ashford, we came to a bronze statue of a man in football uniform. He was holding a helmet.

Fuhrman stopped in front of it.

"He got that when he won the Heisman Trophy," he said, as if it was something I should know. I sneaked a look at Fuhrman out of the corner of my eye. He was staring at that statue with unguarded awe.

I've thought about that moment often. How ironic: Mark Fuhrman, the man who supposedly lived and breathed to frame O. J. Simpson, stood beside me in the bright June sunlight, indulging in a moment of outright hero worship.

Fuhrman would later claim to have found a bloody fingerprint on the back gate at Bundy, as well as an empty Swiss army knife box on the edge of the tub in O. J. Simpson's master bathroom. It's worth noting here that during our tour of Rockingham, he did not *once* mention either the print or knife box to me. (Later we found a line concerning the print in his notes, but by the time those reached my desk, the Bundy scene had long since been washed down.)

"Hey, Marcia, come upstairs. I want to show you something."

It was Brad Roberts. I followed him up the spiral staircase, where the wall was lined with photographs, mostly shots of O. J. Simpson with various white fat cats.

It was on that stairway that I got my first look at the face of Nicole Brown Simpson.

She was blond, with handsome, almost mannish, features. Her hair, teeth, and skin all had that gloss peculiar to the West Side elite. In some of the photos she was with a pair of lovely brown-skinned

children, a boy and a girl. They all wore ski attire. Her face was difficult to read. The expression in all the photos was uniformly happy,
but her eyes were glazed. She had—how would you describe it—a
thousand-yard stare.

By now, I knew that the Simpsons had been divorced for two
years. I found it peculiar that he still had her pictures everywhere. The
photos of *my* ex were long gone from walls and end tables. I peeked
into the master bedroom suite. From that vantage point I could see
only the top and one side of the bed. Brad Roberts knelt on the floor.
He reached under the box spring and, using his fingertips, pulled out a
framed photo. It showed Nicole and her husband in evening dress.

"Is that the way you found it?" I asked.

"Yep," he replied. "Just like that. Facedown. Under the bed."

"Make sure they get a photo of that," I told him.

By now, it was almost one o'clock, and the search team still had not
returned. What the hell was going on? Bundy was on my way to the
freeway, so I decided to swing by. And there I found the real mob
scene. Jammed into the intersection of two winding residential streets
were scores of neighbors, reporters, and lookie-loos straining for
glimpses of a modest Mediterranean-style condo partially obscured by a
screen of foliage. I muscled my way past them to a uniform guarding
the perimeter and gave him my card.

"Vannatter called me," I told him. "I just came from Rockingham.
Any chance I can get in there?"

"Sorry, no one's allowed," he told me apologetically.

I suppressed my irritation. I hadn't been formally assigned to this
case, so I was in no position to pull rank.

"Okay if I look from here?" I asked him.

"Sure," he said. "But watch out for the press."

No shit. Pretty soon they were going to need riot police to keep
this bunch in line.

Relegated to the status of a spectator, I stretched my neck to get a
look past the front gate at what was left of the killing ground. From
outside the yellow tape, I could see the stain that covered the landing
of a set of cement steps. Someone had bled rivers here.

At every crime scene there's some detail that catches your eye. It's not necessarily the most significant in terms of its importance to the investigation, but it's the thing that stimulates your first visceral connection to the case. This time—for me—it was the bloody paw prints of some animal, probably a large dog, that had tracked through the pool of blood on the landing, leaving a cockeyed trail down the walkway toward the street. Had the animal belonged to the victim? The killer? *What had happened here?*

I couldn't see the members of the search team; they were too deep into the property. (Later, I would see many, many photos of the two criminalists, Dennis Fung and Andrea Mazzola, in their latex gloves and shower caps, combing the grounds for evidence.) What I could see was a police photographer standing at the top of the steps, his camera set on a tripod. He was taking careful perpendicular aim at something on the lower landing. I couldn't make out what it was, but I guessed he was documenting the blood trail that Phil had described to me earlier that morning: the shoe prints leading away from the bodies to a gate at the rear of the property—and the drops of blood running parallel to the shoe prints.

It's almost impossible for a criminal to get away from a crime scene without leaving something of himself there or taking something away. Usually, these things are traces, often invisible to the naked eye. In law enforcement circles this is known as the Locard exchange principle. It holds that when you enter an environment, the environment affects you, and you affect it. In this case, the killer had practically left his calling card.

This one could get interesting, I told myself. I couldn't wait to tell David.

David Conn was my boss; he was also my good friend. Head of the Special Trials Unit, David was witty, temperate, and an excellent judge of character. He was a forceful trial attorney and a cunning tactician. But he didn't have the screw-them-over mentality of so many aggressive prosecutors. I admired that. David had real strength.

When I got back to the CCB, I went directly to David's office and dropped into one of his armchairs.

"You're not going to believe this," I told him. I laid out the details. The glove, the bangings on the wall. The blood on the walkway. The blood in O. J. Simpson's foyer.

"Where's he now?" David asked.

"Phil and Tom took him downtown. He's at Parker Center."

David was intrigued, I could tell.

"Sounds good," he said. And a second later, "Do you want to take it?"

I have this superstition about running hard to get a case. Nothing good comes of it. Sometimes trouble will find you when you're just running in place, so why go looking for it? But I'd been hoping for something bigger to fill out my caseload. And if I was going to catch this case eventually, better to be in on it from day one.

"Sure," I told him. "I'm free. I mean, if you think it's okay."

"You've got it, as far as I'm concerned."

"You think Gil's gonna care about this one?"

Technically speaking, it was up to David to make this assignment. But, of course, his choice was subject to approval by the D.A. Frankly, I didn't know if Gil Garcetti would warm to the idea of my taking this case. During my year in management, I'd been assistant to Bill Hodgman, the director of Central Operations. It had been my job to sit in on meetings with the D.A. when Bill couldn't make it. I enjoyed a good working relationship with Gil, but I spoke my mind freely, sometimes a little too freely for the comfort of the brass.

Garcetti couldn't fail to see my qualifications in terms of handling the DNA stuff. I had a strong record of convictions. I was willing to put in long hours. But it was also no secret around the D.A.'s office that I had just filed for divorce, and consequently had incurred all the single-parenting complications that went along with it. I had also bailed out of a management position, which might cause him to doubt my political fealty.

I also knew that Gil had felt burned over assignments he'd made in recent years. The deputies he'd chosen to prosecute certain cases were tough but, from Gil's perspective, too independent. They'd cut him out of the decision-making, and then it was Gil who'd taken the rap for a series of high-profile acquittals. I could see why he might worry about me. I'm no one's idea of a lapdog. It wasn't that Gil couldn't tolerate assertive women; in fact, he went out of his way to promote them. But I could see how he might look at me and think, *Loose cannon.*

"I'll talk to Gil," David promised me. "In the meantime, you stay in touch with the cops."

Patience is not my strong suit. Wherever I go, I bring a file or book with me in case, God forbid, I'm stuck waiting for someone. By now, I was beginning to feel edgy. Nearly five hours had passed since I'd last spoken with Phil Vannatter. I supposed that he and Tom Lange were finished interrogating Simpson and had him in lockup somewhere. Best not to bug them, I told myself.

So I held off calling. As I was looking back over my notes from the morning's conversation with Phil, I suddenly realized I hadn't called my friend Lynn. I'd completely missed the lunch in her honor. I rang her up and apologized.

"No big deal," she assured me. Considerate, given that her upcoming wedding was a very big deal to her.

"So," she said, "what do you think?"

"Of what?"

"Of this guy Simpson."

It was the first of an infinite number of queries about this case that will likely continue until I am lowered into my grave.

"The evidence is looking pretty strong so far," I said. "I can't wait to find out what he's saying to the cops."

As I was signing off with Lynn, David poked his head into my doorway. "Why don't you give them a call?" he said, sitting down across from me.

He was right. Why sit here like some deb waiting for a prom date?

I rang Parker Center.

"Lange, here."

"Tom, it's Marcia. Just called to find out what our man had to say."

"We talked to him for a while. Took his blood. Got some photos." Typical Tom, wasting no words. He did tell me that Simpson's attorney, a local heavy hitter named Howard Weitzman, had gone to get coffee or something, leaving his client to go into the interview alone. That was odd. What could Weitzman have been thinking?

"Did you tape?" I asked him. This was really important. If they got the thing on tape, we wouldn't have to cope with challenges to their note-taking or memories.

"You bet," he assured me.

"So where're you holding him?" I asked.

"We let him go."

Let . . . him . . . go??

I couldn't fucking believe it!

"You let him . . . *go?*" I was looking at David, whose jaw had dropped.

"He's not going anywhere," Tom told me, sounding a little defensive. "He's too famous."

Give me a break. Sure, he was famous. Sure, it seemed unlikely that he might bolt. But we had a lot more to worry about than whether O. J. Simpson could find a place to hide. *"What if he decides to destroy evidence?"* I wanted to ask Tom. *"What if he starts to intimidate witnesses?"* But I kept it buttoned. The last thing you want to do is get into a pissing match with your investigating officers. I told myself, unconvincingly, that Phil and Tom were doing the best they could, considering that they'd been up since at least two or three A.M. Lange handed me off to Vannatter, and I could hear the fatigue in Phil's voice as he summarized, rather disjointedly, the interview with O. J. Simpson.

"Suspect has a golfing date. . . . Suspect attends his daughter's dance recital. . . . Suspect drives aimlessly in his Bronco making calls from a cell phone." From there it was back to Rockingham, a limo to the airport, and then a flight to Chicago.

"I don't know whether you heard about it," Phil paused to say, "but when we met him at Rockingham, he had a big old bandage on the middle finger of his left hand."

Of course. The blood drops running parallel to the footprints on the drive.

"No shit!" I said. "Where'd he say he got it?"

First, Simpson told them he'd gotten the cut in Chicago, which left him having to explain the blood in his driveway and foyer. But then he seemed to cover himself, saying he'd noticed the bleeding before he left, as he was rushing to get to the airport for the outbound flight. The way Phil told it, it was difficult for me to figure out whether we had an incriminating slip or just a confused explanation. I needed to hear that tape.

"What's doing with the search?" I asked him, hoping earnestly that the search team was not rooting around Rockingham unsupervised.

"We're on our way out there now," he assured me.

"Keep me posted."

"Sure thing." Phil hung up.

I looked at David. For a minute, the two of us said nothing, both silently assessing the magnitude of the cops' blunder. Why had they let Simpson walk? It was true that once the police formally arrest someone, they must be prepared to charge him within forty-eight hours. If they're not sure of their evidence, they can cut him loose, then pick him up later when they have something more solid. But why in this case, where the evidence seemed so strong?

I had never seen the cops this jittery. It was not so much what they said as the reticence in their voices. Something in Phil Vannatter's tone reminded me of Mark Fuhrman's as, earlier in the afternoon, he'd gone out of his way to tell me about Simpson's record on the playing field. At one level, I was hearing the perfectly ordinary sound of people talking. And beneath it, the cackle of *It's the Juice, man. Can you believe it? It's the fucking Juice!*

I didn't work late that night. The cops had made it clear that they weren't going to let me into the loop until they were good and ready.

I caught sight of my baby's head bobbing behind the crocheted curtains of the picture window. The sight of him always gave me a rush of joy.

No sooner had I gotten into the house than a tiny hand grabbed mine and dragged me down the small flight of stairs to the crudely appended addition that was my bedroom. I called it the Swamp. Whenever it rained, water cascaded down the wall behind my four-poster bed, causing mold to grow. I was allergic to it. During the rainy seasons, spring and fall, I was sick all the time with respiratory infections. There seemed to be nothing I could do to get rid of either the dampness or the mold.

There on a patch of well-discolored wall behind the bureau was an evil-looking arachnid the size of a pinball. She was starting a web, apparently at home in the squalor.

Oh, swell.

For the millionth time, I told myself, "We gotta get outta this place." What invariably followed was the dismal realization that we had nowhere to go. I was struggling just to make the mortgage payment on this dump.

Thoughts like these usually triggered an orgy of self-reproach. But not tonight. I found, to my surprise, that I was in an indestructibly good mood. True, the cops had cut loose the suspect in a double homicide when they had a mountain of evidence to hold him. True, they were holding me at arm's length. But you work with what you've got.

The fact of the matter was, I loved having a new case. A new case is like a secret lover. You think about it. Plan for it. It infuses unrelated events with a sense of purpose. We ordered in Chinese food that night, and as we struggled with chopsticks, I found myself mentally composing witness lists. That's how it's supposed to feel. Mind and heart engaged, neither tripping over the other. I hadn't been that happy in a long time.

God, Do We Look Like Morons

"Marcia, it's crazy here!"

It was the delicate, nervous voice of Suzanne Childs on my car phone. I'm weaving in and out of lanes, trying to balance the handset against my cigarette. The damned window on the driver's side won't roll up. I'm struggling to hear her over the traffic.

"You won't believe what's going on!"

"Calm down, Suzanne. Just calm down."

Suzanne is our conscientious and permanently agitated media relations director. This is her third call to me that morning, and every one has been urgent. The press was hounding Gil for details about the Simpson case, she said. Please—did I have any more info I could pass along?

"Geez, Suzanne," I told her. "You probably know more than I do."

Which was true. I'd caught some of the press coverage on TV the night before, and right there in my car, the drive-time radio waves were inundated with breathless news breaks about the double murder at the home of the famous former "football great," as the _L.A. Times_ described our suspect in a long page-one story. The alarming part of all this was that the news reports were telling me all sorts of things I didn't know, turning up witnesses I hadn't even heard of. That meant that every attention-hungry wannabe within broadcast range of L.A. was going to be coming forward with "evidence."

When I reached the office about half an hour later, Suzanne was waiting for me. "Do you think you could call Phil or Tom?" she asked anxiously.

I already had. Several times. They weren't calling me back. I motioned Suzanne to follow me into my office, tossed my purse and files on the floor next to my desk, and picked up the phone to dial RHD. No luck.

"Let's talk to Gil right now," I said to her, hoping that by pooling our information, we could stay abreast of events until I could get with the detectives. We walked to Gil's office, which was unfortunately located right next to the pressroom. Frances, the guard who sat by the door to the D.A.'s office, was staring at a gang of reporters who milled around with jittery energy. As soon as they sighted me, the vultures descended. I waved them off.

"Has it been like this all morning?" I asked Suzanne.

"They're driving us nuts," she moaned.

We've got to get a handle on this, I told myself. _It's gonna spin out of control._

Gil was on the phone. When he saw me, he beckoned me in.

"Close the door," he said.

Our first meeting on the Simpson case. I should remember it more clearly than I do. David was there; I know that. He stood with arms folded tightly, as he does when he's under stress. Some of the brass were there, I believe. Frank Sundstedt and Bill Hodgman. Everyone looked agitated except Gil. He sat behind his desk, wearing his usual mask of composure. He looked toward me, a signal to begin the briefing.

Briefing. What a joke. I barely had more than the top-of-the-hour drive-time reports. But I plunged in gamely.

"Here's what we know about the second victim," I told them. "Ronald Goldman. Twenty-five years old. Would-be actor who works part-time as a waiter at Mezzaluna."

I'd never been to Mezzaluna, but I'd noticed it driving through

Brentwood. One of those trendy West L.A. bistros where tourists go in hopes of sitting next to Michelle Pfeiffer.

"The night of the murders, Nicole Brown—"

"Maiden name?" someone interrupted.

"Looks like it," I replied.

To me, that fact spoke volumes. A woman who has children with her ex usually doesn't choose to take back her maiden name unless she's hell-bent upon reasserting her own identity.

David or someone put in that Nicole and her two children had eaten dinner at Mezzaluna, and Goldman happened to be on duty. She'd apparently dropped her glasses or something, and he went to her place to return them.

"Is that *all* he went there for?" I asked. No one had an answer. We'd have to check whether the two were lovers. I jotted this down on my legal pad.

"How about the search?" Gil wanted to know. "Did we find a weapon?"

Nothing yet.

Someone passed around a copy of the *L.A. Times*. It carried a report that Simpson had roughed up his wife one New Year's Eve and that he'd pled nolo contendere, no contest. This is the standard plea a defendant cops to when he's caught red-handed—and wants to save face.

"When was that?" I asked.

" 'Eighty-nine," David replied.

"Nothing more recent?"

"There may be, but we don't have it."

Now, the fact that O. J. Simpson had beaten his wife didn't mean that he'd killed her. Not all the men who beat their wives end up killing them. But my years in law enforcement had shown me that men who kill their wives have often beaten or abused them in the past. Whether that was what we had here, I couldn't tell. The fact that they'd been divorced for two years still bothered me. Do you carry a torch for an ex after the paperwork's done? I remembered the photo of Nicole that Brad Roberts had pulled out from under Simpson's bed. And I remembered the big glossy shots of her and the children mounted on the wall by the stairs. *Yeah,* I thought. *It could happen.*

"Any word from the cops?" Gil asked me.

"I'm on it," I assured him.

For most of the morning, I'd been trying to reach Phil. After the meeting broke I put in a couple more calls. Finally, around noon, he rang me back.

"Phil, man. What is going on?"

He seemed flustered and apologetic.

"It's the brass, Marcia. They don't want us talking to you."

I let loose a choice expletive.

Phil tried to placate me. "Listen, Marcia. It's just temporary. I know we can work this thing out."

I had a pretty good idea what this was all about. The brass at Parker Center had gotten their knickers twisted over Michael Jackson. What a fiasco that had been—a case of child molestation that went nowhere after Jackson's lawyers reached a settlement in January 1994 with the father of the alleged victim. Not a surprising outcome when you consider that the father had been asking for money. But the cops blamed us, thinking we'd stepped in where we didn't belong and botched a perfectly good case. Now that another celebrity suspect was in play, they were freezing us out.

There has never been any love lost between the D.A.'s office and the LAPD. Invariably, there are disputes on the big cases, where everyone starts grabbing for turf. But never before had I encountered a flat-out stonewall. This could seriously damage our chances for prosecution, if and when we got there. The resistance wasn't coming from Phil and Tom's level. Nor did it seem to be coming from the office of the Chief. From where, then? The LAPD has such a labyrinthine hierarchy that it's almost impossible to tell who's accountable for any given order.

I wanted a showdown with the cops right then and there; so did some of the others. But Gil counseled restraint.

"Hang back," he instructed us. "If the evidence is as strong as it sounds, they'll have to pick him up in the next few hours."

So we hung back, each of us working our private sources. I checked the police crime lab and found out they were testing blood samples. I sucked in my breath. Shit. Whenever I had a case requiring DNA testing, I tried to circumvent the Special Investigations Division, the semiautonomous agency under whose auspices the crime lab fell. Instead, wherever possible, I'd reroute samples to Cellmark Diagnostics in Maryland. Cellmark, a private lab, had done an outstanding job for me in that "no-body" case Phil and I had worked together. But now, stuck in hang-back mode, I was in no position to direct the Simpson samples anywhere. I knew the crime lab was doing a relatively simple DNA test called DQ alpha. I could live with that. With the suspect at large, it was crucial to get this screening test done quickly. If the preliminary markers linked Simpson to the crime scene, the police would have plenty of grounds to arrest.

Later that afternoon, we were huddling in the conference room, kicking around our options, when the call came in from SID. I took it. The blood on the walk at the murder scene matched O. J. Simpson's.

Bingo! There was the evidence the cops needed to charge. I grinned jubilantly at David and Gil and held my wrists together, pantomiming handcuffs. I figured squad cars would be rolling toward Brentwood any minute now.

Like hell. O. J. Simpson remained at large.

And when I arrived at work on the following morning, Wednesday, June 15, he was *still* at large. The papers were filled with speculation about the case. Somehow the *L.A. Times* had gotten wind of the blood-test results. But we were still getting the freeze-out from the cops. Normally, we'd be getting witness statements and reports within twenty-four hours of a crime. This time, we hadn't received so much as a single sheet of paper. Even Gil had realized it was time for a showdown, and he'd finally brokered a meeting with the cops for later that afternoon.

"So, what's the deal?" I wanted to know. "Are they going to arrest?"

"I'm not saying that," Gil replied. "Just go in there and meet with them."

"We shouldn't be kissing ass here!" I muttered to David and Bill as we walked the two blocks to LAPD Headquarters at Parker Center. "They should have kept him in custody. We should be looking at a filing. I think we should tell them we're considering the grand jury."

What I meant was this: if the cops wouldn't arrest, we could unilaterally start an investigation of our own by taking the case to a grand jury. That way, the cops couldn't stonewall us because we'd have the power to compel their testimony. Furthermore, if we took the case to a grand jury and got an indictment, the police would have no choice but to arrest Simpson. Still, going grand jury was risky. The cops would take it as an in-your-face insult. My guess was that the very mention of it would drive them crazy.

"Go easy," David advised me. "Let's just see what they have to say." As we rode the elevator up to Robbery/Homicide, I tried to imagine what Bill Hodgman was thinking. He'd been the front man on the Jackson case, a role that had caused him to drop considerably in the LAPD's popularity polls. But Bill was also a very sweet guy and the consummate diplomat. If anyone could soothe the cops' hurt feelings, he could. My concern at that moment was focused more on the police brass—would they continue to hold out? Or would they put an end to this game and work with us?

The Robbery/Homicide Division bullpen was a large room with about twenty desks facing each other in two rows. Consequently, the homicide team that worked on the LAPD's most sensitive cases had absolutely no privacy. Their notes and reports were in plain view of any clerk wandering through—it was Leak City. Tom Lange had repeatedly complained to his bosses about it. But nothing had been done.

I knew the bullpen pretty well. I had been there often to talk with my IOs, investigating officers. I liked it: bare bones; gritty; real cops working tough, nasty cases. I'd always get good-natured ribbing as I made my way through. That Wednesday afternoon, however, I nearly got frostbite.

Someone pointed us to a small room off the bullpen where the brass were gathered. There was Commander John White, chief of detectives; Lieutenant John Rogers, of Robbery/Homicide; and Captain William Gartland, head of RHD. And, of course, Phil and Tom. On the table in front of Tom was a stack of documents bound with a rubber band. Exactly what I'd been waiting for.

"Here're the reports so far," Tom told me. His tone was neutral. I glanced over at Phil, who was looking distinctly ill at ease. Our eyes met. Everything was still okay between us.

"Obviously, there's a lot more to be done," Tom said. "But this should get you started."

"Thanks, Tom," I said, not wanting to appear too eager, but itching to get my hands on those reports. We swapped some observations about the case, making nice. Nobody on the other side seemed willing to bring up the thorny issue of arrest.

So I hit it dead-on.

"When do you plan to bring this for filing?"

"We want to interview more witnesses," Tom said slowly. "We were thinking maybe the early part of next week."

Bill, David, and I were silent. The cops knew that this was not what we'd wanted to hear.

"Well, frankly," I said, "we're a little concerned about letting it go that long." I paused to make sure they were paying attention. "We've been thinking about taking it to the grand jury."

Gauntlet thrown.

"Well, that's your prerogative," Tom replied, looking to his superiors for support. "We can't stop you. But we'd prefer to wait a little longer."

They were not going to budge.

The fire escapes that lattice the exterior of the CCB were a favorite retreat of the smokers among us. The one I used offered a vertical-slatted view of Parker Center and the Federal Buildings. The narrow veranda was furnished with a couple of dinette-type chairs. Someone had dragged out one of those tall cylindrical trash cans, which was always overflowing. There was a broom propped in one corner in case anyone felt industrious and wanted to clean the place up. No one had for a while.

The fire escape is where I headed when I got back with my spoils from the LAPD. Documents and notepads in one hand, cigs in the other.

I took a chair, propped my feet on the other one, and began leafing through the slender sheaf of police reports. Until now, I'd had only a sketchy mental image of how the bodies at Bundy lay.

Now I learned that Nicole, upon whom death and the medical

examiner had bestowed the designation "decedent 94-05136," had been found at the foot of the stairs at the front gate. She was in fetal position on her left side, wearing a backless black dress. No shoes. Her arms were bent at the elbow, close to the body. Her arms, legs, and face were stained with blood. The coroner had found a "large, sharp force injury" to her neck.

Ron Goldman, "decedent 94-05135," had been found to the north. He'd fallen or been pushed backward and was slumped against the stump of a palm tree. He was wearing blue jeans and a light cotton sweater. Lying near his right foot was a white envelope containing a pair of eyeglasses. Goldman had injuries to the neck, back, head, hands, thighs. He'd apparently put up a fierce struggle.

I absorbed the contents of these reports without emotion. Over the years, I'd learned to do that. I imagine that emergency-room physicians approach their work the same way—first treat the symptoms; only after the bleeding stops, notice the human beings. I knew with painful certainty that if I caught this case for keeps, the deaths described in these pages would become personal. And, like it or not, I would begin to grieve for the victims. Just as I'd written to Rebecca's mother, Danna Schaeffer, once you start letting yourself feel, the misery is endless.

But at this moment, the facts were all I needed or wanted.

Cause of death? "Sharp force injuries from some kind of knife or bladed instrument."

I hated that. With a bullet you can match striations to the barrel of a gun and be 99 percent sure that you have the murder weapon. Blade wounds are usually sloppy. The injuries often can't be traced to a single instrument.

Murder weapon? No sign of one yet. The cops had checked trash receptacles and luggage lockers at LAX and were in the process of searching the fields around O'Hare. They apparently had a line on a German hunting knife that Simpson had bought at an establishment called Ross Cutlery close to the time of the murder. Promising, but a long shot. Barring some anomaly—like some pattern on the handle that got pressed into the victims' skin—we would never get a 100 percent match.

Time of death? Coroner still working on that.

Suspect? I lit up a Dunhill and took a deep drag. Then, on a clean sheet of yellow notepaper, I wrote: "O. J. Simpson." And after that, "ALIBI?"

During the first couple of days after the murders, Simpson's attorney, Howard Weitzman, had been telling reporters that Simpson was en route to Chicago at the time of the murders. Weitzman put it at eleven o'clock. Turns out, however, that the red-eye left LAX at 11:45 P.M.

When was Nicole Brown last seen alive? I skimmed a report taken from the bar manager at Mezzaluna. She'd seen Ron Goldman leave the restaurant at about 9:30 or 9:45, on his way to Nicole's house. Goldman had been talking to Nicole on the phone a few minutes earlier, so it was probably safe to say that she was still alive at around 9:45 P.M. O. J. Simpson's plane is lifting off at 11:45. That's a lot of time in between.

What else have we got here?

"FENJVES, Pablo." One of Nicole's neighbors is watching the Channel 5 news at ten. I like witnesses who peg their memories to the *TV Guide*. They're usually reliable. At about a quarter past to half past the hour he hears a dog barking "uncontrollably." The dog continues barking for over an hour.

Nicole Brown's dog was a big white Akita. His name was Kato. I'd learned that . . . God, where *did* I learn it? From the evening news? Probably. Anyhow, I'd learned that Kato—related in some loony but as yet unspecified way to the houseguest, Brian Kaelin—had been wandering the neighborhood with bloody paws when another neighbor walking his own dog had found him.

If you assumed, for argument's sake, that the hound was Nicole's Akita and that he began to bark when his mistress was murdered, that put the time of death—conservatively speaking—somewhere around 10:15 P.M. to 10:30 P.M.

What about O. J. Simpson? Was there any time during which he was unaccounted for?

The witness who seemed to have the most intimate knowledge of Simpson's whereabouts on June 12 was Kato Kaelin. He'd told detectives at the West L.A. Police Station that Simpson had gone to his eight-year-old daughter Sydney's dance recital, which had begun at five P.M., then returned home at . . .

The officers had not noted the time.

Kato then related—in what would become a familiar litany—how he and Simpson had gone out at about 9:30 P.M. to a McDonald's on Santa Monica Boulevard. Kato wasn't sure when they'd gotten back. Ten P.M., he thought. That was the last he saw of Simpson until around a quarter to eleven. Kato was back in his room on the phone to a friend when he heard "a thump" against his wall. When he went out to investigate, Kato said, he saw a white limousine sitting outside the gate.

"Limo . . . limo . . . limo . . ."

I flipped to the police interview with the limo driver who took Simpson to LAX for his 11:45 P.M. flight to Chicago. You've gotta figure that the livelihood of a limo driver depends upon close attention to the clock. Allan Park, as it turned out, was extremely conscientious about time.

He'd been scheduled to be at Rockingham by 10:45 P.M., but just to be on the safe side, he arrived twenty minutes ahead of schedule. After waiting around for a bit, he rang the buzzer at 10:40. He got no answer. For the next ten minutes he continued ringing without success. At 10:50 he called his boss for instructions. He was still on the line three minutes later when he saw a white male walk from the back of the house carrying a flashlight. Obviously, Kato checking out the thumps.

Simultaneously, Park saw a black man—he believed it was O. J. Simpson—walk quickly from the far side of the driveway to the front door. Park got out of the limo and rang the buzzer again. This time Simpson answered, saying, "I'm sorry, I overslept. I just got out of the shower and I'll be down in a minute."

I made a big mark through this with orange highlighter. Here was a crucial witness. One who could attest that up until 10:50 or so Simpson was not answering his buzzer. He could also attest that someone resembling Simpson walked into his house around 10:53 P.M. Shortly after that, Simpson answered the buzzer. O. J. Simpson, it appeared, had lied about having been in the shower!

If you believed Park's account, it placed the suspect in his own front yard at 10:53 P.M. According to my rough calculations, Simpson had been off the radar for close to an hour. If Nicole Brown and Ron Goldman had been killed as early as 10:10, or even as late as 10:40, Simpson would have had time to drive the three miles or so from Bundy to Rockingham.

From where I was sitting, O. J. Simpson had no alibi.

And still, the police would not arrest.

By the next day, Thursday the sixteenth, the tension in our office was pushing into the red zone. I got a call from SID. The stain on the brown leather glove from Rockingham contained genetic markers from *both* victims, with a strong possibility that Simpson's blood was in the mix. They'd also found Simpson's blood on the interior of the door of his white Ford Bronco. The case was getting stronger by the hour. I'd never seen so much damning physical evidence. What were the cops waiting for? A sign from God?

If you ask the LAPD brass, they'll probably tell you they were in no hurry to arrest because they knew exactly where the suspect was that day. In fact, most of the world knew where O. J. Simpson was that day: he was attending the funeral mass of Nicole Brown at St. Martin of Tours in Brentwood, and later, her burial in Orange County.

I caught a few minutes of news showing the Brown family at Nicole's graveside. Simpson was there, all right. And he made a plausible show of grief. The slumping shoulders; dark glasses hinting at eyes too swollen with tears to look fellow mourners in the eye. I felt a jolt of revulsion when I saw him steering his two children toward the bier. They looked so innocent. So trusting. I had a momentary vision of them upstairs sleeping while their mother struggled with her killer.

In the months to come I would flash from from time to time on the image of those children sleeping. Sometimes a photo of them would trigger it. Sometimes it would be a document. Several weeks after the murders, I finally received a report I'd been requesting from an Officer Joan Vasquez. She'd been assigned to escort the Simpson children out back through the garage, never allowing them close to the crime scene.

Officer Vasquez reported that as the children sat in the back of the cruiser, Sydney whimpered, "Where's my mommy? . . . I'm just tired and I want my mommy."

Sydney and Justin stayed at the West L.A. station for almost five hours! Officer Vasquez, clearly a kind soul, tried to distract them with soda, candy, paper hats, paints. Over that long morning, she'd taught the children to spell their names in sign language and to play Hangman.

"I like the Power Rangers because I'm a green belt in karate," six-year-old Justin told her. "My mommy is going to start going with me again."

Sydney knew something was terribly wrong. At one point, she turned to her brother and said, "Justin, you know something happened to Mommy, or she would have come for us by now."

"Why can't Dad just come for us?" Justin asked her.

"Because he doesn't stay with us sometimes," she replied.

At about 6:30, their older stepsister, Arnelle, picked them up, and they left.

When I read this, I found it hard to keep back the tears. That may have been where the misery hit me in earnest. On the day of Nicole's funeral, however, I was simply struck by how surreal it all seemed. You had Nicole's California-perfect mother and sisters embracing and comforting O. J. Simpson. What was going on here?

I hadn't yet met the Browns. Given the media frenzy surrounding this case, we all agreed it was proper that Gil make the first contact. During the chaos of the first week after the murders, however, he and Nicole's father, Louis, had continually missed each other's calls. How the Browns felt about their son-in-law now was unclear. I knew that they had suspicions. When Tom Lange called Denise Brown to tell her of her sister's murder, the first words out of her mouth were "I knew that son of a bitch was going to do it!"

They had to know about the New Year's Eve beating Simpson gave Nicole. And yet there he was being welcomed as a son and brother, holding the hands of his two children, weeping over the casket of their mother. Could the aura of a celebrity blind even the family of a murder victim?

*   *   *

During the four days since he'd been cut loose, Simpson had been the bereaved widower. He'd spent his time in seclusion, "under a doctor's care for depression," according to his new attorney, Robert Shapiro. Bob had surfaced when Howard Weitzman bowed out of the case citing his "personal friendship" with the suspect.

I'd always considered Weitzman a decent guy and a good attorney. I could never figure out why he didn't insist upon being at his client's interview with Vannatter and Lange. (Much later in the case, I found myself talking to Howard at a dinner party in West L.A. He told me that he'd cut out because the cops threatened not to talk to Simpson if he had an attorney present. That made no sense to me. What really happened, I suspect, is that Simpson's colossal ego, combined with his confidence in his ability to sweet-talk and manipulate cops, had led him to dismiss his own attorney from the interview. Weitzman, of course, would have had no choice but to comply.)

When Weitzman dropped out of the picture, Robert Shapiro stepped right in. I was flabbergasted. *O. J. Simpson's got bucks coming out the wazoo, and this is the best he can do?* Weitzman, at least, had credibility. Shapiro, to my way of thinking, wasn't even a serious trial attorney. He had a stable of celebrity clients, Tina Sinatra, Christian Brando, and Erik Menendez among them. Still, he had a reputation around the Criminal Courts Building as a deal-maker, not a litigator. A lightweight.

One of Shapiro's first moves was to write a letter to Vannatter and Lange saying that his client "would be willing to consider" taking a lie-detector test. The cops faxed me a copy and asked for my opinion.

Polygraphs are risky. A subject can dope himself up to pass, which is why cops don't like to administer the test unless they've had the suspect in custody for a while. (Unbeknownst to me or the cops, Simpson had *already* taken a polygraph and scored a minus 22, meaning he failed every single question about the murder. I did not learn this until well after the verdict. Then I shook my head in amazement. It's hard to imagine that a lawyer would be stupid enough to offer his client up for a second poly after he'd failed the first time.)

The offer seemed fishy. My advice: "Stay away from it."

Shapiro also offered the services of his own experts—Dr. Michael Baden, director of forensic sciences for the New York State Police, and

Dr. Henry Lee, director of the Connecticut State Police Forensic Science Laboratory—to "aid in the investigation." Specifically, he was asking permission for Baden to reautopsy the bodies. "We . . . would like you to contact the next of kin for permission in this regard," he wrote, "since I feel it would be inappropriate for me to contact them directly during this period of grief."

I never answered him. But Nicole's mother, Juditha, would later tell me that during the funeral Shapiro came up and flat-out asked her for permission to exhume the body. She was too taken aback to reply. Shapiro, no doubt realizing how unsympathetically this request would be viewed by the public, wisely let the matter drop.

After the funeral, Simpson dropped off the screen. He'd apparently attended a gathering at Nicole's parents' home down at Dana Point before returning to "seclusion" at Rockingham. By Thursday evening, I was climbing the walls. I called the cops to check up on him. That's when I learned, to my amazement, that they did not have him under surveillance.

"Lack of manpower," they said. "Besides, where's he gonna go?"

This was too much even for Gil. He called us all into his office that evening and put the question to us: "Do we go to the grand jury or wait for the police to file?"

We all agreed the case was well past the stage of being filable. The cops were playing strictly cover-your-ass politics, which might have been fine if they'd had the luxury of working without the constant scrutiny of the press. But that wasn't the situation we had here. The media was broadcasting every tidbit it could get its hands on, and a lot of that information was amazingly on target. Some creep with access to documents was leaking like a rusty tub.

As the evidence piled up, so did O. J. Simpson's incentive to flee.

"What if Simpson pulls a Polanski?" I asked Gil.

Film director Roman Polanski—allowed to remain at large while under investigation on charges of statutory rape—had fled to France. Why couldn't it happen here? The clock was ticking, and we didn't want to be the saps who failed to move because the cops didn't give us permission.

There were other concerns as well.

"I'm worried about losing that guy Kaelin," I told the others. "He's very shaky. We need his testimony—now."

"David," Gil said at last, "tell Terry White [our office's grand jury adviser] to arrange to convene the jurors for Friday afternoon. We'll hear Kaelin's testimony."

Finally, we were moving. It wasn't until everyone stood up and began to leave the conference room that Frank Sundstedt finally asked the question that was uppermost in my mind.

"So, does Marcia have the case?"

I held my breath. Suddenly it felt very important to me. While part of me—probably the rational part—recognized that this would not be a smooth prosecution, I wanted to hear that Gil had the confidence to let me handle a big one.

"Marcia has the case," he said finally, catching my eye. "But not alone. She's going to do it with someone else."

There was a nervous shuffling in the room. Someone cleared his throat. Truth is, if you really trust a prosecutor, you make her the lead chair. No doubt what he intended was to pair me with another strong personality who would keep me in check. My pride wouldn't let me show my disappointment.

But as David walked me back to my office, I fumed sotto voce.

"Why does he think I need someone else?"

David urged me to calm down. Think of it from Gil's point of view, he said. The guy's under a lot of pressure and he's probably just hedging his bets. Your feelings are the least of his problems right now.

He was right, of course. For Gil, this wasn't personal. If I had to pair up with someone, maybe Gil would let me have David?

"How about you?" I asked him. He shot back a look as if to say, "In your dreams, babe." David was up to his ears in Menendez. He had all the alligators he could handle in that swamp.

Even before I left the office that night, I was hearing rumors that the LAPD brass were in negotiations with Robert Shapiro to allow O. J. Simpson to surrender voluntarily. Our threat to go grand jury must have lit a fire under them. But the news was a mixed bag. On one hand, the idea of a negotiated arrest made me nuts. Once again, O. J. Simpson's celebrity status had gained him a legal advantage. A negotiated voluntary surrender signals to the public and potential jury pool that the suspect is someone who deserves special privileges. I'd much rather see a righteously arrested suspect step out of a squad car in handcuffs. Still, my annoyance was all relative. Compared to the act of cutting him loose in the first place, a negotiated surrender was a minor outrage. If it worked, we'd all be happy. But what if the negotiations failed? Would the police back down and delay the arrest again? Would they give Simpson a deadline? We wanted to keep our options open—and that meant proceeding full speed ahead with the grand jury.

First order of business: reel in Kato Kaelin. O. J. Simpson was clearly Kato's benefactor. I could just about bet that had Kato known Simpson was a suspect, he would not have spoken so freely about the thump, for instance, and risk dumping his meal ticket. On the other hand, however, I'd had a chance to study his witness statement pretty thoroughly by now. I felt he had to know a lot more about the Simpsons' private lives than he'd told the cops.

Early Friday morning I dispatched a couple of detectives to West L.A. to serve Kato with a subpoena. David and I were in conference with Gil when I got a call from one of the cops on the detail.

"Kaelin's here with us," he said. "But he says he won't talk unless his lawyer's with him."

"Bring him in anyway," I told him.

This was extremely unusual. Witnesses don't arrive in the company of lawyers unless they're worried about being charged with a crime. From what I could see, Brian Kaelin had no criminal liability. The events he'd witnessed on the night of June 12 had clearly occurred after the murders. I was afraid that his request for an attorney meant that Simpson had gotten to him.

The cops brought Kato into my office at a little past nine. I looked up from my paperwork and saw for the first time that wild mane of dirty-blond hair, casual hip clothes, goofy surfer-boy slouch. My first thought: *Zone-out case.*

"Hey, guy," I greeted him. Casual seemed the way to go.

He shook my hand and fidgeted like a puppy.

"Have a seat while I call my boss."

"Hi, sure, no problem."

He plopped down in one of the chairs across the desk from me. David said he'd be delayed a few minutes, to start without him.

I began by asking Kato how much sleep he'd gotten that night. Did he feel prepared to go before a grand jury? He answered in half sentences, nodding a lot, managing to say very little. *Great,* I thought, *this guy can barely handle small talk—what's going to happen when we put him on the stand?*

I cut to the chase: "Do you remember what you were doing when you heard the thump on your wall?"

"I think I was talking to my friend Rachel. Yeah, I was talking to Rachel."

Okay; that was what he had told the cops.

"Did you tell her about what you'd heard?"

"I really don't . . . um . . . you know . . . want to say anything until my attorney gets here. I mean, you seem real nice and all, and . . . um . . . I really want to help you out. But . . . um . . . I really can't talk about the case without him. I'm real sorry, really, Marcia. I am."

His words tumbled over each other as he squirmed in his seat and cast me a beseeching look.

I wasn't buying this act. Kato wasn't as dumb as he appeared. He'd cut off the questioning expertly.

"Kato, I don't get it," I told him. "Why do you think you need a lawyer? As far as I can tell, you have no liability whatsoever. If there's more to it, please say so now and I won't say another word until your lawyer arrives."

"No, no. It's not that. It's just that my lawyer told me I shouldn't say anything unless he's here."

When David finally showed up, he, too, lobbed Kato a few low and slow ones. No dice. Then, Kato's lawyer, a young guy named William Genego, finally arrived and demanded that we stop talking to his client until he could read the witness report. David offered them his office as a conference room. It was only about 9:30; Kato didn't need to get on the witness stand until early afternoon. But Genego said that wasn't good enough. He'd need the whole *weekend* to go over the statement.

That was ridiculous. The statement was only two pages long. David laid it on the line.

"Your client was subpoenaed to appear before the grand jury at one-thirty this afternoon. Make sure he's there."

The tussle with Kato was small-time compared to the trouble brewing beyond the walls of the Criminal Courts Building. I was oblivious to the rumblings until about noon, when I was paged by the office's indomitable senior legal assistant, Patti Jo Fairbanks. Patti Jo had the authoritative air of a four-star general and the voice of a drill sergeant.

"Marcia!" she bellowed. "I need to see you in my office, right now!"

Sounded serious. I walked the few short steps between her office and mine, poked my head in, and asked, "What's the deal?"

"Come in and close the door."

Good news never comes when they tell you to close the door.

"It's Simpson," she said. "He was supposed to turn himself in at Parker Center this morning and he didn't show."

What?

Shapiro, Patti Jo told me, was to have brought Simpson in to Parker Center by eleven o'clock. An hour later, still no sign of him.

"The cops are plenty pissed," she told me. "They're going to send a unit out there to get him."

"I thought they didn't know where he was."

"He's staying over at Kardashian's place in the Valley," Patti Jo replied. She was referring to Robert Kardashian. Up till then, I'd never heard of the guy, but he was apparently a longtime buddy of O. J. Simpson.

Curiouser and curioser. How did so much manage to happen without our knowledge? I'd never seen this before—and it was certainly a bad sign.

The phone rang. Robert Shapiro.

"Let me talk to him," I mouthed to Patti Jo.

"Just a minute," she told him. "Marcia's sitting right here."

She handed me the phone.

I dispensed with pleasantries.

"What's going on, Bob?" I said. "This is no time to screw around."

"Marcia, I promise you. He's coming in. We just need to do a few things," said Shapiro.

"What do you mean?" I shot back. "He's had all week to get his things together. What are you guys doing?"

"He's being checked out by some doctors," said Shapiro. His speech was infuriatingly slow, his tone condescending. "I'm sure you've heard that he's very depressed. We just need to be sure that he doesn't go into custody in a suicidal frame of mind."

"Oh, I'm sure he's depressed." I snorted. "He's got very good reason to be depressed. I just want to hear back from you in half an hour telling me he's left."

Over the next few minutes, there was a flurry of calls between us. Shapiro kept insisting that "It's going to be a little longer than we thought." Simpson would need another hour, he insisted. Then, inexplicably, he passed the receiver to someone else.

"Who's *this?*" I asked the stranger.

"Saul Faerstein."

I knew that name. Faerstein was a forensic psychiatrist who testified in criminal courts around L.A. County. The line on him was good. What the hell was he doing at Kardashian's? Were they laying the groundwork for some kind of diminished-capacity defense? I asked Faerstein for directions to the house and he gave me some convoluted reply. When I tried to clarify them, he became even more evasive. Finally, I lost my patience.

"Doctor, you'd better stop playing games here," I said. "Do you understand that you're obstructing justice? That's a criminal charge, and I don't think you need a record like that, do you?"

He must have tossed the phone like a hot potato; in an instant Shapiro was back on the line. I was in the process of extracting directions from him when Patti Jo signaled me to break away. She had the LAPD's Valley Division chief on the line. They'd finally gotten their own fix on the safe house and were on their way.

*   *   *

Show time. I took a deep breath and pushed through the doors to the grand jury room. I flashed my best warm-up smile to the jurors seated in the little three-tiered amphitheater. I tried not to betray my anxiety as I first welcomed them and then had to explain our departure from ordinary procedure. I would be deferring my opening statement until Monday.

"For today," I said, "we are convened for the testimony of only one witness." And I called Brian Kaelin to the stand.

"Mr. Kaelin," said the foreperson when Kaelin stumbled to the witness chair, "please state and spell your full name, speaking directly into the microphone."

He looked a bit dazed. "B-R-I-A-N G-E-R-A-R-D K-A-E-L-I-N." Well, at least he could spell his name.

I turned to him. "Mr. Kaelin, were you acquainted with a woman by the name of Nicole Simpson?"

He fidgeted a bit, and then looked down at a piece of legal paper. Finally he spoke, in the tremulous tones of a child reciting a poem he doesn't quite understand. "On the advice of my attorney," he said, "I must respectfully decline to answer and assert my constitutional right to remain silent."

God *damn.*

"You seem to be reading from a piece of yellow paper," I said. "Did your attorney write that out for you this morning?"

"On the advice of my attorney, I must respectfully decline to answer and assert my constitutional right to remain silent."

I couldn't believe that this twerp was taking the Fifth! He read from that paper three more times before the foreperson warned him that his refusal to answer questions was "without legal cause" and that if he persisted in his refusal, he would be held in contempt. Now we had to find a judge to do just that, pronto. When Kato stepped down, David and I went down to the court of Judge Stephen Czuleger, a former federal prosecutor who was the designated hitter for issues that arose before the grand jury, to ask him for a ruling on the plea. I'd always pegged Czuleger as smart and forceful and I hoped he'd put an end to this nonsense.

He didn't. At least not 100 percent. While agreeing that Kato's situation did not seem to warrant his invoking the Fifth Amendment, the judge didn't find it unreasonable to allow him and his attorney the weekend to confer.

I humbled myself before the grand jury, apologizing as handsomely as I could for having dragged them in for nothing. I silently prayed they wouldn't hold it against me. Even worse, would they reject any of Kato's future testimony because he had taken the Fifth?

Great. What a way to start.

Shortly after I got back to my office, Phil called. I could tell from the agitation in his voice that something awful had happened.

"Simpson's escaped," he said.

Dear God, I thought, *do we ever look like morons.*

The events of the next few hours defy linear recall. I'd never seen David so furious. And Gil? Poor Gil was in the unenviable position of having been left out of the loop in the surrender negotiations by the cops, and then having to take heat for it. He handled it with his usual cool, even taking pains to defend the police department for a commendable job in preparing the evidence.

Me? It's difficult in retrospect to sort out all the conflicting feelings I had that afternoon. I know I had one secret, unworthy thought. I'd been getting a bad feeling about this case. Maybe I'd gotten myself into something I couldn't handle. Part of me was thinking, *The most graceful way out of all this would be if Simpson went on the lam—and disappeared off the face of the earth. . . .*

News of the escape spread like a Santa Ana wind. The phones in the press office were ringing wild. I felt strangely numb. As I drove home that night, I was too bummed to listen to the nonstop reports on drive-time radio.

The boys were with their father that weekend. I just tossed my bags into a corner and slumped into a chair at the kitchen table, trying to summon the energy to throw something together for dinner. Shoulda picked up fast food. At 6:30 P.M., maybe a little after, the phone rang. It was Phil.

"Turn on your TV," he told me.

There he was. Our fugitive in a white Ford Bronco, ghosting down the freeway, police cruisers following at a discreet distance. Commentators were calling it a chase, but it looked more like a presidential motorcade. Of course, unless he's assassinated, a president never gets this kind of coverage. I surfed the dial. It was incredible. This surreal slo-mo spectacle was being carried by all three networks. (NBC even cut away briefly from the NBA playoff game. This was serious.)

Certain images burned themselves into my memory. The sunlight streaming across Al Cowlings's jaw. The ghoulish frenzy of spectators waving placards: "Go, Juice." An amorphous dark blob in which popular historians would struggle to find the outline of a man holding a gun to his head. Ninety-five million people watching a police drama unfolding in prime time! It was one of those peculiarly American experiences that, for years afterward, would lead strangers to ask one another, "Where were you when O. J. skipped?"

On the evening of June 17, 1994, I knew that I was at the very epicenter of this event, and yet I felt light-years away from it. I couldn't watch for more than a few minutes. I don't know if that was because it was too painful, or because I was just too disgusted. Sometimes you have to distance yourself from things to stay objective. I told myself that the risk to public safety was minimal. Simpson did have a gun, but he was not a serial killer. He would be caught, or he would be shot.

The jerk.

Take Two

I could never bring myself to call him O.J. And it galled me when everyone else did. No one referred to Charles Manson as Chuck. Yet even the people on my own team would talk about "O.J. this," and "O.J. that." I had zero tolerance for it. "O.J.'s the ballplayer," I'd tell them. "This is 'the defendant.'" At one point, we even began fining offenders twenty-five cents each time they slipped. Bill Hodgman set out a big glass jar to collect the levy. The jar slowly filled with quarters. Not one of them came from me.

I didn't hate Orenthal James Simpson. At least I don't like to think of it that way. Hate is not an emotion that a prosecutor can afford. Hate clouds your thinking and distorts your priorities. The public, by and large, doesn't understand that. When they see you standing up in court leveling allegations against the man in the dock, they assume that your conviction must spring from some deep personal animosity. Usually that's not the case. You must never be drawn into a vendetta against the defendant. You can't let it get personal.

Having gone on record with that noble sentiment, let me say that I reserve the right to consider Orenthal Simpson unregenerate, low-life scum.

Prosecutors do not think much of defendants as a class. I'm no exception. I enjoyed a brief and unrewarding career as a criminal defense attorney. After I graduated from Southwestern University School of Law in 1979, I was taken on as an associate by a criminal defense firm, where I was assigned primarily to represent drug dealers. I was okay defending the dopers. After all, I was a child of the sixties. "Skip a little rope; smoke a little dope"—that was my motto. I'd wrap myself in the flag and declaim self-righteously about the Fourth Amendment, how it protected us all against unlawful searches and seizures. I sprang some dubious clients and had few qualms about it.

But after a few months, I started drawing the violent crimes. Now my clients, for the most part, were defendants whose greed or stupidity had wrecked not only their own lives but the lives of everyone around them. For me, the thrill of victory was no longer enough, because every time I scored an acquittal, I had to reckon with the possibility that I might have released another rabid dog onto the streets.

The moment of truth came while I was assigned to help defend a man charged with multiple murders. They were vicious crimes, but the D.A.'s office didn't have the evidence.

To a defense attorney, that's very good news. My assignment was to draft a motion to dismiss. And I did one hell of a job; several days later, my boss, Jeff Brody, came in to tell me my motion had been granted. Instead of feeling jubilant, though, all I could think of was that I might have helped spring a murderer.

My face must have betrayed my conflict. "Don't worry, Marcia," Jeff reassured me. "The prosecution will refile." (Indeed, they did.) And then he gave me a piece of solid advice.

"I think you'd feel more comfortable as a prosecutor."

He was right about that. Every defendant is entitled to competent counsel—but it didn't have to be me. So I got myself over to the CCB for an interview with John Van de Kamp, who was then the D.A. of Los Angeles County. I threw myself on his mercy. "I can't do criminal defense," I told him. "I won't do civil. This is the only job I want."

Van de Kamp hired me and I took the prosecutor's oath to represent the People. Now, *that* was an idea I could get behind. The People—especially those who have been victimized by brutal crimes—

have just as strong a right to advocacy as defendants do. Prosecution was a fierce calling, and one I felt I could pursue with dignity.

I never worried that I'd do my job so well that an innocent man would go to jail. There were too many checks against such abuses. The grand jury wouldn't return an indictment. A judge would throw out the case. And even if those system checks went haywire, there was a fail-safe: my own conscience. I could never throw myself into the pitched battle of a major criminal trial unless I believed in my head, heart, and soul that the defendant was guilty. When the Simpson case fell into my lap, I had been on the job for fourteen years. I had prosecuted literally thousands of defendants. I could feel a clench in my gut when I realized we had the right man.

By the time O. J. Simpson finally surrendered at his home the night of June 17, 1994, there was absolutely no doubt in my mind that he was the one. That familiar twist in my stomach confirmed it. Even before the blood, we had a strong case. But the blood clinched it. His blood was on Nicole's walk. Nicole's blood and that of Ron Goldman were on the glove from Rockingham. My God, the trail of blood *literally* led to Simpson's bedroom. From where I was sitting, it was dead-bang.

Somebody, probably Suzanne, had given me the tape of Robert Kardashian reading Simpson's so-called suicide letter, a travesty I'd managed to catch for only a few seconds when it was broadcast live. I took it home and, on the Saturday after the chase, I ejected a Disney tape from the VCR in my living room, parked myself on the couch, and watched the whole sorry performance.

"Please don't feel sorry for me. . . . I've had a great life, made great friends. Please think of the real O.J. and not this lost person."

He sent his "love and thanks" to all his friends. He started ticking off golfing buddies. Golfing buddies!

Are you fucking kidding? Your children are left motherless and all you can talk about is yourself, the media, and your golfing buddies?

The only pain he could feel was his own. That kind of total preoccupation with self is the mark of a sociopath. I'd seen it before. These guys commit unspeakable acts and yet somehow things get twisted around in their heads so that *they* are the victims. Simpson's behavior hardly surprised me.

The question being kicked around our office by the end of the week was whether or not Shapiro would try some kind of mental defense. Would he try to claim a temporary insanity that absolved Simpson of responsibility—switching the penalty from life in prison to an indeterminate spell in a mental hospital? Gil was convinced that Simpson would do this by asserting some Menendez-type plea; at the very least he would argue it was a crime of passion. Over the weekend, on *This Week with David Brinkley*, Gil said, "It wouldn't surprise me if at some point we go from 'I didn't do it' to 'I did it, but I'm not responsible.' " (It made me a little nervous that Gil was speaking so frankly to the media, but I trusted his judgment; I also understood that the defense, with its own outrageous pandering to the media, was forcing Gil onto the hustings.) David and I also thought there was a pretty good chance of a mental defense. I was actually hoping Simpson would try it. I had cut the legs out from under Robert Bardo, and I knew the drill—even a sociopath knows the difference between right and wrong.

Over the weekend, Simpson had been placed in the high-security wing of the Men's Central Jail, under a suicide watch. Reporters were scratching and clawing for information about him. And Shapiro cheerfully obliged them by slinging them maudlin slops. Sunday was Father's Day and Simpson, he said, had started to weep at the thought of not spending this day with his children. The press lapped that drivel right up. It was incredible. Here you had two people slaughtered like animals and yet the media coverage was actually creating sympathy for the suspect.

That weekend, I was working at home, sitting cross-legged on my bed with my laptop cradled between my knees. The phone rang. It was Shapiro.

"Hey, Bob, when's the real lawyer coming in?" I needled him. On the surface it was good-natured, but after the chase—a debacle for which he bore no small responsibility—I really wasn't joking. I figured that he'd be stepping aside to let a high-octane criminal attorney take over.

"I'm staying with this case, Marcia," he said, seeming to ignore the taunt. "I'm in it to the end."

"Stop it, you're killing me," I said. Now I got totally serious. "Come on, who's the real lawyer going to be?"

"I mean it: I'm staying with the case."

"Well, we're filing the complaint on Monday. Are you going to ask for a continuance?"

He said they probably would. This was standard procedure. Defense attorneys usually try to postpone the plea to give them a chance to review the evidence and see whether there's room for negotiation. And so I expected that when we all went down to Municipal Court, the hearing would last only long enough for the judge to set a new date for arraignment. From there, we would head straight back to the real show—the grand jury.

The next morning, David and I had taken our places at the counsel table when the bailiffs brought Simpson out of the holding cell. I didn't have to look up to know he'd entered the courtroom. Spectators rustled in their seats. The reporters snapped to, straining forward to see the sheriff's deputies and, finally, the prisoner enter the court. I raised my head and got my first glimpse of O. J. Simpson.

He looked like he'd been sleeping on the street. He wore a dark suit that seemed to sag on his body. In accordance with rules of the suicide watch, he wore no belt or shoelaces. His features were slack, his manner distracted. I suspected he was tranked. He looked half-angry, half-scared, utterly deflated. In the coming months I would watch an alert, carefully coached O. J. Simpson put on an affable, confident face for the jury and the world to see. And I would remember the way he looked this first morning. A common thug, collared.

Shapiro stood close to him, patting his shoulder, whispering in his ear, fawning. Seemed to me he wanted to be close enough to his client to make sure he was in the photos. The municipal judge, Patti Jo McKay, took the bench and we all sat down. When she asked Simpson if he was ready to enter his plea, I opened my calendar, ready to pick a new arraignment date. And to my shock, I heard Shapiro answer, "Yes, Your Honor, Mr. Simpson is ready to enter his plea."

No continuance. The son of a bitch.

Had Shapiro deliberately misled me? Fortunately, an arraignment is a routine procedure that most prosecutors can do in their sleep. I looked down at the complaint:

Count 1: Orenthal James Simpson willfully, unlawfully and with malice aforethought murdered Nicole Brown Simpson on or about June 12, 1994, in Los Angeles County. . . .

Count 2: Orenthal James Simpson willfully, unlawfully and with malice aforethought murdered Ronald Goldman on or about June 12, 1994, in Los Angeles County. . . .

Everything was standard, except for one thing. David and I had carefully worded a clause invoking "special circumstances." As I've explained, this means that the crime was particularly heinous—in this case a double murder. Invoking the clause allowed us to consider the death penalty.

"Orenthal James Simpson, is that your true name, sir?" I asked him.

He wouldn't meet my eyes. He mumbled "Yes."

"To the charges stated in Counts One and Two of the complaint, how do you plead, guilty or not guilty?"

Simpson's reply of "Not guilty" was jumbled. In fact, it was barely coherent.

Then Bob Shapiro did something that shocked me—something that prefigured the Grand Guignol that this case was destined to become.

Shapiro beseeched the court to allow Mr. Simpson to redo his plea.

You could have scraped me off the floor. Did he think this was a goddamned soundstage? "Simpson plea: take two!"

I watched helplessly as the judge allowed Shapiro's outrageous request. This time Simpson, drawing on the thespian skills doubtless honed by his work in *The Towering Inferno*, reached down inside himself and hit the mark. He restated his plea of "Not guilty" in a clear, strong James Earl Jones cadence. Enraged, I watched as Shapiro, his comically heavy eyebrows knitted in a show of concern, patted his client on the shoulder, congratulating him on his improved performance.

And then suddenly, without warning, it was my turn to perform. Suzanne Childs grabbed me outside the courtroom. "Marcia, you've got to go downstairs with David and Gil," she said. "The press is waiting."

It wasn't that I was a novice in front of the cameras. Bardo, you'll recall, was one of the first cases broadcast live on Court TV, and the Hawkins case had received its share of headlines as well. I had never gotten comfortable with press conferences and interviews; the media had become such an intrusive presence in judicial proceedings that you could deplore them, but hardly ignore them.

This appearance would be particularly difficult since my own role in the case remained ambiguous.

For the past week, the media had been referring to me as "lead prosecutor." Yet as Gil had emphasized so pointedly at Thursday night's meeting, I was nothing of the sort. I was more of a co-prosecutor, with a partner to be named later. And so I was feeling overwhelmed and unsure of my mandate. I also felt that my energies should be focused not on this little tap dance but on the chamber upstairs where twenty-three jurors were twiddling their thumbs, waiting for me. Didn't matter. I found myself being herded toward the cameras.

Press conferences were usually held in an antechamber off the D.A.'s office, but this one had been slated for the much larger western lobby on the ground floor. David and I took the slower-than-weight-loss freight elevator for a few final seconds of strategizing. Suzanne Childs fussed with my hair and straightened my suit. "There's going to be a lot of press," she warned me. That was the under-fucking-statement of the year.

The elevator door opened onto a mob scene. The lobby was jammed wall-to-wall with bodies—broadcast androids trying to muscle out the print scruffs. Photographers were dangling from the mezzanine. I don't think there had been a crush like this at a D.A.'s press conference since the death of Bobby Kennedy.

For a moment I thought fright would get the best of me. That my voice might quaver. But then something remarkable happened. As I drifted toward that sea of reporters and cameras, I was enveloped by a sense of calm. All my life I'd felt sure that something would happen to me that would make my life bigger, more profound. As I walked toward the lectern, I felt I wasn't even moving under my own power. To say that I felt a sense of destiny might be overstating it. But I do remember thinking, *This is it. You were meant to do this.*

"It was premeditated murder," I heard myself saying. When one reporter asked me if the killings might be considered an act of passion, a "spontaneous meltdown," I shook my head. "It was done with deliberation and premeditation. That is precisely what he is charged with, because that is what we will prove."

"Are there plans to charge anyone else?" someone called.

"Mr. Simpson is charged alone," I answered, "because he is the sole murderer."

I'd blown it. Man, had I blown it. What I had meant to say, of course, was that Simpson was not the sole murderer, but the sole *suspect*. I realized my slip almost immediately, but by then I was fielding other questions and correcting my error would only call more attention to it. I was sure I'd take heat for not using the word "suspect."

As it turned out, I did get heat—but not for that. The word that Robert Shapiro almost instantly seized upon when reporters spoke to him later that day was not "murderer," but "sole." The D.A.'s office was not investigating other suspects, he charged. In fact, this was completely untrue; the investigation was still wide open.

That was no excuse for my blunder, however. I should have said that O. J. Simpson was the "prime suspect." That first news conference alerted me to the unique perils of this case. I knew that from this point on, every word I spoke would be analyzed, scrutinized, and dissected in detail. Lesson learned. I had to move on. The grand jury was waiting.

Normally, I have weeks or even months to prepare for a grand jury. By the time a session formally convenes, I will have interviewed every witness at least once, often more. But now, the clock was ticking. We had to get the grand jury indictment within the ten days before the preliminary hearing was set to begin. If we didn't, we'd have the same set of witnesses running between two courts to testify. You can imagine what a mess that would be. On the other hand, if we could just get that grand jury indictment, the entire matter would be settled. We could dispense with the preliminary hearing altogether. And so the need for haste.

David and I would have to grab our witnesses as we could get them. We went into court virtually cold, with only a few mounted photographic displays. These, as I look back upon them, were pretty damned impressive, considering we'd had to pull them together over the period of a couple of days.

Almost all of our first meetings with witnesses, even our expert witnesses, had to be done on the day of their appearance. David and I would usher them into the small conference room off the grand jury room, or, if there wasn't even enough time for a fifteen-minute session, we'd huddle in the hallway. I'd do a quick rundown of the witness's story, and try to make an instant assessment. Much of the time, really, was spent instructing them not to give any indirect evidence that might taint the record: "Only answer the question—don't volunteer anything, don't tell me what anybody told you," I'd advise them. "That's hearsay, and it's inadmissible."

It was a sobered, marginally more cooperative Kato Kaelin who returned to testify the morning of June 20. I led him back through the story of how he had met Nicole and convinced her to rent him the guest house. And I had him explain why, when Nicole later moved to Bundy, Simpson balked at Kato's taking a room there. "He said it would probably not be right to be in the same house," said Kato, who then accepted Simpson's offer of quarters—rent-free—in the Rockingham compound.

Kato had mentioned to police that he'd witnessed a scuffle between Simpson and Nicole in the fall of 1993. Only later would I get the police report documenting that fight. A unit from West L.A. responded to a 911 call from 365 Gretna Green and found a terrified Nicole. "He's in the back," she told them, "He's my ex-husband, he's O.J.—*I want him out of there!*" She showed them to the back door, which, she said, Simpson had smashed. "French doors—wood frame splintered, door broken, still on hinges," the cops wrote. Simpson was railing angrily out back in the guest house. "She's been seeing other guys!" he yelled to the cops. The cops had recorded that Kato had apparently been trying to calm him down.

But today, Kato downplayed the episode. "I saw maybe an argument," he admitted, twitching insistently.

"Do you recall the nature of the argument, or just that it was one?" I asked.

"That it was one," he said. He insisted that he didn't know about any other fights.

Still, Kato's testimony advanced us a few notches. He had admitted that Simpson was a jealous guy. Certainly jealous enough to manipulate his wife by buying her friends' loyalty. And during my questioning about the night of the murder, Kato had substantially widened the time period during which Simpson was unaccounted for. Now the window was open between 9:45, when they'd returned from McDonald's—which was fifteen minutes earlier than the estimate Kato had given the cops—and about 10:53, when Simpson responded to the limo driver.

Kato also gave a fuller account of the now-famous thump on the wall of his guest house, which he now recalled as a "three-thump noise." I asked him to demonstrate what it sounded like, and he made a fist and pounded three times on the table in front of him. "Like that," he said. It had been strong enough, he added, to tilt a picture on his wall, and scary enough to make him search the grounds for an intruder.

He would never actually say "intruder." Back in the office when I'd tried to get him to tell me what he thought had caused the thump, he'd danced all around the question.

"Uh, uh . . . I don't know what I was looking for."

"A prowler," I probed.

"Uh, I don't know. Maybe."

(Later, he would volunteer for the benefit of the plaintiffs in the civil trial that the thumps sounded like a body falling against his wall.)

On the stand, however, he did reveal, for the first time, having seen a "knapsack" lying on the grass. What happened was this. Kato had rounded the corner of the main house, flashlight in hand. He checked out the area behind the garage and, finding nothing, started back toward the front yard and then opened the gate to let the limo driver in. He noticed a golf bag on a bench by the front door. He went back to check the area behind his own room, and by the time he ventured out front again, Simpson himself was talking to the limo driver. But now Kaelin noticed something else on the grass near the driveway. It was "like, a bag," he said, in Kato-speak. He didn't recall the color, except to say it was dark.

"To the best of my recollection, it was like a knapsack-type bag," he said.

That knapsack had not been found among the pieces of luggage Simpson brought back from Chicago. Could it have held evidence from the crime scene?

Not bad for a recalcitrant witness. But I was convinced even then that Kato knew a lot more than he was telling.

Outside, in the waiting room beyond the grand jury chamber, were a half-dozen prospective witnesses, crowded on benches like applicants for passports. These were Nicole's neighbors, the limo driver, Ron Goldman's co-workers, and our own technicians and criminalists.

Since I'd had the experience with DNA evidence in other cases, I told David I'd take the criminalists. Meanwhile, David debriefed the coroner, Dr. Irwin Golden.

Had this been a preliminary hearing, we wouldn't even have bothered calling the coroner. Cause of death is almost never in dispute, so the defense usually agrees to stipulate to the medical examiner's testimony. The prosecutor usually reads the coroner's conclusion into the record. Since there are no defense attorneys present at a grand jury proceeding, however, a prosecutor has to protect the record, and the rights of the defendant, by giving all the witnesses a critical questioning.

Neither David nor I had worked with Dr. Golden before. The truth is, most coroners are not Quincy. After all, what happens if they screw up? The patient lives?

The morning we put Golden on we had not given his file a thorough going-over. David, in fact, received the report only minutes before putting him on the stand. One thing immediately struck us as strange. The coroner's investigator had reported that Nicole Brown Simpson was alive at eleven P.M., when she had spoken to her mother. If this were true, of course, Simpson would be in the clear, since he had been spotted at Rockingham at that hour. The coroner's estimate seemed too late. (In fact, phone records would show that Nicole and her mother had spoken at around 9:45 P.M.) Now, a coroner's report is not like a police investigative file, and these kinds of mistakes are common. Still, they give the defense something to seize upon. And we would learn, in the days and weeks ahead, that the coroner's report was, in fact, riddled with errors.

I sat at counsel's table while David questioned Golden, a serious, horse-faced man whose speech was marked by long pauses. What I remember most about the testimony that afternoon was not the witness, but the exhibits—the pictures of the victims. David had organized and mounted the autopsy photos on a strip of cardboard. It was a stroke of superb lawyering. Up until then, I'd been busy with the criminalists and hadn't even seen those unforgettable, gruesome photos.

"Good God," I whispered to myself. For the first time, I saw the wreckage of Ron Goldman's body. The gashes to the head, the gaping slices cut into his neck from ear to ear. Stab wounds to the left thigh and abdomen had soaked his shirt and pants in blood. In death, his eyes remained open. The killer had waged a merciless assault against an unarmed, unsuspecting victim, a victim who was rapidly trapped in a cagelike corner of metal fencing and slaughtered. Whether the motive was sexual jealousy or the need to eliminate a witness, this killer had made a ruthless determination: Ron Goldman would die.

While Goldman's wounds suggested that the killer had been in a frenzy to kill him, Nicole's did not. The attack had been swift, smooth, and efficient. There were no hesitation marks, no half cuts or superficial throat wounds that might have shown uncertainty. Her killer did not romance the deed. Nicole had apparently been swept up, thrown down, slashed at the throat, and dropped at the foot of the steps.

I had looked on literally thousands of coroner's photographs over the years. None were worse than the last pictures taken of Nicole Brown. Her face was a grotesque white—no wonder, since she'd bled out nearly 90 percent. The slash across her neck had nearly decapitated her. She lay there, disjointed, like a marionette discarded by the puppeteer. I had a mental flash of the photo of her that hung by the stairs at Rockingham. I recalled her bright, glossy features. That was a rich man's wife, someone to whom I couldn't relate. Now, as I saw her frail and broken in death, I felt a surge of helpless anger.

I fought back the feeling. Times like this call for cool reason. The last thing you can afford is too much feeling.

*   *   *

I drove home that night feeling dejected. Next to me was a stack of files and documents high enough to qualify me for the car-pool lane. The cell phone rang, but I didn't pick it up. I'd answer calls when I got home, after the kids were asleep. That was when the night shift began. First priority was the grand jury. But I also had to start drafting replies to a blizzard of motions coming our way from Shapiro's office. Most of them were absolute garbage. I didn't get to sleep until the early-morning edition of the *L.A. Times* was hitting the streets. On the front page, a story that read:

> The task facing Dist. Atty. Gil Garcetti in the O. J. Simpson case is daunting and unparalleled: he must try to win murder convictions against an American sports legend well-known to the public for his grace and charm.

You're tellin' me.

If the grand jury was to indict, we needed to demonstrate that O. J. Simpson had the opportunity to commit these two murders; then we'd have to place him at the scene of the crime. That's why I led Tuesday morning's session with Jill Shively. Jill, a clerk for a film-supply company, had called the police the preceding week and told them she'd spotted O. J. Simpson in a white Bronco speeding north-bound on Bundy right around the time of the murders. Talk about an alibi killer!

Jill Shively, I must say, seemed like a real gem. She was dressed neatly and conservatively for her testimony. She was articulate. She was confident. In fact, Scott Gordon, one of my fellow D.A.s, knew her because their children went to the same school.

Just before she took the stand, David asked Shively if she had told anyone that she had been called to testify. "No," she told him. "Just my mother."

"Are you sure?" he pressed her.

"Absolutely," she said without hesitation.

If she could pin Simpson to that location, in that car, at that hour, it would be almost as good as having an eyewitness. So it was essential to nail down the time she saw him. On the witness stand, she did this beautifully. "I left my house at ten-forty-five P.M.," she said.

"Why are you so certain?" I asked.

"Because I was trying to get to the store that closed at eleven and I wanted to get something to eat," she said. Bingo. Vannatter and Lange had even checked with the store to confirm their closing time— another assurance that Shively was on the level.

Then she told her story. "A white Bronco runs the red light and goes through the intersection and almost hits me," she said.

"Were you able to see the person seated in the Bronco?" I asked.

"Yes, I was," Shively said. "It looked like he was mad, or angry." She explained that the Bronco driver was unhappy because a third car—a Nissan—blocked his path. The Bronco driver screamed at the Nissan, "Get out of the way! Move the car!" Finally there was room to pull around the Nissan, and the Bronco sped away.

"Now, that whole intersection where you witnessed all these events, is it dark or is it well lit?" I asked.

"It's well lit by streetlights and a gas station there," she said.

"So were you able to see the driver very clearly?"

"I recognized him right away."

I paused for a beat, because I wanted this next answer to have some dramatic effect.

"And who is he?" I continued.

"I saw O. J. Simpson," she said.

You get a jolt of adrenaline from a nice courtroom moment.

There was no reason to believe that I had just presented the grand jury with a flat-out lie.

But I had.

The next morning, I'd barely stepped out of the elevator on the eighteenth floor when reporters began asking me whether I'd seen the tabloid TV show *Hard Copy* the night before. It turns out that Ms. Shively—our alibi killer—had made an appearance. Despite having insisted to us that she had told only her mother about the Bronco incident, our star witness had found time to address several million television viewers, proudly displaying her grand jury subpoena for the cameras.

The news sent me reeling. But things got worse. On my desk was a fax from a television actor named Brian Patrick Clarke. He was claiming to have lost money to Shively and considered her a consummate liar.

Normally, you take the imprecations of a disgruntled business partner with a grain of salt. But Clarke's story had a paper trail to back it up. According to Clarke, Jill had presented herself to him as a screenwriter and asked him to read a script she had purportedly written. She'd said a production company was about to buy it for $250,000, and she wanted Clarke to star in it. Before this bonanza arrived, though, Jill allegedly managed to borrow $6,000 from Clarke. And guess what Clarke later discovered? The script wasn't Shively's. In fact, it was the screenplay for a film in pre-production titled *My Life*, which starred Michael Keaton and Nicole Kidman. Clarke filed a suit against Shively in small-claims court and won a judgment of $2,000.

"Get that woman back in here!" I hissed to Phil.

We hauled Shively back into David's office and started grilling her about *Hard Copy*. It turned out that she'd done the television interview the day before her grand jury appearance—for $5,000. At the time she appeared before the grand jury, she explained nervously, the show hadn't aired. It wasn't going to air until afterward. She thought it was okay. She just "forgot." She hadn't slept well, and she was nervous, and she "really wasn't thinking."

We'd been duped. This was a serious screwup. We had no choice but to cut Shively loose.

I was more loath to do this than anyone. I did not, as one commentator would later suggest, ditch her in a "fit of pique." There was a far more serious principle at work here. If I allowed Shively's testimony to stand without amendment, suspecting as I did that it was fraudulent, the grand jury proceeding would be tainted. If an indictment against Simpson resulted, the defense would be entirely justified in asking that it be thrown out. It was my responsibility to preserve the integrity of the record.

And so I made Ms. Shively return to the witness chair the next day and made her repeat her squirming explanations to the grand jury. It was an uncomfortable experience, cross-examining my own witness and watching her credibility crumble.

Then I took a deep breath.

"Ladies and gentlemen of the jury," I said, "because it is our duty as prosecutors to present only that evidence of which we are 110 percent confident as to its truthfulness and reliability, I must now ask you to completely disregard the statements given and the testimony given by Jill Shively in this case."

It was a tough lesson for us, but a necessary one. In the Simpson case—as with no other case in history—there was an incentive for people to come up with phony stories in order to cash in on sudden fame.

In the end, the loss of Shively, thank God, was not ruinous. We had other time-line witnesses, and they turned out to be first-rate. The very best of the lot was the limo driver, Allan Park.

As usual, I got to talk with Park for only a few minutes before putting him on the stand. He struck me as a real straight shooter, well-groomed, well-spoken. He wasn't eager to be there, but he wasn't resisting. And unlike Kato Kaelin, he wasn't beholden to Simpson and he had no ax to grind.

I had prepared a diagram of the Rockingham estate, and once Park was on the stand, I walked him through his story, marking where the limo was, and his line of sight, at every moment. He told the grand jury how he'd arrived at Rockingham twenty minutes before the 10:45 P.M. pickup time, and waited until 10:40 to ring the buzzer on the front gate.

"Did you notice any car parked in front?" I asked him.

"No, I did not," he replied.

This was important, because Simpson had told police that the Bronco had been parked there since early evening.

Park recounted his repeated, futile buzzing, calling his boss, seeing Kato wave. He recalled seeing the black male crossing the lawn. In the police report, he'd pegged the time at 10:53. Since then, we'd had the opportunity to consult cell phone records, which placed the sighting of the black man at around 10:55 or 10:56 P.M. A minute later, Simpson answered the buzzer.

Park then described a bag that he had seen sitting by the Rolls. Kato, he recalled, had reached for it, but Simpson said, "No. No. That's okay. I can get it." This had to be the missing "knapsack" that Kato had mentioned earlier.

On the way to the airport, Park testified, Simpson kept complaining of being "hot." He'd rolled his window down and turned on the air-conditioning. In fact, the night was unseasonably cool. Simpson then asked Park where the light was. In the rearview mirror, Park could see that Simpson was "checking his bags." What was in those bags, I wondered. Perhaps . . . a murder weapon? Bloody clothes? I could see the grand jurors focusing closely on Park's words; were they wondering the same thing?

All in all, Park's testimony dovetailed snugly with Kato's. And it had the effect of strengthening both.

Mezzaluna's weekend bar manager, Karen Crawford, was up next. She testified that Nicole and her party left the restaurant between 8:30 and nine. Shortly afterward, she'd gotten a call from "the older woman in the party"—obviously Juditha Brown—saying she'd lost her glasses. Karen found them lying by the curb outside the restaurant and sealed them in an envelope.

"About five minutes later, there was another phone call," she said. This one from Nicole.

"What time was that, approximately?" I asked.

"I would say it was between nine-thirty and nine-forty-five," she answered. Crawford called Ron Goldman over to the phone to make arrangements to deliver the glasses. Then he left the restaurant carrying the envelope.

So where did that leave us in terms of time? Nicole and her mother spoke at around 9:45 P.M. Police had talked to the neighbor, Pablo Fenjves, who had reported being bothered by the wailing of a dog on the night of the murders. The barking, he thought, had begun between 10:15 and 10:30 P.M. By midnight the victims were dead. That's when Sukru Boztepe and his wife, Bettina Rasmussen, came upon the body of Nicole Simpson.

Sukru and his wife were one of those Mutt-and-Jeff couples. He was large, burly, and dark, with a long ponytail. She was slender and fair, her blond hair cropped short just below her ears. The few minutes I had with Sukru before testimony were tense. He still hadn't gotten over his discovery of a murder scene. He stammered and groped for words until finally, when he got to the point of telling how he'd first seen the body, his voice broke and he covered his eyes with one hand.

Taking the witness stand somehow seemed to calm him. He told how he'd come home to his apartment on Montana Avenue—only about six hundred feet from the crime scene—at around 11:40 P.M. He found his upstairs neighbor sitting with a big white Akita. This, though Sukru didn't know it, was Nicole Brown's dog, Kato. Sukru and Bettina offered to keep the dog until they could get it over to an animal shelter the following morning.

"How did it behave in your apartment?" I asked.

"He was pretty nervous, and he was going to the doors and windows, running around in the house."

"Did you see anything unusual about his legs or his body?" I asked.

Sukru swallowed hard. "On the legs, there was blood."

About midnight, the couple decided to take the animal out to see if they could find its owner. The animal headed toward 875 Bundy. Home.

"When we got closer to the place, he started to pull me a lot harder than normal," Sukru said. "We were walking on the right side of Bundy and the dog stopped and turned right and looked at—"

There was silence in the courtroom as Sukru tried to go on.

"—and I turned right and looked, too. And I seen her body."

The Akita's role in all this was eerie, to say the least. You had to wonder what that poor animal had witnessed. Had he tried to defend his mistress? Probably not. Police canine experts later examined Kato, summarizing their conclusions in a "witness statement." Kato, they concluded, was such a low achiever that he probably could not have defended himself, let alone a human. The chief trainer for the LAPD's K-9 unit reported that Kato had a "very nice disposition . . . [but] inadequate instincts or courage to protect his territory, owner or himself."

Thanks to his primitive loyalty, however, we were able to postulate that the murders had occurred between the time he began to howl and the time he was discovered wandering on Bundy with bloody paws—a window of perhaps an hour. That dog, it seemed, had a better handle on time of death than the coroner did.

I only wish he could have spoken for the criminalists.

*   *   *

A case like this—with no eyewitnesses save, possibly, a white Akita—clearly would hinge on physical evidence, especially blood evidence. That's why I had been so concerned from the start about which criminalists we could get assigned to the case. It was critical that we establish two things: first, that the blood samples had been collected and preserved properly; and second, that the samples had undergone reliable analysis. The criminalists had to do their job competently, and it was essential that they be able to present themselves credibly to a jury. Phil's tepid assurance that criminalist Dennis Fung was "okay" had set off alarm bells in my head.

My first meeting with Dennis Kirk Fung had been on Monday, June 20, in the waiting room outside the grand jury chamber. He'd come with Collin Yamauchi; Fung was the criminalist on the scene, and Yamauchi the criminalist/analyst in the lab. They'd handed over their reports to me, and I'd scanned them quickly, trying to envision them as testimony that would be coherent enough for a juror to follow. Fung's task was relatively straightforward: to tell where he collected the blood and how he packaged it. I'd told him to review his reports so he'd be prepared when I took his testimony later in the week. He bobbed his head up and down as I spoke.

Then I'd turned to Collin Yamauchi. In theory at least, he had the more difficult task.

The LAPD crime lab had just recently begun to do DNA testing. None of its technicians was all that experienced in the process. They were perfectly capable of performing the simplest test, called PCR DQ alpha. But it had to be done correctly. When contamination occurs, you get wildly erratic results. That was why I breathed a sigh of relief when I read Collin's report: in this case, the results were perfectly consistent. Every blood drop on the trail at Bundy displayed O. J. Simpson's genetic markers, and *only* his genetic markers. Bull's-eye.

It was even possible that his blood was on the Rockingham glove. Preliminary tests indicated that this was the case. We had already found markers on that glove from Ron's and Nicole's blood. If we could establish that the glove bore a mixture of blood from both victims *and* from the defendant, that would be very powerful evidence. For that, however, we would need to send the samples away to Cellmark for more sophisticated testing.

On the witness stand, Collin turned out to be pretty effective. He handled the glove business well, leaving open the possibility that it had been stained with a mixture of the blood of both killer and victims. He did stumble at explaining the fundamentals of DNA testing, but it is very complicated stuff and he hadn't much experience on the stand. I assumed he would get better with practice.

Dennis Fung was another story.

When Dennis took the witness stand on Wednesday, June 22, I led him through a pro forma description of how he collected the blood samples by wetting swatches of cloth with distilled water, then applying them to each bloodstain. We established that he'd handed them over, as the protocol required, to Yamauchi, back in the lab.

"Are you familiar with what is known as a stride analysis?" I asked him.

"Yes, I am," he replied.

Whenever shoe prints or footprints are found at a crime scene, the criminalist may decide to do a stride analysis to determine whether the suspect was walking or running. Fung claimed he had done such an analysis. Naturally, I asked him if he could tell us whether the person making the footprints was moving quickly or at a normal pace.

"Not really," Fung said.

The stride analysis may also say something about the size of the person, based on the size of the print and the distance between the steps. The prints at Bundy were from size 12 men's shoes. And so, when I asked Dennis if the bloody footprint on the walk at Bundy seemed to come from a man or a woman, all I expected was a very qualified answer that tended to favor a man. Either it was a really big woman, or a little woman or man in a pair of big man's shoes, or a big man. There weren't that many realistic options.

"I haven't been in the shoe analysis assist unit for about three years," he replied. "So I'm kind of rusty on that aspect."

I was stunned. If he was too "rusty" to make such no-brainer observations, what the hell was he doing at a murder scene as our criminalist? This was not good at all.

"So you are disqualifying yourself?" I asked him incredulously. "Telling us you are *not* qualified to render an opinion as to that because of a lack of experience or training?"

"Yes, at this point," he replied.

At that moment, I realized that I had no idea what might come out of Dennis Fung's mouth next. I was flying blind. All I could do was continue questioning him, and hope that there were no more ugly surprises.

No such luck. Throughout the testimony, I watched helplessly as Fung fumbled through his notes, constantly losing his place. We went through all the presumptive blood tests he had taken. A presumptive blood test is simply a quick, though not infallible, procedure to determine whether a stain is indeed blood. Several stains at Rockingham had given a positive result, including stains in the foyer, on the door handle of the Bronco, and on the glove found on the south pathway. Fung had also done the tests on the drains in the master bathroom sink and shower—and they, too, had indicated blood! This could mean that Simpson had washed himself off before heading to the airport.

But Fung blew it. As we got deeper into the questioning, I learned to my dismay that he had not tested *all* the drains at Rockingham, only those that had appeared to be in "recent use." When you do presumptive tests for blood, you should always be aware that the results can be impeached in court, because they can sometimes also give a positive result for things like rust and vegetable matter. Fung's failure to test all the drains would play right into the defense's hands. I could already hear opposing counsel crossing him: "Oh, you mean you didn't test the other drains? So you don't know whether they, too, might have given a positive result, do you, Mr. Fung? And if they had, you might have concluded that the positive result you got in my client's bathroom was nothing more than rust, isn't that so? Or would you try to tell this jury, Mr. Fung, that blood had been washed down every sink in that house?"

Fung had failed to obey the criminalist's first commandment: be thorough. His tendency to test selectively would later cripple our efforts to get important blood evidence into the record. And his demeanor on the stand wouldn't give a jury the confidence that he could change a lightbulb, let alone supervise a forensic investigation.

After he left the stand, I called my people and said, "This guy's a fucking disaster."

Here's the bottom line: Fung and his colleague, Andrea Mazzola, a trainee with only four months' experience, should have been supervised as they went over both crime scenes. Tom and Phil should have returned to oversee that search. When I'd spoken to them mid-afternoon after they'd interviewed Simpson, they'd assured me they were on their way back out to Rockingham. They didn't make it back there until after five. Too late. By that time Fung and Mazzola were packing up and heading home.

We'd be doing damage control on that sloppy search for a long time to come. We still are.

At the outset, I had assumed we would be offering the cops' taped interview with Simpson into evidence. But there was more foot-dragging by the LAPD. Not until the week the grand jury hearing began in earnest did I finally get the cops to fork over the cassette tape of that interrogation.

In the privacy of my office, I slipped the tape into my player, grabbed a legal pad, and pulled my knees up into my oversized leatherette chair to listen to what I assumed was at least a two-hour interview. It was a shock, therefore, when after thirty-two minutes, I heard Lange say, "We're ready to terminate this at 14:07," and then heard nothing but the white fuzz of unrecorded tape. I didn't get it—Simpson had spent three full hours at the station. What could they have been doing all that time?

I was even more disturbed by what was on the tape. Phil and Tom both sounded exhausted—that was understandable. They'd been up since three the morning of June 13. But that was no reason to allow a potential suspect in a double murder to set the program for the interview.

Any Monday-morning quarterback can now see that Simpson lied to Tom and Phil all through that interview. Of course, some of the lies weren't apparent to them at the time. For instance, Simpson claimed that he'd been invited to dinner with the Brown family after the recital, which Nicole's mother would later deny. Tom and Phil couldn't have known that yet. But on other, more elemental points, like where and when he'd parked the Bronco, there was plenty they could have done.

Lange: "What time did you last park the Bronco?"

"Eight something," replied the suspect. "Maybe seven, eight o'clock. Eight, nine o'clock. I don't know, right in that—right in that area."

The follow-up should have come hard and fast: "Well, what the hell was it? Seven, seven-thirty, eight, or nine? You knew you had a flight to catch, so shouldn't you have been aware of the time? What time did you park? What did you do then?"

And what about Simpson's apparent lack of concern after Kato told him that he'd heard thumps on the wall? Kato was so worried that he'd taken a dim flashlight and searched the grounds for an intruder. And yet Simpson seemed strangely unconcerned—he was more intent upon finding a Band-Aid for the cut on his finger. On that one Vannatter and Lange should have dug deep: "Did you check it out? Did you call your security people to check it out? Why not? Wasn't your daughter Arnelle staying at Rockingham? Weren't you concerned for her safety?"

Such pointed questions would have highlighted Simpson's evasiveness. Instead, the detectives responded to Simpson's tentative statements by saying "I understand," or simply "Yeah," or "Okay," or a mumbled "Mmnh-hm." On some fundamental level, I think, Tom and Phil wanted to hear a plausible explanation that would eliminate Simpson from suspicion.

Just when they got a big opening, they'd move on to something else. For instance, when they ask Simpson if he would take a lie-detector test, he vacillates:

"I'm sure I'll eventually do it," he says, "but it's like, hey, I've got some weird thoughts now. And I've had weird thoughts—you know, when you've been with a person for seventeen years, you think everything. And I don't—" He stopped himself.

And what do Lange and Vannatter say? "I understand." Not once but *twice*. And then they drop the subject!

Why didn't they swoop down on that? "What sort of weird thoughts? Thoughts of hurting Nicole? Did you ever share those thoughts with anyone?"

I'd seen plenty of people whose family members had been murdered. An innocent man who's just learned about the death of his children's mother—when the children were asleep in the house—would most likely be stunned, distraught, even hysterical. And he wouldn't hesitate to take a polygraph. He'd be demanding, "How can I help you catch this monster?"

But the O. J. Simpson who emerged from that police interview struck me as cold and detached—fundamentally unaffected by the news of his ex-wife's murder.

Simpson chuckles as he shoots the shit about his relationship with his girlfriend, Paula Barbieri. He volunteers a story from after his last breakup with Nicole. She had returned an expensive diamond bracelet he'd given her as a birthday present. Simpson then presented it to Paula and pretended he'd bought it for her. Scamming one woman immediately after his breakup with another, who, at that moment, was lying on a cold metal coroner's table! I couldn't believe the way he told Vannatter and Lange about that. "I get into a funny place here on all this, all right?" he says. *Wink-wink, nudge-nudge.* "Yeah," they chime back. You could practically hear the towels snapping in the men's locker room.

That jocular, almost flippant tone pervaded the entire interview. Simpson tells them about how an endorsement deal gets him Bugle Boy Jeans for free—"I got a hundred pair," he brags. He also tells them his preference in sneakers—"Reebok, that's all I wear." He even gives a little rap, referring to himself in the third person, about how he rushes for a plane, just like in the Hertz commercial—"I was doing my little crazy what-I-do. I mean, I do it everywhere. Everybody who has ever picked me up says that O.J's a whirlwind at the end, he's running, he's grabbing things."

In defense of Phil and Tom, I do know there's something to be said for developing rapport with your suspect to get him talking. It's just that at some point, push has to come to shove. And during this interview the shove came way too late and way too gently.

"O.J.," Phil says uneasily. "We've got sort of a problem."

"Mmnh-mmh," the suspect replies.

"We've got some blood on and in your car. We've got some blood at your house. And it's sort of a problem."

Tom puts in, "Do you recall having that cut on your finger the last time you were at Nicole's house?"

"No," Simpson replies. "It was last night."

"Okay, so last night you cut it?"

"Somewhere after the recital . . ."

"What do you think happened?" Phil asks him. "Do you have any idea?"

O.J. subtly puts the detectives on the defensive.

"I have no idea, man. You guys haven't told me anything. I have no idea. . . . Every time I ask you guys, you say you're going to tell me in a bit . . ."

"Did you ever hit her, O.J.?"

"Uh, we had—that one night we had a fight."

"Mmnh-mmph."

"That night—that night we had a fight. Hey, she hit *me*."

"Yeah."

"You know, and—and, as I say, they never took my statement, they never wanted to hear my side. . . . Nicole was drunk, she did her thing, she started tearing up my house, you know. And I—I didn't punch her or anything, but I—I—you know—"

"Slapped her a couple times?"

"No. I wrestled her is all I did—"

"Uh, okay."

Nicole is dead, his children have no mother, he's talking about the time he was arrested for beating her—and once again, Simpson is whining about how *he* feels mistreated. As I sat listening to this crap, I thought: *This guy is going to deny everything all the way. He's never going to confess.* There wasn't one shred of remorse there; not enough real soul for him to need to unburden it by telling the truth. Some killers have a need to confess, at least to themselves. But I don't think he ever did.

That interview was one of the worst bits of police work I'd ever seen—but I kept my thoughts to myself. I couldn't afford to alienate my chief investigators. Besides, it was spilt milk. Complaining about their ineptitude would not help me get through this case.

I had serious qualms about playing this interview tape before the grand jury. And in the months to come I would debate endlessly whether to play it at trial. It was a very risky gambit. That decision would rest largely upon the composition and sentiment of the jury. If we ended up with jurors who were star-struck by the defendant, would they be offended by his callousness toward his wife and lover, or would they be beguiled by his crude jocularity? Would they take his loss of memory and vague responses for evasion, or would they see an innocent man willing to talk to police despite his pain and exhaustion, and who got nothing but suspicion in return?

I decided to hold off.

Instead I had Phil summarize the interview. He touched briefly on Simpson's self-pitying explanation of the beating on New Year's, 1989, and then on what Simpson called an "altercation"—the 1993 incident that had also resulted in a 911 call. "I kicked her door or something," Simpson had said.

That was as far as I intended to go into the issue of domestic violence for now. I'd handled DV cases before, and I knew they were very tricky. Husbands usually do not batter their wives in front of others. If a wife is killed, there is rarely an eyewitness to the murder. Or to the years of abuse that preceded it.

In this case, there was just too much we still didn't know. Had friends ever seen them fight? Had they fought since the divorce? How recently? What were the flashpoint issues between them? I was willing to put domestic violence on the back burner for the time being—until Keith Zlomsowitch forced our hand.

Zlomsowitch, a thirtysomething restaurateur, was passed on to us by the LAPD. He claimed to have witnessed O. J. Simpson stalking and harassing his wife. Zlomsowitch lived out of state and was due to board a plane home the next day. Like it or not, David and I had to bring him in before the grand jury to preserve his testimony.

I had no idea what Keith Zlomsowitch intended to say, and didn't get a chance to find out before he took the stand. Instead I spent our pre-interview trying to make sure he didn't taint his testimony with hearsay evidence. Since his story involved the victim, I had to make sure that he didn't repeat anything she might have said to him.

"Keith," I told him, "please listen very carefully to my questions. Anything that you heard O. J. Simpson say is fair territory, but don't tell me anything which Nicole may have said to you."

Zlomsowitch said he understood.

So I wound up listening with innocent fascination—along with everyone else in the courtroom—as Keith told how he had met Nicole in Aspen about two years before her death. At that time, he was director of operations for the Mezzaluna restaurants' Colorado and California operations. Nicole was legally separated from Simpson then and living at Gretna Green. In the spring of '92 he and Nicole became lovers, but only for about a month. During that time, Zlomsowitch said, O. J. Simpson would follow Nicole when she went out in the evening. Once Nicole and a party of friends showed up at the Mezzaluna in Beverly Hills, where Zlomsowitch was on duty. As he was sitting with her at her table, he noticed O. J. Simpson pull his car up to the parking attendant. Simpson came in and went directly to Nicole's table. He leaned over, stared at Zlomsowitch, and said, "I'm O. J. Simpson and she's still my wife."

"How would you describe his tone of voice?" I asked.

"Serious, if not scary," he said. "Just deep, threatening to the point of—yes, we were very intimidated."

Zlomsowitch told of another incident, in April 1992, which occurred at a restaurant called Tryst. After waiting for a table, Keith, Nicole, and a few of Nicole's friends had just sat down when Simpson appeared. This time, he walked past them and took a table about ten feet away. He pulled the chair around to face them and just stared. And stared. That freaked Zlomsowitch out.

Not long afterward, Keith went on another date with Nicole, this time to a comedy club where a friend of hers was performing. From there, they went dancing at a Hollywood club called Roxbury. They had been there less than an hour when Nicole said, "O.J. is here."

I had to tell the jury to disregard the statement attributed to Nicole. At that point, though, they seemed to be hanging on Zlomsowitch's every word, breathless to hear what happened next.

"We went back to Nicole's house," he continued. "We lit a few candles, put on a little music, poured a glass of wine, and we . . . began to become intimate." After they'd had sex, Nicole told him she thought it best if he went home and she went to bed.

The following day, Zlomsowitch came back to the house and sat with Nicole by the pool as her children swam. She complained of a stiff neck; they went into a bedroom off the swimming pool where he began to give her a neck message. After about five minutes, Zlomsowitch recalled, O. J. Simpson appeared two feet in front of them and said, "I can't believe it. . . . Look what you are doing. The kids are right out here by the pool."

According to Zlomsowitch, Simpson went on to say, "I watched you last night. I can't believe you would do that in the house. I watched you. . . . I saw everything you did."

Then he demanded to speak with Nicole alone. Zlomsowitch, who was still sitting on Nicole's back at that point, eased off slowly. He told us that he didn't want to make any sudden moves that might incite Simpson to anger.

At Nicole's urging, Keith left her alone to talk to her estranged husband. Several minutes later, O. J. Simpson emerged from the bedroom. Keith said he was frightened, but then, to his surprise, Simpson stuck out his hand. "No hard feelings, right?" he said, shaking Zlomsowitch's hand. "I'm a very proud man."

As Zlomsowitch spoke, I stood there with my mouth open in amazement. O. J. Simpson was spying on his wife in the bushes while she was having sex, then, the next day, shakes the hand of her lover? That was the weirdest thing I'd ever heard. (Since then, I've had a chance to learn a lot more about the nature of domestic violence. Batterers only rarely blame other men. It's usually the wife or girlfriend, "the bitch," who takes the heat. But at the time I first heard this story, Simpson's behavior struck me as utterly incomprehensible.)

All in all, Zlomsowitch seemed an honorable guy. He'd been a pallbearer at Nicole's funeral, and all he seemed to want out of this was to see justice done. The fact that he had been willing to recount events favorable to Simpson, like the handshake and apology, was reassuring proof of his honesty. And he had given us valuable new evidence— including the information about the stalking episodes—of Simpson's behavior as a jealous husband.

David was as relieved as I was that Zlomsowitch had panned out. You take a risk putting *any* witness on blind, and here we were throwing one after another on the stand without a vetting.

"I can't believe it," David groused to me as we ate lunch on the afternoon break. "We have five minutes to put this case together for the grand jury, and law professors across the country are going to take months dissecting and critiquing every word."

Man, if he only *knew* how true that would be.

Actually the grand jury was going pretty well. The only real screw-up was Shively. I told myself we'd been lucky to find *any* witnesses whose testimony had not been tainted by pretrial publicity. The important thing was to proceed step by step and not be distracted by the babble of media around us. The grand jurors had been admonished to do the same thing. "Turn off your radio, don't turn on your TV, don't pick up a newspaper, don't scan headlines at a newsstand."

Grand jurors usually take their charge very seriously, but they are also human and as curious as anyone else. On Thursday, June 23, we were wrapping up the testimony and I had already started drafting my closing statement. I'd give it on Friday, and we'd be done. I think the jurors would have had more than enough evidence to give us the indictment. Then this hysterical pace would subside, at least until the trial started, which would be months from now. Maybe I could even go back to eating dinner at home again.

These were my thoughts as I walked down the hallway toward Suzanne's office. I checked in with her at least once a day, usually around six o'clock. We'd kick back and shoot the breeze, or in more hectic times, like these, she'd fill me in on any brushfires that needed extinguishing. That night, I could smell smoke even before I reached her door. Suzanne and a visitor, a local television reporter, were sitting in front of the TV, riveted to the screen. There wasn't much to see, as I recall. Just the staccato sound of a tape being played. The voice of an anguished young woman filled the room.

"He broke my door. He broke the whole back door in. . . ."

A second voice, apparently that of a 911 operator, interrupted her: "And then he left and he came back?"

"Then he came and he practically knocked my upstairs door down, but he pounded it and then he screamed and hollered and I tried to get him out of the bedroom 'cause the kids were sleeping there. . . ."

"What the hell is this?" I asked Suzanne.

"Nicole," she replied without taking her eyes from the screen. "A 911 tape."

"What 911 tape?"

I knew that there had been police reports on the New Year's Eve of

1989 and the door-kicking incident of 1993. Both had been triggered by Nicole's calls to 911. But I was under the impression that the audiotapes of those calls had been destroyed in a routine recycling procedure.

My impression was wrong. It turns out that the city attorney's office, which prosecuted that '93 case, had kept its own copies of the tapes. The press had tracked them down and petitioned under the state Public Records Act to get them. And somehow, they had gotten those tapes released—before I had even heard that they existed.

Suzanne's reporter buddy handed me copies of the police reports on the tapes. I hadn't seen these, either.

"Oh, great," I fumed. "Now I'm getting discovery from the press!"

Within the space of an hour it seemed that tape was everywhere. You couldn't step within earshot of a radio without hearing Nicole's pitiful, quavering pleas for help. It was on all the television news shows, and they didn't play it just once, but kept repeating it, in a sick parody of MTV's heavy rotation.

"My ex-husband or my husband just broke into my house and he's ranting and raving. . . . He's O. J. Simpson, I think you know his record. . . . He's fucking going nuts. . . . He's screaming at my room-mate about me . . . about some guy I know and hookers . . . And it's all my fault, and now what am I going to do. . . ? I just don't want my kids exposed to this. . . ." When Nicole begged Simpson to calm down, for the sake of the children, his anger only increased. "I don't give a shit anymore! Motherfucker! I'm not leaving!"

The backlash was immediate. Our lines were flooded by outraged callers. And most of them took the side *not* of the panicked 119-pound woman, but of the out-of-control former football player who was ter-rorizing her. They said, "How can you do this to that poor man?" Everyone assumed that the release of the 911 tape was part of a cynical scheme hatched by the D.A.'s office, the LAPD, and the City Attorney's office to spin public opinion against Simpson.

What a joke. Believe me, there wasn't enough solidarity among these camps to coordinate a beer run, let alone an offensive like that. For days afterward, we would all point fingers at one another, Gil lit into the city attorney, James Hahn, for releasing the tape. Hahn insisted that he had acted in the belief that the LAPD had gotten approval from the D.A.'s office for his office to release the tape. The LAPD would say it was against releasing the tape, but felt it hadn't gotten support for that position from the D.A. In our office, it was David who took the fall. The cops had called, asking him if they should authorize release of the tape under the Public Records Act. And he had told them, "Do what you normally do." It was the right instruction—but the result was disastrous.

The worst part of it was watching Shapiro exploit this screwup. He filed a motion to halt the grand jury hearing on grounds of excessive publicity. At a hearing hastily convened on Friday in the courtroom of a former prosecutor named Lance Ito, Shapiro was preening like a peacock in full plumage. He accused the D.A.'s office of misconduct in making "improper expressions of personal opinion." He cited my "sole murderer" slip as well as Gil's speculation that Simpson might cop an insanity plea.

I couldn't let this pass.

"Robert Shapiro has lost no opportunity to exploit coverage in this case to get sympathy for his client," I told the court. "He has been no stranger to the spotlight."

But the barbs exchanged by Shapiro and me were at that very moment being rendered irrelevant. That morning, our grand jury adviser, Terry White, had come back to Gil with reports that a couple of jurors were discussing the 911 tape. That cinched it. If we did get an indictment, it could be thrown out on the strength of this revelation alone. Gil himself had no choice but to file a motion to dismiss the grand jury. Superior Court Judge Cecil Mills heard the motion and began interviewing the jurors to see if they had read or heard anything that might affect their judgment. He concluded that they had, and granted Gil's request to recuse the jury.

It was over.

In some ways I was not unhappy to see this grand jury go bust. The case had drawn such intense public interest that I was uncomfortable seeking an indictment in a closed proceeding. I felt we'd always be susceptible to the charge that funny things were happening behind locked doors. Better to bail out early and try for a better result at a preliminary hearing in open court. Besides, the grand jury had been a useful dress rehearsal for what was to come—sort of an overture to the opera. By totally immersing us in the case, it sharpened our perceptions of its weaknesses and strengths. I'd even prepared a grand jury summation that was a very early first draft for a closing statement.

Still, the suddenness with which the grand jury was disbanded came as a shock. None of us could remember such a thing ever happening before. It also put us in a very tough spot logistically. Normally, we have weeks, or even months, to pull these things together. But the deadline mandated by law was upon us. We had less than a week to prepare for a preliminary hearing.

A prelim is like a little trial where the witnesses you put up can be cross-examined by the defense. This means you have to go back, re-interview each one of them—after comparing their statements to the grand jury to those made to police. We couldn't afford any unpleasant surprises. No more Jill Shivelys. It would mean sorting through the complex physical evidence and figuring out a comprehensible way to present it. We'd be clocking fifteen-hour days, at least.

This was a really low moment. The only way I could keep my spirits up was to hold on to my fantasy that Gil would relent and let me keep David on the team. That night, Gil called us both into his office. He looked straight at me, and something in that look told me it was hopeless.

"Marcia," he began firmly, "you're going to have to pick a partner. I'll try and accommodate any reasonable request, but I want you to find someone who's as strong as you."

What he meant was I couldn't bring on some baby D.A. who would just carry my books. Even though I knew what the answer would be, I turned toward David and inclined my head in his direction.

"No," Gil said flatly. "I need David on Menendez."

I could feel hairline cracks fanning out in crazy patterns all through my confidence. With David by my side I felt strong and sure. Having him to strategize with would be a dream come true. But there was no appealing Gil's decision. I'd have to find another partner. Someone who had real strength. Someone who could brace me against the coming storm.

Although I admitted this to no one, I was scared to death.

War Games

He has to say yes—there's no one else.

That was my mantra as I walked down the hall from my office to the corner office occupied by Bill Hodgman. I was about to change his life. Right now he was in a relatively low-stress post as the director of Central Operations; if he accepted my offer, and Gil approved, he'd be subject to unprecedented heat. I think he knew I was coming. I almost expected to find a sign on his door that said "Leave me alone." I wouldn't have blamed him. But I also wouldn't have known where to go next.

There were only seven deputies besides me in the Special Trials Unit, and all of them were either already trying a case or about to start one. I'd thought a bit about Brian Kelberg, a thin, intense man with a goatee and dark glasses. Brian was almost pure intellect. He had spent a little time in medical school before switching to law. It would be terrific, I thought, to have him as a sounding board for the complex evidentiary issues of the Simpson case. But I knew having him as co-counsel wouldn't work. Though Brian was brilliant, he was a loner. He'd always felt that the team approach to prosecution wasn't an effective way to try a case.

Then my thoughts had turned to Bill. We'd worked together in management, and we'd clicked. I was brassy and often abrasive; Bill was gentle, a conciliator. We laughed a lot together—and a sense of humor would be as essential as a law degree in a pressure cooker like this one. But most important, he was one hell of a lawyer.

Bill had started out in Long Beach, one of the branch courts. Shortly after he arrived Downtown, he prosecuted savings-and-loan executive Charles Keating. The resulting conviction (though ultimately reversed) was a thrilling triumph in an office starved for victories, and for a while Bill was the golden boy. He'd been with us only about a year when Gil appointed him director of Central Operations. He was the first real trial lawyer I can recall who ever held that job. His placement had been a boost in morale to all of us on the front lines.

All the same, Bill's experience with Downtown juries was fairly limited. I'd done some of my juvenile work in Long Beach: the community was conservative, so the jury pool tended to be law-and-order types. The judges pretty much mirrored that point of view. As a result, criminal trials were relatively orderly affairs, seldom the grueling battles that were the daily experience of deputies Downtown.

The Simpson case was shaping up to be the ultimate Downtown case. I didn't know if Bill was up to the rough-and-tumble. I didn't even know if *I* was. Of one thing, however, I was certain: Bill Hodgman had a gift for evaluating the strengths and weaknesses in evidence. Bill and I had talked through a number of cases in the last year, and I had come to admire his instincts.

I needed him.

His door was open, and I leaned in. "Got a minute?"

"Sure, partner, come on in."

Bill took a seat behind his huge desk, framed by a postcard-worthy panorama of downtown L.A. It was very luxurious by county standards. It was even carpeted.

"Bill," I said, "remember how we've talked about wanting to try a case together?"

He nodded. I couldn't read his expression.

"How would you like to do Simpson with me?"

He smiled.

"I have been kind of anxious to get back into court," he said slowly. "I don't know how my wife will take it, and I hate to miss my time with Alec."

I knew what he meant. When Bill had been trying Keating, I'd been knee-deep in Bardo. We'd find ourselves in the office on weekends slaving away at our respective witness lists, and we'd commiserate about how our cases were cutting into family time. I remember him telling me that his son, Alec, then four years old, was taking his absences hard.

But Bill was too intrigued by this once-in-a-lifetime case to let it pass. "Let me talk to my wife, see how she feels about it," he said finally. And we left it at that.

I don't know what went on in that conversation, but when Bill showed up at my office the next day, he gave me the thumbs-up. We went down to Gil's office to get his blessing. We received not only that but our marching orders.

"I want you two to work as equals," said Gil. "No first- or second-chair situation."

I didn't like that. It wasn't that I felt competitive, but for strategic reasons, every team needs a capo. Otherwise, you lose too much time negotiating over every little disagreement in approach. I also admit that it was disappointing to have Gil zing me like that. Again. I thought I'd hidden my feelings, but apparently not. Bill pulled me aside and said, "Marcia, it's your case. I know what the realities are." And during the months to come, he was as good as his word. Bill knew someone had to lead.

We needed to move fast. Shapiro was demanding that the preliminary hearing be held within the time set by statute, ten days after the arraignment. That meant we would have to be ready to go within a week. We knew that the media were gearing up to cover these hearings extensively; they would be beaming testimony into the homes of our jury pool. Our office has an official policy about cameras in courtrooms: don't object to it. So I had no choice in the matter. This left no room for the fumbles or rough spots that in normal circumstances are routinely tolerated at an early stage of a case. No more flying by the seat of our pants.

I'd told Gil earlier in the week that we should assemble a team of experts from our office to analyze the case—a sort of war council. That way, deputies with different specialties could lend us their expertise for formulating strategy. Gil thought it was a good idea, and called a meeting for Saturday, June 25. On Friday, Gil and I hashed out who should attend. He first suggested Curt Hazell, the head of the Narcotics Unit. Hazell was an expert on search and seizure, and we needed someone who would help us deal with problems arising from the search of Simpson's house.

I also wanted to hear from Lydia Bodin, our expert on domestic violence; she, I thought, might help us use Simpson's history to show that Nicole's murder was premeditated, rather than an impulsive act of passion. Lydia would team with Scott Gordon, a deputy whose experience in the Sex Crimes Division had led him on to a personal crusade against spousal abuse. He'd even drafted legislation on the issue.

To shore up the blood work, I wanted Lisa Kahn, the deputy who had given me tutorials in DNA on that no-body case I'd done with Phil. We still didn't know if Simpson would try a mental defense, but if he did, I wanted to have someone in the wings with medical training—and Brian Kelberg, whom I had briefly considered as a trial partner, would be perfect.

Bill would be there, of course. And I was happy when Gil said that David should attend as well.

On Saturday morning, June 25, about fifteen deputies and brass all met in the conference room next to Gil's office. Most wore jeans and workshirts, though I'd rejected my usual weekend attire of leggings, Reeboks, and an oversized T-shirt in favor of slacks and a blouse. While the clothes were casual, the atmosphere was tense.

"Go ahead, Marcia," said Gil, abruptly cutting off small talk. "Brief us on what we have so far."

I laid it all out, beginning with the centerpiece of our case: blood. That's what the Simpson case would be about.

Nicole's blood.

Ron's blood.

O. J. Simpson's blood.

Blood would tell the truth. I was convinced it would convict.

"Here's how it breaks down," I began, speaking from notes I'd scribbled on a yellow legal pad. "The police lab did DNA testing on the blood drops at Bundy leading away from the victims—and they all come back to Simpson. The bloody shoe prints to the right of those drops are a size twelve—Simpson's size. The blood on the Rockingham glove seems to be a mixture of Ron's and Nicole's blood, and possibly Simpson's. We'll send the samples to Cellmark for more sophisticated testing."

I glanced around the room to make sure I hadn't lost anybody. Nope.

More results were coming in, I told them. There was a bloody shoe print on the driver's-side floorboard of the Bronco. We were preserving it for shoe-print comparison before we did the DNA testing. The knit cap found between the victims at Bundy, I told them, was set to be examined for hair and trace evidence, but nothing had been done on it yet.

On the chalkboard mounted behind Gil's seat, I sketched a diagram of Rockingham. *That's* where Simpson parked the Bentley, I showed them. *Here's* where Allan Park pulled his limo up to the gate. And *here's* the back wall of Kato's guest house.

They began pelting me with questions:

When exactly did Simpson leave for the airport?

Where did Allan Park first see the black male walking toward the door?

How could Kato not have seen him, too?

I could address some of these questions, but certainly not all of them. When I didn't have an answer there would be an uncomfortable silence, then more questions, with a slightly more aggressive tone. In fact, even though many of the people in this room were my friends, the questioning at times was not entirely friendly. It wasn't just that everyone was feeling the pressure. It wasn't just that the reputation of our office was at stake. Maybe they wanted not only to see where the weak points lay, but to test *me*, to see if Marcia Clark could stand up to a pummeling.

"Give me a *break*," I whispered to David when I finally got back to my seat.

We had to make a decision. What precise crime would we charge O. J. Simpson with? Three options were open to us: murder one, which required establishing premeditation; murder two, for which we would have to show intent to kill, although the killing could be on rash impulse; or manslaughter, which meant demonstrating an intent to kill mitigated by the heat of passion. The crucial question is whether the evidence shows a clear intent and decision to kill. I felt that it most certainly did. You could not look at those photos of the murder scene and think otherwise.

"I'd like to charge the defendant with two counts of murder in the first degree," I said.

Not everyone agreed.

"You're looking at an uphill battle to ask a jury to tag O. J. Simpson with anything," said Peter Bozanich. Peter was director of Branch and Area. I respected Peter, who was among the best in sizing up the strength of a case.

"You got him, there's no question about that," he said, in a resigned, almost philosophical tone, "but the guy's a hero, and people aren't going to want to drop the hammer on him."

Peter was right. I knew it. Hell, we all did. But I felt that as a matter of principle, we should ignore O. J. Simpson's celebrity in our decision to charge. A defendant, regardless of personal popularity, should be held responsible for his acts.

Brian Kelberg felt that second-degree murder was the more legally correct choice. "I basically see this as a rage-type killing," he said. "I think he did not go there planning to kill her."

"But what about the fact that he brought the knife, the gloves, and the ski cap?" I countered. "Not to mention the fact that he conveniently had a flight to catch immediately afterward."

"I think he went there intending to scare her," Brian insisted. "And when he saw Ron Goldman walk up, he became angry and things got out of hand."

That didn't feel right to me. Simpson had packed a knife with a blade at least five inches long, along with cashmere-lined winter gloves and a ski cap—in the middle of June. This went beyond intent to scare. It was a plan to commit murder. It may well have been that the food run Simpson had taken with Kato was part of the planning, too. It seemed out of character for him to dash out for fast food with a houseguest *cum* lackey.

"Remember," I told my colleagues, recalling what Kato had said about that night, "Simpson had never done that before. The whole thing has the feeling of an alibi setup."

Gil looked to his two other top assistants, Frank Sundstedt and Sandy Buttitta, who hadn't weighed in yet.

Frank was a big teddy bear of a guy with curly blond hair and a mustache. He was someone I'd grown to like and respect during my days in management. He really cared about the deputies and agonized like an overly concerned father over decisions affecting their welfare.

"First—at least, that's what it looks like to me," he replied.

Then everybody turned to Sandy. She was a strong, no-nonsense professional, the first woman to be appointed chief deputy. At that point, I'd had very little interaction with her, and had no idea what she'd say.

"I think it's first-degree," she said.

Gil's silence was affirmation: we had a decision.

The case of Ron Goldman was a bit different. Nicole was obviously the intended target. Goldman, it appeared, was a visitor who happened onto the scene at the wrong moment. His death could have been classified as either first- or second-degree murder. But I was pushing for first-degree. "Remember," I said, "the number and nature of his wounds alone show premeditation." Everyone in the room understood what I meant: under the law, premeditation cannot be measured in time. It's there or it's not, even if it occurs mere seconds before the crime. The fact that Ron's killer did not dispatch him with a single blow, but a series of them, to me showed deliberate intent.

"Also," I continued, "it's reasonable to assume that Ron's murder was not the rash impulse of a jealous ex-husband, but the calculated elimination of a witness to Nicole's murder." That, of course, would also justify a charge of murder one.

No one objected. Most significant, Gil Garcetti once more tacitly agreed. There was a brief silence as we all recognized that the first momentous decision in this case had been made. We would charge Orenthal James Simpson with two counts of murder one.

*   *   *

Next item on the agenda: strategy for the prelims. The big question concerned how much evidence to put on. Normally, a preliminary hearing is a bare-bones production. The prosecutor submits just enough evidence for a judge to find probable cause that a suspect should be bound over for trial. If you go beyond that, you're unnecessarily allowing the defense early access to your case and your strategy; the conventional wisdom says that you should make them work for it through discovery motions. But this case was anything but normal.

In effect, the defense already had access to our case: they were entitled to receive the grand jury transcripts. They'd be able to prepare themselves for most of the witnesses we intended to call. So now that we'd lost the advantage of a bare-bones strategy, I argued, we should present a relatively complete case—that way, we'd not only make sure that the public realized the strength of our case, but the municipal judge would feel more confident binding Simpson over for trial.

"Our evidence is strong," I told my colleagues. "I think we should just lay it out there for the world to see."

This meant that we would call the dog-bark and time-line witnesses for sure. And, of course, the blood witnesses.

Oh, God. That meant Dennis Fung.

"We'll need to do some remedial work with the criminalists," I mumbled, shuddering slightly at the prospect of watching Fung shuffle through his reports in front of millions of viewers. Still, he had collected the evidence. I'd have to spend some serious prep time to whip him into shape before the prelim. But there was no choice but to put him on.

Collin was another matter. I had confidence that Collin would turn out to be a pretty good witness at trial. (And, indeed, he was.) In the meantime, however, he needed some prep time to get down the lengthy technical explanations of DNA. I felt it would be better all around to hold off on DNA testimony until trial, when we could put on the sophisticated results from Cellmark. In the meantime, I suggested to my comrades, why not go with more conventional tests? I knew the person to do them.

"Think Special Investigations would let loose of Greg Matheson?" I asked, looking around the room.

Greg was a highly esteemed serologist at the Special Investigations

Division. He was scrupulously honest, and I knew from his previous appearances on the witness stand that if we used him to augment Fung, he could present the evidence in a simple, straightforward way. He could also fend off attacks on cross without becoming irritable.

Someone asked whether Greg's tests might use up too much of our blood samples. Good point. If we tested all the blood drops taken from Bundy for the prelims, we'd consume too much to allow for both the prosecution and the defense to do separate tests later on. And I *wanted* to have enough for both sides to do their own tests. Maybe it was a throwback to my days at the defense bar, but I always felt the prosecution should welcome independent verification of its lab work. If their results supported ours, we'd be golden.

Brian Kelberg offered a suggestion: "Why don't you have Greg test just *one* of the blood drops at Bundy?" he asked. "A single drop on the trail would be enough to establish identity for the prelim. And if those drops are Simpson's, he's made."

I saw nods all around the room. I scrawled a note to pull whatever strings necessary to get Greg Matheson assigned to us.

For the time being, we decided to hold off on one major category of evidence: DV, domestic violence. We all agreed that the physical evidence alone demonstrated enough premeditation to warrant murder in the first. That meant we did not necessarily have to introduce any battering incidents to support the charge. And to tell you the truth, I was just as glad to stay clear of this issue for the moment. The only way DV might be thrust to the fore was if Simpson attempted to plead insanity, or tried to float some other kind of heat-of-passion defense. In that case, we had to be ready to refute. Lydia Bodin authoritatively cited several cases in which murders that arose from violent domestic quarrels were nevertheless prosecuted at first-degree. So even if Simpson tried to worm his way out of this by claiming temporary insanity, we could still charge murder one.

Early the following week, we served a second warrant on Rockingham.

I began to write this one myself, but thankfully, Curt Hazell took over to make sure that it was airtight. This was an abundance of caution, but caution was necessary. By now, of course, I had had an opportunity to read carefully through Phil's affidavit in support of the first warrant served on Rockingham the morning of June 13, and was distressed to find several glaring errors.

Phil had written, for instance, that Simpson had left town unexpectedly, when, in fact, his trip to Chicago had been planned in advance. Phil had apparently gotten that misimpression as the result of asking Kato where Simpson was. Kato had passed him off to Arnelle, who'd said something to the effect of "Isn't he here?"

Phil had described the stain on the Bronco's door handle as "human" blood. But the criminalist had only done a presumptive test, which showed the presence of blood. In theory, it could have been animal blood.

The most serious thing I saw in that warrant, however, was not an error, but an omission. For whatever reason, Phil had failed to put in the affidavit that they'd had to leap the wall that morning to unlock the gate. He certainly hadn't mentioned it to me when he'd called me for advice on the warrant. I was seriously annoyed by this.

Even though the warrantless entry seemed, under the circumstances, justified, the omission of it on the affidavit could serve to seriously undermine his credibility.

Both Curt and I knew that come the preliminary hearing, we would end up doing battle to justify the cops' entry and defend their integrity. For now, I was content to see that the second warrant was done right. I wanted a thorough search for the items we now knew Simpson had on the night of the murders. Principally, we were looking for the knife from Ross Cutlery and the dark sweats Kato had seen Simpson wearing during the early evening, neither of which had turned up. I also wanted to search the Bentley. If we found no blood there, it would indicate that Simpson had not wounded his finger until after the outing to McDonald's; that, in turn, would place the cut closer to the time of the murders.

The five of us—Tom, Phil, David, Bill, and I—arrived in a single car at Rockingham on the morning of Tuesday, June 28. Reporters blocked the gates. Overhead, I could hear the thrum of copters. The scene looked like something out of *Apocalypse Now.*

"Did you guys request those?" I asked Tom.

"It's the media," he replied, disgusted.

We parked on Rockingham and were ushered in by a couple of uniforms. I met up with John Stevens, a photographer for the D.A.'s office, whom I'd asked to come on this search to videotape the grounds. I wanted him to record Allan Park's view of the driveway and front door from his position facing the Ashford gate. This would allow me to demonstrate to a jury how Park's vantage point allowed him to see Simpson entering the house. I also showed John a couple of other areas we should document—for instance, the south pathway where the glove had been found. If a case takes months to come to trial, you can forget little details of layout. You find yourself clinging to frames of videotape. It's essential to capture those images right away.

As Tom and I walked through the kitchen I noticed a pretty young black woman standing in a small desk-and-bookcase nook. She looked uncomfortable. I hadn't expected any civilians, so at first I assumed she was a cop.

"Marcia," Tom said, "this is Arnelle Simpson. Arnelle, Marcia Clark is the D.A. on the case."

Arnelle had no reason to like me. I'm sure she saw me as just one more intruder tramping through her home. I didn't know what to say except "I'm sorry for all this. We'll get out of your way as soon as possible." She said nothing—just smiled weakly and shook my hand.

When Tom and I got to the pool area, we found Phil and Mark Fuhrman standing near a round glass table. I thought we might be able to grab a few minutes to talk. Sometime before the hearings we would all have to sort out the events of the detectives' first trip out to Rockingham on the morning of June 13. I would need a solid, lucid accounting, not only of their actions, but of their frame of mind, in order to defend that search.

But as we spoke, the din of the news copters grew so loud that we were having to shout in one another's ears. We stopped that when someone warned us that the media might have parabolic mikes pointed in our direction. "Let's try writing notes to each other," I shouted at Mark, and he nodded back, pulling out his pad. But before he'd managed to set anything on paper, one of the detectives motioned to us that some eye in the sky might be able to read them. I gave up. We agreed to meet later in my office to finish the interview.

We retreated inside, where I happened to glance at a television mounted on the wall in Simpson's living room. The day's news fare was . . . us. Local programming had been canceled in order to bring the viewers of Los Angeles a live, on-the-spot broadcast of the scene at Rockingham. The image on the screen was the exterior of the house. And I was inside the house, watching them watching us. Could this get any weirder?

I went through that house room by room to see how the search was going. Simpson's bedroom was thoroughly tossed, but the day's results were to be measured mainly in the negative: No knife; no bloody sweat clothes. Nor were there bloodstains in the Bentley.

We did, however, seize some additional pieces of evidence, among them a single leather glove, this one black, which I'd seen lying on a table in the living room during the first search. It had a different lining from the pair found at Bundy and in the south walkway, but both the single glove and the bloody pair in evidence had been manufactured by Aris. I thought this would tend to suggest that Simpson favored the brand.

When I reached the foyer, a cop called out to me, "I found his divorce file." He handed me a letter typed on the letterhead of "O. J. Simpson Enterprises." It was from Simpson to Nicole and was dated June 6, 1994. It put her on written notice that she did not have permission or authority to use his permanent home address at 360 North Rockingham as her residence or mailing address for any purpose, including tax returns. "I cannot take part in any course of action by you that might intentionally or unintentionally be misleading to the Internal Revenue or California Franchise Tax Board," he wrote. It was signed "O.J." and cc'ed to his attorney, LeRoy Taft.

Until now Simpson had been claiming that at the time of Nicole's murder, his relationship with her had been amicable. But in this typed sheet I was holding, he was ordering her in icy legalese to steer clear of Rockingham. This pair had been divorced for two years, and they were still arguing over assets. When I saw the letters "IRS," I knew we had our flashpoint.

I took the letter outside to show David. His eyes widened as he read it.

"See the date?" I asked him.

"Incredible," he agreed. But neither of us knew exactly how to proceed.

After a moment of silence, David looked at me. I could tell what he was thinking. This piece of evidence lay in a gray area. The letter was clearly not specified in the warrant. There had been no way we could have been aware of its existence. And yet we were standing with a piece of evidence that went clearly to the defendant's state of mind during the days before the murders.

"I think the law is on our side," David said finally. "I think we can take it."

So we did.

Months later, at trial, the trial judge would thwart our first attempts to present the IRS letter as evidence. Because it was not mentioned in the affidavit to the search warrant, he ruled, it was inadmissible. He was right, or course. But by then I'd figured out a lawful way to procure that document. I promptly sent Attorney Taft a subpoena for the letter.

I was not losing that letter. No way. No how.

I set about our preparations for the prelims with my usual anal-retentive devotion, but it was like trying to neatly crayon in one of my sons' coloring books while riding in a bumper car. I'd just get up to speed, and I'd be knocked outside the lines.

Case in point: it took a lot of phone calls and a lot of politicking before I finally persuaded SID to assign Greg Matheson to do the initial blood analysis to determine whether the blood might be Simpson's. Conventional tests will usually narrow the number of possible donors to only 10 to 15 percent of the population. In a city like Los Angeles, with nearly three and a half million people, that's still a whopping 450,000 candidates.

But we caught a real break. The blood type that came up on the drop at Bundy was fairly rare: it could have come from only one half of one percent of the population. Only one person in 200 had that blood type. And Orenthal James Simpson was one of them. Yes!

I carried my good news down to a meeting with Bill and some of the brass. But before I could utter a word, I was stopped dead in my tracks by their somber faces.

"I've got rather disturbing news," Bill said to me. "The knife salesman sold his story to the *National Enquirer*."

Jose Camacho was the salesman who'd told the cops how Simpson had purchased a stiletto only days before the murder. He had testified before the grand jury, where he'd come off as a pretty decent guy. Now he'd pulled a Shively? Oh, damn! How many times had we told our witnesses to stay away from the media? We'd even admonished them not to talk to *anybody,* because in this overheated atmosphere you couldn't predict who might sell a story heard secondhand. But what good were our threats? If someone wants to talk to a reporter, there is no legal way to stop him. When the hand holding the mike is dangling a $10,000 check in front of a witness who barely makes minimum wage, it's easy to see how abstractions like justice and integrity can get shoved aside.

Camacho's interview-for-profit now limited our options. Technically, we could try to prosecute him for contempt. Unlike Shively, Camacho had sold his story *after* testifying before the grand jury, where he was instructed not to discuss his testimony with anyone. But I doubted that we could get a contempt ruling to stick. Camacho was a Spanish-speaking witness; he was already setting the stage to claim that he did not understand the admonition. Which was nonsense. Camacho had felt confident enough of his English to testify without an interpreter at the grand jury hearing. In fact, his English was excellent.

Was he ruined as a witness? Anything he said on the stand would be tainted by the fact that he'd sold his story, a story that was worth more to the tabloids if it incriminated Simpson. If we had the knife itself, it might have been worth our effort to overcome this taint. But we didn't have the knife.

"I say we don't call him," I blurted. I looked around the table for reaction. Gil, as usual, was hard to read. Dan Murphy, one of the D.A.'s top assistants, was leaning back in his chair, eyes turned to the ceiling, hand to cheek. Frank Sundstedt was slumped into his chair, hands folded together against his chest—his characteristic contemplative pose.

"Trial's a long way away," Frank said finally. "By the time you start picking a jury, this story won't even be a blip on the screen. If we do turn up the knife, Camacho's testimony will be important. I think we ought to preserve it, just in case he takes a powder."

Frank had a point. If a witness testifies at a preliminary hearing, that testimony is usually admissible at trial even if the witness has absconded. That would be useful if by some chance we found the knife. Gil agreed: we'd put Camacho on. I understood their reasoning, but I doubted it would be worth the nasty hits we were going to take for putting on such a damaged witness. More specifically—the hits *I* was going to take. It was one thing to agree in principle around a conference table. But somebody has to stand up there with a straight face and present this opportunist as a witness for the People.

Our whole team worked like maniacs preparing for the prelims. I had no time to worry about how big the case was getting; it was all I could do to gather and organize all the material. After all, we had a week to do a job that normally we'd have had three months to complete. The day before the prelims were set to start was especially hectic. Shapiro filed his motion to suppress the evidence seized at Rockingham before Phil tried to get a warrant. We'd expected this, but just not so soon. So we got a judge to postpone testimony on the motion until we had some time to prepare. Then we went back upstairs to work.

We stayed until after nine on the eve of the prelims. I was sure that most of the press would have retreated to their respective hotel bars by then. Instead, as Suzanne, Bill, and I walked out the back of the CCB, we saw that the parking lot was more crowded than a tailgate party on homecoming weekend. For the past week, it had been jammed with vans, satellite dishes, and lunch wagons. ABC, NBC, CBS had all erected scaffolds that resembled medieval assault engines. The correspondents themselves, however, displayed the more modern enthusiasm of fans vamping behind the bleachers before the big game.

Suzanne wasn't surprised: for the past few days her office had been handling hundreds of calls every hour, from every corner of the world. Just about all the callers, of course, wanted interviews.

Out of nowhere, a reporter with a video cameraman behind him shoved a mike in our faces.

"How do you feel tonight? Are you ready for court tomorrow?" he asked.

Bill tossed off an innocuous one-liner as we hustled out of range.

I'd begun to realize that no matter what happened in court, the sheer amplitude of media coverage would distort these proceedings like never before. It made me feel out of control, angry and helpless.

I tried not to dwell on those things the next morning as I scrambled to get Matt ready for school and organize my thoughts at the same time. *Just do what you always do,* I told myself. I would repeat that many times to myself in the next year.

I arrived on time that morning. I believe I was even early. Bill and I had witnesses stashed all over the eighteenth floor and we ducked in and out of offices, touching base with them, reassuring them. Our last stop was the room used for press conferences. When Bill opened the door, I found myself face-to-face with a roomful of strangers. They were tense, their faces expectant. The victims' families.

Usually, I meet with the next of kin almost immediately after I get a case. I go out to their homes or they come in to the office to meet me. Wherever they feel more comfortable. It's important to make that connection right from the start. The unusual circumstances of this case had caused me to proceed more cautiously. For most of the first week after the murders, the case was not officially mine. It was a bad idea, I thought, to make contact and set about establishing rapport with these deeply hurt people when there was a chance that I might not be assigned to the case for keeps. The District Attorney's office should convey to a victim's family the feeling of strength and certainty. And that could not happen if they were being passed around from deputy to deputy.

The cops had interviewed them, of course. Gil had spoken to them to convey his sympathy. They had been commended to the care of our "victims' coordinator," whose job it is to accompany them to court and answer their questions. I had had brief phone conversations with the Browns and the Goldmans several days earlier, but only to introduce myself. I was hoping they would forgive the awkwardness of meeting under these circumstances.

On one side of the room were the Browns, awesomely handsome and erect. Lou and Juditha, flanked by Denise, Dominique, and Tanya. The suspect was their son-in-law, their brother-in-law. Exactly what stance they were taking toward him was still unclear to me. I found them very hard to read.

On the other side of the room stood the Goldmans. Ron's father, Fred; his stepmother, Patti; and, of course, Kim, a reed-thin girl whose pretty features were red and swollen from crying. Looking at her made me recall the pang I'd felt upon seeing her brother's face for the first time, in the coroner's photos.

"What's going to happen now?" asked Patti Goldman. She was a petite woman with large, lovely green eyes. Fred stood with his arm draped around her protectively.

"We'll have some motions to begin with, nothing major," I said. "The defense has filed a motion to suppress evidence, but that will be heard later during the hearing."

"Suppress the evidence!" Denise Brown snapped. "What do you mean?"

I could understand why this idea offended her. She would later express her concerns to reporters in even stronger terms. "If he's innocent," she would ask, "why does he want to suppress evidence?"

"It's a motion we see a lot," I explained. "The defense claims the police got evidence illegally, and they've asked the judge to throw it out. We're prepared for that and I don't think there's any chance that the judge will grant it."

We talked a little more about the sorts of things that the defense was likely to do. No matter how hurtful it might seem, I told them, they shouldn't take it personally.

Easy for me to say.

At 9:10 A.M. on June 30, 1994, Judge Kathleen Kennedy-Powell bade us good morning and looked over her courtroom. It was packed—the hottest ticket in Hollywood. Only ten seats were available to the general public, and the media folk had to scramble to secure one of the twenty-five seats set aside for them. But no one had to miss a thing: the best seat in the house was reserved for the cameras.

I'd never appeared before Judge Kennedy-Powell before, but I'd actually worked with her in the eighties when she was deputy D.A. I knew her as a hardworking, conscientious prosecutor who took her job very seriously. She looked at ease on the bench. But we couldn't get down to business. Someone was missing.

"Well, I guess the defendant is not out yet," Judge Kennedy-Powell observed.

"This is the quietest courtroom I've ever been in, Your Honor," Shapiro quipped, trying to fill the dead time.

"I don't know how long that will remain, but we'll see," Kennedy-Powell smiled.

At last, the door opened. The courtroom went silent. O. J. Simpson strode in, impeccably dressed, looking surprisingly fit. What an impressive transformation from the bedraggled, confused defendant who had appeared for his arraignment. His new role was the O.J. You Know and Love, Falsely Accused. And no Shakespearean actor would play this one better.

Judge Kennedy-Powell asked the record to reflect the defendant's presence and asked counsel to present themselves.

"Marcia Clark for the People," I began.

It's hard to believe that my first act that day was arguing about the hairs on O. J. Simpson's head. But it's true.

We'd requested hair samples from Simpson, so we could determine whether his matched several found at the crime scene. Shapiro had offered us a ludicrously insufficient number: three. It was up to me to argue first.

Oblivious to the hype and cameras, I launched right into my reasoning. This was my job; I had been doing it for years. Carefully, I explained how we needed samples from various parts of the head; the usual quantity is a hundred hairs. But only the criminalist taking the samples could determine how many were needed.

"Mr. Shapiro?" asked Judge Kennedy-Powell.

"Your Honor," he said soberly, "according to Dr. Henry Lee, our chief criminalist, who is the head of the Department of Criminology in Connecticut, he tells us one to three hairs are sufficient."

Judge Kennedy-Powell mused aloud that she had never seen a case where the prosecution was limited to a sample of three hairs. But then she faltered. She would not let us take more than ten hairs unless we could present expert witnesses who could establish how many hairs were required for a valid sample.

I was ready. Our expert was Michele Kestler, director of the SID crime lab. She backed me up in saying that a case like this commonly required seventy-five to one hundred strands.

On cross-examination, Shapiro immediately assumed the glacial pace that would become his trademark. He insisted upon a detailed recitation of Kestler's credentials, her résumé, her experience— everything but what she ate for breakfast. He had her recite all sorts of minutiae about her profession and the specific samples of blood and hair she had received from our searches. Shapiro again cited the source for his contention that only a single hair was required.

"Are you familiar with a gentleman by the name of Dr. Henry Lee?" he asked her.

She was.

"Have you seen his fifty-page curriculum vitae lately?" he asked. *Give me a break.* And then Shapiro asked Kestler what sources *she* had relied upon for her opinion that seventy-five to one hundred hairs were required.

Michele produced a book co-authored and edited by none other than Dr. Henry Lee.

Judge Kennedy-Powell gave us our hundred hairs.

I savored that small victory even as I realized what this skirmish meant: nothing in this case would be conceded without interminable bickering.

Bill, bless his heart, had agreed to put on the knife salesman, Jose Camacho. It was predictably painful. Bill walked Camacho through a straightforward account of selling the stiletto to Simpson the morning of May 9. Then Bill fronted the *Enquirer* business. The clerk seemed like a harmless little man. I don't think he was a liar, just a sellout. How he would have looked in the eyes of a jury, I don't know. That question was rendered academic by the advent of a mysterious manila envelope.

It seemingly materialized from thin air. One minute, in the middle of Camacho's testimony, Judge Kennedy-Powell left the courtroom, and the next minute she was back, producing with a flourish a yellow manila envelope containing some sort of solid object. She'd received, she said, an envelope containing evidence collected by a special court master at the defense's request. She intended to open it. Shapiro shot out of his seat with an objection. I chimed in with one of my own. You didn't have to be Hercule Poirot to guess what was sealed inside: a knife. But I couldn't be sure. And for months down the road I wouldn't be sure. Periodically, we would file motions to compel the defense to reveal the contents. The defense would object and our motion would be tabled. This happened time and again.

We were well into the criminal trial by the time we were allowed to learn that the envelope did indeed contain a stiletto. The report said that it had been discovered by Jason Simpson in the medicine cabinet of Simpson's bathroom. Then it had been turned over by Shapiro to a special court master, who gave it to Judge Kennedy-Powell. (Shapiro was unhappy that she introduced it at the prelim—apparently he'd been hoping to blindside us with this evidence during the trial.) The knife's discovery was supposedly made *after* our second search of June 28.

I never believed the medicine cabinet story. I'd been at Rock-ingham all through the second search, and the rooms had been taken to pieces by officers looking specifically for that knife. But the question was largely academic. The knife didn't matter. It is too easy to boil a knife to destroy traces of blood and tissue. It is not difficult to go out and buy a duplicate. No coroner could say with certainty that it was the murder weapon. Knives, unlike guns, do not smoke: they do not leave proof-positive evidentiary calling cards. If I'd really pressed to get it into evidence, however, I'm sure that all I would have gotten was a spanking-clean knife, property of a known collector of weapons. In the end, we let the stiletto rest in its eight-by-eleven manila envelope—where, I believe, it remains today.

Eventually, I imagine, O. J. Simpson will reclaim it and auction it off on *Larry King Live*.

After the knife interlude, we were finally able to begin proving that there was sufficient cause to charge our defendant. We clicked through the civilian witnesses briskly. Shapiro's cross-examination was uni-formly ineffective, so there was little or no cleanup needed on redirect. Every single witness helped our presentation.

One key witness was Steven Schwab, the dog walker who had first encountered Nicole's Akita running loose in the neighborhood. We hadn't been able to get him up before the grand jury, but his testimony was crucial to our time line. If the murders were committed after eleven o'clock, Simpson would be home free: he couldn't possibly have done the killing and hooked up with the limo driver in time. The problem was that the first time Schwab talked to police, he said that he believed he'd first seen the Akita around 11:15 P.M. This statement was made to the cops at about five on the morning after the murders; Schwab had been awakened from a deep sleep and was slightly confused about times. Upon more clear-minded reflection, however, he realized he'd actually seen the dog at about 10:45.

Usually a prior inconsistent statement by a witness is a credibility killer. At best, you're left doubting the witness's memory; at worst, his honesty. But Schwab was so sturdily forthright you just knew he'd made an honest mistake. He endeared himself to the spectators in court by recounting the process by which he had verified in his own mind the Akita encounter. He had an unvarying nightly routine, centered on old reruns. A cable network showed his favorites and he always watched the *Dick Van Dyke Show*, which ended at 10:30. Then he would take his dog for a half-hour walk, returning in time to catch the opening minutes of the eleven P.M. showing of *Mary Tyler Moore*.

Such banal details mark all of our daily lives and give our days some predictability. Schwab's recitation drew laughter, but no one could doubt the truth of his testimony. He had seen the dog at 10:45, *not* 11:15. Our time line was secure.

Pablo Fenjves was my essential "dog bark" witness, the neighbor who heard the Akita's "plaintive wail" starting at 10:15 P.M. His description of that sound lodged in the memories of reporters and public alike. Taken in tandem with Sukru Boztepe and Bettina Rasmussen's solemn, emotional account of finding Nicole's body, it seemed to cast an eerie spell over the gallery. We were still in that state of morbid dislocation when Judge Kennedy-Powell dismissed us for the Fourth of July weekend.

I spent very little of that weekend at home. I worked all day Saturday. And on Sunday morning I drove out to Bundy, to the little condominium on the downscale side of Sunset.

For the past few days I been increasingly anxious to scope out the condo. I had not been to Bundy since the morning after the murders, and then I'd been detained at the perimeter, like a bystander. The condo's various appointments—the security gate, the dog leap stairway, the landing where Nicole lay, the fenced-in corner where Ron was killed—had all become part of the public's collective consciousness. Yet to me they remained abstractions.

I met up with Tom Lange and Phil Vannatter at the rear of the condo. Bill was there, too, as were Patti Jo and several officers from Robbery/Homicide. We were all silently relieved that the media hadn't trailed us.

We'd gathered in the lane at the rear of the condo, when Lieutenant John Rogers noticed blood—drops of blood, on the back gate. What the hell? We stopped dead in our tracks and looked at one another. Could Dennis Fung have overlooked this crucial evidence on the morning of the thirteenth? We stopped everything and called for a criminalist.

The realization that we'd probably just stumbled upon another incredible fuckup cast a pall over the party.

Tom led us down the walkway toward the front of the condo. I could still see some of the blood droplets and the faint outlines of the bloody shoe prints, mere ghosts of the images I'd seen countless times in photographs. What had it been like, I wondered, for the officers that night to see all this evidence lying before them? I'd never seen so much left at a crime scene. This murder was obviously the work of an amateur.

At the front of the condo I stood on the upper landing and looked down on the area enclosed by the front gate. It was cramped and dark, even smaller than photos could convey. I turned to Bill and said, "The jury has to see this. When they realize how small it is, they'll understand how impossible it would be for two men to have fit in here to commit the murders."

"Yeah, no kidding," he replied, clearly as moved as I was. Then, ever practical: "We'll have to get a motion going on it."

We'd been told by Nicole's friend Ron Hardy that the intercom controlling the lock on the front gate was broken. If Nicole had wanted to let a visitor in, she'd had to go down and open the gate manually. If this was true, it was easy to conceive how Nicole and Ron were both at the front gate when Simpson moved in for the kill.

He could have attacked Nicole from behind, hitting her on the head, making a quick cut to her neck, and slamming her into the staircase wall. She would have been knocked unconscious long enough for him to deal with Ron before going back to dispatch her with the coup de grâce.

Frankly, I favored a slightly different scenario: Nicole Simpson hears something outside—the sounds made by her ex-husband lurking in the shrubs around her condo. Nicole steps outside to investigate. She ventures down to the front gate, looks down the walkway and into the shrubbery to the north. Nothing. And then, when she turns to mount the steps, to reenter the house where her children are sleeping, she walks right into him, smack into the man who she had vowed would no longer be the center of her life. He is dressed for silent combat—dark sweats, knit cap, gloves. He has come to take her life.

Somewhere during this time, Ron Goldman, on his innocuous errand, appears. Perhaps Ron has come up the walk while Simpson is in the midst of his stiletto mêlée. Why doesn't he flee? Perhaps he has come too close and can't escape. Or perhaps—and this seemed a stronger likelihood—Ron feels compelled to come to Nicole's aid. He is about to engage in an act of selflessness that will lead to his death.

In either case, my strong feeling is that Simpson did not have to confront both of his victims simultaneously.

He murders first one, then the other.

The blood pools on the sidewalk.

The dog howls.

How many minutes for each?

How many times on other cases had I worked through this same gory calculus? You can never quite capture the factor of pain.

Like Rockingham, the interior of Nicole's condo at Bundy was white with some muted pastels for accent. It had the tranquil, static quality of a photograph from *House Beautiful*. The kitchen was tidy, nothing out of place. In the center of the sunken living room sat a large square table. On it stood several candles, which had been burning on the night of the murders. The spent wax had dried in a pool around them. But everything in that room seemed like wax. Cold. Solid. Lifeless.

Nicole's bedroom was done in the same white and pastels, but the room felt anything but tranquil. Attached to one of the posts of her large four-poster bed was a pair of toy handcuffs. Something else interested me about the bed: the blankets and sheets. They lay in a rumpled heap, just as they'd been found by the first officer on the scene. Until now I had left open the possibility that Nicole had sexual designs on Ron. If so, I figured it had been a spontaneous idea, occurring after Juditha Brown lost her glasses. But the sight of Nicole's messy bed made me doubt this theory. What woman plans an intimate night with a man and leaves the bed unmade? You just wouldn't do it. Not even if you intended to limit your fooling around to the couch downstairs.

Ordinarily I would not have allowed myself such intimate speculations about a woman I'd never met. And yet a couple of times of late I'd been surprised by a sense of connection to Nicole. Looking back on it, I don't know why it seemed so improbable that I might identify with a woman who was taking her first toddler steps into the world after divorce. And yet it seemed strange to me at the time. The sight of Nicole's chaotic bed and the cold dead wax of her candles chilled me. So did the memory of her pale, bloodless face. And so I did what I always do with emotions too painful to confront: I pushed them to the back of my mind.

Things continued going well for us the following week. The limo driver, Allan Park, was concise and unimpeachably credible. I even managed to extract some new information from the eternally stumbling Kato Kaelin. His recounting of Simpson's activities that night preserved our time line, and the description he gave of the thumps outside his cottage and the confusion around Simpson's attempt to hook up with the limo driver made a clear pitch to the judge—and to millions on television—that something undeniably suspicious was afoot at the Rockingham residence.

Then, late on Tuesday, July 5, we began arguments on the defense's search-and-seizure motion. A lot was riding on it. The main target, of course, was the Rockingham glove. Shapiro would have tried any kind of crazy stunt to keep that out of the record. At the heart of his argument to suppress was the allegation that all four officers went out to Rockingham that morning believing Simpson was a suspect. In that case, they might have needed a warrant to enter the grounds.

By now I'd looked thoroughly into these allegations. In follow-up interviews, all four detectives led me through their individual movements during the early-morning hours of June 13. I'd read all of their reports and made notes on my informal conversations with each of them.

What I heard was encouraging: the four were acting under official orders to make a humanitarian notification—and that in itself went a good distance toward discrediting the defense's claim. In murder cases, you *always* try to notify the next of kin personally. Sometimes cops will drive two hours to make the contact. And when the case involves a celebrity, there's even more urgency—you don't want the first notification to come from the media.

The officers had just come from a scene where two victims had been savagely slain. Simpson's two young children had been roused from their beds at Bundy and were at West L.A. Station waiting for their father or some other member of the family to pick them up. Where was he? Was he all right? The uncertainty mounted when they reached Rockingham and rang the buzzer at the Ashford gate. No answer. For nearly ten minutes, no reply.

Finally, Ron Phillips got Simpson's phone number from the private security service. He called it on his cell phone, letting it ring over and over again. No response. The detectives fell back to try and figure out what kind of situation they had. It didn't feel right that the place should be deserted at 5:30 in the morning. Especially considering that the lights were on and cars were in the driveway.

They were reviewing their options when Mark Fuhrman walked down to the white Ford Bronco parked just outside the Rockingham gate. The way it was parked, rear wheels jutting out from the curb, struck him as odd. He pulled out his penlight and began to examine the vehicle more closely. A package in the cargo area was addressed to Orenthal Productions. Fuhrman moved around the car with his penlight and when he came to the driver's door he stopped. On the clean surface he noticed a tiny dark spot. He called Phil over. They both agreed: it looked like blood.

There was a real possibility that someone was in danger. Their choices: leave and get a search warrant, in which case precious minutes would be lost, or go in right away and hope they weren't too late. Everything spelled urgency. Phil decided to go in. He asked Mark, who was the youngest and fittest of the four, to climb over the wall and open the gate. Fuhrman did so and opened the gate from inside. The detectives knocked on the front door and got no answer, so they went to the back of the house, fanning their flashlights around the pool area looking for signs of disturbance—or more victims. Nothing.

I asked all the cops whether they'd done a thorough search of the grounds—waded through shrubbery or gone inside the pool house. They all told me no. That wasn't their goal. They were looking for bodies or for someone who could tell them how to reach O. J. Simpson.

When they found Kato Kaelin and Arnelle Simpson in their respective guest houses, they learned that Simpson wasn't there. Mark told me how he and Ron Phillips had approached the first of the guest rooms at the back of the house. Ron looked through the glass door and saw someone on the bed. When they knocked, a white man in his thirties came to the door. He appeared dazed and confused.

I laughed to myself when I heard this. Kato always seemed that way. Mark had shone a penlight into his eyes to see if he appeared to be under the influence of drugs. Not visibly. Mark then checked his clothes and boots for blood. Clearly, Mark, at least, considered him a potential suspect. Kato told Mark Furhman about the thump on the wall. When Mark went outside to investigate, he saw a small lump, barely visible, on the ground. As he drew nearer, the lump began to take the shape of a glove. Earlier that morning, he'd seen a glove lying on the ground between the victims at Bundy. *Was this its mate?*

Until that point, no one inside the house had been searching for evidence. Only when Mark returned to tell them what he'd found did that change. Fuhrman escorted the others to the site, one by one. By the time it was Phil's turn, the sky had lightened so that he was able to see without the aid of a flashlight. As he looked toward the Bronco parked just outside the Rockingham gate, he noticed spots on the cobblestoned driveway. He moved for a closer look. Again, blood. The drops stretched between the Bronco and the front door.

That was enough for Phil. He declared Rockingham a crime scene and called for a criminalist. Shortly after that, he left to prepare the warrant.

The big question seemed to be whether Vannatter, Lange, Fuhrman, and Phillips had gone to Rockingham early that morning to notify Simpson—or to investigate him. Believe me, I grilled Phil with plenty of hard questions.

"Phil, man," I said. "You're tellin' me straight that you didn't think that Simpson might be a suspect when you went out there?"

Phil was unshakable. All that he would say was that Simpson was a "potential suspect," just like everyone else who had come in contact with the victim. He was not an actual suspect, meaning they had no actual evidence linking him to the murders.

"We took Mark and Ron along so they could stay with him, get his kids out of the station, and calm him down when we went back to the crime scene," he insisted.

"Yeah, I know," I said. "But really, Phil, didn't you consider him a suspect after Mark told you he'd been out to the place before?"

This was one aspect of the case that puzzled me. Back in the mid-eighties, when he was still a patrolman, Mark Fuhrman had been called out to 360 North Rockingham for some unspecified family-dispute call. This was a fact that he apparently had confided in his superior, Ron Phillips, on the morning of June 13. Ron, in turn, told Phil, who professed not to know quite what to make of it. Later I would receive, among documents sent over by the City Attorney's office, the copy of a letter Fuhrman had written at that office's request to shore up its 1989 battery case against Simpson. In the letter, Mark had mentioned how he'd come upon O. J. Simpson pacing in his driveway. Nicole sat on the hood of a Mercedes-Benz, its windshield shattered, apparently by Simpson wielding a baseball bat. When Fuhrman inquired as to what had happened, Simpson replied, "I broke the windshield . . . it's mine . . . there's no trouble here." Fuhrman had asked Nicole if she'd wanted to make a report, and she'd said no.

The most curious part of the letter was its closing: "It seems odd to remember such an event, but it is not every day that you respond to a celebrity's home for a family dispute. For this reason this incident was indelibly pressed in my memory."

This squared perfectly with the Mark Fuhrman I had seen admiring the bronze statue of Simpson on the morning of June 13. Clearly, Fuhrman adored the Juice and was not about to arrest him if he didn't have to. Still, didn't the mere fact that Fuhrman knew of prior domestic violence between the Simpsons color the cops' thinking about Simpson as a suspect on the morning they left Bundy for Rockingham?

"Frankly, all I remember was him saying he'd been there a long time ago and it may have involved domestic violence. It was a passing remark and it didn't mean much at the time. A call from ten years ago sure didn't add up to what we saw at Bundy."

Do I think Phil was naive? Yes. Do I think he was lying? No. That conviction grows stronger as time wears on. What you had in this situation was four cops who, on one hand, worshiped O. J. Simpson— and on the other, were seriously shaken by the mayhem at Bundy. I believe in my heart that they were actually resisting the idea that the Juice could have caused this horror.

Everything about the situation bore out their story. They'd left Bundy without so much as a whisper to anyone to advance the investigation. They hadn't even called the coroner. Why? They thought they'd be right back. Their actions at Rockingham were also consistent with their story. Once over the wall, they'd done nothing more than check the grounds with their flashlights, looking for other victims, until they reached Kato. When Arnelle let them into the house, they waited as she tried to locate her father. They didn't so much as open a drawer in all that time. They didn't venture upstairs. How did that conform with the notion that they'd come to Rockingham to grab their number-one suspect? It didn't.

As a witness in the preliminary hearings, Mark Fuhrman was simply splendid. He remained poised and patient in the face of defense attorney Gerald Uelmen's pedantic and long-winded cross. He sounded like a model cop.

The public has long since forgotten this fact, but the press had begun lionizing Fuhrman even before he left the courtroom. They followed him down the corridor, clamoring for sound bites. As I watched this scene unfold, I had an uneasy feeling. Now I know why. I've come to recognize reflexive adulation as the kiss of death.

Suddenly Mark turned and waved off the reporters. He looked my way and motioned me over. We pulled away from the crowd.

"I've got to talk to you," he said urgently. "But this has to remain confidential. I can't tell anyone but you."

What, I thought, could be so damned urgent? I was hip-deep in motions and had no time for distractions.

"Can't it wait?"

"No. I've got to tell you now," he replied. He sat down on one of the benches that lined the court hallways. This forced me to stop and sit beside him. I glanced conspicuously at my watch.

"Marcia, you have to know about this because the press is going to pick it up any minute," he continued. "A long time ago, I thought I wanted to leave the force. I was strung out over my divorce and feeling burnt out. I put in for a stress disability claim. There's a file with some shrink's reports in it. Mine claimed I said things that I never said. He got it all wrong. I tried to get them to take it out, but I couldn't. When the press gets hold of it, they'll smear me to kingdom come."

"Well, what exactly did you say . . . or did he claim you said?" I asked. I was hoping this was a tempest in a teapot. It is not an uncommon thing for government employees, especially cops, to try and get out early, with their pensions and benefits intact, on a stress disability claim. They would invent stories about how they were falling apart, couldn't handle the job, were suicidal. The claims were often nonsense. And everybody knew it. "Anyway, I don't know how anyone can get a shrink's files," I told him. "I thought that stuff was privileged."

Why did he seem so certain that the press would get to it?

"I don't know, but I know they will," he insisted. "I just wanted you to be prepared."

At the time, Mark's concern sounded to me like paranoia. I couldn't imagine what would be in those reports that would be so awful, nor could I understand how it could all become public knowledge as easily as he implied. As for being prepared, Mark was not helping me out with specifics. Once I got clear of the prelims, I would have to get that file myself. Certainly Mark could request it. For the moment, however, I wanted reassurance on one point only.

"Mark," I asked slowly, "is there anything in that file that would affect the truth of what you said on the witness stand? Is your testimony all accurate?"

"Oh, absolutely," he told me. "This has nothing to do with this case at all. That stuff was a long time ago."

I've been asked a million times since why I didn't know all about Mark Fuhrman and his disability-claim file. The truth is simple. No one told me. Phil Vannatter swore to me afterward that neither he nor Tom had a clue. I believe him. Cops generally do not gossip outside their own divisions. A guy from the Wilshire Division isn't going to tell tales about the guys from his office even to cops in another area of town.

Frankly, I didn't know what to do with the information Mark had given me. In hindsight, of course, I should have requested the file immediately. But in the heat of the moment, I just made a mental note to check it out. To be honest, it seemed that Mark was just getting a bit panicky at being thrust into the spotlight. I certainly had no reason to think that it would turn into a major issue. At that moment, the most important thing was getting back to the courtroom, where Phil Vannatter was due on the stand. If we lost the search-and-seizure motion, all the Mark Fuhrman evidence wouldn't matter.

Gerald Uelmen had argued for the defense. The officers, he charged, were not so much interested in notifying Simpson or attempting to stop a potential crime in progress as in conducting an illegal investigation. He wound up by quoting Justice Louis Brandeis, hinting darkly that the Fourth Amendment itself was at risk.

When I took the podium I congratulated Uelmen on his rhetoric.

"But none of . . . the fine quotations can change the facts as they existed on those early morning hours," I said. "He attempts to depict in very graphic terms the search . . . as though a Sherman tank were being driven through the backyard and being plowed in through the doors. In fact, nothing could be farther from the truth." I refuted his arguments point by point, walking the judge through the June 13 events as the police saw them: Their vision of the scene at Bundy. Their uncertainty about what was happening at Rockingham. The blood. The thumps of an intruder. How quickly it all happened. How, if someone had been bleeding and cops had waited for a warrant, we now would all have been calling them derelict and incompetent.

Judge Kennedy-Powell agreed. She upheld the warrant.

I felt that we were home free. We'd already established a time line, and the next step was putting Simpson at the scene of the crime. That's where the blood expert I had worked so hard to get on our team, Greg Matheson, came in. His testimony was pure dynamite. Only 0.5 percent of the population could have left the blood in the trail at Bundy. And Simpson was one of that tiny group! It was hard evidence that linked Simpson, and very few others, to the crime scene. Of those others, how many had blood in their cars and blood on their driveways? How many knew the victim, Nicole?

On Friday, July 8, Judge Kennedy-Powell ruled. "The court has carefully considered the evidence in this case and the arguments of counsel," she said. "There is sufficient cause to believe this defendant guilty."

I can't represent it as a stunning victory. It was the outcome I'd expected. And yet, in this season of the unexpected, who knew?

For the next few days, as we ramped up preparation for the trial we now knew would be held, things almost seemed normal.

And then, suddenly, the timbers collapsed beneath our feet.

It was the third weekend in July, a little over a week after the end of the prelim. I had taken the kids to play at the home of one of my fellow D.A.s, who also had children. We were in the backyard when my beeper went off. I didn't recognize the number, but that wasn't unusual—I had been bombarded by calls since this case began. I went inside to return the call. It was Mark Fuhrman.

"I guess you know about *The New Yorker*," he said glumly.

Dread started its prickly progress up my spine.

"What are you talking about?" I asked.

"I'm sitting here with a couple of executives from Channel Seven. They want to give me a spot to tell my side of the story. Marcia, I really think I should do this."

Mark thought his new friends at Channel Seven were real "straight shooters," and he handed me over to a young woman who proceeded to read to me from an advance copy of a *New Yorker* article by a writer named Jeffrey Toobin: "An Incendiary Defense."

In it, a lawyer for the defense, who spoke on condition of anonymity, laid out how the Simpson team intended to portray Fuhrman as a racist rogue cop who had planted the bloody glove at Rockingham in an attempt to frame Simpson. *Shapiro,* I thought. *It had to be Shapiro.* The idea that he would even attempt such a thing was monstrous. My nausea deepened when the cheery TV producer read me quotes from Fuhrman's psychiatric file. *How out of control is this? Not only am I first hearing this information from the press, but even that account is secondhand.*

How on earth did a reporter get hold of a cop's psychiatric records? The only legal way I know of getting into an officer's personnel file is by bringing what is called a *Pitchess* motion. The defense usually files one when a defendant is charged with assault on a police officer or with resisting arrest. If the defense can show that the cop had a history of such misconduct, it's a great way to pump up the credibility of that claim. But that wasn't an issue in this case. Fuhrman hadn't even seen Simpson, let alone arrested him.

According to the story, Fuhrman had been an enthusiastic marine, but he had purportedly told Dr. Ronald Koegler that he had stopped enjoying his military service because "there were these Mexicans, niggers, volunteers, and they would tell me they weren't going to do something." He told another shrink, a Dr. John Hochman, that his work among street gangs in East L.A. had given him "the urge to kill people that upset me."

I just couldn't imagine Mark having said things this awful. I couldn't believe that was how he felt. I asked the producer for the date of the report. It went back to the early eighties. That was a long time ago. Had he really believed all that, or was he just saying something outrageous to support a disability claim?

After Mark had made his urgent but vague references to this file in the hallway after his testimony, I'd made a note to follow up. A week later, it was still on my "To Do" list.

I've thought about that a lot in retrospect. And when I find myself beating myself up over it, I stop myself and ask, "Would history have been changed so radically if I'd run right down and filed a request for that disability file right after Mark told me about it?" Probably not. After all, it was too late to keep Mark off the stand. He'd already testified. About the only advantage I would have had was not being blindsided by this call from Channel Seven.

"Let me talk to Mark," I said to the producer firmly. My tone must have scared her; she put him back on immediately.

"Do you believe that shit, Marcia?" he asked me.

"About planting the glove? That's ridiculous. But it may not matter what I think once people get a load of those shrinks' reports."

"I never said that stuff! That's what I was trying to tell you before. I just told him I hated gang bangers. I couldn't stand the way they screwed over innocent people. I don't know how he got all that shit in there."

"Is that how you feel now?"

"Hell, no. I'm no racist, Marcia. You can ask anyone. Some of my good friends are black. Shit, ask Danette Meyers if you don't believe me."

I knew Danette Meyers, a striking African-American woman who was a D.A. in Santa Monica. She was smart, feisty, and nobody's fool. She certainly wouldn't tolerate racist crap from anyone. I needed to talk to her. But for the moment, I had to take a very, very deep breath and think this through.

What were the actual chances of Fuhrman's shrink report coming into evidence? Pretty slim. I felt I could successfully argue that a shrink's report from a decade before the crime in question was too ancient to be admissible. But in practical terms, what would it matter? The article, with all the attendant publicity, would ensure that anyone out there with a pulse would know about Mark's statements to his psychiatrists. Which is exactly what Shapiro wanted when he planted his poison with a stooge holding a press card.

So the nightmare began. It was, however, not unprecedented. In countless cases involving a black defendant, the defense makes some effort to play the race card. But in this case, one would have thought that this particular odious card just wasn't in the deck. It just seemed so patently inappropriate: O. J. Simpson lived a rich man's life among friends who were, by and large, white. His ex-wife and current girl-friend were white. His entire legal team was white. How, I wondered, could Shapiro or Uelmen sell a racial defense?

As for the planting theory, it was more bizarre than anything I'd heard of so far. How would Shapiro account for the fact that other cops had been at the Bundy crime scene and viewed the evidence before Mark arrived?

"So what do you think about my talking to Channel Seven?" Mark asked me again.

"I want to talk to Gil about this," I told him. "Tell them to sit tight for now."

I don't think I'd ever paged Gil Garcetti before. "Sorry to bother you on a weekend," I told him when he called me back, "but there's something you should know about." I laid out the damage.

He had no instant panacea, and who would have expected one? This isn't one of the situations they teach you about in law school. "Just when you think you've heard them all . . ." he finally said, his voice trailing off. "Let me think about this. I'll call you back."

Gil phoned me again about a half an hour later and told me to deny Mark permission to do the interview. "I think we have to keep playing by our usual rules," he said. Mark wasn't happy when I told him, but he agreed to go along with us. I promised him we'd talk on Monday.

Outside in the sunlit yard, the children were giggling uncon-trollably. I shut out everything for the moment except the sweetness of that scene. Fortunately, they hadn't a clue about the misery that could befall adults. I needed to regain my perspective. In the months to come I would find myself grasping at the strangest diversions to restore that precious clarity. But at the moment it was enough to join the kids on the swing set and let them push me until I could see my feet against the sky.

Strange Days

On most days Jim Morrison hovers on the periphery of my consciousness. During my last few years as a deputy, I kept a four-foot-high poster of him mounted on the wall behind my desk. Jim is onstage, wearing tight leather pants and that signature pout. As a teen, I was a big fan of the Doors, and Morrison's expression just hooked me. Here was a guy who looked Strangeness in the eye without blinking. Well, ultimately he did blink. But it was my guess that throughout the preliminary hearings, Morrison was parked on a couch in the Valhalla of dead icons, watching CNN and grinning.

This is the strangest life I've ever known. It was Morrison's line, but I found myself saying it over and over. In the days following the prelims I could not believe what was happening. What a freaking spectacle. In the space of three weeks this case had grown from a straightforward double homicide—which incidentally concerned a celebrity—into a national obsession. It was like Desert Storm with a docket number. Why is the American public such a sucker for any drama unfolding live? Will Baby Jessica make it out of that well? Will the baby killer whale make it to open sea? Will O. J. Simpson blow his brains out? The lure, I suppose, is the honesty of an uncertain outcome.

But even now, in the cold gray light of hindsight, I still don't fully understand the appeal of this case. I know that the Bronco chase offered a powerful rush. *The first hit is free. . . .* Liking the jolt it got during those two hours of unprogrammed airtime, the public came looking for another. And another. The media fed the addiction, covering every twitch in the case as a "stunning new development." By the time we got through those preliminary hearings, nothing was ordinary. Nothing was *allowed* to be ordinary. It was all reported at the same hysterical, accelerating pitch.

God forbid there should be a slow news day, or the press would settle its frenetic, predatory attentions on me. No one ever came right out and asked the question on everyone's mind: "Why'd Gil Garcetti pick a *girl* for this job?" The subtext, however, was clear: Criminal prosecution is guy's work. You gotta be tough. And for a case this big you gotta be real tough. You gotta put your best man in there. Is your best man really a woman?

I've never been one to cry sexism. But I know the score. I know that I have to be tougher and better than the guys I work with. My attitude has always been, So what? Having to be tougher and better makes me just that, tougher and better. And I tried looking at this particular situation philosophically. I knew that anybody Gil picked for this job was going to come in for a lot of scrutiny and a whole lot of grief. But the kind of grief I got was the sort I thought had gone out of fashion with foot binding.

After that blast of exposure during the prelims, my appearance became the subject of seemingly endless speculation. (You remember, don't you?) The circles under my eyes. When I'm tired, I tend to get circles under my eyes. People I scarcely knew would come up and say, "When are you going to do something about those circles?" And I'd tell them, "I'll do something after the trial. I'll get some sleep." During the prelims, my facial features became one of the leading indicators of the prosecution's fortunes. As in, "Marcia's looking hagged out; the prosecution must be having a bad day."

Once I wore a short-sleeved white dress. There was no significance to it except that it was clean, comfortable, and not something I usually wore in front of a jury because it was just a little too casual. Since we were in pretrial motions and didn't even have a jury at that point, I could choose comfort over formality. And so, as I got off the elevator, reporters started hectoring me: "Marcia, what is the significance of the dress? What does it mean?"

What does it mean? The dress means nothing, but the fact that you have to ask means a lot. It means there sure as hell is such a thing as pink coverage versus blue coverage. It means "She may be the CEO of General Motors, boys, but she's still a woman."

The debate inevitably descended to the length of my skirts. Drive-time radio jocks wore themselves out complaining that my hems were "too short." Let me explain something here. When I'm on my own time I wear my skirts any damned length I please. And that is usually about three inches above the knee. It's not an attempt at seduction. It's not the Dance of the Seven Veils. But when it comes to what I wear in front of a jury, I have always been conservative. I wear what I consider to be smart, lawyerly suits with hems slightly above the knee. Now, if you check the hems of the other female D.A.s, I suspect you'll find a number of them at precisely the same length. (But, of course, while the controversy over my skirts was at full boil, none of them came forward to say "Check out *my* hems.")

The real problem was that I was overexposed. During a single week, my image had been beamed for some seventy hours into the living rooms, bedrooms, bathrooms, and kitchens of strangers. That's about five years' worth of *Seinfeld* episodes in seven days! No wonder strangers felt a false sense of intimacy with me.

One day after work I swung by the grocery store to pick up some ground turkey and green peppers for dinner. By the time I got to the checkout counter, my cart was loaded with stuff, including the obligatory Popsicles and Cheerios. The girl at the counter looked up at me and said, "What are *you* doing here?"

Meaning, "Big shot like you must certainly have people to do this kind of stuff for you."

I felt like telling her, "Look, honey. I live in a rat hole with a leaky bedroom. My car window is busted. I can't pay the mortgage. My nanny doesn't drive. Who do you suppose runs my errands?"

But I didn't. Some kid who makes $4.25 an hour bagging groceries probably doesn't care about the distinction between Princess Diana and a public servant who stumbled into the spotlight.

*   *   *

Like it or not, I was a celebrity. I guess I was getting a taste of what drove my man Morrison nuts. Everywhere I turned, people seemed to be grabbing at me. They felt that they were entitled to interrupt me, no matter what I was doing. When I went out to dinner, they'd come over to my table. Or worse, they'd make that cute gesture of sending a waiter over with a glass of o.j. I'd try to be gracious, but I'm not an extrovert by nature. And I found dealing with these flat-footed overtures very depleting.

Everywhere I looked, there were hands. Hands wanting to shake mine. Hands wanting autographs. Hands wanting to touch me. It was getting to me. I had a recurrent waking nightmare that one of those hands reaching out to me, slow motion, held a gun pointed at my heart.

This was not some irrational, free-floating anxiety. During the Rebecca Schaeffer case, I'd learned about the pathology of obsession from Gavin de Becker, a security consultant and perhaps the world's wisest authority on the psychology of stalking. Gavin helped me develop a psychological profile of Rebecca's killer. When the Simpson case broke, I didn't even have to call him. He phoned me to see if I was okay.

"Marcia"—Gavin's mellifluous voice is unmistakable—"have you been receiving mail?"

I had, in fact—by the box load. I hadn't read it. I didn't have the time. Gavin offered to sort through it for me to see if there was anyone to watch out for. He also told me how to mitigate the risk factor in signing autographs: "Never sign more than your name," he warned. Even a meaningless expression like "sincerely" could give encouragement to an unbalanced fan. If a situation seemed the least bit weird— a guy looking twitchy, avoiding eye contact—I should get the hell outta there.

"Kind of ironic, huh, Gavin," I told him. "Whoever thought I'd be on the receiving end of this bullshit?"

There were others looking after me, too—like Lieutenant Gary Schram, a big, barrel-chested ex-marine who was in charge of the D.A.'s investigators. Schram was this sweet, wonderful guy who worried over me constantly. He assigned his men to follow me around. If I was out on the freeway, I'd look up and see one of them in my rearview mirror. If I changed lanes without thinking and lost my escort, my car phone would scream almost instantly. It would be Schram, chewing me out for my carelessness.

At Gary's insistence, I began carrying a handgun, a .38-caliber Smith & Wesson revolver. I wasn't opposed to the idea in principle; a lot of criminal prosecutors carry guns. And I was certainly no green-horn when it came to firearms. My ex-husband had been a gun enthu-siast, and we'd gone out to the range together now and then for some target practice. Since I'd been living alone, in fact, I'd kept a handgun on the upper shelf of my kitchen cabinet.

Having one in your purse, though, is a whole different trip. It requires a CCW, a permit to carry. Schram took me down to the police firing range in the hills behind Glendale. The old cop who ran the range gave me a quick refresher on cleaning and loading proce-dures. We reviewed safety tips that I already knew. I fired a few shots at a silhouette to demonstrate I could aim at Van Nuys without taking out Long Beach.

It usually takes weeks to get a permit, but Schram and his buddies had one laminated and in my hands before I left the range. On the way out, Schram fixed me with his steady blue eyes. "I want this in your purse at all times," he told me. "It won't do you any good in your desk drawer."

I kept forgetting it. It was a form of denial on my part, I suppose. If I wasn't in danger, I wouldn't need a weapon. Right? Schram didn't buy this pretzel logic. If I happened to pass the lieutenant on the way out of the office, he'd hold me up for a random inspection. If he didn't find the Smith & Wesson in my purse, he'd send me back to my office to get it. I finally got used to carrying that gun as a matter of habit.

I'd gotten word through the rumor mill that one of the networks was having me tailed, that the *National Enquirer* was having me tailed, that O. J. Simpson's private investigators were having me tailed. All of them were presumably competing for lane space with my own security detail. Every time I climbed into my car I felt like Goldie Hawn in *The Sugarland Express*.

It was no longer possible for me to walk down the hall to the

D.A.'s office and take a meeting with Gil Garcetti. Now, the sight of me opening those glass doors excited too much speculation. So Gil showed me a back way. There's an entrance on the north side of the building that lets you circumvent the reception area and enter the D.A.'s office unobserved. I'd spent ten years in this place and nobody had ever bothered to tell me about it.

Used to be that Bill and I could jump in a car and go visit a witness. No fuss. No armed escort. Now, we couldn't leave the CCB together without staging a major military operation. One day, Bill and I had to interview a witness named Danielle Rose. She was a friend of Kato's girlfriend, Rachel Ferrara. Danielle had called us about a conversation she'd had with Rachel a day or two after the murders. According to Rachel, Kato had seen Simpson outside the house within moments of hearing the thumps on his wall. It was hearsay on hearsay, but we still had to check it out.

Danielle was nervous about coming to our office. She'd seen how reporters pounced on anyone they suspected had been speaking to the prosecution, and she wanted no part of it. This distinguished her from any number of wannabe starlets who'd had even fleeting contact with any of the main players in the case and now were coming out of the woodwork and selling their stories to evening newsmagazines. This one wanted anonymity. Cool. We came up with a plan to meet her in an alley a short distance from the apartment of one of her friends.

Bill and I got into Phil Vannatter's car, D.A. investigators flanking us before and behind. As we drove, Phil kept in radio contact with our escort. So far, so good. No tail spotted. I was beginning to think that we could all use a few weeks in therapy to lose the paranoia. No sooner had we pulled into the alley, however, than Phil pointed off to the left. Two men in sunglasses sat in a parked nuthin'-special car. One of the investigators checked them out—sure enough, they were reporters from a local TV station. He shooed them off like cowbirds.

We didn't mention this little episode to Danielle. Poor kid was freaked out enough as it was. And all for nothing. As she stammered through her story it became clear to me that she might have simply misunderstood Rachel, whose main concern was not what Kato had done when, but that he had dragged her into this mess at all.

On the drive home, I was still boiling about the leak. What had alerted the station? A phone tap? A comment overheard in the hall? We never did find out. But after that we doubled our precautions. No more talking on cell phones. We had our cars and offices swept for bugs. From that point on, there was no more talking about the case in public. Not in the halls, not in the elevators, not even in the johns.

Meanwhile, the Fuhrman controversy showed no signs of slackening. It irritated the hell out of me to be drawn off the preparation of the case by diversionary tactics of the defense. But I also knew we'd never get back on track until we faced the problem head-on.

It did not seem logical to me that Fuhrman would try to frame O. J. Simpson with as little information as he'd had at the time he'd found the glove. How, for instance, could he have known that Simpson didn't have an airtight alibi for the time the murders occurred? How could he know whether an eyewitness, or even an ear witness, might come forward to identify someone else? What if someone stepped forward to confess? How could he know whether Kato had already gone far enough down the south pathway to see the area where the glove was found? Did Fuhrman even have the *opportunity* to move evidence?

I'd asked the LAPD for a list of all of the officers who'd arrived at Bundy *before* Mark. There were sixteen of them. Only four had gotten beyond the perimeter to see the evidence near the bodies: Officer Robert Riske, first officer on the scene. Lieutenant Frank Spangler, one of the highest-ranking officers supervising the scene. Sergeant David Rossi, in charge of the patrol officers. And Detective Ron Phillips, Fuhrman's supervisor, who arrived at precisely the same time Mark did. I interviewed those four men personally, and each was very clear about one thing: there had been one glove, and one glove only, lying between the bodies.

Except for Phillips, none of these guys knew Mark well. They would hardly risk their jobs, not to mention an indictment, to protect him. If their testimony was to be believed, it was a physical impossibility for Mark Fuhrman to have planted evidence.

From where I was sitting, Fuhrman was in the clear. I did my best to reassure him of that. But he was very anxious. Very paranoid. He complained about being treated like a "goddamned suspect." He complained that the defense was targeting him, trying to destroy him. Things took a turn for the worse when the FBI found a single Caucasian hair on the glove from Rockingham. It most likely belonged to Ron Goldman, but no one could establish this conclusively. The defense asked for hair samples not only from Fuhrman, but from Phil, Tom, and Ron as well.

When I passed this request along to the cops, they went absolutely ballistic.

"We're not going to be treated like goddamned suspects. Next they'll want to take our blood," they huffed.

I warned them that their refusal would look bad, but I said, "Fine. I'll fight it." I got myself charged up to oppose a court order for the hair samples. But before I could strap on my armor, the cops had a change of heart. Their attorneys had told them that in refusing, they'd appear to be hiding something. So they agreed to give the hair samples.

I got on the horn to Shapiro. "You won't need a court order for the hair, Bob," I told him. Fine, fine. Everything's cool. I had barely gotten off the line when the cops did another flip-flop. "We're not giving samples," they insisted. "We're not goddamned suspects." Finally, they complied. And, thank God, when the results came back a few weeks down the line, nobody matched the mystery hair.

The thing that annoyed me was that I'd really gone to bat for those guys, and still they went around grousing that I was disloyal. I could already see the police distancing themselves from this case. By late September, Tom and Phil were "too busy" to do anything I asked. Finally, I just quit calling them and used our D.A. investigators instead.

Annoyed as I was with Tom and Phil, I felt very sorry for them. They'd been beaten down by a barrage of idiotic requests and make-work motions coming their way from the defense team. Shapiro had started his own "investigation" to find the real killer or killers. He'd set up an 800 number that during its first two weeks of operation drew over 250,000 calls. Most of them seemed to come from psychics, psychos, and general cranks who'd had dreams about where the knife was hidden. "Look in the sandbox." "Look in the tree by the playhouse."

Like we hadn't thought of that? We got our share of crank callers as well. My favorite was the one who theorized that Simpson, Nicole, and Ron had all sat around in a circle stabbing one another. Crazy stuff. But Tom and Phil had to follow up every lunatic lead or risk being harangued by the defense. After a couple of weeks of this, their expressions were hangdog, their eyes tired. I could just about tell what they were thinking: "We're too close to retirement to take this bullshit."

Naturally, Shapiro's make-work motions ended up on my desk. He wanted murder logs. He wanted dispatching logs. He wanted records of all the people treated for dog bites at emergency wards. The message of this last request, I guess, was that any resident of West L.A. who'd been bitten by a dog during the late hours of Sunday, June 12, 1994, was a potential suspect in the murder of Nicole Brown and Ron Goldman. That one gave me a laugh. The perpetrator of a grisly double homicide is going to walk into an emergency room to get treated for a dog bite?

As primary litigator, I shouldn't have been saddled with these day-to-day distractions. I should have been concentrating on building what is called the case-in-chief—the essence of a presentation that proves the defendant committed the crime. But there was absolutely no time for overall planning or, indeed, any creative thought about this case.

After the prelims were over, I'd expected to have a little breathing room to sit down and organize the mountains of evidence gathering around my desk. A case like this one usually takes a year or more to come to trial. Generally, the defense wants to delay things as long as possible to give themselves time to prepare. They are also hoping that key witnesses will die or disappear in the meantime, so they'll ask for postponement after postponement until either we or the judge says, "Enough, already. Let's go."

Shortly after the prelims, however, Shapiro announced that his client intended to invoke his right to a speedy trial.

When the news reached me, I just put my head on my arms and moaned. "Speedy trial," by law, means no more than sixty days after an arraignment. It was a good strategy. In fact, I'm surprised that more defense attorneys don't use it. What it meant was that we had to be ready in eight weeks. It was an absolutely impossible deadline.

I knew that Shapiro was no more ready than we were, but he didn't have to prepare a case to prove his client's innocence. All he had to do was stand by and be ready to kick us in the shins. He wouldn't have to present any evidence until we finished our case. We were at a bigger disadvantage than he was.

The clock started running on July 22, the morning of the defendant's second arraignment. (A second arraignment is standard. A prosecutor may have acquired more information that would change the charges. In this case, however, they remained the same.)

Simpson arrived at court that morning sporting an expensive dark suit and an irritating swagger. This was new. I remember thinking that his handlers must have adjusted his medication because he was clear-eyed and alert. He appeared confident, which gave me odd comfort. My guess was that Simpson's confidence often led him to do stupid things. He seemed in the mood to bluster. I wondered if he was being coached to display that swagger in hopes that press and public would remember that the guy in the dock here was the ostentatiously confident O. J. Simpson.

"Do you understand the charges against you, sir?" asked the supervising criminal court judge, Cecil Mills.

Simpson stood up straight and answered as if breaking from a huddle. "Yes, Your Honor."

"How do you plead?"

Simpson snapped to full attention and boomed, "Absolutely, one hundred percent not guilty."

You asshole, I thought. *You unregenerate, scum-sucking creep.*

I watched Simpson as the deputies led him out of the courtroom. He gave the crowd a thumbs-up. *Beneath that three-thousand-dollar suit he's just one more sadistic punk,* I told myself. *You've put a lot of those away. He's no different.*

But, of course, he was.

By my estimate, O. J. Simpson had already sunk more than a million dollars into his defense, and the case was barely six weeks old. Shapiro alone must be pulling down a retainer well into six figures. Possibly seven. With each passing week, the defense team seemed to be doubling in size. There were at least three private investigators we knew of working for the team, with scores more P.I.s on the freelance pad. Their names kept turning up in the press—as did those of defense attorneys around town looking to get some ink.

One of those was Johnnie Cochran.

Johnnie's name began circulating through the rumor mill almost immediately after Howard Weitzman dropped out of the picture. At first, Cochran demurred: he was too close to O. J. Simpson to take the case. "He's a friend," he would later be quoted as saying. "And that's a mess, when you start trying to represent a friend."

I was not surprised to hear that Johnnie knew Simpson. Johnnie knew just about everybody worth knowing in L.A. Smooth, affable, urbane, he was one of those guys who seemed welcome wherever he went, whether it was a political fund-raiser, a film screening, or the courthouse corridors. Johnnie joked and glad-handed like a pol. "Howyadoin? Howyadoin? Howyadoin?"

Everybody wanted to be his friend. He'd done a short stint in the D.A.'s office as an assistant to John Van de Kamp. That was a political plum; his duties were largely ceremonial and administrative. As for private practice, no one in our office could recall his trying a single, big murder case, save one. During the early seventies he'd defended Geronimo Pratt, a Black Panther who'd been accused of murdering a white schoolteacher. He lost; Pratt was sentenced to life in prison.

Rather, Johnnie had made his reputation as a litigator in civil suits—ones brought against the city by blacks and other minorities who claimed they'd been roughed up by the LAPD. On the wall of his office hung larger-than-life blowups of the seven-figure settlement checks he'd won for his clients. Bill Hodgman had, in fact, tried an attempted-murder case against Johnnie and lost. To Bill's way of thinking, Cochran was no legal scholar, nor was he a particularly clever tactician. But he was smooth and charismatic and judges seemed to love him. Bill warned me early on that Johnnie would play the race card. Johnnie always played the race card.

I doubted that Cochran would risk his reputation as a pillar of the community for the likes of O. J. Simpson. The defendant was not some brother who'd been shaken down by cops for driving in a white neighborhood. O. J. Simpson could have jogged nude through Bel Air without being arrested. He hobnobbed with white golfing buddies, married a white woman, lived in a mansion, and had effectively turned his back on the black community. He had, moreover, committed two murders of horrific savagery.

Johnnie certainly realized this. At age fifty-six, Johnnie was one of the best-known and best-respected black men in the county. He was in a position to be one of those conciliators to whom both blacks and whites could turn in times of racial distress. A word from him could help calm the waters. Why risk a citywide race riot to promote O. J. Simpson as a cause célèbre?

Shows you what I know. On the morning of O. J. Simpson's arraignment, I walked into court to find Johnnie Cochran sitting at the defense table.

Johnnie, with his dark good looks and strange iridescent suits, was hard to miss. He was one of the most animated men in public life, and yet the thing that struck me that morning in late July was how quiet he seemed. He was hunched in an upholstered armchair, his chin resting on the tips of his index fingers, in a posture of deep thought. He appeared almost withdrawn. Shapiro was clearly running the show, and Johnnie wasn't used to being anyone's second chair.

From the moment he logged on as attorney of record, Johnnie was causing mischief. Word filtered back to me that he was telling reporters that Fuhrman should be grilled on his racial attitudes. "Give me one black on that jury," he was reported to have said. He didn't need to finish the thought. Clearly, Johnnie figured that even one African American would be enough to hang a jury.

Not long afterward, Johnnie announced—in open court—that there was a witness who purportedly would clear Simpson and provide an "important lead" on the "real killers." Johnnie said this evidence was "totally inconsistent with the theory of a lone assailant. And is entirely inconsistent with the fact that Mr. Simpson is that assailant." He suggested that the LAPD had given this witness short shrift. As it happened, the "witness" to whom he was referring had already been checked out by the police. Frank Chiuchiolo, a self-described prowler who had called in shortly after the murders, said that he'd seen a pair of heavyset white men running from the rear alley at Bundy. Before the police could even dispatch detectives to the guy's house, up north in a town called—I just loved this—Happy Camp, the media had sniffed him out and exposed him as a chronic liar and publicity seeker. This goon—the Happy Camper, we called him—had also surfaced in the Polly Klaas abduction-murder case, where he'd *also* tried to give the cops phony information. And yet here was Johnnie using this shaky lead, proclaiming that the cops and the D.A.'s office had over-looked crucial evidence in their "rush to judgment"!

You might think that pulling a stunt like this would erode a lawyer's credibility. But Johnnie Cochran would make these far-fetched or unsupported allegations time and time again, and the media never really held him accountable. Johnnie realized that journalists, by and large, have the attention span of gnats; the important thing was grabbing the headline. In the mad rush of events, he wagered that no one would follow up. And he won the bet, nearly every time.

Something more powerful than principle was operating here. Attorneys who should have known better were being drawn to this case like moths to a floodlight. By the time Simpson was bound over for trial, F. Lee Bailey was being cited as a possible addition to the defendant's all-star team.

Shortly after joining the team in late June, Bailey gave an interview to NBC's *Today* show in which he made ridiculous assertions about what the prosecution could and could not prove. He quoted misinfor-mation inadvertently passed to the defense by Juditha Brown—that Nicole had spoken to her mother at eleven P.M. Bailey proclaimed tri-umphantly that this proved Simpson could not have committed the murders and that the case would soon be thrown out. It was a foolish, sloppy mistake. We'd already gotten phone records that showed that the call had been made at 9:45 P.M., not eleven, which gave Simpson plenty of time to kill two people and make the five-minute drive back to Rockingham. I don't know what possessed Bailey to shoot his mouth off like that. I just think the guy could not resist an impulse to grab the limelight.

Neither, apparently, could others.

Early on, probably during the first or second week of the case, I'd seen Alan Dershowitz do one of his talking-head numbers on national TV. It seemed to me, at least, that he was convinced of Simpson's guilt. To PBS talk-show host Charlie Rose, he professed indignation at the "excuses" defendants use nowadays to absolve themselves of guilt. He cited "cop-outs" such as the "battered-woman syndrome" and the "abused-child syndrome." He predicted that the defense in the Simp-son case would most likely mount a mental defense. "The Juice Excuse," he would call it. Then, the next thing I hear, he's being touted as one of O. J. Simpson's "legal strategists."

Do these guys think no one is listening?

People still ask me whether the sight of those big guns rolling onto the field intimidated me. "Didn't you dread coming to court every day to face these guys down?" they say. The answer is no. Whenever we heard the press referring to this crew as the Dream Team, Bill and I just rolled our eyes. The idea that these were special forces carefully recruited by Commander Shapiro, a sort of Dirty Dozen of the bar, was ludicrous.

Because what you had, basically, were a set of incompatibly grandiose egos—lead horses who by definition could never pull easily in the same harness. As early as the week of the arraignment, Shapiro was already looking worried that Johnnie would muscle him out of the limelight. It didn't take a psychic to predict procedural chaos if this bunch were not held in check by a strong judge. What we needed was someone who would be temperate but decisive. Someone who would be consistent. Someone who knew enough law and had enough confidence to rule from the bench. We needed the ump of all umps. A square-jawed, rock-ribbed referee with *huevos* of steel.

Instead, we got Lance Ito.

The announcement was almost anticlimactic after Simpson's "absolutely, one hundred percent not guilty" performance. When Judge Mills announced, "I'm assigning the case to Judge Lance Ito," I cast a quick glance at Bill. He seemed as taken aback as I was.

Judge Mills had about six to nine names to choose from. These were drawn from a pool of judges who were available for so-called long-cause cases, complex cases, usually murder trials, that were expected to go longer than a month. The lawyers on both sides get to look over the list of judges to see if there's any candidate so objectionable that one side or the other might have to "paper" him. "Papering" means filing an affidavit of protest. It's a little like a peremptory challenge; you can reject an appointment without offering a reason. The only problem is that you're obliged to take the next name you're given.

There were at least two candidates so awful they made the hair on my neck stand on end. I would definitely have papered them. And then there were three or four others who would have been terrific. But Lance Ito? He'd never, ever occurred to me.

"You've gotta be kidding," I whispered to Bill. Why, I wondered, does the judiciary never pick its brightest stars for these cases?

Lance was certainly no bright star. When he was chosen for the Simpson case, he was presiding over the master calendar court, which sends cases out to be tried. It was a useful but mundane assignment. The judge in calendar either tries to get the sides to plea-bargain or sends the case out for trial. It's strictly an administrative position, and one that takes a judge out of the loop of trial work. It's certainly not the sort of assignment that would prepare one for dealing with the pressures of the Simpson case.

Lance always struck me as an overgrown adolescent. He was the only judge I knew who wore running shoes under his robes. I'd worked with him briefly in the D.A.'s office—he'd been a prosecutor during the eighties. His reputation as a gun enthusiast preceded him. According to office lore, he'd been looking over a handgun with another D.A. when somehow the piece went off and fired a bullet into the ceiling—which happened to be the floor of the Public Defender's Office.

Lance was one of those guys who can sniff out a new source of power in the office and always manage to attach themselves to the unit du jour. He got himself assigned to the Hard Core Gang Unit when it was a hot political baby. He prided himself on political correctness. His wife, Captain Margaret York, was the highest-ranking female officer on the LAPD. I could never figure that pair out. It became clearer and clearer to me as the trial went on that when it came to gender equality, Lance was stuck in a tar pit.

In his seven years on the bench, Ito had shown himself to be a typical ex-prosecutor judge. Don't get me wrong. Some old prosecutors go on to the bench and turn out to be terrific judges, fair and decisive. A number of them, however, treat the D.A.s who appear before them very badly. If the prosecutor is any good, the judge feels competitive. The ex-prosecutor judge is usually so eager to show that he has no lingering loyalties to the D.A.'s office that he'll kiss the toes of the defense.

I hadn't argued a case before Ito, but Bill had: the Keating case. I could remember Bill grousing about Ito at the time. He thought Ito had bent over backward to accommodate the defense and dismissed a lot of counts he shouldn't have. But in the end, Bill and his team won a guilty verdict. It's not unusual for a D.A. to be tweaked by a judge's day-to-day rulings, only to recall him as a fine and thoughtful jurist when the outcome is favorable. Bill felt Ito had done a tolerably good job on Keating, which was by anyone's reckoning a complicated long-cause trial. Keating, however, was strictly white-collar crime; accordingly, everyone kept his gloves on. The Simpson case was shaping up to be a sort of break-your-bottles-and-go-at-it street brawl. We would need a judge who could step in and keep the peace. I didn't believe Lance had the fortitude for that.

My first inclination was to refuse him. But Judge Mills added a complication. He noted that Ito was married to a captain on the LAPD.

"In the event that either side desires him to do so," he explained, "no affidavit will be required on the request of either side. He will recuse himself from handling this matter."

Thanks a lot. Now, if we refused him on the grounds that his wife was a cop, what kind of message would that send? It would telegraph to our prospective jury pool that we didn't think much of the LAPD, or that Lance had some inside information about the LAPD that would hurt us. The only politic option was to decline Judge Mills's offer, use our one challenge to boot him, and hope for a better draw. Of course, then we'd have to accept the next name to come up. No arguments; no appeals.

I'd have papered him in a hot second if I hadn't known there were a couple of worse judges in the building. (Although, looking back, it's hard to see how they could have been *much* worse.) Instead, I turned to Bill, who knew Ito better than I did.

"What's your gut tell you?"

He sighed and gave me a thumbs-up.

I wish that one of us had been endowed with some mystical gift of prescience that would have warned us off this train wreck. But you make your decision with the best information you have at the time.

Only four days after he took the case, Lance and I locked horns for the first time. It was bitter and it was public. The defense had filed a motion that would have required us to give them 10 percent of each of our blood samples so that they could do their own testing. I couldn't let that happen. Some of the samples contained so little DNA that if we gave up even 10 percent, we might not be left with enough blood to get a test result. This was particularly true for the more sophisticated tests—for instance, the one that utilizes the RFLP method is very reliable but requires a fair amount of DNA. Remember, by law the defense is not obligated to come forward with their results—so if their tests proved Simpson guilty, they could and most assuredly *would* hide the information. On the other hand, if our diminished sample failed to yield a result, we'd wind up with nothing. So if we gave the defense a portion of bloodstains off the top—a concession that was based on no legal requirement—we might well destroy crucial evidence.

I was almost certain that Ito would reject the defense's motion out of hand. Any reasonable judge would. Just to be certain, I drafted a proposal that would make it even easier for him: let the *defense* do all the testing. I was willing to go out on a limb like this because I knew the defense's blood expert, Dr. Edward Blake, and I both respected and trusted him.

What I proposed was to give Dr. Blake the entire sample. Let him do all the testing—*provided* the defense would share his results with us. If the Dream Team was sincere about getting an honest result, they'd go for my compromise. The only possible reason for turning me down was if they knew the results would hang their client. My counter-motion, in essence, would call their bluff.

Get it, judge? They don't want the truth; they want to hide evidence.

Sure enough, the defense flatly rejected my proposal. That figured. What surprised the hell out of me was the subsequent ruling from Ito. He granted the defense's ridiculous request: 10 percent, he decreed, would be "available to the defense for their own testing."

I leaned over to Lisa Kahn, the deputy who was handling DNA for our side, and whispered, "Did he say what I think he said?"

Lisa just shook her head in disbelief.

"Your Honor." I jumped up, interrupting Ito in midsentence. "May I ask the court to take some further evidence?"

Ito fixed me with an icy glare.

"I think that perhaps defense counsel has misled the court as to the nature of the testing that is going to be performed. You're depriving us of ever conducting the poly-marker test completely by giving that ten percent to the defense. . . . You are taking evidence out of our hands forever."

Ito seemed embarrassed and angry. I'd put him on the spot. On national TV no less. He must have realized that he could not safely ignore my objection. What if I was right? What if this screwy order wound up trashing all the blood evidence? So he ordered a hearing during which experts from both sides would testify as to how much evidence we had and what we could afford to give up.

I've wondered over and over again if I should have taken him on so boldly so early in the game. But every time I replay this scene in my mind, I come to the same conclusion. No good attorney would sit by and watch a judge throw away evidence. Meanwhile, the message was clear—Lance Ito lacked good judgment. If he'd strayed afield on such an obvious no-brainer, what could we expect on the complicated rulings?

We'd soon find out.

The defense had committed what I considered a serious tactical blunder by challenging the warrantless search during the preliminary hearing. Under California law, with rare exception, you are entitled to challenge a search or warrant only once. Shapiro and Gerald Uelmen had taken their shot before Judge Kennedy-Powell during the prelim, and she'd denied their motion. But now the defense wanted to mount a new assault upon that search in Superior Court.

Their grounds? "New evidence" had come to light involving police misconduct. They petitioned Ito to reopen debate on the warrantless search. He wasn't, apparently, impressed with their showing and denied the motion. The defense then attacked the warrant, saying it was faulty and misleading.

In order to make any headway here, the defense would have to show that the warrant misstated or omitted crucial facts and that an accurate version, if corrected, wouldn't have shown probable cause. And they *must* file a declaration itemizing those things that they considered errors.

In anticipation of this motion, I had put fellow D.A. Cheri Lewis to work on a set of tight, logical arguments showing how anyone could have made these mistakes under similar circumstances. The mistakes were, in legal terms, "merely negligent." This phrase sounds more ominous than it is. It's essentially an "oops": mistakes anyone could make. They were not "reckless," which means the cop knew or should have known what the truth was, but put down something else.

Cheri and I marched into court on September 21 loaded for bear. To our amazement we discovered that the defense team had not even produced a declaration listing the errors. Any judge with his eye on the ball would have admonished them for this omission and then ordered them home to write a proper motion. But not Ito.

And so we listened to Gerald Uelmen, former dean at Santa Clara University School of Law and one of the most boring speakers on earth, drone on for hour upon excruciating hour, before he got to his point: Phil's claim that there had been "human" blood on the Bronco door was so devastatingly reckless that he'd misled a magistrate into granting the warrant.

Huh? You mean finding a bloody glove matching the one left at the crime scene wouldn't be enough?

Uelmen concluded on a bit of tortured logic: getting a search warrant must have meant the cops considered Simpson a suspect, right? So why didn't they arrest him when he got back to Rockingham on the thirteenth?

I wanted to stand up and concede the point. *You know, Gerry, you're right. They should have arrested him right then and there, but those nasty old conspirators let him walk right out the door. Phil Vannatter lied all over the warrant just so he could nail O.J. . . . and then what does he do? Lets him slip right through his fingers. Yeah, I get it.*

Far from making a persuasive argument, Uelmen had only underscored the cops' innocent intentions.

In the end, Lance upheld the warrant. He really had no choice. He, like Judge Kennedy-Powell before him, had seen that the cops, acting under extreme stress in emergency circumstances, had performed imperfectly but properly. And yet Lance could not resist a gratuitous slap. He could not, he said, make a finding that Phil's actions were "merely negligent." Instead, he termed them "at least reckless."

Even as I think back upon this now, it makes my blood boil. This episode was, for me, an education in the ways of Lance Ito. Lance, I was beginning to see, was so indecisive, so fearful generally of the "big guns" at the defense table, that he didn't dare give us a decision without handing the defense something in return. Split the baby. Apologies to Solomon, it was Ito's Law. In this instance, the cost of appeasement was high: a cop's good name.

Throughout August and September, and into the early part of October 1994, prosecution and defense continued to wrangle over blood evidence. The defense claimed we'd intentionally delayed sending about two dozen blood samples from Simpson's home and Bronco off for DNA testing. They claimed we were trying to buy time. That was ridiculous. If you measured our progress by any normal pretrial schedule, we were proceeding at the goddamned speed of light. The amount of evidence we'd managed to pull together and submit to date was staggering. But the labs had their own backlogs to deal with. Ito just didn't get this. He felt somehow that the world should shut down for the Simpson case. The defense had dropped its request for a portion of our samples. This, however, only complicated matters because we had been ordered by the bench to have the testing conducted only at those times when the defense's own expert, Dr. Blake, could be present. It had turned into a scheduling nightmare.

It was D.A. Lisa Kahn's job to explain this to Ito. Unfortunately, she and the defense's own DNA point man, a scrappy little New York import named Barry Scheck, could scarcely conceal their contempt for each other. Day after day she and Scheck went at it, he accusing us of bad faith, she accusing him of filing a flood of motions to confuse and mislead the court. The press dubbed these running hostilities "The Lisa and Barry Show."

I could see that both of them irritated the hell out of Ito. Under the best of circumstances, Lisa wasn't inclined to suffer fools, and she'd copped a snippy attitude with the judge.

One afternoon I was upstairs trying to get some of my own work done when a law clerk came running into my office.

"Marcia, have you seen what's happening in court?" she gasped. "You'd better get down there ASAP. Ito's furious at Lisa!"

I grabbed a pad of paper and flew downstairs, but court had already adjourned for the day.

Later, back in my office, Lisa gave me the unpleasant details. Ito seemed to be leaning toward keeping out blood samples, so she'd snapped, "If the court wants to make such a ruling, the court is entitled to . . . although I don't believe there is truly any authority to support it."

This had infuriated Ito.

"Fuck him, if that's the way he wants to be," she said angrily.

"You're gonna have to do some begging and pleading to shore up our position," I told her.

She wouldn't do it. She wasn't going to kiss butt for a motion she felt we shouldn't have to argue in the first place. I sympathized with her, but I knew this intransigence would get us nowhere.

Ito was set to rule four days hence on whether our delays had been deliberate. If he found they were, he could impose sanctions that would exclude as many as two dozen blood samples. Among them was the blood of Ron Goldman, which had been found in the Bronco. It was a devastating piece of evidence against the defendant. And its loss would be terrible for us.

I knew we had to do something to pull Ito back toward the center—and fast.

I sat Lisa down and we drafted a letter, calmly laying out our position. I promised that I would take the letter in myself and spare her the humiliation of bowing to Ito's wishes.

Friday morning, October 14, I took a deep breath, put my head down, and marched into court. I handed the letter to Ito's clerk, Deirdre Robertson. This was going to be ugly.

When Ito took the bench I asked permission to address the court. He granted it curtly.

This is not the time to stand on your dignity, I told myself. *Fall on your damned sword.*

So, on behalf of the People, I apologized profusely for any slight His Honor might have suffered during Tuesday's hearings, and I implored him to consider the letter we'd submitted. I begged him not to cripple the People's case by keeping out evidence when the testing delays were really no one's fault.

Ito was still petulant. Why, he asked, couldn't Lisa have answered him civilly and satisfactorily when he'd asked her for explanations? He continued to take out on me all the animosity he felt toward her.

"I don't know if I can telegraph this ... more openly. You're about to lose," he warned me.

We all went home that weekend in very low spirits, thoroughly expecting that next week, Ito was going to cut our legs right out from under us.

But then Lance did another of his classic turnarounds. On the following Tuesday morning, when we reconvened on the matter, he announced that he'd found no deliberate attempt on our part to sandbag the defense or the court.

Defense motion denied.

I glanced over at the defense table. Johnnie looked stunned. Barry Scheck looked like somebody had killed his dog. I was nearly weak with relief.

It was only as we were basking in the afterglow of this victory that I let myself reflect on the dynamic that had turned the situation around. Lance Ito had really enjoyed watching me grovel.

I'm sure Gil thought twice before asking me to take a meeting with Don Vinson. He knew that I had very little patience with frivolous interruptions. Ever since this case had started I'd found that people in high places would find any excuse to "meet" with me or Bill. Often these meetings came in the guise of some kind of help or favor they wanted to offer, but what I suspected people really wanted was to pick up insider gossip on the case and pass it along at cocktail parties. Media biggies arranged for Suzanne Childs to bring them by my office in hopes of getting an interview. Under other circumstances I would have gotten a kick out of that. Some requests I could deflect with a polite refusal; others required that I break from my work and chat for a few moments for the sake of diplomacy. Each of these interruptions probably took less than ten minutes. But the minutes added up.

The meeting with Don Vinson was not so easily avoided. Vinson was the founder of DecisionQuest, a firm that specialized in jury consulting. After the hung verdict in the Menendez case, Vinson had volunteered his services to our office for the retrial. Gil was touched by the gesture. Apparently, both he and David Conn were impressed by Vinson's work, and when Vinson offered to consult gratis on the Simpson case, Gil thought we should go for it.

Now, I do not particularly like jury consultants. As far as I'm concerned they are creatures of the defense. They charge a lot, so the only people who can afford them are wealthy defendants in a criminal trial or fat-cat corporations defending against class-action suits. As a matter of principle, I don't feel that the government should be in the position of market-testing its arguments.

Not long after the preliminary hearings, however, we'd heard that Simpson had retained a topflight jury consultant named Jo-Ellan Dimitrius. Jo-Ellan was a heavy hitter who'd been used successfully by the defendants in both the McMartin Preschool and Rodney King state and federal trials. The line on her was good; she was a decent person and a hard worker who handled everything for her clients, from drawing up a profile of the ideal juror, to writing the ideal juror's questionnaire, to evaluating responses and rating prospective juror candidates. No doubt about it, the Dream Team had hired themselves a great big gun.

This had Gil very worried. There were a number of tricky currents in this case: race; public attitude toward the LAPD; the defendant's celebrity. If the defense was out there gathering intelligence to help them navigate these waters, then, Gil's thinking went, so should we. In this case I agreed. I wanted all the help I could get.

Vinson suggested that Bill and I meet him for lunch at the very conservative, very exclusive California Club in downtown L.A.

I balked.

"If they have ideas for us, let them come in here and hand them over," I groused to Bill. "I'm in no mood to clink glasses."

Bill, ever the voice of reason and conciliation, coaxed me out of my lair with the promise that if Vinson didn't offer anything of substance, I'd be off the hook for future invitations.

In a private dining room within that very private club, we found Vinson, a heavy, florid man with huge jowls. Thin wisps of white hair had been combed into submission across his pate.

"Ms. Clark," he greeted me, in a drawl that suggested an *haut bourgeois* pedigree. When he rose to shake my hand, I caught the flash of gold cuff links. Bill noticed them, too. They became our private joke. After that, any time we ran into something pretentious, we'd refer to it as "very cuff link."

Vinson was full of grand plans. He urged us to let him try out our case in front of a mock jury. It would work this way: He'd recruit a demographically diverse group of people to serve as jurors. He'd make a videotape of me giving a final argument for the prosecution, and Bill giving one for the defense. The jurors would deliberate and vote to convict or acquit. We would be allowed to watch them through a one-way mirror.

Bill frowned. I knew that he, like me, favored doing things simply, without all the flash. But I just sipped my Chardonnay and tried to sort out my thoughts before speaking. It was absolutely imperative that the results be kept confidential. Bill and I would have to lay our evidence on the line. We certainly didn't want that leaked to the press.

"Oh, don't worry," Vinson told us confidently. "We've never had a problem before."

So, against my better judgment, and in deference to my boss, I gave my okay to this plan.

This would require some work. After all, pulling together a closing argument was not easy to do. At that point we did not have the DNA evidence back, so I would have to cobble something together from the prelims. It took time we didn't have, but Bill and I completed our respective arguments, and taped our presentations one evening down in the conference room. Then we sent them off to Vinson.

Several days later, Vinson called me to say that he could not use my tape. It was important that the mock jurors not know which side, prosecution or defense, was sponsoring the testing. I had become "too famous," he said. If he showed my tape, we'd give ourselves away. He now wanted to redo my argument, with one of his male associates presenting it.

On Saturday, July 23, 1994, Gil, Bill, and I met Vinson at an office building near the airport. The consultant ushered the three of us into a darkened room, where we got the first peek at our "jurors" through a one-way glass. There were ten. Four black, two Hispanic, two Asian, two white. They'd been warned to base their decision solely on the evidence, but they quickly tossed that admonishment to the wind and began kicking around the question of whether Mark Fuhrman could have planted the glove. The battle lines were drawn. Blacks were convinced he had; the others professed neutrality or disbelief. Then they moved on to the juicier, yet totally tangential issue of whether Kato and Nicole had been lovers.

"They were supposed to be talking about our videos, not gossip from the six o'clock news," I complained to Vinson.

He stepped into the room to remind the group to confine its comments to the evidence.

"Well, yeah," they argued. "But everyone knows about all this stuff anyway."

Reluctantly, they agreed to try again. Within two minutes they were off and gossiping on another subject not mentioned on the tape—the Bronco chase. Black jurors believed Simpson had only wanted to visit Nicole's grave. When one of the more neutral jurors suggested that it might—just might—have been the escape attempt of a guilty man, one of the female blacks shot back with a defense of Simpson, referring to him as "my man O.J."

"My man?" I thought to myself. *The only way he'd be your man is if you were white, twenty-five, and built like a centerfold.*

The racial divide did not come as any great shock to us. As early as the second week of the investigation our grand jury adviser, Terry White, had come to us warning that a couple of black female jurors seemed protective of Simpson. They'd gone so far as to say that Nicole "got what she'd deserved." What was disturbing to me was how the popular media had permeated the thinking of the mock jury. Not a soul among them seemed capable of critical thinking. If it was on TV, it must be true. Of course, many of the reports they'd seen were based upon nothing more substantial than a loose comment dropped in the hallway outside of court, but they had entered the canon as God's own truth.

The jury hung, five to five.

Naturally, we were deflated. For my part, I was content to take what lessons we could from the session—specifically, the reaffirmation that black females would be a hard sell—and cut our losses. Not so, Don Vinson. He insisted we try again. This time, he wanted to go with a full-blown facsimile of a trial. We'd present more of the scientific evidence and maybe get an idea of how to simplify it. It was likely, he said, that a more detailed presentation would elicit more specific opinions than the knee-jerk loyalties we'd gotten in the first go-round.

I was uneasy about this. It was August now, nearly two months since the murders. If this case had had the normal life cycle of a major criminal trial, the media frenzy would have been slackening. But the madness was actually intensifying. It was a miracle that the results of the first mock jury had not gotten out. How would we keep the details of an even more elaborate dress rehearsal from leaking to the press?

Vinson agreed that keeping the experiment under wraps would be difficult. But the jurors, he said, were required to sign an oath of confidentiality.

"And what do we do if they violate this agreement?" I asked him.

Well, there was really nothing anyone could do, he conceded. But no one in his experience had ever breached an agreement of this kind. To assure secrecy, he proposed doing it out of state—specifically, in Phoenix, Arizona. No one would follow us there, he assured me. People weren't as hot on this case outside Los Angeles.

So, on August 18, Bill and I met at the airport to catch a flight to Phoenix. When the idea of this trip first came up, Vinson had talked about flying us out on a private jet. He never came through with that. Instead, we were booked on a commercial flight. This should have been our first tip-off to the troubles afoot.

Bill and I hid out in the terminal bar, the only dark, quiet corner that would afford us some privacy while we waited for our flight. Immersed in reviewing our notes, we lost track of the time. Bill looked at his watch and yelped, "We'd better hustle." We gathered our bags and sprinted to the metal detectors that separated us from the jetway. Just as I was about to send my purse through the metal detector, it hit me:

"Shit, I've got my gun in there."

I'd forgotten to get clearance to carry it on board. Bill and I looked at each other, neither of us quite knowing what to do.

"Keep it for me," I begged the security guard at the station. "I'll get it on my way back."

"No can do," she told me. "You've got to fill out the paperwork." One look at her face told me she would not be moved.

"Go without me!" I shouted to Bill. Then I raced back to the ticket counter to find someone who could help me. One agent, a sweet and sympathetic woman, agreed to hold the gun for me. I thanked her breathlessly and was headed for the metal detector when I saw Bill walking toward me, forlorn, his suit bag over one shoulder.

"Stand down, partner," he said. "We missed our flight."

Man, did I feel stupid.

The airline gave us its conference room, where we spent a little time going over prospective presentations. Then we napped. The pace of this thing was sapping both of us.

When at last they called our flight, we were making our way wearily to the gate when I heard someone call my name.

"Do you ever read the *National Enquirer?*" the disembodied voice asked. I was about to say, "Are you crazy?" when I saw a guy with cameras slung around his neck. The tabloids! Somebody had dropped a dime on us. Bill and I turned and ran all the way to the gate.

"It's over," I told him. "News'll be all over the place in about five minutes. They couldn't have sent us on a private plane?"

"Stupid," Bill muttered. "Just plain stupid."

When we landed in Phoenix, I spotted the burly bearlike form of Frank Sundstedt, who'd arrived in Phoenix early and was now waiting for us at the gate. We told him about the reporters.

"How about a disguise?" he asked, only partly in jest.

"Hell," I told him, "I'll wear dreadlocks if you think it will help."

On the way to the hotel, we nipped into a drugstore and I picked out a pair of clunky reading glasses. I looked at myself in the little round mirrors clipped to the top of the rack. Great! Pistol-packing nerd. I kept my head down as we entered the hotel where Vinson had booked our rooms. Frank went to check on our reservations. They'd been booked under our real names. Swell. Reporters had been calling the hotel asking about us. Once again, we'd been made.

That was it. There would be no mock jury. The only thing we could do was to turn around and go home.

God damn this case, I thought. I'd missed a night at home for this? I would have loved to be singing lullabies right now. You wouldn't catch *me* humming Brahms. It would probably be something more like "Angel Baby."

Bill, Frank, and I met Vinson for dinner at a restaurant near the hotel.

"It's over, Don," I said. "Call it off. The press is all over us."

"No, no, no," he protested. Vinson, I suspected, could see his claim to glory as guru to the Simpson prosecutors slipping through his fingers. He argued. He cajoled. He begged us to reconsider. I cast a glance Frank's way. I could see that he, too, was hoping to salvage something from this debacle. After all, seventeen recruits were due to arrive tomorrow morning at a conference room in the hotel. I suggested a compromise.

"Why don't you just go in and ask them what they think of the case so far? Ask them what they think of the witnesses, the evidence. Maybe even what they think about the lawyers. But no mock trial. No ballots. No verdicts."

Vinson entertained this proposal. I could see that Frank and Bill were warming to it. Finally, we all agreed that Don would chair a discussion by a panel that had now been officially downgraded from "jury" to "focus group." Bill, Frank, and I would watch on a TV monitor in an adjoining room.

I crawled back to my room that night, already feeling the strain of battle fatigue. I looked at the clock. Four A.M. I'd get only about four hours of sleep before I had to be up and going again. I turned out the light and was asleep before my head hit the pillow.

The phone was ringing. I reached blindly for the receiver.

" 'Lo," I croaked.

"Marcia, you're late." It was Frank speaking in soft, urgent tones. "They've already started—you'd better get down here."

I squinted at the digital radio by my bed. Nine A.M. I'd forgotten to set the damned alarm!

I pulled on a pair of leggings and boots, threw on a shirt, and, grabbing a legal pad and a few binders with case reports, ran out the door. I quietly let myself into the viewing room and found a seat next to Bill. Vinson was on the monitor. He sat at the mouth of a U formed by conference tables. The seventeen panelists were seated around it. The breakdown, as I recall it, was about nine blacks or Hispanics and eight whites. Most of the blacks were women.

"What did I miss?" I whispered to Bill.

"Not much," he whispered back. "They're still getting acquainted."

I remember one of the men saying something like "It don't make no sense. Why would someone who had it all just throw it away over a woman?"

I'd heard that one before. To a guy who punches a time clock it probably seems incomprehensible to risk a fortune because you've been jilted. But that didn't take into account the fact that even a guy who had everything could flip out in the throes of sexual obsession. I made a note to confer with our domestic violence people about this one.

As I wrote, Vinson's voice penetrated my concentration. He was asking our focus group what they felt about the death penalty.

I stiffened with alarm. We'd given him a list of topics, and that most certainly wasn't on it. They were not supposed to talk about sentencing issues. I looked over to Frank, who was already on the case. He whispered something to one of Vinson's assistants, who promptly entered the conference room and in turn whispered to the boss. Vinson excused himself and came in to see us, chastened.

Vinson apologized, saying he did not know it would be a problem. "There's been no decision on whether we'll seek death or not," Frank told him. "That subject is strictly off limits."

By this time, all of us in the D.A.'s office knew that we wouldn't be seeking the death penalty. It just wasn't an option. No jury—not even one composed of white, middle-aged Republican males—was going to sentence O. J. Simpson to death.

Now, I know there is a school of thought that in a capital case, the district attorney should ask for the death penalty as a tactical ploy. If you have asked for the death penalty, every juror empaneled must be "death certified"—in other words, willing in principle to vote for death. And so, the reasoning goes, if you can pack a jury with law-and-order types, they will be more willing to convict.

I never believed that. What you're likely to get, in my view, is a panel of tough talkers who, when push comes to verdict, can't bring themselves to convict. Why? Because it has only just dawned on them that their actions may result in a person's death.

There was an even more compelling reason for not asking for the death penalty in this case. I didn't feel—and I don't believe that any of my colleagues from the brass on down felt—that it was warranted. Apart from the incidents of battery, Simpson did not have a prior criminal history. Over the course of his life he had not shown the kind of callous disregard for society's rules that you look for in a hardened criminal. O. J. Simpson was not an incorrigible, nor was he a danger to society at large. Under those circumstances it would have been immoral to seek his death.

Chastened, Vinson now steered the conversation onto another course.

"What do you think of the lawyers on the case?"' he asked them.

Of Robert Shapiro—*Oily, insincere,* said the nonblack jurors; *Smooth, smart,* said the black ones.

Bill Hodgman? A couple of jurors thought he was "smart" or "nice." But the majority didn't seem to recognize the name.

What do you think of Marcia Clark?

I found myself pulling my knees up to my chest to shield myself from the blows.

"Bitch!" two black women answered almost in unison.

I'll make no bones about it. That stung.

Let me pause for a moment. I don't want to make myself out to be some hothouse petunia who withers in the face of criticism. God knows I'd been called "bitch" before. But it was usually during the rough-and-tumble of trial work. And the taunts came from men, usually behind my back. They're livin' in a dream world if they think that stuff doesn't reach my ears. Being called a bitch by some old-time gender bigot doesn't bother me. In context, it's a compliment. It means I've stood up to him, I haven't let him have his way, and now he's throwing a little tantrum.

But from women?

We all knew—virtually from day one—that a racial divide existed in this case, but I figured I could talk to women. In cases past, I'd always been able to reach them somehow. White, Hispanic, Asian, black. It didn't matter. Even when they had failed to convict, I didn't feel that they had it in for me personally. But *these* gals were ready to eat their own.

Interestingly, none of the men used such slurs in describing me. Most of them, including one black man, found me strong, smart, and tough. That didn't count, somehow. It was the "bitch" remark that sailed right through the walls of the conference room and reverberated over the wires. So much for confidentiality. The story was out before we even made it back to L.A. The headlines all read that a Phoenix "jury" had voted to "acquit." Of course, it was complete nonsense, since no vote was ever taken. But one thing that was true—the "bitch" business—was reported with rabid glee.

On the flight home, I gave serious thought to withdrawing from the case. I am not a quitter by nature, but, I thought, if my style, my gender, or my race could actually subvert the process of justice, I should offer Gil the chance to dump me gracefully. So I asked for a meeting with Gil and Don Vinson.

Now, I should say here that in the months since the verdict, Don Vinson has been quoted more than once as saying that his research showed that black women would be too turned off by me to render a fair and impartial verdict. He's claimed to have counseled our office to downplay the domestic violence issue on the grounds that black women didn't consider it any big deal—and that I resisted him, clinging to the delusion that I could make them care.

Reality check. By the time I returned from Phoenix, I knew perfectly well what I was up against. And if reaching jurors meant emphasizing physical evidence over DV, I was perfectly willing to do it. The domestic violence aspect of the case had gone largely undeveloped. It wasn't that we'd neglected investigating the essential leads. Early on, we'd been in touch with the City Attorney's office, which had handled the 1989 battery incident. We'd collected files of documents generated by that case as well as those from the 911 call from 1983. Throughout the fall I would conduct extensive interviews with prosecutors and cops who had spoken to Nicole on both occasions. But I hadn't been able to get beyond the basic facts or to talk to domestic violence experts who might help us to interpret those facts.

I hadn't a spare moment to deal with it. My concentration and energy had been centered upon blood and other physical evidence. I was also experiencing some emotional resistance within myself—which I was hard-pressed to explain, though the reasons for it would become plainer to me as time wore on. The idea that I was on some wild-eyed feminist jag is one of Vinson's self-serving fantasies.

Vinson's misrepresentations of me, when I later read them in print, seemed all the more fantastic in light of the little speech he actually delivered to me in the very presence of Gil Garcetti.

"Marcia," he assured me unctuously, "those responses are nothing to worry about. When you're in the courtroom, they'll get to know and like you. I know they will. No question about it."

I looked to Gil. He paused for a moment, then said, "I agree with Don."

Gil Garcetti could have bailed on me, and he didn't. I will always be grateful to him for acting so honorably. I think he wanted to send a message that neither race nor gender should disqualify a good prosecutor. Gil also realized, as a purely practical matter, that anyone he chose was likely to meet resistance from jurors like those who'd branded me a bitch. A white man would be written off as a representative of the power establishment. A black man would be reviled as an Uncle Tom. A black woman? Black female jurors would fucking lynch her. Bottom line, if we drew a panel of jurors who were determined to acquit O. J. Simpson, they were going to kill the messenger.

For several weeks, the mock-jury results were a hot topic of gossip. The "bitch" comment took on a life of its own. I could hear tongues wagging: Clark's a bitch. Clark's a hothead. Is it any wonder she doesn't get along with the judge?

By now the Barry and Lisa Show had given way to the Lance and Marcia Show. Lance and I probably didn't do nearly as much wrangling as it seemed from the headlines. But whenever there was a flare-up, the five scrappiest seconds would make the ten o'clock news. In fact, Ito and I spent a lot of calm, normal moments together doing business-as-usual courtroom stuff. Sometimes we got along well; other times, not. We didn't have great chemistry, but if we'd been left alone we probably could have arrived at a wobbly truce.

But that was never going to happen. Lance was just too sensitive to his own press notices. He saw that the media had set up the two of us as sparring partners and he wanted to make damned sure the public knew, the reporters knew, and *I* knew who was running the courtroom. Whenever I raised my voice to make a point, he scowled or dressed me down. While he always spoke respectfully to the defense, referring to them as "Mr. Cochran" and "Mr. Shapiro," I was usually "Marcia." I felt that I had to draw the line early and break him of the habit of condescending to me before this case came to trial. If a jury picked up his cues, they'd tune me out before I could finish my opening statement.

Gil had been watching all this from the sidelines. A week or two after the "bitch" episode, he called me into his office for a heart-to-heart.

"Why don't you try laying back?" he suggested. "Don't be so tough."

I was flabbergasted. What the hell did he want me to do? Go in there with a pinafore and pigtails and threaten to hold my breath if Lance didn't treat me better? I had a job to do, and if I was to represent the People properly, I had to show a little strength. Either that or be an empty chair.

I was tempted to say all this, but I held my peace.

Gil smiled. "Just try lightening up a little."

I left Gil's office pretty hot under the collar. The thing I found galling about the "lighten up" business was my suspicion that these suggestions had probably come straight from Don Vinson. By this point, Vinson had zero credibility in my book. If he'd offered his etiquette tips directly to me, I would have told him to go fuck himself. But they didn't come from him; they came from my boss. I had a lot of respect for Gil Garcetti. He seemed to have faith in Vinson, and once I'd had a chance to calm down, I realized it was probably not a good idea to blow him off.

There were slight alterations I could make in my approach. I could couch my objections more deferentially. I could smile more. That wouldn't be insincere, would it? In my private life, I am warm and gentle. At least, I can be. But being made to display, on command, a side of my nature that I normally don't bring to the counsel table seemed awkward.

I went over and over this in my mind, trying to figure out what was right. Vinson told Gil that the people he'd polled perceived me as "hard." I should speak more softly. I should get a softer hairdo. I should lose the business suits in favor of—get this—dresses. Just think about the logic here. Vinson claimed that black middle-aged women were carrying a grudge against me. And so the way to defuse them was to gussy myself up like Vanna White? Vinson's line of reasoning was unapologetically sexist. It was demeaning to me personally. And in the end it was meaningless psychobabble. But we were spooked by a set of odds that were definitely not in our favor.

So I got a goddamned haircut. It was *not* a makeover. The style I'd been wearing to date was frankly unflattering. My hair had always tended to be thin, so I'd had it permed. Suzanne Childs took me to her own hairdresser, Allen Edwards in Studio City. He specialized in soft, natural styles. Allen saw exactly what had to be done. He pulled my fuzzy hair back to the nape of my neck and declared with a flourish, "This must go."

The transformation was not, in my opinion, miraculous. In fact, it took several visits to Studio City to get it right. But even I had to admit that it was an improvement. My features appeared softer, less matronly. And let's face it—who's going to complain about being made to look younger? According to the wisdom of consultancy, these changes should have had a subliminal effect. I would come across as fresher, younger, and, as a consequence, less annoying to middle-aged black women. Go figure.

The "makeover" was big news. A week or so after the cut I drove into a car wash. The radio was on and I heard Howard Stern and Robin Quivers discussing my new 'do. Howard thought it looked like I'd had chemotherapy. I have to say, I found it amusing. Some of the best commentary to come out of this trial actually came from those guys. But the point is, the buzz would not die. Every time I went in for another trim, or made the slightest alteration, there was another flurry of public commentary about my hair.

Several months down the line, I got my perm straightened. (I'd actually wanted to let it grow back to its natural straightness, but I'd put it off, fearful of calling attention to myself.) The next day, when I got off the elevator at the ninth floor, reporters gave me a standing ovation.

Look pleasant, I told myself. *They mean well. At least they're on your side.*

When I walked into court, Lance did a double-take. He noticed the stir my altered appearance was causing.

"Miss Clark . . . I think," he quipped.

There was laughter in the courtroom. I joined in, although later I felt uncomfortable about it. The experience produced in me that awful naked feeling of being a teenager changing her hairdo to please the popular crowd. And the irony of it was that this beauty offensive left me feeling more vulnerable than ever before.

A UPI reporter whom I've known for years pulled me aside in the hall and said, "Marcia, let me give you one piece of unsolicited advice. Don't change. You know what you're doing, just do your thing."

Do your thing. I used to have a pretty good idea of what my thing was. Even when my private life was a mess, I could come into the courthouse of a morning and count on doing my thing. And I did it pretty damned well. Now my thing had turned into this weird and seedy game show. And when you're standing confused and blinking in the klieg lights, it's easy to lose sight of yourself altogether.

But of one thing I was certain. I couldn't undo four hundred years of social injustice with a pretty dress and a soft voice.

Robert Bardo stalked and murdered actress Rebecca Schaeffer.

Rebecca's mother, Danna Schaeffer, and me, after the guilty verdict.

My first husband, Gaby, 1979.

Homestretch of the infamous Bronco "chase." I couldn't watch.

HARTOG/THE OUTLOOK/SIPA

The June 28 search at Simpson's Rockingham home. Phil Vannatter and I direct the D.A.'s photographer to shoot the Ashford gate, where the limo driver was parked.

AP/WIDE WORLD PHOTOS

ABOVE: *Nicole Brown Simpson, looking to a brighter future that never came.*

ABOVE, RIGHT: *Ron Goldman, whose selflessness cost him his life.*

RIGHT: *Simpson, subdued, at his first arraignment; his old arrogance would soon return.*

LEE CELANO/REUTERS/ARCHIVE PHOTOS

Gil Garcetti, David Conn, and I give statements on the day we filed the complaint. Reporters overflowed the western lobby of the CCB for what was reputed to be the largest press conference since the death of Robert Kennedy.

Johnnie Cochran. In his hands, the race card trumped justice.

GILLES MINGASSON/GAMMA LIAISON

SIPA PRESS

ABOVE: *Shapiro jealously guarded his photo ops by sticking to Simpson like glue.*

RIGHT: *Judge Lance Ito. He and the Simpson case were a devastating mismatch.*

GILLES MINGASSON/GAMMA LIAISON

Denise Brown. She spoke from the heart, and the jury received her tears with hostile skepticism.

Kim, Fred, and Patti Goldman, the conscience of the trial. They barely missed a day of the lengthy ordeal.

Phil Vannatter and Tom Lange.

Scott Gordon was our domestic violence mentor.

I couldn't get a trim without causing a buzz.

With the prosecution team in the War Room,
December 1994. Bill Hodgman is to my right.

Our science team: they masterfully presented the evidence
that should have put the murderer in prison.

© RON SEIB

The glove demonstration sparked a nationwide response from photographers around the country, all with pictures of Simpson sporting an identical pair. Here I'm pictured with one of those photographers, Ron Seib, in my office.

American Tabloid

I don't mean to sound like a whiner. I know there are lots of people who would trade a kidney for a few seconds of celebrity. In fairness, I'm willing to concede that under some very special circumstances it can be flattering to be the center of attention. It's a nice little perk. You feel important for a moment; then you go back to work.

But the escalating media frenzy in the Simpson case filled me with a sense of foreboding. The attention didn't stop at my work, or even at the length of my skirts. The reporters who besieged Suzanne Childs and her overworked public relations people were interested in "Marcia Clark, up close and personal." Read: What gives with Marcia's personal life? I told Suzanne to hold them off. I did whatever I could to discourage them. When I heard that the *L.A. Times* was looking to profile me, I kept ducking the reporter. Poor guy finally threw in the towel and ran something called "The Reluctant Headliner," which was a piece about how I avoided publicity. Whenever reporters asked Gil about my personal life, he'd say, "I don't even know if she has a family." Most of my friends and colleagues were similarly discreet.

Around the middle of July, the *National Enquirer* published its first piece about me. It was a sweetly inaccurate story about how, in my private life, I was a homebody in the June Cleaver mold. They'd found some eight-year-old neighbor girl who was supposed to have said, "What I love best is when Mrs. Clark lets me make cookies with her. . . . She says little girls are the best helpers when it comes to making cookies and that makes me feel special."

That one had the guys in my office absolutely howling. For the record, I bake cookies about once a year. As for the kid, I wouldn't know her to pick her out of a lineup.

All in all, it was pretty harmless fluff. But what worried me was the fact that they would be out there talking to my neighbors at all! Was it because I was going through a divorce? The *Enquirer* had already gotten hold of it. A divorce filing must send out some kind of subliminal alert to those dissolute Brits who run the American tabloids.

Under ordinary circumstances I would not even consider talking about my private life. In fact, when I sat down to write this book, I didn't intend to touch upon anything personal at all. I've had second thoughts about that. So many absurd things have been published about me that I feel I owe you an honest accounting of myself. By "honest," I do not mean exhaustive. But there are some things about me that I can and should discuss. Things it's important for you to know. And when you read on, I think you'll understand why.

Marcia was a very reserved person who came from a very orthodox Jewish family. She would sometimes have her face covered with a veil and before . . . marriage was even chaperoned by another woman who spoke no English.
                                            National Enquirer, August 2, 1994.

I was born Marcia Rachel Kleks, daughter of an Israeli immigrant. We were most emphatically not Orthodox. We rarely went to temple. I spent my babyhood in the Bay Area. At the age of three or four I decided to become an actress.

It was more than some preschooler's daydream. Joel Grey was a distant cousin on my mother's side—though I only met him once, when I was eight. My mother herself was a classical pianist. By the time she was eighteen, she'd made a recording. She never went on to perform professionally. She married. All the time my brother, Jon, and I were young, she kept that recording locked away somewhere like an old love letter. I never heard it.

When I was six my mother started me on piano lessons. I was a nervous, fidgety kid and had a hard time sitting still long enough to practice. Unfortunately, I was blessed with a good ear, which allowed me to be lazy. I would listen to my teacher play a piece, and then I'd learn it by ear so I wouldn't have to be bothered figuring out how to read music. I took lessons off and on until I was nine years old, when both my mother and I conceded defeat. But then, I'd discovered dance, a passion that would last a lifetime.

I have a faint recollection of practicing ballet in the living room while my mother played the piano. Unfortunately, I don't have many of those mental snapshots. For the most part, the memories of my early years are chaotic and incomplete. My father was a chemist with the FDA, and his job required us to move at least ten times while I was growing up. I'd just get settled into a place—then, *wham,* uprooted again. I could never afford to let myself get too attached to anyone or anything. There's a lot, I'm sure, I've never let myself remember.

When I was ten or eleven we moved back to the Bay Area into a new development called Foster City. It was touted by its developers as a sort of Shangri-la laid out along a string of lagoons. The showcase homes had their own boat docks. Ours didn't. It sat across the street from a beach. We did get a Sunfish, and I learned how to sail. The area was raw and undeveloped in those days. My mother would send me to the store in my sailboat to pick up milk and other small items. As I look back on those days, I realize that I enjoyed a remarkable amount of freedom. And when it wasn't given to me, I went to great lengths to steal it.

Foster City didn't have its own school system, so in seventh grade I was bused to a junior high in a very rough neighborhood. I wasn't exactly born with a silver spoon in my mouth, but I'd never seen anything like this. These kids were all wise in the ways of the streets. Here I was in knee socks and pleated skirts, with long, straight brown hair, sitting next to babes wearing ass-hugging skirts, black fishnets, a pound of makeup, and hair teased into humongous lacquered swells. They smoked in the bathroom, swore like sailors, and didn't give a damn about their grades or what their parents would say. *Très* cool. I wanted some of that.

I knew *my* parents would throw a fit if they saw me in fishnets, so I came up with a plan to get around them. I went shopping with a school friend who helped me pick out a low-cut V-necked sweater that exposed my nonexistent cleavage. I borrowed a tight black skirt that was way too long for me. I think it was something my friend's older sister had outgrown. I fixed the hemline problem by rolling up the waistband, then hid the bulge under the bulky sweater. I scored a pair of black hose and doctored the runs with pale pink nail polish. And I bought a pair of cool black pumps. This became my uniform. My secret uniform.

I'd leave the house every morning in normal clothes. Then, when I got to school, I'd duck into the girls' bathroom, dig into my knapsack, and pull out my finery. There were usually several friends willing to help me tease my long, straight hair to an acceptable height. The black eyeliner, applied with a canoe paddle, and pale pink lipstick completed the transformation. I was ready for class.

Back then the student population was divided into two groups: "surfers" and "greasers." I liked the greasers, car-addicted, chain-smoking tough guys who swore at the slightest provocation, wore tight jeans, pointed boots, and leather jackets, and poured more oil on their hair than in their engines. I attracted the attention of the leader of the pack. Tom was fifteen—an older man by the standards of a twelve-year-old. He wore his hair slicked back with a ton of lubricant and sported a black leather jacket, his trademark. He was reputed to be epileptic; this somehow only added to his mystique. He had a pair of deep brown eyes, full sensuous lips, and a sexy macho attitude that made him *the* premier catch of the school. Shortly after my own transformation, he decided we had to go steady.

This seemed a very cool thing to do. It was a sure way of getting accepted by the fast crowd and proving how tough I was to boot. So I took Tom's ring, a heavy metal number that was way too big for me. I tried the prescribed remedy of wrapping yarn around it to improve the fit, but that made it so bulky, I ended up wearing it on a chain around my neck. My steady didn't mind. He considered it proof of his manliness that his ring hung loose on his woman's skinny finger.

At recess he'd let me wear his leather jacket, which hit me at the knees. We'd stand together, his arm around me. Periodically, he'd plant an ostentatious kiss on my lips. He'd linger long enough so that everyone could see we were a couple. What they couldn't know was that he'd repeatedly invited me to go out on dates—usually to Saturday matinees—and that I kept finding ever more creative excuses to decline. Quite apart from the fact that I'd never be able to carry off an actual date under my parents' noses, I learned that I could expect to be "felt up" and "felt down." That prospect terrified me. I knew that eventually I'd have to put out or get out. I wasn't quite sure how to do either.

It was one of my steady's jealous ex-girlfriends, Linda, who settled the matter once and for all. She sent out the word that she was going to knock out my lights. Tom told me he'd "take care" of her. One day, at noon recess, I went into the girls' restroom. I'd just finished patting my hair into place when Linda burst through the door, cornered me, and threw a punch. I was agile enough to duck, or she would have knocked me out cold.

"You little bitch," she growled. "You can't have Tom; he's mine. Get it?" She was leaning forward with clenched fists. It would have been funny, it was so trite—except I was scared to death. What had happened to Tom's promise to "take care" of her? It was clearly up to me.

"Take him, he's yours," I told her, in as rational and assertive a tone as I could muster. She seemed surprised, but she backed off. And so I slipped out of a rumble *and* a sticky romantic entanglement within the space of a minute.

My career as a greaser was cut short by my family's next move, this one to Michigan. I had just turned thirteen. I found to my dismay that the quiet suburb we now called home had no great appreciation for fishnet stockings. The kids in my new high school worshiped all things Californian. They wanted to be surfers. There was only one real "in" crowd. All the rest were wannabes. By my third day, the popular clique—operating upon the mistaken assumption that because I was from San Francisco I must be a surfer girl—took me under its wing. I was ceremoniously escorted to their table in the lunchroom and introduced all around. The girls were all dyed-in-the-wool Heathers. You know the type.

Before lunch was over, they'd set me up to join them for Cokes at a local hangout on Friday, go shopping with them on Saturday, and visit someone's house on Sunday. The kicker came when one of the girls called me at home that night to announce that I would be going steady with one of the freckle-faced rich guys I'd met at lunch. I was stunned. I'd heard of arranged marriages, but this was ridiculous.

The next day at lunch, I deliberately chose to sit at a table of outcasts—those who'd either abandoned all hope of ever being popular or had never cared much to begin with. One girl leaned over to me and asked, "Do you realize how pissed off they're going to be if you sit with us?" Of course I did. I actually enjoyed watching the Heathers glower at me from their privileged position. They didn't like the idea of being rejected. *Serves you damned right,* I thought.

I did okay on my own terms. That year I got into gymnastics. I would have liked to try out for the women's gymnastics team, except there wasn't one. Instead, I became a cheerleader. Co-captain of the squad, in fact. Before I could really get into the season, however, we moved again. This time to Maryland.

I was prepared to hate the place, but I ended up loving it. The apartment complex we moved to was populated largely by families as transient as my own. They came from all over the world. In the afternoons and on weekends I'd play soccer in the central courtyard with kids from India, Chile, Argentina, and England. They were kindred spirits. Most of them had lived lives as unsettled as my own, and they had no trouble welcoming a newcomer whose tenure was uncertain. I faced the usual trauma of having to make new friends, but the transition was easier than ever before. Within two months I'd become part of a congenial crowd, with a few close friends among them.

That interlude of contentment, however, ended abruptly with yet another move, this time to New York. The announcement devastated me. I'd been so happy in Maryland. For the first time in my life I hadn't felt like a freak. Maybe it was the feeling of having no control over my life, or maybe it was just the prospect of having to start all over again, but when I got news of our impending departure, I marched upstairs to my room, closed the door, and ripped up every book I could lay my hands on. Then I threw every fragile object I owned against the wall. When my belongings lay in ruins around me, I dropped onto my bed in a fit of sobbing.

We moved to a development on Staten Island, where we bought a large house. That, at least, made me happy. I had the whole downstairs floor to myself. It had its own entrance, which gave me more freedom than ever. The bad news was that the kids in my new high school regarded me with outright hostility. The California mystique didn't mean spit here. The only group that would accept me were the hippies. They were not junkies or hypes or anything, just basically good kids who, like me, didn't fit in anywhere else. I helped them organize the distribution of the *High School Free Press* and agitated for the abolition of the school dress code. And I smoked a little dope, something I admit without a twinge of regret or guilt. When I see a politician squirming when asked to admit he sneaked a toke as a kid, I just want to shake him and say, "Grow up, Junior." The way I look at it, toking was just one more rite of passage.

One night my friends and I met at a local park that was one of our favorite hangouts. We were just sitting around acting cool. One guy brought his guitar and we were singing Dylan songs badly. Suddenly a crew-cut man wearing a Ban-Lon shirt, cutoffs, and a peace symbol approached us and flicked on a flashlight.

"This is a bust, everybody," he barked. "Stand up."

I thought it was a joke. I mean, he had to be kidding, especially in that getup.

"I mean it," he repeated. "I'm a cop."

"Oh, yeah? Well then, where's your badge?" I taunted him. I was perfectly sober but high on attitude.

He produced a badge. We promptly stood.

The cop marched us out to where several other officers had stationed themselves in the middle of the park. Another girl and I were handed over to an older cop who questioned us apart from the others. I was scared. I was enough of a middle-class Jewish girl to know that an arrest would be terrible for me in every way. But I also knew that I'd done nothing wrong.

"Why are we getting busted?" I asked him. "We were just singing."

"Don't give me that," he sneered at me. "We found a bunch of hype kits and Baggies of heroin right over there." He pointed to some bushes.

Heroin! The thought of pushing a needle into my arm made me physically ill.

"You must be kidding," I said in complete amazement. "We don't do heroin!"

"Oh, yeah?" he said right into my face. "Well, let's see your arms."

I was wearing a sleeveless top, which, as I think back on it, should have told the cops right off the bat that I was no junkie. But I stretched out my arms obediently. The officer examined them and pointed to a small scratch on my right bicep. "You see," he said triumphantly, "that could be a skin pop."

Skin pop? What the hell was that?

The sickening realization swept over me that this guy could say anything he wanted. He could manufacture any evidence he wanted. No matter how innocent I was, he could send me to jail if he wanted to. To him I was just a scruffy piece of shit.

I don't want to sound melodramatic, but that sense of total helplessness stayed with me long after I became an officer of the court. For a prosecutor, it's easy to become annoyed at a criminal justice system that seems to be stacked so ridiculously in favor of defendants. But you have to have been on the downside looking up at the face of the law before you realize how thin those defenses really are. Once you've been there, you can't honestly begrudge a defendant any help he can muster.

That night in the park, I had no cards to play. So I did the only thing I could. I begged. I pleaded. And as fear and frustration overcame me, I began to cry. The other girl watched this performance in silence, but when I glanced at her out of the corner of my eye, I saw she looked as terrified as I felt. When I'd run out of words and courage, I stopped.

The officer stood looking at us for a moment, confused. Then he said, "All right, you two, get out of here, and fast. I don't want to see you anywhere around here ever again. You hear me? Now beat it!"

I looked at him for a moment, unsure of what I'd just heard. I looked at my friend. She nodded, and together we turned and began to walk away, expecting to be stopped at any moment. After the first few steps, we broke into a sprint that had our hearts pumping. We didn't stop running until we got to a bus stop about a mile from the park. And there we parted ways. Neither of us said a thing to the other. And after that evening, I never saw her again.

I never figured out what happened that night. How the heroin—if it really was heroin—got there. Whose it really was. The word around school was that the cops had planted the drugs as an excuse to bust us because neighbors had complained about noise in the park. The boys were booked and charged. No one got any jail time, but after that we all pretty much lost touch with each other.

My life was already drifting in another direction.

Shortly after we'd moved to New York, I'd started taking weekly acting classes at a small repertory theater in Greenwich Village, Circle in the Square. I absolutely lived for those classes, especially during the first six months of the school year while I was still battling the stigma of being the "new girl." The acting teachers at Circle in the Square were terrific; they gave me the opportunity to cut my teeth on Shakespeare. When we worked on readings from *Othello*, I chose to play the maid rather than Desdemona. No mystery as to why—Desdemona was an ingenue, a sheltered little girl. Emilia, the maid, was an older woman, wise in the ways of the world and the streets.

My teachers seemed to think I was pretty good. At the end of the course, we put on a showcase and I was given the female lead, Emily, in a short segment from *Our Town*. I also had two roles in Dylan Thomas's *Under Milk Wood*, which was more than anyone else got to play. While waiting to go on, I was paralyzed with stage fright. It was like being underwater, that queer sense of dissociation from the physical world. I would suffer that same crisis of nerves many times in years to come—in fact, any time I had to deliver an opening statement. But the resolution was always the same. Once I actually set foot onstage, the fear drained away. I became totally immersed in the moment. Onstage the imaginary characters overtook me and I felt the rush of bringing them alive for a few moments. Heady stuff for a fifteen-year-old.

From my first trip into the Village, I felt at home. It was exciting. Exotic. I just couldn't get enough of it. During the summer between my sophomore and junior years, I found a way to spend more time there: I got a job. Well, sort of.

One afternoon after school, I wandered into a leather shop—I'd always loved the smell and feel of leather—and struck up a conversation with a man who turned out to be the manager. He asked me if I'd like to make a little extra money. I was wary. "Like to make some money?" sounded like a preamble to "Take off your clothes." The manager saw my reaction and laughed. He was looking for someone to distribute advertising flyers. He'd pay me five bucks an hour to walk up and down the street and hand them out to passersby.

It was too perfect. I'd be right in the middle of the action, and making money at that. I accepted on the spot. He handed me a stack of flyers and I hit the pavement with a big grin on my face. I did this for about two months until I got a job as a salesgirl at a low-end fashion boutique. I was really good at it. I could talk to people, size up types, and put together great outfits. Low-riding, hip-hugger bell-bottoms, tight T-shirts and halter tops.

For the next two years I worked at several shops on the Lower East Side. Artists and entrepreneurs had moved in and begun transforming what was basically a slum into another hip venue. It would come to be called the East Village, but in those days it was still a pretty raunchy part of town. The boutiques where I worked stayed open until one or two A.M. on Fridays and Saturdays, which meant that I was out on the streets in the small hours of the morning. On the way home I had to run a gauntlet of winos, junkies, and speed freaks, all looking for a handout. I knew better than to stop and reach into my purse on those dark streets. I decided I'd better get myself some protection. Not a gun—camouflage. I bought the scruffiest leather air force jacket I could find, as well as a pair of funky, threadbare jeans. Add to that a really beat-up suede saddlebag. I'd change into my grungy getup, pull a scarf over my hair and face, and adopt a speed-freak lope all the way to the subway. Worked like a charm. Even the winos gave me a wide berth.

By now, my old school chums were history. I wouldn't date high school boys. I didn't have to. Village dudes were invariably more attractive to me than high school geeks. I'd finally found someplace where I belonged. Then, once again, the ax fell. We had to move again—back to the West Coast, this time to Los Angeles. I was too young to stay in New York and finish high school alone. I had to go with my parents.

That next fall, when I started college at U.C. Riverside, I was suffering from depression. I hated the place. I hated life in a girls' dorm. You can understand why. I'd just come from the Village, which was on the cutting edge of everything from street fashion to politics. Now all of a sudden, here I was, stuck in a dormitory where my floormates wore curlers and fuzzy slippers and agonized over whether boys should be allowed to use the girls' bathrooms during Sunday visits.

I had fun shocking people. I still dressed in my Village clothes, which consisted mostly of velvet and leather. The only thing I would consider wearing to bed was an ivory satin gown, Jean Harlow–style, fitted to the hips and flaring out into a swirl around the ankles. I'd found it in a thrift shop. The Sandra Dee types viewed me with suspicion, and I avoided them like the plague. After two weeks I transferred to a coed dorm where I had a much better time.

The coursework was easy and I found a terrific jazz dance class. It was taught by Joe Tremaine, a slender redhead who had an impressive list of professional credits as both a dancer and a choreographer. It was just dumb luck to have run into someone that good. Joe gave me religion. One day the class was doing a combination he'd just demonstrated when he suddenly stopped the music and glared at us.

"You all think you can just get out there and wiggle your fannies and have a good time, don't you? Well, you look sloppy and amateurish. Anyone can see it. I can tell who's had ballet. I can tell who's trained and worked, and who hasn't. There's no substitute for real work. If you're not working, you're not fooling anyone but yourselves."

I knew he was right. Whether I ever danced professionally or not, I knew I wanted to do it right or not at all. The next day I got myself into a ballet class and continued to study ballet for the next twelve years. I danced until the rigors of trial work, and later, motherhood, made it impossible for me to keep up.

The following year I transferred to UCLA. I cut classes as often as I could get away with it. I don't mean to leave the impression that I was a slacker. Far from it. I just preferred to study on my own. In fact, I took a heavy load each semester so I could graduate as soon as possible. I also worked several nights a week as a waitress at a local steak house. I hardly dated at all. To make up for the absence of a social life, I started folk dancing, which was a real craze back then. I made a few good friends, mostly women, and we started going out together on the nights when there was no good place to dance. Our favorite watering hole was on Fairfax Avenue.

This was the early seventies; the Six-Day War, which had ended in a huge victory for Israel, was still fresh in the minds of American Jews. Israeli males who streamed to the States in its aftermath carried with them not only the aura of foreignness but the macho allure of the conqueror. Most of these hotshots found their way to Jewish communities, where they felt most at home. In Los Angeles, that was the Fairfax district.

Fairfax Avenue was jammed with small restaurants that served falafel and shuwarma. They were in constant and largely unsuccessful competition with Cantor's Delicatessen, the flagship anchored on the busiest part of the thoroughfare. Cantor's was the premier hangout for newly arrived Israelis, as well as for Americans who wanted to meet them. Young Jewish girls who were bored by the nice Jewish boys they'd grown up with were thrilled by the prospect of these exotic specimens. (How strenuously, after all, could one's parents object? These Israelis *were* Jewish—and war heroes to boot.)

The Israelis were perfectly well aware of their allure, and took full advantage of the many romantic opportunities it afforded them. Some were honorable; some weren't. The rogues among them left a trail of broken hearts and bitter stories that eventually saddled the whole lot with reputations as womanizing bastards. When I came on the scene, that rep hadn't yet evolved; we still had reason to believe that they could be okay guys.

My girlfriends and I tended to congregate at a joint across the street from Cantor's. It had only about ten glass-topped tables, seating forty at most. On the walls hung posters of Israel. A tape of popular Israeli music played nonstop. The owners didn't object to patrons nursing cups of coffee for hours rather than spending money on dinner. This made it a great favorite of the Israelis, and of the girls looking for Israelis.

It was there I met my first husband.

*   *   *

I wasn't looking for a husband, or even a boyfriend. I had no desire to be added to anyone's list of conquests. My friends and I had finished eating when I was aware that one of the sharks was cruising our way. I was about to warn my friends to ignore him when he pulled up a chair and sat down next to me.

It was one of those heavy-handed advances so typical of Israeli men. I signaled to my group to ignore him, but he'd already started chatting up one of the girls. She was getting all shiny-eyed and breathless and had taken it upon herself to make introductions. I half-turned to say hello—and sitting next to me was the most incredibly handsome man I had ever seen.

He had glossy dark curls and enormous green eyes. His features were angelic and yet strongly masculine. Gaby—that's what his friends called him—was doubtless a womanizing cad. But he was very charming. And he was incredibly funny. Gaby's wit was never self-deprecating; the joke was always at someone else's expense. But it was always right on the mark. I was charmed by him despite myself. He spoke to me only in Hebrew, which seemed more intimate than English. About a hour after we'd met he told me, "I'll take you home."

It was not an offer. It was an order.

All my life I've had this thing for bad boys. I'm embarrassed even having to think about this, let alone talk about it. But I got turned on by that tired old macho come-on. Worldly as I considered myself, I was still a kid. I was wildly confident one moment, withdrawn the next. And so when I ran smack into this handsome, assertive man who seemed to know exactly what he wanted, I saw in him only what I wanted to see: real strength.

I let him take me home to the studio apartment I was sharing with a friend near campus. We began seeing each other. In less than a month I was living with him.

Gaby and I made an odd pair. Here I was, a grubby college student in jeans, whose idea of high fashion was the latest shipment at the army-navy surplus store. I studied all day and ventured out at night only for folk dancing. Gaby was flashy, always dressed to the nines in body-hugging suits. He seemed to have plenty of money. He slept all day and went nightclubbing all night. I found his lifestyle very glamorous, and allowed myself to be swept along by it.

Gaby played backgammon for a living. I'd never even heard of the game before I met him, but Gaby took great pains to teach it to me. He instructed me not only in the basic rules, but in theory and strategy as well. He spent hours explaining the various plays and how to size up your chances of winning at any given point. The sizing-up business was important, because the stakes of the game could be raised over and over again by "doubling." One player could challenge by offering to double the stakes. If the other player refused, the game ended and the challenger scored a point. The stakes could range from a quarter a point to hundreds or even thousands of dollars a point. When you consider that fifty or sixty points can be easily racked up in one sitting, you can see how some heavy coin could change hands, fast.

I soon learned that backgammon was a real hot pastime with the rich. The craze was in its infancy when Gaby and I first met. Two years later, when I started law school, it had become a full-tilt mania. Bars and clubs everywhere had at least one or two tables. Some clubs devoted themselves exclusively to it. The most popular of these was Pips, in Beverly Hills. Pips catered to the rich and famous. The name of the club was inlaid discreetly in brass to the right of the large double-doored entrance. Muted lighting, thick carpets, and dark, paneled walls lent the place an air of understated opulence. The room devoted to backgammon was right off the foyer. It had ten tables and its own bar. I liked Pips more than other places on the backgammon circuit because it was relatively quiet and had cushiony, well-upholstered chairs. There, I could park myself and study while Gaby played.

Gaby and I would drop into Pips every other night or so while he tried to hustle up a "pigeon," the pro's term for a novice who played for high stakes. It wasn't easy to get a game at Pips. The fashionable set usually played with their friends and were understandably leery of a flashy stranger with an Israeli accent. So if he failed to score, we'd move along to the Cavendish.

The Cavendish, located on the border between West Hollywood and Beverly Hills, was a private club that had been devoted largely to bridge and gin rummy. Gambling, of course, was illegal, and I'd heard that the Cavendish had been raided a couple of times—but as far as I could tell that hadn't slowed down the action. During the early seventies, the entire back room was given over to backgammon. The

Cavendish was not the plush playground that Pips was. It was located in an office building, two flights up. There was no elevator that serviced the club. Nor was there any sign visible from the street to announce its existence.

The first thing you saw when you came in was a long counter where club personnel would check to make sure you were a member in good standing. To the left of that counter was a lounge with a couple of sofas and coffee tables. If you passed through the lounge, you'd walk into a large room filled with bridge tables. To the back was a partition of wood and glass; beyond that, backgammon.

Gaby never had trouble finding a game here. In fact, he made a lot of money. The tabloids later portrayed Gaby as a chronic cheat. I should tell you that backgammon is a game of cutthroats, and it was very common for players to accuse one another of cheating. So you have to take those stories with a grain of salt. All I can say is, I never saw him cheat.

At the beginning, I loved doing the clubs with Gaby. The nightlife reminded me a little of my time in Greenwich Village—which I still think of as the happiest, most carefree part of my life. But looking back on it, I can see that my life with Gaby was a weird existence by any standard. Gaby would play all night; then we'd hit a twenty-four-hour diner. By the time we got home, it would be four in the morning. We'd be too keyed up to sleep, so we'd watch TV until at least five or six A.M. Of course, then we slept until one or two in the afternoon. We'd start out again at seven or eight. It was common for us to see the sun only as it was setting or rising.

I skipped classes. Actually, I'd never gone much, to begin with. I'd check in for a few sessions at the beginning of the semester and then spend the rest of the term reading on my own. That suited me better. My grades stayed high. Everything worked out fine.

After the first year, however, I found the charm of the nightclub circuit wearing a little thin. Nocturnal living left me isolated, dependent almost solely upon Gaby for love and companionship. That wouldn't have been so bad, except that he and I fought a lot. Sometimes the conflicts were subtle—he'd get sarcastic over something as small as my not making dinner the way he liked it. But that was usually a pretext for deeper irritation, like the fact that I'd come home from dance class later than I was supposed to. He didn't like being alone. He couldn't stand not knowing where I was. He'd say he was afraid that whenever I wasn't with him, I was seeing other men.

We'd scream at each other in Hebrew. Once he barricaded the front door with chairs and sat down on one of them, arms folded, refusing to let me out. I'd lock myself in the bathroom to get away from him; once, he literally kicked the door in. I tried to leave him so many times. One time in particular, we'd been fighting about God knows what, and I decided I'd had enough. I threw some clothes in my dance bag and ran out of the apartment. Gaby ran after me and caught me just as I reached my car. He grabbed me by the arm and tried to pull me back with him across the street. He yanked me so hard the he knocked me off my feet. As he dragged me over the ground, I screamed "Let me go!" over and over. Finally, a neighbor opened a window and shouted, "If you don't knock it off, I'm calling the police!" That sobered us up real fast.

But the brawls continued. I'd try to leave; he'd try to stop me. Once as I was headed for the door, he pushed me onto the bed. I got up and pushed him back. As I tried to make for the door again, he grabbed hold of me. The next thing I knew I was flat on my back on the floor and he was standing behind me. I wasn't thinking. I was just reacting. I swung my foot up behind me to ward him off and I felt it connect with his body. For one startled second I waited in dread for the retaliation. It didn't come. I leaped to my feet and, without so much as looking at him, I ran to the balcony, climbed over the railing, jumped, and hit the ground running. Thank God, we lived on the first floor. I ran hard, convinced I'd hear him gaining on me. After about five minutes, I realized that he wasn't following. Winded, chest heaving, I stopped and looked back. He wasn't there.

I was puzzled. This was a first. I'd never run out the door without Gaby hot on my heels. Maybe I was mistaken. Maybe I hadn't kicked him. After about an hour, I figured it would be safe to test the waters. I entered the apartment warily and found Gaby sitting in a chair in the bedroom, slumped over, ashen-faced. What had I done?

"Are you okay?" I asked him timidly.

"You kicked me in the balls, damn you," he managed weakly.

I started to apologize, but he waved me away and limped over to the bed.

"Just leave me alone."

I felt so guilty that I stayed. Things went back to our peculiar idea of normal. That meant rolling from the heat of battle to the unnatural quiet that settled over us after we'd wrung ourselves dry. Then we'd drift for a while into a loving period when we'd actually laugh and have fun together. And then it would all start up again.

Gaby never slapped or punched me. Things never escalated past the shoving stage, which was almost always the result of my trying to leave and his trying to restrain me. Once, during an argument, he pushed me against the wall, pinned my shoulder back with one hand, and tapped my cheek in a mock slap. Then he grabbed my chin. I asked him tearfully to let me go. He looked in my eyes and said, "I hold you like this because I love you. You make me act this way. I'd never get this way if I didn't love you so much."

And I accepted that. Somehow, we'd both come to equate a display of physical aggression with a demonstration of love. When our fights escalated to the point that I tried to walk out the door, his efforts to restrain me were actually a form of reassurance for us both. It was the way we proved to each other that we were still in love.

I spent half the time wishing I could get away from him; the other half of the time I felt that all I wanted to do was be with him. I hated myself for being so weak. I seemed to have no real personality of my own. Gaby was the mirror in which I saw myself. I'd changed my habits to fit his convenience. I'd pegged my expectations to his. I had never had a job other than waitressing or salesclerking. I knew that those menial jobs paid barely enough to live. I felt like a hamster on a wheel, unable to see a route out.

I had a vague, unformed, yet undeniable realization that having a job was where it was at. If you had well-paid work, you had some power in a relationship. You could be independent. And if you had a well-paid job that was interesting and satisfying? That almost took the place of a relationship. But how the hell did you get a gig like that?

By now, I'd realized I would never make it as an actor or a dancer. I had some talent, but not the insane drive you need to make it to the top. I had enough sense at the time to realize that I needed a profession. But I didn't have any clear idea what that was. I was so clueless that I actually applied to United Airlines for a position as a flight attendant. (In those days we were still calling them stewardesses.) The

airline called me back for a second interview. I'll never forget it—
about ten of us sitting around the table. They started asking us our
political views. Everybody's sitting there simpering, "I don't know, I
mean, I don't really care." Then I weighed in with a few strong opinions. I never heard from United again.

I fell back to reconsider. I could be a diplomat. Sure. Why not?
This was admittedly an odd choice for someone as impulsive and con-
frontational as I am, but I already had a couple of languages under my
belt. I could speak French and Hebrew. I applied to work in the For-
eign Office in the State Department. During my first interview some
functionary informed me that I would have to take an entry-level post
as a secretary. I thought, *I don't see how that works. Secretary to
diplomat? No. I don't think so.*

In the spring of 1973, after graduating from UCLA, I took a job
with a law firm that specialized in estate planning. My God, was that
dense. I did accounts receivable and reception work. Basically, I was a
girl Friday. At the outset, I approached the job rather too casually for
my employers' taste. I came in late, showed up when I felt like it.
Before long, my supervisor called me in and warned me that I was
about to be fired.

That brought me up short. "Man," I thought, "I don't mind getting fired from a good job, but I can't get fired from a job this tacky."
So I cleaned up my act, became prompt, innovative, a real dynamo.
They came to love me. I started thinking, *Maybe there's some future for
me in the law.*

It was not such a leap. An actor seeks validation from his audience.
An attorney gets his validation from judge and jury. (Many trial
lawyers, I've concluded in the years since, are frustrated actors.) I took
stock of my abilities. I had a good memory. I could write well. I could
think on my feet. So I got a book from UCLA Law School that was
supposed to help you prepare for the LSATs. On the night before the
test I looked through it. Then I went out and got drunk. Maybe I
wanted to sabotage myself, or perhaps I wanted to give myself an excuse
if I failed. Anyway, they give that test early in the morning. I stumbled
in, three sheets to the wind, barely able to pencil in a blurred succession
of circles. Somehow I did well enough to be accepted by Loyola and
Southwestern in Los Angeles and Hastings in San Francisco.

Gaby was threatened by the whole idea of my going into law. He refused even to consider the prospect of my moving, or our moving, to San Francisco, so Hastings was out of the question. His objections were just enough to undermine my confidence. I put off sending in my applications until it was too late for Loyola. Southwestern accepted me for the fall of 1973.

I grabbed onto law school like a drowning woman clings to flotsam. It was to become my salvation. Law school took more effort than undergraduate work. I had to study. I had to memorize. I actually had to attend classes. I found that I was well suited to analytical thinking. Briefing cases came easily to me. You take a case decision of fifty pages written in the densest legalese and have to figure out: What's the issue? What's the rule? What's the conclusion? I enjoyed the intellectual exercise of taking something very complicated and reducing it to its essence.

I cannot say that the law loomed before me as some mystical, meaningful vocation. A sense of principle did not kick in until a few years down the line, when I realized my real calling lay in the D.A.'s office. But from the start, studying law served as an absorbing and invigorating counterpoint to my life with Gaby.

The deeper I got into law, the more I withdrew from him. We continued living together—we were going on five years. But the screaming matches and the physical skirmishes ended. The reason was simple. I was no longer really there.

Sensing that I was distracted for long periods, Gaby'd ask me, "Where's your mind? Where are you?"

I'd always had the ability to distance myself at will from reality. During our first year together, I recall, I had an unwholesome penchant for romance novels, real bodice-rippers like *Lust in the Weeds*. I read them voraciously. And I lived in a dream world.

But now, my emotional disengagement from Gaby took on a different quality. It was convenient, in a way. He liked me best when I was docile and submissive. I'd made that discovery the first year of our relationship, when I'd gotten a terrible cold. I was weak and exhausted and Gaby couldn't have been sweeter to me. He was at my side almost constantly. He tended to my every need and even carried me to the bathroom. My dependence galvanized him into chivalry. Subconsciously, I dragged out my illness to extend that peaceful interlude as long as I could. The problem was, I couldn't stay sick forever.

I remember so many nights I'd come home from a study session or the library and peek into the bedroom to see if he was there. If he wasn't, I'd hop into bed as fast as I could in hopes that I'd be asleep before he got home.

As I look back on it all now, I realize that I was suffering from a true depression. I was unhappy with Gaby, but my perspective was so distorted that I couldn't imagine being happy with anyone else. I repeated to myself all those bromides that I'm sure a lot of couples repeat to convince themselves that they should stay together rather than get out and look for something better. Like: "There's no such thing as the perfect mate." "You can't find it all in one person." "You always have to compromise." What I didn't understand at the time was that in order for compromise to work, both parties have to be essentially compatible. They shouldn't be spending 90 percent of their time together brawling. There should be something in each that enhances the other. Still, whatever it was that Gaby and I had, I thought it was the best I deserved, the best I could hope to get from life.

Even now, I'm hard put to explain why I married him. I'll be the first to admit that a lot of what I've done in my personal life has been impulsive, has seemed to run counter to the dictates of common sense. But in its own weird way, getting married made sense at the time. If we were having trouble, the thing to do was to bind ourselves closer to each other so we'd have to get along. Right?

Well, no, actually.

Still, Gaby was a pragmatist. He needed a green card and he'd get one if he married me. Since we were obviously going to stay together, didn't it make sense to do it in a way that would give him citizenship? I saw the logic of that, though Gaby knew how down I was on marriage in general. I agreed on one condition—that no one but the government would know about it. We'd run out to Las Vegas and get a piece of paper and keep our lips buttoned. He agreed. And that's how we got married the first time. It was just a formality.

Gaby kept his end of the bargain. Our secret never leaked. I never told anyone, and no one ever knew—not even my brother, who was my closest confidant.

A year or so passed this way and Gaby started to talk about doing it properly. The idea of a wedding seemed to make him happy, so I gave in. On November 6, 1976, we were married again. My father's father, a very devout Jew, came over from Israel, and for his benefit we had an Orthodox wedding in my parents' home. I remember standing at the altar, nearly delirious with a 102-degree fever, telling myself, "This is not happening." The rabbi's words washed over me. I was barely conscious.

We spent our three-day honeymoon in—where else?—Las Vegas. On our first night, we went out to dinner at a swanky restaurant. It dawned upon me that we were alone. Really alone. There were no distractions. No backgammon cronies. No games to jump into as soon as dinner was over. We gave the waiter our order, and when he walked away I looked across the table at Gaby. I experienced a moment of absolute emptiness, realizing that I had nothing to say to him. *My God,* I thought. *What have I done?* This man, whom I had publicly vowed to cherish, etc., till death do us part . . . this man felt no closer to me than the waiter who'd just taken our order.

I wandered through casinos on Gaby's arm. I laughed too loudly, played the part of the happy newlywed. When the strain became too much, I laid claim to a chaise longue by our hotel pool and drank piña coladas until I was stuporous.

I continued to be the dutiful camp follower. Whenever Gaby had an out-of-town tournament, I'd bring my law books and study while he played. One week before my final exams, he had a big tournament in Las Vegas. Again, I brought my books and spent all day alone in our hotel room studying before I went out at night and joined him for the tournament. You would hardly think that those conditions would have made for distinguished academic achievement. But I made the dean's list that year. On the surface, everything seemed to be working out fine.

It's just that our marriage was hollow at the core. I didn't care if Gaby saw other women, as long as he left me alone. I got a clue to the depth of my own disengagement when a woman called the house one day asking for him. The tone of her voice made it clear that she was no business associate. I asked her if she wanted to leave her name, and she hung up. I had every right to be angry. Not only was he cheating on me, but he'd had the gall to give his girlfriend his home number. But I didn't care. I truly did not care.

We had some good times left. After I took the bar exam, we treated ourselves to a trip to Europe. I'd been studying nonstop for two months and during that time we hadn't even gone to see a movie together. Gaby wanted us to take a real vacation, as opposed to the usual backgammon jaunt. I'd been going to law school on a federally insured student loan and I had some of that money left over. We splurged on a week-long trip to Italy and France.

After those two months of sensory deprivation studying for the bar, I was exhausted and ready for a blowout. The sights and smells of southern Europe were intoxicating. I couldn't do or see enough.

Gaby had a way of going up and talking to people. He could speak a little Italian, a little French. He regaled strangers with his back-gammon exploits until they were eating out of his hand. Anyway, he struck up a conversation with the conductor of the sleeping car we took from France to Italy. He was a young guy with a sweet face and large warm brown eyes. When we arrived in Rome, the conductor took us home to have dinner with his mother. And he offered to act as our unofficial tour guide. On one outing he took us to a topless beach. I thought it was an absolute riot. I've never been the inhibited type. In fact, shortly after we got there, I shed my own bikini top. Gaby put his arm around my waist, and our Italian friend snapped the picture. I was happy and smiling in that shot.

When we returned from Europe, I withdrew into myself again. Gaby and I lived more or less separate lives. I got a job as an associate lawyer with the firm I'd been clerking for. And there I discovered the healing powers of work.

I like to think that having a real career awakened some semblance of self-esteem and an independent identity that gave me the strength to confront the truth. Perhaps I'm wrong. Maybe it was just the growing-up process, which would have happened regardless of whether I'd found a profession. Whatever the reason, I grew stronger. More confident. I liked myself a little better. And I realized then that my days with Gaby were numbered.

I agonized about leaving him. I knew I should just pick up and go, but I was hamstrung by guilt. Just as my career was taking off, his fortunes were taking a downturn. The backgammon mania was subsiding. It became clear that gambling would not provide him with an identity—or even a living—very much longer. All he'd ever been was a backgammon pro. A teacher at best; a hustler at worst. His entire image of himself was built around being pretty and having a fast, flashy lifestyle. His looks were going. His money was going. He was depressed. We spent long nights discussing his childhood, his past, and his uncertain future. I knew that if I was ever going to find it in my heart to leave him, I was going to have to get him back on his feet. But I'd suffered from bouts of depression myself. And trying to deal with Gaby's problems left me feeling overwhelmed.

Gaby needed professional help. I begged him to see a psychiatrist, but he wouldn't hear of it. Then I remembered something from my days in Greenwich Village. The managers of the leather shop I'd worked for had been Scientologists. They'd talk to me now and then about their beliefs. The church gave them very specific suggestions for learning to be assertive and confident. A lot of that teaching struck me as pure common sense, but it seemed to provide them with a source of strength.

As it happened, one of Gaby's star pupils was into Scientology in a big way. His name was Bruce Roman and he was one of the few genuinely good guys I met on the backgammon circuit. Bruce was a tall man whose athletic build and curly blond hair contrasted strikingly with Gaby's dark good looks. When they went out together, women would stop dead in their tracks and stare.

Bruce was passionate about backgammon. He just couldn't get enough. He initially gravitated toward Gaby in order to learn the game, but over time the teaching relationship grew into a close friendship. When Gaby refused therapy, I turned to Bruce for help. He'd already noticed the change in Gaby, though he didn't realize the extent of his distress. At my urging, Bruce suggested to Gaby that he might look into Scientology.

At first, Gaby was reluctant. His attitude was basically "What can they tell me that I don't already know?" I knew that he didn't like the idea of being treated like someone's crazy aunt. So I offered to go check it out with him. That idea appealed. He agreed to enroll in a few courses and we went together to sign up for the first class.

At first Gaby was gung-ho. We'd go a few nights a week, although we ended up taking different classes. For me the experience was interesting, though not earthshaking. Scientology, as I saw it, was really kind of a ragbag of truisms from the world's great religions. But Gaby's spirits seemed to be improving. After only three or four weeks, however, I heard that he was close to getting thrown out. Apparently, he'd been hitting on the women in his classes and they didn't appreciate it. They complained to the supervisors, and Gaby was put on notice that he'd have to clean up his act or get out.

That did it for me. I realized right then and there that I couldn't waste my life if he wasn't going to get serious about his.

It was around that time that I met the man who would become my second husband.

I'd gone down to the church's administrative offices to sign up for a new set of courses. A pleasant young man was assigned to help me. His name was Gordon Clark.

"What's your job?" he asked me.

I told him I was a lawyer. I wanted courses that would stress interpersonal relations. I was looking for something that would help me to size people up and evaluate them from an attorney's point of view.

Gordon cracked a joke or two about lawyers, something I'd gotten used to during the year since I'd passed the bar. The conversation wound its way around to ourselves. I learned that Gordon was an officer in the church. He lived right in church housing and worked twelve- to fourteen-hour days. He lived, breathed, and ate Scientology. He also seemed very upbeat, not just about Scientology, but about life in general. I responded to his energy and enthusiasm and to what I took at the time to be spirituality. I came away from our first meeting feeling lighter than I had in years. It was just the way a person should feel, I told myself. Happier, lighter, focused upon the betterment of the self instead of on an unending quest for big scores and fast times.

I knew that I was attracted to Gordon Clark. And I could tell he was attracted to me. I suppose anyone looking at us from the sidelines could tell what a mismatch this was. For one thing, I was a twenty-six-year-old attorney. He was a twenty-two-year-old without a college degree. But he seemed to hold out the promise of happiness. I looked at him and I saw, or thought I saw, stability.

I knew what I had to do and I steeled myself to do it. One evening, I waited for Gaby to come home. I wasn't nervous or frightened. I was sitting on the stairs and he was in the living room below me. He started to discuss a trip we'd been planning to take to Monte Carlo, where he was to play in a backgammon tournament.

"Gaby, I'm not going to Monte Carlo with you," I told him.

"What are you talking about?" he asked me, mildly exasperated. "It's all planned."

"I'm not going," I told him in a voice so calm it surprised even me. "Gaby, I want to get a divorce."

He stared at me in silence for a few seconds. Ordinarily there would have been blame-swapping, finger-pointing intended to intimidate me. Instead, I found calm acceptance.

"Can't you give me another chance?" he asked.

"No, Gaby. It's too late. I just want a divorce."

It was over. We both knew it.

There was one small problem. I had no place to go. I had no money. I could have gone after community property, but all I wanted was out. The sentiment was noble—but hardly practical, given my current circumstances.

I was in between jobs and on unemployment. And the nine-month grace period on my student loan repayment had expired several months before. I'd thought Gaby was making those payments, but shortly after I moved out, I learned that he hadn't paid a dime; I was several months in arrears. That nonpayment had been reported to all the credit agencies, so I had no credit cards and no way to get one. I couldn't have passed a credit check even if I'd been able to afford an apartment. How could a woman with a law degree be so helpless?

Luckily, friends of mine knew a man who was converting some apartments into condominiums. He agreed to let me stay in one rent-free for a month or two until I could get on my feet. I packed up my clothes. Gaby gave me an old TV and I moved out. I wrote the bank a letter explaining that I was going through a rough period and that I had no intention of defaulting on my student loan. I assured some faceless bank official that as soon as I was employed I would catch up on the delinquent payments and make all future ones on time. I made good on that promise. After a year of timely payments, I wrote another letter to the bank asking them to clear my credit rating. And to my surprise, they did. (If whoever was responsible for that act of kindness is reading this, I'd like to say thank you. That gesture meant more to me than I can properly express. It didn't just boost my credit rating, it was a vote of confidence.) Someone had cared enough to look past the data sheet and see that I might actually shape up to be a responsible member of society.

When I left Gaby, however, I was destitute. In spite of that, I was happy. I felt I might actually be able to make it out on my own. Not long after moving out I landed a job with the law firm of Brody and Price doing defense work. I loved my colleagues. They were wonderful, ethical people. I was well on my way to making it on my own. And yet within three months, I was married to Gordon Clark. How did that happen?

Why didn't I take some time to enjoy my newfound freedom and experience life as a single, independent adult for a while? What the hell was the rush?

The relationship with Gordon had taken off like lightning, but marriage was definitely not on the agenda as far as I was concerned. The Church of Scientology, however, didn't allow romantic liaisons between its officers and members of the public. If Gordon wanted to stay on the staff and keep seeing me, we'd have to get married. The problem was that I was still legally married to Gaby. One of Gordon's fellow Scientologists told us how to get a quickie divorce in Tijuana. It was supposed to be perfectly legal, but I wasn't so sure. On the other hand, so what if my marriage to Gordon wasn't strictly kosher? We were only going through this charade to appease the church hierarchy.

And so I made the trip to Tijuana. My brother came along to keep me company. Two weeks later Gordon and I got married in a friend's apartment. The Scientology minister who married us was Bruce Roman, who, strangely enough, managed to remain friends with Gaby. Having a friend do the honors made it seem less frightening. It was quick and casual. Gordon immediately went back to work.

Thinking back on it all, I can see both the pattern and the reasons for the facade weddings, the race from one marriage to the next. The truth was, I didn't know how to be alone. I didn't have a self to be alone with. As long as there was a man in my life, there was someone to cater to and mold myself around. As long as I had a man to define me, I didn't have to confront the uncomfortable issue of discovering my own identify. It's funny. People used to tell me how they never really felt they knew me; that I was mysterious to them. If I'd been a little more in touch with myself, I would have looked inward to see what the hell they were talking about. But I never got beyond being puzzled by my own actions.

I look back on those days of obscure identity with great sadness. If only I'd found the strength to stand on my own for a while, to endure the loneliness, to handle the challenges of daily living as a single adult! I might have learned, among other things, to enjoy my own company. I might have discovered a real person who didn't need another to find definition. That must be what happiness is all about. It's not a life without problems. It's the ability to handle those problems. It took me two marriages—and two divorces—to figure this out.

Four or five months after I'd left Gaby I was driving through Beverly Hills when I saw him walking somewhere. His expression was so sad. I'd heard that he'd gotten into a fight with someone who accused him of cheating at backgammon. Gaby had been punched in the face. It was the only time I'd ever heard of a backgammon row ending in real violence. Gaby was apparently sinking deeper.

I didn't hear anything about him for another seven years or so. One morning I saw a small article in the *L.A. Times.* A man named Gabriel Horowitz had suffered a gunshot wound to the head. I sat stunned, reading and rereading the lines of print, not quite comprehending. Gabriel Horowitz? *My Gaby?* It had to be.

I knew that for my own peace of mind I had to get the whole story, so I asked a detective I was friendly with to check it out for me. A few days later he reported back. Gaby'd been visiting Bruce Roman and the two of them were looking at guns—they were both collectors—when the gun Bruce was holding went off and the wild shot found its way into Gaby's head. It had been a freak accident. The shot had ricocheted off the ceiling and hit Gaby on the rebound. It left him paralyzed.

Such a bizarre twist of fate. For weeks, I walked around in a daze, barely able to concentrate. The guy had put me through a lot of pain, but when I thought of him confined to a wheelchair for life all I could think was "Poor Gaby." I never thought I'd say that.

My sadness was so deep, it was inexpressible.

Admittedly, my private life has taken some unusual turns. And whenever I can manage to climb onto a plane of semidetachment, I see why the tabloid press ended up pursuing me with such cruel enthusiasm. I had no defenses. All I could do was steel myself for the worst-case scenario. In late July 1994, just as we were gearing up for the harrowing business of jury selection in the Simpson case, I got word from Suzanne Childs that the tabs were rooting around my marriage certificates and divorce papers. A couple of weeks later, the *Enquirer* published an opus entitled "O.J. Prosecutor's Tragic Secret Life," which alleged, among other things, that I had "dumped" Gaby after receiving my law degree. It also detailed the shooting incident at Bruce Roman's, leaving the casual reader to imagine that I was somehow involved.

The stories presented me in absurd caricature, but anyone could see that they contained nuggets of truth. I was so humiliated. I'd never confided the details of my first marriage to anyone at the D.A.'s office except my friend Lynn. My "past," as I saw it, was not an opportunist's upward scramble, but a painful, private struggle. As far as I was concerned, I was a survivor. I had surmounted my personal difficulties through acts that took considerable initiative and will. In the summer of 1994, I was not Marcia Kleks, the gambler's girlfriend. I was a lawyer—an intelligent and accomplished one at that. I was a damned good mother. And everything admirable that I'd accomplished seemed threatened by this disturbing and unsolicited celebrity.

I knew that the only chance I had of coming off with any dignity was to stay calm and keep silent. I thought, *If I just concentrate on my job, I can get through this. They'll get tired of me. I can ride this out.*

But the tabs didn't get tired of me. In September I picked up new rumblings: the *National Enquirer* was working on a story that I had been a battered wife. They'd apparently turned up a pair of backgammon promoters who were claiming that once, during a tournament-organizing event, Gaby got angry and threw a chair at me.

They'd also found some dingbat who'd once been a neighbor of Gaby's and mine. She was claiming that I walked around in long-sleeved dresses all the time so that no one would see the bruises from Gaby's beatings.

The news threw me into a state of near panic. Of course, I knew what the truth was. Gaby never threw anything at me in public. His pride would never have allowed him to let people see that we fought. We did all that in private. But even during those arguments behind closed doors he never beat me. Never. He pushed, I shoved, we wrestled. That's as far as it ever went.

Don't misunderstand me. The pushing and the shoving were bad enough. But I always gave as good as I got. It wasn't right to let Gaby take the rap when I'd done so much provoking. I was not a battered woman! I was not a victim!

I have always hated the culture of victimization. It seems that everyone nowadays has some personal trauma to explain away his own character failings. It's something I can't tolerate. I believe people have to take responsibility for themselves and their actions. This seems a reasonable position for a prosecutor to take on matters of human conduct.

My approach to domestic violence cases over the years was one of extreme caution. I've never gotten up on a pulpit to spout a feminist line. I never rushed in and charged spousal battery without a full set of facts in hand. The Simpson case was no exception. From the beginning I'd hung back on the DV. I felt there was too much we didn't know. As of July 1994, the personal history of the Simpsons was still too murky. From a strictly legal standpoint, we would never have needed to address their history of marital violence. True, the fact that a man has beaten his wife over the years may go to motive if he is accused of murdering her. But the state isn't required to establish *why* one person killed another, only that he intended to do it. It is perfectly possible to get a conviction strictly on the physical evidence. And in the Simpson case, the physical evidence was so amazingly strong, I felt that we could probably put him away relying on that alone.

The domestic violence aspect of the case, by contrast, left me deeply conflicted. The photos of Nicole, her voice on the 911 tape—

these produced in me sensations of dread. When the police and city attorney's reports arrived in my in box, I scanned them hurriedly, professionally, then pushed them to one side. Later, when Scott Gordon would collar me in the hall, as he did at least seven times a day, with, "Marcia, we've got to get to work on DV," I'd say "Yeah, yeah, Scott. Why don't you write me up a memo on that?"

Every time a reminder of Nicole's physical suffering came up, I felt headachy. Sometimes a little sweaty. I'd knock the feelings away and keep pushing on. There were so many brushfires burning around me that it was easy to postpone dealing with the issue indefinitely. I'm sure I knew that, when the time came, I'd have to confront my personal history as well. Which gave me added incentive for not facing the demon down.

By late September 1994, this new threat from the tabloids to invade my personal life left me feeling desperate. If things proceeded on a crash course and the *Enquirer* was allowed to publish such a wildly distorted account of my troubled marriage to Gaby, the fallout could be disastrous. O. J. Simpson's defense would charge that I had some political agenda for going after their client. This was not a time to work through my personal *mishegoss*. I had to take some kind of action. But what, I didn't know.

My good friend and fellow D.A. Lynn Reed came to my rescue.

"You have to go and see my friend Mark," she instructed me firmly. "He's an entertainment lawyer. He helped out a friend of mine who's been chased around by the press, and he really knows what he's doing. If the tabs start hearing from your lawyer, they might decide it's not worth it. Trust me on this one, kiddo."

She gave me his number.

This whole thing seemed so weird to me. How does it happen that a D.A. in the course of prosecuting a class-one felony comes to need an entertainment lawyer? Come to think of it, have you ever heard of a prosecutor whose private life has made it into a tabloid banner? I haven't.

Anyway, I gave Mark Fleischer a call and we agreed to meet at a downtown restaurant called Checkers.

I arrived at six o'clock. The place was almost empty. Businessmen and bureaucrats had already decamped for home after downing their "freeway flyers." I lurked apprehensively in the foyer until the maître d' directed me to a table in the farthest corner of the room. Mark rose to greet me. He was a slender, dapper man reminiscent of Fred Astaire. He had twinkling blue eyes and a firm yet gentle handshake. I liked him on sight.

"I'm the one who bakes cookies and collects husbands," I told him.

Mark laughed. "I'm aware of your financial situation," he said. "One of my dearest friends works in your office. Scott Gordon."

Scott! I felt a pang of guilt for having ducked him every time he tried to get me moving on the domestic violence issue. My neglect of the issue was, of course, all the more ironic in light of my current predicament. I was about to become poster girl for the battered women's movement, for no good reason.

"I'm going to help you out as a favor to the D.A.'s office," Mark told me. "I've always admired you guys and I'm going to take this opportunity to put my money where my mouth is. There will be no fee for my services."

Had I heard correctly? A lawyer was going to take on a client who might give him nights and weekends of grief—absolutely gratis? The man was a freaking saint.

"We're probably not going to persuade them to leave you alone," he warned. "Only time and some new scandal will do that. But we *can* discuss the possibility of a lawsuit. We don't want to come at them unless we feel fairly sure of winning. That means I'll need you to do some homework."

Homework. Exactly what I did not need at this moment. The Simpson case was already threatening to bury me under an avalanche of paperwork. Every night I'd carry home a couple of satchels of documents. Then, after the usual bedtime routine, I'd spread my papers out on my bed and work into the early hours of the morning.

"I want you to get one of those little pocket recorders and document each article and how it affected you," Mark continued. "It would be best if you could manage to do that every day. The more detail the better. Spare yourself nothing. This will describe the emotional distress and the damages we ask for."

He told me to keep the tapes in a secure place. And if I didn't have one, I should give them to him to put in his office safe.

"When am I going to do all that?" I asked him.

"You spend a lot of time in your car, don't you?"

I did as Mark asked. I bought myself a microcassette recorder. It sat for a few days on the dashboard of my Maxima. Finally I picked it up and made my first faltering attempts.

"Well, Mark," I began, "here goes. It is . . . what *is* today? September thirtieth, and I'm leaving the courthouse. It's about ten after nine and I'm exhausted. . . .

"The stress has been building and building and building . . . the stress of this trial . . . and, of course, going through a divorce and everything . . . I always feel like I'm being pounded. And it's real hard to focus because when I'm at work during the week there's always people coming in my door and calling on the phone, just one after another. . . . I feel like I've been beaten to a pulp. . . . The only time it really feels good to go to work is on a Saturday or Sunday when there's no one there to bother me and I can focus on my job. . . .

"There's so much to organize. I just wish I could stop the clock for about three weeks and put everything together in a nice, neat, tidy order. Do all the things that I usually do to prepare for a trial. I am beginning to [be] very pessimistic about my ability to put it together the way I ordinarily would. And in this, of all cases, where I need to do more than I usually would—it's frightening. . . . Ah, God. I don't know how I'm gonna survive this. . . ."

When I replayed the tape, the distress in my own voice took me aback. I was also surprised by the relief it gave me to vent my frustrations. I continued to record, not every day, but every few days. I found that getting into my car was like entering a confessional. I talked, and talked, and kept on talking to that mute, whirring confidant. I reflected and I flamed.

A tape recorder is a patient listener. It passes no judgments.

Double Solitaire

CAR TAPE. *October 2, 1994. Everything's coming back to him. He's got her blood on his socks in the bedroom. We've got her blood and Ron's blood in his Bronco. We've got her blood and Ron's on that glove at Rockingham, and maybe Simpson's blood too. After we finish the testing we'll know more. Now it seems we've even pinned down the shoe print to a style of Bruno Magli shoe. . . . The same size as the defendant's shoe! I mean, it's just unbelievable!*

The defense is gonna come up with their space invader theories. It's gonna be like something out of the National Enquirer. *You know, police bungled and fumbled and goofed everything up. And so, right, that's how the evidence all came back to him. If it's a frame-up, why frame him, of all people? Couldn't you think of somebody less likable to frame? I mean, who wants to try a case against Yogi Bear?*

You shoulda tried this case in Santa Monica.

Gimme a break.

Ever since the verdict in the criminal trial, TV and radio commentators, print pundits, old armchair warriors with a whole lot more ego

than common sense have weighed in with their theories about what
went wrong. First off, they would have you believe that we blew it by
not taking this case to the suburbs. What they mean—but never have
the guts to come right out and say—is this: "Why didn't you go shopping around for a congenial, white jury who'd convict the son of a
bitch?"

The grumblers are usually people who should know better—
former prosecutors like Vincent Bugliosi, who actually faulted us for
moving the trial *from* Santa Monica. Gil Garcetti filed this case *exactly*
where he should have filed it: downtown L.A.

Regardless of where a crime occurs, long-cause cases, as they're
called, virtually always end up downtown. In June of 1994, when the
Bundy murders took place, this was not even discretionary; it was
policy. Set by the Superior Court. Several years earlier, a panel of
assignment judges put their heads together to try to figure out how to
clear the backlog in the branch courts. One of the tougher measures
the judges took to rectify this problem was to require that any case that
stood to go on for longer than four weeks be filed Downtown, where
the D.A. has deputies, clerks, and support services to handle it.

(People have asked me why the civil trial was tried in Santa
Monica. The answer is simple: Civil litigants get to pick their forum.
They don't get directed to a particular venue at the command of the
bench the way criminal cases do.)

Only by a fluke does a long-cause criminal case ever end up in one
of the branch courts. The trial judge in the Rodney King case, for
instance, was downtown but transferred to Simi Valley and dragged
the case along with him. The results were disastrous. An all-white jury
acquitted four white LAPD officers of beating King even though
the crime was immortalized on videotape. Los Angeles erupted into a
race riot.

Every time I hear about Bugliosi or some other clown mouthing
off to the press, I have to grit my teeth and count to ten. *You shoulda
tried this case in Santa Monica.* Do they realize what they're saying?

To suggest that the D.A.'s office should have ignored standard
procedure and filed this case elsewhere for purely tactical advantage is,
in my opinion, a shameless and inexcusable display of racism. It pre-
supposes that only a white, upscale, West Side jury can deliver justice.

Wrong. Dead wrong. I've seen Downtown juries made up of poor blacks and Hispanics do justice time and time again.

By the time the Simpson case landed on my desk, I'd been trying cases Downtown for more than ten years. I'd had defendants and juries of all races. I'd tried twenty homicides and won nineteen of them. I'd tried scores of lesser felonies. Won most, lost some. None of the verdicts seemed completely off the wall to me. Whenever I'd gotten to talk to jurors who'd delivered unfavorable verdicts, I found they'd had their reasons, usually good ones.

To Vincent Bugliosi and those who share his worldview, a good prosecutor is apparently a slick operator who works the angles. And the prescribed angle in this case would have been to steer clear of dark skins, particularly those belonging to middle-aged black women. Sounds ugly—because it *is* ugly. As well as impractical, unethical, and unconscionable.

One of the proponents of this embarrassing thesis seems to have been none other than our own jury consultant, Don Vinson. After the trial, he apparently met Bugliosi for lunch at—where else—the California Club. Like Cassandra spurned, Vinson wailed that he'd warned the D.A.'s office of the dangers of picking middle-aged black women as jurors. When word of this got back to me, I just shook my head. I would like to take this opportunity to ask Don Vinson, "Exactly what would you have had me do?"

It must have been apparent even to someone as stubbornly ignorant of the law as Vinson that you cannot mount a campaign to target black women. It's illegal, for God's sake. And assuming for the moment that it was not illegal, excluding them would be an impossibility. Blacks accounted for over half of our eventual jury pool. A full three quarters of those blacks were women. Like it or not, black women were going to be a powerful presence on this jury.

I didn't need Vinson to tell me that black women—or at least certain black woman—would be a tough sell. As I mentioned earlier, our grand jury adviser, Terry White, had let me know that a couple of middle-aged women among the grand jurors had seemed maternally inclined toward Simpson. Terry is a black man and had been one of the prosecutors on the Rodney King trial. He is infinitely better informed on issues of race and the law than Don Vinson. The fact is, Terry thought we could bring them around. We'd both seen many juries of black women who were more than willing to convict black men.

For my part, I was perfectly confident that if O. J. Simpson had been some black sanitation worker who had killed his white wife in a fit of rage, a jury of twelve middle-aged black women would have convicted the jerk in a heartbeat. The bedrock issue here was not race—but race coupled with celebrity. It was not so much that Simpson was a black man; he was a *famous* black man. And a well-loved famous black man. Black jurors of either sex were going to feel reluctant to knock an African-American icon off his pedestal. And in combination with race, celebrity complicated this case in ways that none of us had ever before had to consider.

That's why so much was riding on the jury questionnaire.

Jury selection in the Simpson case was set to begin on September 26. Ito had ordered up an unusually large pool, one thousand candidates. He clearly foresaw a long, drawn-out contest and wanted to make sure we had the bodies to cover it. The first step was elementary triage: he would call in the whole bunch and hand out a one-page screening questionnaire to determine if serving on a long case would cause them hardship.

I always hated this phase. It was during hardship questioning that a lot of the better-educated, solid-citizen types would find a way to get themselves excused from service. People with steady jobs and career commitments can't afford to take time off, because employers won't cover their salary for more than ten days of jury service. Once they heard the estimated trial time for a long-cause case, as many as 70 percent of them would walk right out the door. These people, the ones with with steady jobs and career commitments, are usually pro-prosecution jurors. It was so ironic. The lengthy cases were by and large the most serious ones, often death-penalty cases where you want the most intelligent jurors possible. And yet if one candidate with a college degree ever made it through hardship and the gauntlet of defense challenges, we always regarded it as a miracle.

The survivors of hardship questioning—in this case a pool of three hundred—would receive the full-blown questionnaire containing questions submitted by both the prosecution and the defense. The questions themselves had to survive a rigorous weeding-out process: both sides would submit questions and, after a lot of angry rhetoric and head-banging, the judge would decide which ones made the cut.

By the time we got to drafting questions, Bill and I had already given the questionnaire a lot of thought. Our questions had to be blunt enough to hit the hot-button issues head-on: "Have you ever been beaten by a spouse?" "Have you ever been arrested by the LAPD?" "Do you fantasize about being O. J. Simpson's date at the Rose Bowl?" That sort of thing. They had to be tactful enough to avoid offending anyone we might have hoped to win over. They had to be sly enough to trip up anyone who was lying. Usually you'll find people who'll lie like crazy to avoid serving. But here we had to entertain the possibility that the opposite would occur; at least some opportunists out there might be looking to cash in on their stint in the jury box at the Trial of the Century.

After we'd spent God knows how many hours clinking glasses with Don Vinson, I expected that he would at least send us a list of questions, if not a completed questionnaire, for our review. Jo-Ellan Dimitrius, after all, did the entire thing for the Simpson team. But the deadline for submitting our draft to the court was approaching, and Vinson had sent us nothing.

"What's he waiting for," I groused to Bill, "an engraved invitation?"

Bill promised he'd give Vinson a nudge; I assumed he did. But days passed. Nothing came by winged messenger from DecisionQuest. What Bill finally received was one question scribbled on a piece of legal paper. I don't even recall what it was. I do recall it was not even remotely useful.

In the end, Bill and I just had to knuckle down and do the thing the way we normally did it: by ourselves. We recruited our DV experts, Scott Gordon and Lydia Bodin, to work on domestic violence. Our DNA expert, Lisa Kahn, oversaw the science part. Everyone pitched in on the celebrity issue. Question on the table: How do you get at the issue of fame? It's one thing to prosecute a defendant who's notorious—someone who's well known but not particularly well liked, like Charles Keating, or the prosecutor's dream defendant, Charles

Manson. With a flaming psychopath in the dock, all you have to do is get up and recite your Social Security number to win a conviction. This was not the case with a sympathetic figure, one idolized the way O. J. Simpson was. I didn't know of anyone who'd ever tackled a problem of this magnitude. Somehow we'd have to get the jurors past the defendant's public image and get them to acknowledge that all they knew about O. J. Simpson was a slick facade.

We all agreed that we should seed the questionnaire throughout with celebrity questions, some direct, others indirect. First we'd ask jurors where they got their news: TV, radio, print? A juror who got most of his news from tabloids and watching evening news magazines like *Hard Copy* would obviously be a problem for us. Not only would he have been fed a steady diet of misinformation, but his viewing preference might show that he had a more than average interest in the cult of celebrity itself.

Some celebrity questions suggested themselves.

"Have you ever asked a celebrity for an autograph?"

"Have you ever written to a celebrity?"

Certain questions taken together provided internal checks. If, for instance, a juror wrote that he watched news on three channels daily, and yet insisted that he had no knowledge of the Simpson case, we'd have some reason to believe that he was being less than truthful.

I have to say that in this instance Lance Ito really came through for us. He gave us almost every question we asked for. Of course, he gave the defense almost everything *they* asked for, as well. The result was a document at least an inch thick. It was the longest questionnaire that either Bill or I had ever seen. Seventy-five pages each! I heard that when prospective jurors first saw it, they groaned. And I thought, *What are you complaining about? You're not gonna have to go through each and every one of these suckers comma by frigging comma.*

One afternoon during the last week in September, a law clerk wheeled a steel cart into my office and unloaded four cardboard boxes of completed questionnaires. Three hundred of them. Bill and I just looked at each other. It was a look that said, *The journey of a thousand miles begins with the first step.* He took half. I took half. Then we burrowed into our respective offices and started to work.

The job wasn't as simple as reading through the questionnaire once and jotting down notes. I had to flag key responses and then summarize them on a separate ten-page form that Bill and I had devised for the purpose. We'd also come up with a system for grading each juror on a scale of 1 to 5, 5 being the best. It was incredibly clumsy, but we had no precedent for a job this large.

I lost track of the time. When I finally put my pen down and looked up, it was dark outside. *My God*, I thought. I'd started at three o'clock in the afternoon and it was already past seven. And I'd only gotten through three of these monsters!

I walked down the empty halls to Bill's office. To tell you the truth, I liked this place a whole lot better when it was deserted. The feeling of being alone in the office gave me a sense of freedom that I found invigorating and at the same time peaceful. But right now I was feeling low and needed bucking up.

Bill's door was open. I could see him hunched over his desk, poring over a document tidily flagged with Post-its.

"How many have you gotten through?" I asked him dourly.

"Only two. I can't believe it."

"We've gotta find a better system," I told him.

We heard a rustle in the hall, and just then Jonathan Fairtlough stuck his head in the door. Jonathan, a freckled young Irishman with an unruly shock of brown hair, had been one of our first picks for the team. He was full of energy, optimism, and expansive ideas for graphic presentations. Jonathan was also an electronics genius, whom we called in whenever the computers or even the copiers went on the blink. He never seemed to get tired. At least not at that point.

"Hey, boss," he said. It was directed at both of us. "Anything I can do for you?"

"As a matter of fact," I told him, "we're trying to come up with a way to streamline the summaries. Any ideas?"

Jonathan thought for a moment.

"Why don't you just dictate the important stuff into a mini-cassette? Then get the secretaries to type them up for you."

Bill and I looked at each other. Out of the mouths of babes!

After that, we picked up our speed a couple of knots, but we still remained in danger of drowning beneath swells of detail. We needed some way to make the task more concrete, more visual. I recalled a system I'd had picked up from another D.A. named Pat Dixon. He'd tried a lot of long-cause cases, and he'd devised a system for jury selection. Before voir dire, he would make up a pack of yellow cardboard cards, about three inches by three, one for each juror in the pool. He'd jot down pertinent information about each one on the front. Then he'd deal the cards. Twelve of them arranged in two rows of six, a simulated jury box. This helped him to visualize what those twelve people, each with his own history and set of prejudices, might look sitting next to the others. He'd take one candidate—maybe a crotchety contrarian—and try to figure out the rating each side would give him. Then he'd try to figure out which side was likely to get him struck for cause and which would have to use a peremptory challenge. The contrarian would stay, or he'd go. Pat would do this until he had combined the cards in all their plausible permutations. Whenever I went past his office, I'd see him sitting, staring hour after hour at the cards before him, playing this game of lawyer's solitaire.

So I made up a pack for Bill and me. Three hundred yellow cardboard cards. In the late afternoon, or whenever we had a few moments, Bill and I would meet in one of our offices and pull out the pack and start dealing. We'd add a juror to the rotation to see how he or she fit into the mix. We'd rotate the least desirable candidate out. We kept looking for the perfect ensemble. Or at least an acceptable one.

It was dismal going. Any way you shuffled the deck, this was far and away the worst pool of jurors either of us had ever seen. Few of these people had ever taken college courses, let alone gotten a degree. Many were out of work. No one had anything good to say about the LAPD. An uncomfortably large percentage of them either knew someone who had been arrested or had been arrested themselves. The Bronco chase seemed to arouse in them nothing but regret for the sufferings of the defendant. "Poor guy, gone to visit his wife's grave and all he gets is grief from the law." At the very worst, Simpson's actions were seen as "bizarre." Almost no one believed that he had been trying to escape.

Before the questionnaires came in, Bill and I had been going back and forth on whether we should introduce the Bronco chase as evidence. Do we offer up the eight thousand bucks, the passport, the fake mustache and beard? To us, of course, these items seemed very incriminating. But in light of the responses we were getting on the questionnaire, introducing them carried substantial risks. First of all, the money had been found on Cowlings, not Simpson. The goatee, mustache, and passport were found in Cowlings's Bronco. Proving that Simpson even knew about these items would be difficult. I was convinced he did, but demonstrating it was another matter.

Worse, if we introduced the Bronco evidence, it would give the defense an opening to slip in the records of the calls Simpson had made from his cell phone while motoring up the 405. We'd get the tape of Tom Lange talking him in off the freeway, telling him what a wonderful guy he was, how his children needed him; in the background, we'd hear Simpson's groans of anguish. We'd get a parade of witnesses who would recall the tearful protestations of innocence and grief. All the defendant's denials would come in through the back door of these phone-call witnesses. O. J. Simpson would be allowed, in effect, to offer emotional testimony on his own behalf without ever having to take the witness stand. (In a criminal trial, only the defense can call the defendant to the stand.) Whatever hope we had of getting to cross-examine Simpson would wash right out the courtroom door in a river of crocodile tears.

To make the risk worthwhile, we'd needed to offer proof of flight so unequivocal that it would expose the phone calls to family and friends as the shams they were. Now, *I* might hear one of these tapes and think, *You sniveling bastard; what about the pair you murdered?* But to our prospective jurors—at least the ones who revealed themselves in these questionnaires as an unchartered chapter of the Juice Fan Club—he would appear nothing but sympathetic.

During the months since the verdict, I've gotten hammered repeatedly for "failing" to introduce evidence from that chase. Certain old armchair warriors have gone so far as to call it a breach of prosecutorial responsibility. Let me set the record straight. No prosecutor is compelled to produce evidence that he feels might work to his detriment. There is no right or wrong in this matter. It's a judgment call. I decided to keep it out; another prosecutor might have decided differently. But once he'd made that call, he'd better have been prepared to take the consequences should the thing jump back and bite him in the ass.

If I had it to do again, with the jury God saw fit to grant us, I'd make exactly the same call.

CAR TAPE. *October 2, 1994 . . . Constant anxiety . . . I feel like I can't breathe thinking about all the work I have to do, and I don't have the time for it. I'm so tired. Tired of seeing my face in the magazines and . . . tired of everything. Just plain tired.*

By the time I'd read through eighty of the questionnaires, I was so depressed I could hardly speak. On our scale of 1 to 5, only ten ranked as high as a 4. The rest of the pool was grouped down around 2 or $1^1/_2$.

But the worst of it was the lying.

An anthropologist reading through these questionnaires would probably conclude that he'd stumbled upon the remnants of some lost civilization. In the midst of the most media-saturated city in the world, we'd somehow managed to find three hundred human beings who claimed never to watch television, listen to the radio, or read newspapers. These pristine souls insisted that they didn't know anything about a case that permeated every streetcorner conversation between East L.A. and Santa Monica. Under questioning, however, this astounding phenomenon would prove illusory. When we pressed the jurors for specifics about the Bronco chase, it would come out that they'd read and seen a great deal. But on the questionnaires, they told us anything they thought we wanted to hear, just to get on the jury.

My head ached. My eyes were burning. Why, on this of all cases, did we wind up with the fucking jury pool from hell?

For the three weeks it took to collate those questionnaires, I dragged myself home each night in a stupor of fatigue, bowed under the weight of the knowledge that I'd have to go in there and fight every day in a battle that might already be lost.

There seemed to be no safe corner. During my waking hours the phone was constantly ringing, or my beeper was going off. Every ten seconds someone was knocking on the door of my office saying, "Got a minute? Got a minute?" Patti Jo Fairbanks, our senior legal assistant, did her best to run interference for me. She screened my phone messages, handing over only the ones with top priority. She posted signs on my door that read, "Don't Knock. Keep Out!"

At the end of three mind-numbing weeks, I completed my summaries of all three hundred questionnaires. I picked up Bill's to compare our observations—and was stunned. Bill had uniformly rated all the jurors much higher than I had. In one instance he had given a 5 to a juror I'd rated a 0! Was I losing my mind?

That night I went down to his office. "Bill," I asked, "have you noticed a discrepancy in our grading?"

"Yeah." He looked glum. "Let's talk."

I pulled the problem juror—his 5, my 0.

"What about this one?"

He glanced over the summary. His face fell even further. "I don't know what I was thinking," he said. "Maybe I'm just trying to convince myself that we've got a chance."

I knew exactly what Bill was feeling. He was in denial. I think we both were. The prospect of a bitterly fought trial we knew we could never win was just too much to bear.

You can't acknowledge that a situation is hopeless. It destroys your will to fight. And so Bill and I reached a tacit arrangement in which we ended up supporting each other's delusions about the candidates filling out those questionnaires.

Yeah, maybe this one isn't so bad. Maybe we can get her to listen, even though she considers the defendant a "hunk" and named her firstborn Orenthal. Yeah, yeah. It might happen.

Something might happen. There might be a miracle.

Meanwhile, Bill and I racked our brains trying to come up with ways to keep the jury pool from being contaminated by the avalanche of misinformation issuing from the press daily. Normally, it's the judge's job to protect the jury pool from such pollution, but Lance didn't seem to have a clue. We begged Ito to put off jury selection until after we finished arguments on admissibility of DNA, something that stood to be a long and complicated public brawl. Why pick a jury and then send them home, where they could listen to the defense belittle the science of DNA testing? But Lance didn't see the problem.

Ito set voir dire for October 12. At the very least, we pleaded with him, bring the jurors into the courtroom one at a time. If you don't, we told him, you're going to have jurors discussing gossip and half-truths right in front of the whole pool. Once again, motion denied. It would be a cattle call, everyone sitting together, every juror questioned right out there in the open.

On the Wednesday morning we were to start voir dire I had arrived early and shut myself in my office to practice my questions. When finally I looked at my watch, it was half an hour to show time. *Odd,* I thought, *I haven't heard from Bill.* Patti Jo knocked on my door. She looked worried.

"Bill's sick," she told me. "He can't make it in today."

"You're kidding, right? Tell me it's a joke. We're supposed to start voir dire in about twenty-seven minutes!"

It was no joke. Bill had been looking haggard and drawn lately. I knew he hadn't been sleeping well. The stress was taking its toll on him. Come to think of it, it had kept him home on the first day of hardship questioning, too. Now this! If Ito didn't grant me a continuance, I was screwed.

When I got to court, with my heart in my throat, I asked to postpone the proceedings. Shapiro objected but, to my utter amazement, Lance backed me up. He pointed out to Shapiro that if "Mr. Cochran [were] similarly afflicted . . . I would exercise the same discretion and allow you to trail it a day."

Lance caught me totally off guard.

I was so grateful and relieved that I couldn't even manage a gracious reply. Maybe Ito wasn't such a bad guy. Just in a little over his head.

Bill returned the following morning. Nothing to get alarmed about, he told us. Just a touch of the flu. He looked pale, but reasonably fit. Ready to kick ass.

The rail is the three-foot-high wooden divider that separates the lawyers and parties to the action from the spectators. But its importance far transcends that of a physical barrier. The rail is an unofficial line of demarcation separating the players from the watchers.

Don Vinson wanted to sit with us at counsel's table. I was opposed to that. The last thing we needed, in my opinion, was our jury—most of whom perceived their fortunes as blighted by accidents or crimes of social injustice—associating us with this well-fed, monogrammed, cuff-linked fat cat.

Vinson's gall seemed all the more amazing in light of his record of broken promises. He'd assured us that he would come up with a way to give us a computerized profile of each juror. But when we'd sent him the questionnaires, he couldn't deliver. The format, he said, didn't lend itself to that kind of analysis. And Vinson apparently didn't have time to read through them all himself, so he sent a kid fresh out of college to help us.

"How many jury trials have you observed?" I'd asked the kid.

"None," he replied.

Bill and I looked at one another.

"Let him do his thing," Bill whispered to me.

So we listened as this boy read dutifully through his notes. His efforts were well intentioned, but there was nothing there that two seasoned prosecutors could not have intuited on their own.

I thanked him for his efforts and sent him home.

As for Vinson, we didn't hear from him again until a few days before jury selection. He'd called to say that he wanted to present the results of his "findings." This time I demanded that he come to our office. We met in the room we used for press conferences. Vinson spread out a set of elaborate pie charts and graphs on the table in front of us.

His staff, he explained, had conducted phone surveys in which they had compiled demographic and personal data on those who refused to believe Simpson was guilty, those who were undecided, and those who were leaning toward guilt. His findings showed a wide racial divide. Caucasians tended to feel Simpson was guilty; African Americans tended to think he was not.

Duh.

I waited for some fresh insights, the flashes of revelation that would cause the scales to fall from our eyes. The most original of the lot?

"We found that people involved in bowling leagues tend to be anti-prosecution," Vinson announced.

I couldn't restrain myself. I burst out laughing. Even Bill was having a hard time maintaining his respectful poker face. Bowlers! *That's* what we'd been waiting for?

The real shame of it all was that Don Vinson probably could have contributed something of value, if he'd had a clue. Instead of warning us off black women as a class—an utterly pointless exercise since we were going to have black females on that jury no matter what—he should have helped us fine-tune our questions in such a way as to identify the most reasonable and reachable African Americans, male and female, in our jury pool. Then, he could have offered some advice on how to reach them. Our biggest frustration stemmed from the fact that our repeated entreaties for that kind of help fell on deaf ears.

Now this guy was angling to sit in front of the rail! He wanted to be on national TV!

"No," I said. "Absolutely and unequivocally no!"

But Garcetti reminded me that Vinson's company had provided us with a terrific set of graphics. Which was true. And now wasn't the time to alienate him, Gil insisted. So Bill and I packed up our notebooks and trekked down to court, followed by two law clerks, Vinson, and a parade of others from our office, all of whom wanted a front-row seat on the action.

By the time we got there, the cramped, plywood-paneled courtroom of Department 103 was packed to capacity with the jurors who had made it past hardship screening. The bailiff called the court to order. Ito's clerk, Deirdre Robertson, pulled eighteen names at a time. The candidates took their place in the jury box. First the judge would question them. Then the defense. Then we would.

In California, it's routine to have a judge ask jurors the tough questions, which in this case meant those concerning police credibility, domestic violence, and race. Conventional wisdom holds that jurors are more likely to be candid with a judge than with the lawyers. Jurors are generally impressed with the power the judge wields and will think twice before lying. Some of the questions, like "Have you or any family member been arrested?" could arouse personal resentments. Better they resent the judge than the attorneys.

Ito, however, seemed reluctant to assume the role of the heavy. He couldn't bring himself to ask the tough questions. If, for example, he asked a juror, "Have you or anyone in your family been the victim of domestic violence?" and the answer was yes, he should have been prepared to press:

"Who was involved?"

"My father hit my mother."

"Were the police called?"

"Yes."

"How did that make you feel?"

"Pretty terrible . . ."

And so on.

But Lance was too delicate, too fearful of offending, to probe.

He floundered politely for a while, then finally said, "Ms. Clark?" He was turning the questioning over to me.

And so I stood to face the twelve in the box. No surprises here. The first batch was largely black, largely female. I had no illusions about this group. Their questionnaires indicated that they believed overwhelmingly that Simpson was innocent. But they'd be damned if they'd say that to me. I tried to get one young black guy to admit that seeing a celebrity on camera didn't mean that one actually *knew* him— the point being that someone who seemed to be a real nice guy on the tube could still be capable of drawing a knife across a woman's throat.

You've seen the defendant on television, according to your questionnaire, right? I asked him.

I could see from the look on his face that he regretted admitting even that much.

A couple of times, he replied.

Do you feel that you know him?

I don't know.

Well, has he ever invited you over to dinner?

No.

Have you ever gone out to the movies with him?

No.

Have you ever met his family? Ever talked about the weather, politics, or religion?

Of course, this elicited a litany of *no*s.

So, do you think you know him?

I guess not, came the reluctant reply.

Jurors begrudged me even the most obvious answers for fear they'd say something that might get them dismissed. Bill seemed to fare no better. I was so frustrated that I even turned to Vinson to see if he had any suggestions. He was slouched in his chair, twirling his glasses, wearing a detached, supercilious expression. He looked to me like some indolent white plantation owner. I was astounded to see that he'd taken no notes. On the other side of the room, perky little Jo-Ellan Dimitrius, jury consultant to the stars, was busy scribbling on Post-its and passing them to Shapiro and Cochran.

When it came the defense's turn at the plate, I was curious to see who'd lead off. Officially, Shapiro was still at the helm, although rumors reached me daily about the internal conflicts on the Dream Team. Cochran, I heard, would call for a meeting, and Shapiro would refuse to go. Or Shapiro'd insist on meeting at *his* offices, and Cochran would refuse to attend. This struggle carried over into the courtroom. Every time it was the defense's turn to do something, you'd see Cochran and Shapiro muttering to one another about who would take it.

This time Shapiro must have won the flip. It was clear that Bob had gotten some heavy coaching. His style was still phony and self-important, but he handled himself surprisingly well. He zeroed right in on the sensitive topics and hit them head-on.

Of one well-educated and fairly conservative white woman he asked, "You also saw the freeway incident?"

"Yes . . ."

"And your conclusion was that O. J. Simpson was fleeing?"

"Yeah. I think he was. Yeah."

"And then, after all of this was done, your opinion that he was probably guilty was made even stronger, was it not?"

"From what? I am sorry."

In three more questions, he had her admitting that she did indeed think it made Simpson look guilty.

She was excused for cause.

Perhaps I should take a moment to explain this business of excusing jurors. Each side gets a certain number of peremptory challenges. In this case, we got twenty. These allow you to excuse a juror without giving a reason. If you don't like the way he parts his hair or don't approve of the books he reads, you can exercise one of these strikes, as they are also called, to send him packing. Once your allotment is used up, however, you can't go to the cashier and get more. That's why we guard our peremptories like thousand-dollar chips in a poker game.

What we prefer to do is challenge for cause. But for that you need grounds—for example, the fact that a juror has already formed such a strong opinion about the case that he or she can't promise to render an unbiased decision. It's important to note here that the law does not *require* that a juror be excused simply because he's got an opinion about some part of the case—or even because he's got an opinion about the defendant's guilt or innocence. The question is whether or not the juror can set that opinion aside and entertain the evidence with an open mind. If he says he can, and you can't prove otherwise, there is no basis for cause.

The number of challenges for cause is unlimited. Naturally, it's better to get a juror booted for cause than to use up a valuable peremptory. So even when the grounds seem shaky, attorneys for both sides will pop up with "Excuse for cause, Your Honor." It's then up to the judge to decide whether to allow it.

Here Ito gave the defense wide latitude. He gave us virtually none. If, for instance, a juror had written that he found Shapiro "slick," he was gone in a heartbeat, kicked for cause. If, on the other hand, a juror found me "pushy, too aggressive, too strident," Ito refused to dismiss him. If we wanted that juror out of there badly enough, we'd have to use a peremptory.

If a juror uttered a remark that was even remotely pro-prosecution, that was grounds for excusal. I'm thinking of one young black man who theorized that Kato would probably be loyal to Simpson because he'd given him a place to live rent-free. I thought this guy would make a great juror. The defense moved to excuse him for cause, and Ito granted the motion. I objected that his opinion was a matter of logic, not bias. But it didn't matter; he was gone.

The defense didn't want anyone with an IQ above room temperature. They were kicking jurors simply for being too smart. This happened to one of the alternates, a chemistry student from UCLA. This guy was absolutely brilliant. I knew that he sure as hell was going to understand our scientific evidence, and you could see that he gave the Dream Team *agita*. Sure enough, they struck him with a peremptory.

The UCLA student had another drawback from the defense's perspective: he was Japanese. People from Asian backgrounds, courtroom wisdom goes, are law-and-order types. Naturally, we try to get them on juries, and the defense always tries to keep them off. Defense lawyers have to be savvy about this, because if they appear to be targeting jurors on the basis of race, we can file what's called a *Wheeler* motion. If it's successful, the entire jury panel may be dismissed and jury selection will begin all over again. It doesn't stop there. If a judge grants such a motion, he's required to inform the state bar, and the offending lawyer can be reprimanded or fined, or both. It's a real bad mark on your record. But it didn't keep Shapiro from going after Asians.

There was one elderly Filipino man whose questionnaire indicated a law-abiding attitude. Bill and I knew the defense would find some way to get him off. Since there was nothing in his background that gave grounds for cause, they'd have to use a peremptory. Shapiro should have just struck the guy and moved on. Instead, he went out of his way to humiliate the man.

"Give us your definition of reasonable doubt," Shapiro commanded imperiously.

It was an obvious attempt to demonstrate the man's supposed language deficiencies. But asking him to define reasonable doubt? Not even legal scholars can agree what it is. The poor juror blushed, stammered, and asked Shapiro to repeat the question, which he did in an even more challenging tone.

I was absolutely furious. How could Lance, whose own ancestry was Asian, allow minority jurors to be treated like this? In fact Shapiro treated all nonblack jurors with this same sneering contempt. If either Bill or I had tried a stunt like that, we would have been called up to the bench so fast it would have taken your breath away.

Johnnie's approach was entirely different. He was warm and smooth with every juror. He came from the "call and response" school of voir dire. Johnnie was stupid like a fox. His questions were general, nonconfrontational ones that required only a yes or a no. He made no attempt to draw out a juror's real thinking. If you're sure you have a jury pool stacked in your favor, the last thing you want to do is let them talk enough to let slip a basis for cause. Judging from the answers I'd seen on those questionnaires, the pool was packed with O. J. Simpson fans. Why expose them by probing too deeply?

Still, I liked Johnnie, if only because he gave me somebody on the defense side that I could talk to. By that I mean someone who could tack through the choppy swells of a criminal case without losing his sense of humor. Squaring off against Johnnie was fun—at least in the beginning.

He'd come into court and greet me with that big, easy smile. "You're looking very lovely today, counselor," he'd say. And I'd reply, "No lovelier than yourself, Mr. Cochran."

Once, at a sidebar, I grumbled about "this fucking case—TFC"; Johnnie thought that was hilarious. He picked it up from me. His colleagues picked it up from him. By the end of the trial everyone was referring to this case as TFC.

The press caught on gradually to the realignment in our respective camps. At first, the talking heads tended to see this contest as Clark versus Shapiro: Bob and I were the combatants who scrapped with each other in court while our more levelheaded counterparts, Bill and Johnnie, sat back and steered the steady course. As we got further into voir dire, however, that perception changed. My office was still billing Clark and Hodgman as co-counsel, but that didn't fool anyone. The press could see that I was too aggressive and loud to be anybody's second chair, or even co-chair. I was the de facto lead on my side. And Johnnie was the lead on his. He'd pulled away, leaving Shapiro in his dust.

It was inevitable, I suppose, that the easy give-and-take I enjoyed with Johnnie should be misinterpreted as a flirtation. There was one very amusing incident that occurred a few weeks after the trial started in earnest. One of the tabloids published a sequence of still photos of Johnnie and me at a public hearing. The jury wasn't present and I'd been at the podium arguing to introduce some evidence that might have established Ron Goldman's time of death. This caught Johnnie off guard, and he rushed to argue against in. In the process he put his hands on my elbows and gently moved me away from the microphone.

The gesture took all of three seconds. The camera caught me looking surprised, which I was. It is unusual for lawyers—particularly men and women—to touch each other in court. My guess, if I know Johnnie, is that he did it solely to throw me off my game. Good lawyers sometimes use guerrilla tactics. Okay, fair enough. I can roll with it.

CAR TAPE. *October 1994. I don't see how we can ever get a decent jury on this case. Every misstep in the world that could be made is being made, because all the judge and the defense attorneys care about is looking good in the press.*

I'm really appalled at what's going on, at the deepest level. I really fear for our system of justice. I don't know how the jury system can continue without some serious revamping. It's hopeless—we cannot rest easy with the knowledge that a jury will use its common sense and follow the law and the evidence to come to the right verdict. If popular opinion and celebrity and fame and the politically correct view is going to be what really sways the jury, if the jury will disregard the law, disregard the evidence, and everyone expects it to happen, then why bother?

Have you ever had a dream where you try to run but your feet are weights? That was what voir dire was like. Jogging through molasses. Lance had hoped to get through twenty jurors on the first day. We managed only four. We tried to move faster, but Lance, Johnnie, me, everybody seemed to have fallen under some kind of malaise.

On October 18, we were jolted out of our dream state by a bulletin from the real world. That morning on my way into court, I bumped into Ito's clerk. Deirdre Robertson, a tall, stylish black woman in her thirties, was a classy lady. She had a young daughter and we used to talk about our kids a lot. Deirdre thought that O. J. Simpson was guilty and told me so. She was somebody I'd end up going to a lot for encouragement and solace during the trial.

"You put on the evidence," she'd tell me. "All you can do is put it in front of them."

I could tell by her face this morning that something ominous was afoot. We'd be starting late, she told me. Something had come up. When I asked her what, she just shrugged. A few minutes later, Ito huffed in, looking very agitated.

A tell-all had just hit the newsstands. The author, a friend of Nicole's named Faye Resnick, had written some very damaging things about O. J. Simpson. Ito had worked himself into a lather over the possibility that our jurors might have seen the book. He sent Deirdre out to buy copies for each of us. Then he suspended the voir dire until we could all read it and assess the damage.

I'd already talked to Faye—or at least I'd tried. Early on in the case I'd hooked up with some of Nicole's buddies, notably Kris Jenner, the former wife of Robert Kardashian, who had since married Olympic decathlon champion Bruce Jenner. Kris was an absolute gem, and she didn't seem to care much for her ex. She had the strange habit of referring to him as "Kardashian." I got the feeling they stayed on speaking terms only because they had four children in common. Kris and her friend Candace Garvey put me in touch with several of the Brentwood crowd. Among these was Cynthia "Cici" Shahian, who, coincidentally, was a cousin of Kardashian's. She'd been elusive at first: I'd leave messages that were never returned. But after a couple of months, she showed up in my office, flanked by Kris and Candace. Cici was extremely valuable. She'd been standing next to Nicole when Nicole got Simpson's letter threatening to turn her in to the IRS. Cici had been able not only to identify the letter, but to describe Nicole's furious reaction to it.

During the first few weeks of the case, Kris and Candace had been working on my behalf to reel in Resnick. Faye, a wealthy divorcée and, as she was most often described, a "West Side socialite," was a friend of the Jenners. Kris had introduced her to Nicole about two years earlier. Faye, too, was elusive, but Kris managed to coax her into my office late one night in July.

During that first encounter Faye Resnick came across as childlike and wary. She was a thin, waifish woman with an enormous mane of dark-blond hair. There was certainly nothing about her to prefigure the self-possessed siren who would eventually hit the talk-show circuit, to say nothing of the cover of *Playboy*. In fact, she sat almost curled up in a ball, staring at the floor.

"If it's Simpson you're afraid of," I told her, "the best thing to do is come forward." Even as I said it I was aware of the half-truths I am often forced to tell. Sure, she might be safer physically. But I had a feeling that if the defense got her on the stand, they'd cut her up pretty good. Clearly, this had occurred to Faye as well.

"You don't want me for a witness," she told me. "The defense will trash me for my drug habit. They'll make me out to be so bad it will ruin your case."

Faye's "drug habit" was supposedly a thing of the past, but Simpson's attorneys were already floating stories, claiming that she and Nicole had borrowed money from Colombian drug lords to open a coffee bar. Supposedly, that led to Nicole's being murdered.

"Let me worry about that," I told her.

If all she had to offer was hearsay, she'd never make it to the stand anyway. But any information at all was helpful.

"Faye, if you have anything that could help our case, please share it with us," I said. "Do it for Nicole's sake."

Faye said she'd think about it. I didn't put too much pressure on her that night. Kris had warned me that it would probably take at least one more meeting to draw her out. This meeting, at least, had served as an icebreaker. Before she left, I gave her a supportive embrace.

But now this! Deirdre handed me my own personal copy of *Nicole Brown Simpson: The Private Diary of a Life Interrupted*.

I took the slender volume back to my office and began to read. To my surprise, Faye devoted her first chapter to our interview. Her version wasn't exactly as I remembered it, but was impressively accurate. She even described how I'd hugged her "warmly" before she left.

I read on, intending to underline and annotate the book for future reference, and as I did, my eyes grew wide. Faye asserted (as the defense team would later) that Nicole had been carrying on a secret affair with football star Marcus Allen, who was O. J. Simpson's best friend. (Allen denied any romantic connection with Nicole.) This was not, strictly speaking, news. The rumors about Marcus Allen were out there from day one. I was just shocked that she came out and said it. I figured that O. J. Simpson would be way pissed off about that.

Faye wrote that she'd begged Nicole to cut off the affair with
Marcus and warned her, "You may be signing your death warrant."
During the weeks before her death, Nicole apparently told her about
beatings and abuse that had never come to the attention of our investigators. Once while they were staying at a Las Vegas hotel, Simpson
allegedly flipped out, grabbed Nicole by the hair, and flung her into a
corridor. She lay in the hallway sobbing, mostly naked, until a security
guard found and rescued her. But the worst beating, Faye claimed,
occurred about a year before their son, Justin, was born. Nicole had
found a jewelry box in one of her husband's drawers. It contained a
pair of diamond stud earrings. Assuming he had bought them for her
birthday, she put the box back. But the birthday came and went; no
diamonds. Later, according to Faye, Nicole learned that one of Simpson's steady mistresses, a former Miss New York named Tawny
Kitaen, had been wearing them around town. When she confronted
him about it, he punched and kicked her, and then locked her in a
closet. For hours after that, she lay quivering. And what was O. J. Simpson, American hero, doing? Lounging in the other room, watching
some sports special. Every so often he would come back to the closet,
open it, and kick her some more.

I thought Faye's book would be tabloid nonsense—*Life and Times in
the Brentwood Fast Lane*—but it wasn't. It impressed me. I believed
she was speaking honestly; the book had the ring of truth. From a
prosecutorial point of view, however, it was frustrating. Much of the
information it contained, unfortunately, *was* hearsay. We'd have
trouble getting it admitted at trial unless we could get independent
corroboration. I began to focus my reading, trying to find isolate
things that could be introduced as evidence. And about three-quarters
of the way through the book, I found something. Around April 1994,
Simpson and Nicole were on the rocks again. He'd extracted some
bizarre promise from her that she wouldn't see other men until
August, when he was due to leave for New York to start a new sports-
casting contract with NBC. Even though they'd broken up, he simply
couldn't bear the humiliation of seeing her, or others seeing her, with
other men, at least when they were on the same side of the Mississippi.
Simpson had called Faye in a fit of distraction. "If . . . I find out

she's with any other man before August," he allegedly told Faye, "I'll kill her."

If Faye herself had indeed heard Simpson make this explicit death threat, it would be admissible. I believed she had. I just didn't know whether Faye Resnick had sufficient credibility to testify for the People.

The drug problem that Faye had alluded to during our first interview was only the first of several difficulties a jury would have with her. I could work with the drug history, maybe even turn it to our advantage by pointing out that it was Nicole who arranged for the intervention that finally got Faye into a rehab clinic. Our victim was a compassionate woman. A caring and responsible friend. The fact that she had intervened to stop Faye's downward spiral also seemed to indicate that Nicole was not some wild-eyed cocaine freak.

But Faye gave the defense more ammunition as well. I knew they would zero in on chapter 18, where Resnick wrote, "How can I describe the intensity of my relationship with Nicole, particularly toward the end? We had become more than friends. Call it what you will, bonded sisters, soulmates, confidantes . . ." Yes, they were lovers, if Faye was to be believed. Resnick laid out a fairly graphic—and, she claimed, one-time—episode in which she and Nicole made love while listening to Madonna's *Erotica*.

Airing this stuff in court would be disastrous—the defense would use it not only to attack Resnick's credibility, but to damage Nicole Brown Simpson's own image in the eyes of the jury. By the time the defense was through with Resnick, the jury would be writing off Nicole as one of those West L.A. cocaine bitches, who probably got what was coming to her.

Still, that was no excuse for Faye's not telling us what she knew. It could have put us way ahead on the domestic violence part of the investigation. But what did she do? She squirreled away her nuts to sell in a confessional memoir. Didn't she feel some kind of real duty to Nicole? Didn't anyone in this case feel a duty to justice?

While the Resnick shock waves reverberated through the media, the Dream Team was going through the motions of a serious freak-out. Shapiro sputtered to the court that he'd been blindsided. He wanted the trial postponed for a year to let some of the frenzy around Resnick's book subside.

Blindsided, my ass. I learned from a conversation with Resnick's own publisher, Michael Viner of Dove Books, that Viner had run into Shapiro at a party over a month earlier. Viner claimed to have told Shapiro that the book was coming out the week of October 17; he told me the lawyer had not appeared particularly concerned. Now that the book was out, however, Shapiro was weeping and moaning that his client couldn't get a fair trial. He not only wanted the case held over for a year, but he wanted Simpson to spend that time free on bail, his activities monitored by "private security" that Mr. Simpson himself would provide.

Not a chance, Bobby. A defendant charged with a capital crime is ineligible for bail under state law—even if the D.A. has decided not to ask for the death penalty.

But we couldn't look to Lance Ito for decisive action on such an obvious ruling. Resnick's *Private Diary* had knocked the judge off his moorings. He called in the jurors one by one to ask what, if anything, they knew about the book. Nearly every one of them admitted, either voluntarily or after some strenuous questioning, to having some knowledge of it. Ito sent the jury pool home for two days—a particularly boneheaded move under the circumstances, since it sent the message that the book was a very big deal. Any of them who hadn't read it, of course, were headed straight for Barnes and Noble.

The next day, Ito held the bail hearing, closed to the public and press. I got up and argued that the option put forward by defense counsel was "unacceptable to the People," since what the defendant was asking for was impossible under state law. Even if it that hadn't been so, O. J. Simpson had already demonstrated before about 95 million fellow citizens that he had a propensity to flee. I reminded the court about the pursuit up the 405. I reminded Ito about the cash, the passport, the disguise. This defendant had made one obvious attempt at flight. It showed his consciousness of guilt. What would stop him from making another one?

"If the defendant wants a continuance," I said, "he should remain in custody as would any other defendant charged with a double homicide and special circumstances."

As I turned to leave the podium, I caught Simpson out of the corner of my eye. He was shifting in his seat, his face contorted with— what was it? Rage? Frustration? Disbelief? His lawyers had probably told him that he had a good shot at making bail. And here I'd gone bringing up all that Bronco business. Being at the mercy of a woman had to be O. J. Simpson's personal idea of hell. That gave me at least a moment of satisfaction. But as so often happened in TFC, even my smallest triumphs were short-lived. Johnnie did an end run around me, announcing that his client wanted to "address the court."

If the defendant has counsel there to speak for him, he shouldn't be allowed to speak directly to the court unless he's prepared to take the witness stand.

I started to object, but it was too late. Lance had granted the request.

"How do you feel?" he inquired amiably of Simpson, who now stood, hands clasped in front of him, the very picture of wounded virtue. *How did he feel?*

"Well," he complained, "I feel I've been attacked here today."

Attacked? Does he not get it that he's the defendant in a double homicide?

"I'm an innocent man," he continued. "I want to get to the jury. . . . I want to get it over with as soon as I can. I have two young kids out there. That's my only concern. . . . I've got two young kids out there that don't have a mother. . . ."

It disgusted me to the point of nausea to hear this man use his children this way.

And then Simpson turned toward me. I didn't meet his eyes—not because I was intimidated by him; I just didn't want to give him the satisfaction of knowing he had my attention.

"Mrs. Clark, Miss Clark, said I was trying to run," he fumbled. "Everyone knows that I called my father-in-law. . . . I admit I was not in the right frame of mind at the time, I was trying to get to my wife. . . ."

"Excuse me," Shapiro broke in, apparently agitated. It seemed to me that he was trying to create the impression that his client was straying out from under his control.

"I was headed back home," Simpson continued.

Shapiro reared up theatrically and threatened to resign if his client kept talking. Finally, Simpson said, "Thank you," and sat down.

Man, I thought, *I'd love to get him on the witness stand.* That monster ego of his would trip him up so bad. He wouldn't be able to keep his cool with a woman firing hostile questions at him. He was too unstable. If the Dream Team had an ounce of sense, they'd keep him off the stand and try to sneak in these unchallenged statements wherever they could. Just like this one. The saving grace of this outburst, I told myself, was that this hearing was closed and the transcript sealed. I sure didn't want Simpson's self-serving spiel reaching the ears of the jurors.

There was a curious atmosphere in the courtroom that day. It was actually pretty relaxed. The cameras were gone. Everyone loosened up a little. Both Shapiro and I let down our guards and vented our frustrations about the jury pool. Bob complained to the judge that jurors wanted to get on this case so badly, they were telling the court whatever they thought we wanted to hear. His implication: they were lying to get on this case so that they could convict O. J. Simpson.

I agreed that they were telling tall tales, but for quite the opposite reason.

"Many, if not most," I argued to Ito, "are lying to the detriment of the People because they are sitting there as the fans of this defendant saying, 'We want to get on this jury . . . so we can acquit this man, no matter what.' . . . I wish that we could only put all the jurors on polygraph, because if the People could get just twelve fair-minded, impartial jurors to listen to the evidence, then we know what the outcome will be."

The "polygraph" remark was a joke. Inside the courtroom that day, it was taken as a joke. Johnnie even laughed out loud. I didn't think any more about it. I was more self-conscious about having accused our jurors of lying. But, again, I comforted myself with the fact that this session was closed, the transcript sealed. I had no reason to believe that that L-word would ever reach their ears.

By the time the session came to an end, Ito had checked the penal code, which confirmed what we all knew. The law would not allow bail for O. J. Simpson. End of debate. But not the end of mischief.

Bill requested that the transcript of this closed hearing be kept under seal.

Shapiro rejoined, "We want it open." The defense clearly wanted Simpson's unsworn testimony to become public for the edification of the jury pool.

"Judge, you can't do this!" I protested frantically. "This is very incendiary . . . both sides accusing the jurors of lying. The defendant making an uncross-examined, unsworn statement about his innocence. None of this is fair. None of this is right."

Ito released the transcript.

As I look back upon this episode, I still can't figure out what possessed Lance. I know he was coming under a lot of pressure from the media, but that's not enough to have caused him to act so unwisely. Lawyers need to know that there is someplace they can talk where their statements will be held in confidence. They shouldn't be lulled into a false sense of security, then have the rug pulled out from under them. He could have kept the transcript sealed and never worried about being reversed on appeal. I think his heart was in the right place, but he was so weak. He let himself get pushed around by the defense.

I was totally screwed. I'd accused the jurors of lying. Can you imagine having to go back in and talk to these people after they read the L-word in their morning paper? I learned my lesson: never say anything in chambers or closed hearing that you wouldn't say in public.

By the next day, those transcripts were everywhere. Shapiro exploited the opportunity to hold me up to ridicule. Oddly, it wasn't the L-word he seized upon. I guess that's because he, too, had accused the jurors of lying. No, it was the P-word. The "polygraph" comment, he told reporters, "was the most idiotic statement ever made in a court of law."

Johnnie Cochran knew perfectly well that my polygraph remark was intended as a joke. But now he joined Shapiro in insisting that the remark had been serious. I just shook my head and thought, *I've lost all my respect for you, Johnnie. You're a two-faced, hypocritical bastard just like the rest.*

CAR TAPE. *October 1994. I'd like to see us abolish the jury system. Why leave the fate of our nation in the hands of these moon rocks?*

After the Resnick fiasco, a lightbulb popped on in Lance's brain. He realized, finally, that he had to do something to protect the jury pool from taint. So he started bringing jurors in one at a time for questioning—as we'd asked for from the start. And for the rest of the voir dire he limited the press to one pool reporter in the courtroom. The pool arrangement, however, only served to make the reporters now milling outside the locked doors more desperate for news from the inside. Johnnie and Bob took full advantage of this situation. Each convened his own daily press conference to fulminate over some new outrage. And on October 27, they dealt Bill Hodgman an ugly, low blow.

Bill had been questioning an elderly black man from South-Central L.A. He'd asked the guy, "Do you know what a polygraph is?" What he was trying to get at, of course, was whether the fellow had read my jurors-are-lying-their-heads-off comment and whether he had been offended by it.

The man shot back, "You're pumping me as if I'm on trial or something. So I don't like that. You are sort of riling me."

Bill ended the questioning as gracefully as possible and sat down. He was stunned. So was I. Bob and Johnnie saw their opening. During the next break, they ran out and held a pair of press conferences. Bill, Shapiro charged, was trying to get jurors removed for cause "because they are black, because they have black heroes and because O. J. Simpson is one of them. There is no other reason."

On another floor of the courthouse, Johnnie was busy making the same baseless charge. "We're really concerned about the tenor of the questions and the way they go after certain jurors," he said. "If there is a pattern, we'll be asking the judge to look into it."

I couldn't believe it. *They harass Asians, they boot nonblacks at every turn, and they accuse us of targeting minorities?* Blacks made up nearly 60 percent of the initial jury pool. We couldn't have gotten rid of them if we'd wanted to. The defense ended up bringing a raft of *Wheeler* motions against us, but we came prepared with a list of reasons for every black juror we excused. And they couldn't make a dent in us.

It was clear that Johnnie and Bob's intent was to poison the jury pool with insinuations of racism. And they succeeded. Several days later, Bill drew a black woman to question. We really had high hopes for her. She wore a smart, tailored business suit and had smiled at me warmly during the hardship questioning. Bill had just begun his very gentle questioning when she fixed him with an angry glare. "I don't know. You make me feel like I'm on trial here, really."

She'd obviously read the news accounts about the juror who'd felt "riled" and decided that she, too, would jump on the race bandwagon.

A look of shock and panic passed over Bill's face. He struggled to find words to reassure her and then defuse the situation. But he was mortified.

I could see that this process was just tearing him to pieces. After that, we agreed that I would question nearly all the remaining black jurors.

We finished the formal voir dire early in November. By now the jury pool had been winnowed down to under fifty bodies. We had one last shot at them. Each lawyer was allowed seventy-five minutes to make an eleventh-hour pitch, hoping to evoke a reaction that might help us in the final selection. I decided to throw away the rule book and shake these people up a little. Somehow, I had to get them to confront their own racial anger. I needed them to consider how hero worship might distort their judgment. But how could I get them to admit to me things they might not even have admitted to themselves?

When it came my turn to speak, I hesitated a bit. I looked at the faces. Again, mostly black, overwhelmingly female. It was important to start off on the right foot. Whatever happened, I didn't want these people thinking that I was condescending to them because they felt some sentimental fondness for the defendant.

"We've all seen *Naked Gun*," I told them. "He made us laugh. . . . We've had him referred to as the all-American hero. . . . And that's why it's so very difficult to have to present to you that someone of this image can do a crime so terrible."

They were looking at me as if to say, *We can't believe she's saying this.*

He's such a famous guy, I continued. He's such a popular guy that there's going to be a real temptation to do something different than what the law requires. This is a horrible situation, none of us like it, but that doesn't mean we suspend the rules of evidence. Just like in a football game—it's always a hundred-yard game no matter who's playing it. It doesn't matter if Mr. Simpson's on the team, it's still a hundred-yard game. It doesn't become an eighty-yard game, and it doesn't become a hundred-and-twenty-yard game, either. Rules are rules.

I reminded them that there were a whole lot of angles to this case: interracial marriage, a black defendant, white victims, spousal abuse. Which one of these do I have to worry about with you? I asked. Are you guys going to vote on the basis of one of these agendas? Are you going to try and even some score you've got in mind? You all agree with me that that would be wrong? That the place to even the score is the ballot box, not in this courtroom?

A few of them nodded yes.

"Is there anyone here . . . rooting for one side or the other?"

No nods this time. I continued:

"I don't care which side it is. If you are sitting there rooting for 'guilty' right now, I want you to get up and have the honor and the decency to excuse yourself from this panel." Same thing, I told them, went for those who were sitting there rooting for a verdict of "not guilty." "If you've decided how this case should end, then you cannot be fair."

And how about all these conspiracy theories? I continued. The Mafia did it. A Colombian cartel did it. A crew of white burglars did it. Are you going to make me convene the trial of the People versus the Mafia? Are you going to make me shoot down all these screwball theories before you'll listen to the evidence? How many trials do I have to do here? You could make the evidence fit anything, but that's not justice. I reminded them of Rodney King.

That case was in trouble from the very start, wasn't it? Because it had an all-white jury in a police community. And with a videotape, the most slam-dunk case you could possibly imagine. Our office lost that case, and we all know why.

"Do you know that had something to do with the fact they were being tried . . . by a jury that was all white? That it was tried in a community where a lot of police officers lived?"

Murmurs of "Probably . . ." "Yes . . ."

That's what happens when you don't listen to the evidence, when you vote on the basis of some private agenda.

Bob Shapiro objected to what he called my "unprofessional conduct." It is against the canon of ethics for a prosecutor to criticize or comment on a verdict to a potential juror. My comments, he said, were deserving of "severe sanctions."

That was technically true. So I apologized to the court. Then I looked at the jurors point-blank. "I hope I did not offend you with any of the comments I made concerning the Rodney King verdict. . . . Have I?"

The whole bunch of them smiled and gave me a rousing "No."

Shot yourself in the foot, Bobby.

For a moment there, I felt those jurors were with me. I'd gotten right up there in their faces, but they didn't seem to hold it against me. They seemed galvanized. I really felt that some current was flowing between us. Bill leaned over.

"Little white girl up there talking about race issues," he said. "One of the most dramatic moments I've ever seen in a courtroom."

The following day, we went in ready to kick and pick. That's the term we use for the last volley of the twenty peremptory challenges to get the pool down to twelve. So Bill and I got right in there and mixed it up. We kicked and we picked with a vengeance. And what we ended up with was one white woman, one man who described himself as "half American Indian," two Hispanics, and eight blacks. Six of those blacks were females.

By the end, we still had four of our twenty peremptory challenges remaining. That's right: we didn't use every single one that we were entitled to exercise. I can understand why a casual observer could assume that we missed an opportunity because of this. And, in fact, our detractors seized upon those four unused challenges, claiming that we could have kicked some of the clinkers and fill the slots with better prospects.

No, we couldn't. Let me explain.

During our nightly bouts of solitaire, Bill and I had kept precise tabs on the rotation of candidates within the pool. As days passed, the rating of the average juror in our pool—going by that 1-to-5 scale we'd developed—kept getting lower. Originally, our population had a very strong contingent of middle-class, educated citizens. But remember: the first round of elimination—the "hardship" phase—drastically changed that. The solidly employed middle class had no appetite to serve on this case, and Judge Ito let them off without looking back. There went most of our potential 5s and 4s. Then the defense began their attacks on two categories of jurors: those who were educated and those who were weren't black. Ito let them strike many without using their peremptory challenges. We were left with virtually no 4s and 5s, and only a few 3s.

By the time the defense's peremptory challenges had been exercised, we were down to our 2s. We were playing a defensive game, and we played it as cunningly as we could. The best we could do was make sure that the very worst jurors didn't find their way into the box. And the way the numbers broke down, if we used even one more challenge we would have called up a batch of even sorrier prospects who would outnumber the peremptories we had left. What would be the sense of knocking off one of our 3s or even 2s if most of the bodies who would take their place were 1s, people who wouldn't have voted to convict if O. J. Simpson stood in front of them with a knife in his hand and shouted, "I did it"?

The process of picking a jury had been so exhausting that when we finally got the twelfth juror, both sides of the room broke into cheers. We were kissing, shaking hands, hugging each other. It was unbelievable. Especially when you consider that only one side really had anything to celebrate.

Bob Shapiro ambled over to our table for some chat. He and Bill and I laughed and joked about the questionnaires. As I suspected, none of the Simpson team had ever had to soil his fingers flipping through those things. Their consultant had done it all for them.

"Gil made you read your own questionnaires!" Shapiro declared, astounded and amused. "He should give you hardship pay!"

Tell me about it.

Then Shapiro gave me a cartoon he'd drawn of me. There were two stick figures: "Marcia Before the Trial," showing me with long hair and a short skirt. Then, "Marcia After the Trial," where I had short hair and a long skirt. It was pretty funny. I kept it.

On balance, I'd never expended so much of myself picking a jury.

The exhilaration that came from completing that phase, along with the positive feedback I'd gotten from my speech the previous day, led me to a false optimism. That night, on the way home, I spoke into my little tape recorder:

We knew we'd wind up with an almost all-black jury. . . . We were guaranteed to have basically a female black jury and we do. But I think overall, we're not unhappy with the jury. I think there's enough strong, fair ones that we'll get some kind of fair shake. I mean, it's certainly not the best panel I've ever seen, but maybe they'll rise to the occasion.

I know I was livin' in a dream world. But you have to leave yourself a little hope.

Fever

There were times I could have drowned Suzanne Childs in a gunnysack. This was usually when the D.A.'s media relations adviser ignored the signs on my door reading "Leave Me Alone!" and "Go See Patti Jo" and bustled in with her handful of message slips.

"Well, CBS wants . . ."

"Suzanne!" I cut her off. "I don't have time for this."

I didn't mean to give her a hard time. It wasn't her fault that she was the bearer of unwelcome tidings.

Actually, I depended on Suzanne a lot, and considered her a great friend. She's a beauty—tall, thin, and laced with nervous energy. During the seventies she had been a weekend anchorwoman on the local CBS affiliate. She'd also been married to Michael Crichton. That was before he was such a big deal. Their marriage ended in a rather public divorce. As a result, Suzanne knew what it was like to be a much-stared-at single woman in L.A. I think that's why she took pity on me.

I had no personal life to speak of. Except for the nights when there were other arrangements at home, I usually left the office in time for dinner. Then, after the house was quiet and the toys all put away, I'd burrow in to the makeshift office in my bedroom. We'd started this case off-balance, and because of the defendant's insistence upon a speedy trial, we never really had a chance to take a breather. We were like greyhounds chasing a mechanical rabbit.

Beaten down though I was by my workload, I felt I should take at least a baby step toward an actual life. I'd spread the word among my friends and associates that I wouldn't mind going out on a date, if anyone knew of a moderately intelligent, heterosexual male. In other words, I was available.

One day, when I came back from court feeling whipped, Suzanne met me in the hall and gave me the once-over. (After two months, the "makeover" she had supervised was already beginning to fade.)

"You should get out a little," she told me.

"Great idea, Suzanne. Could you get me a life, maybe a few extra hours in a day?"

"I could get you invited to a party," she told me. It was at the home of some director—I didn't recognize the name. "It's a little get-together. About ten people. You could go right from work."

Suzanne gave me the address, which was in Beverly Hills. I found myself driving north of Sunset, deeper and deeper into the heart of mansion country. I was about to run into some serious glitter. Me, in my believe-me suit, driving a Nissan. The window on the driver's side still wouldn't work and it looked like it was going to rain. I pulled my little Maxima into a huge open drive and parked it next to a Mercedes. The only other car as crappy as mine was a county-issue Ford Taurus. I knew that Suzanne had arrived.

My God, what a place! A white-pillared entryway framed a pair of huge double oak doors. I'd barely rung the bell when it was answered by a butler in full livery. Behind him stood the host, who pumped my hand warmly and introduced himself as Ray Stark. Over the course of the evening, I came to realize that he was a big-deal producer, something I probably would have known right away if I hadn't had my head stuck inside of law books and autopsy reports for the past ten years. This little dinner party was also a private screening of *Legends of the Fall*.

Suzanne took me by the elbow for a quick turn around the place, past a wall of windows that looked out onto a yard of marble statues and topiary. Then, into the screening room. At the rear was a wet bar with all kinds of fancy chocolates set out in silver serving dishes. As we moved, Suzanne made easy introductions to some celebs and semi-celebs. God, I couldn't believe it—there was Kirk Douglas. To my amazement, Kirk (May I call you Kirk?) turned to me and said, "I'm such a big fan of yours." And I'm like, "I've been watching your movies since I was a kid."

The irony did not escape me. Suppose I'd stuck to acting. About now I'd be an aging bit player, who would have given up what was left of her virtue to be invited to a party like this. But here I was. And Kirk Douglas was angling to meet me! I felt like I'd been dropped onto another planet. There was David Geffen on my left, Kirk D. on my right, Ron Meyer on one end of the table, and Betsy Bloomingdale on the other.

The best part of it was that someone, probably Suzanne, had spread the word that the Case was off-limits for cocktail chat. An O.J.-free zone! Everyone was very cool about it. I've discovered since that the one advantage of mingling with the glitterati is that they've all had to wage their own battles against tabloid headlines. They observe a sort of gentlemen's agreement with respect to one another's privacy.

Ray Stark made sure I was introduced to Alan Greisman, who, I learned, had been head of Savoy Pictures and was the former husband of Sally Field. He was also handsome, and apparently available. He asked me out, which probably took some guts considering all this bull-shit mystique that now surrounded me. Now, I still thought I could date like any other soon-to-be-divorced mother of two. Obviously clueless. The following item appeared a few weeks down the line in a New York tabloid:

Transformed by her new hair-do, Marcia Clark at 41 has finally emerged outside the O.J. courtroom as a veritable siren, and with her new softer, prettier looks, the prosecutor in the Trial of the Century has even managed to find romance amid her grinding schedule.

According to sources, Clark has recently linked up with ac-tress Sally Field's ex-hubby, Alan Greisman, through mutual friends. . . . "They have been lovey-dovey all over Los Angeles," says a source. "I don't think they even attempt to keep their relationship a secret; they are dining out most nights."

In fact, Alan and I had only one date. I met him for dinner at a little Italian place in Beverly Hills. We talked for most of the evening about divorce. And by the dessert course I knew that nothing could come of it. Alan was intelligent and charming, but he ran with a flashier crowd than I thought I could handle, at least with the Simpson case on my hands. We parted amiably, without having managed to see any part of Los Angeles together beyond the inside of a restaurant.

I made a couple of other stabs at dating. A friend of a friend introduced me to a single guy she knew. He turned out to know Fred Goldman, but he seemed to enjoy no other claim to fame. *Hmmm,* I'm thinking. *This one's a good bet, not a fast-laner, not wired to the media.* I think I saw him twice; it was barely a friendship. But then one of the tabs found out that we knew each other and asked him if there was a romantic relationship there. He didn't confirm it; but he didn't deny it, which seemed dishonest to me.

After that I pulled in my antennae. I was safer with my own kind. From November until the verdict came in twelve months later, I limited my social life to late nights with my co-workers.

CAR TAPE. *November 17. I don't feel like I ever get more than four hours' sleep, constantly fighting this cough and this cold. I have not a minute to myself. If I'm not working, I'm with the kids. If I'm not with the kids, I'm working. . . .*

I don't really feel very good about our chances in this case, I just don't think we can get the jury to get over their emotional response to seeing their hero being taken down for this, and the evidence is so compelling. I don't feel like it's gonna matter. I feel like I'm going to be standing up there talking to myself, you know? . . .

But Chris Darden, boy. I pat myself on the back all day long for putting him on the case. What a gem. What a gem! The guy is smart, resourceful, creative, got lots of energy—because he hasn't been beat up like we have all this time. I'll give him a little time in front of this twelve-headed monster, and he'll get tired and beat up too. But he's wonderful. . . .

Thank God for Chris Darden.

As far as the public and the press knew, Chris Darden joined the team in early November. In fact, he'd been working with us behind the scenes for more than three months.

As I look back on it, I find it amazing that I didn't think of Chris when I was first drawing up that short list of D.A.s to partner with. He hadn't even occurred to me. That's because you tend to think of the people right under your nose. Chris was down on the seventeenth floor in SID.

Eight years earlier, he and I had worked together in calendar court. We had a lot in common. Like me, he was a hard charger, ambitious, tenacious. Back then, after work, Chris and I and a handful of other deputies would all take out the bottles from our respective desk drawers, down a couple of shots, and swap war stories into the night. Then we'd be up early the next morning, ready to charge all over again. During the years since calendar court, Chris and I had gone our separate ways: I to Special Trials; he to the SID, where he handled complaints against cops. We'd see each other from time to time in the courthouse and we'd laugh and joke and talk about the old days.

One summer morning soon after the preliminary hearings, he stuck his head into my office unannounced.

"Hey, Clark," he hailed me. "Any time for the working class?"

It took me a minute to focus. Cool shaved head. Malcolm X fuzz. "Chris! C'mon in, man!"

He seemed relieved that I'd recognized him. By the time he took the chair he was having trouble making eye contact. Chris always did have trouble making eye contact. Not just with me, but with judges and juries. Down deep, he is a very shy guy.

Chris gave a detailed account of our reunion in his excellent memoir, *In Contempt*. He recalled me in a dense cloud of my own cigarette smoke, at a desk fit for a CEO. "She leaned back in her huge brown leather executive chair with the diamond tuck in the back, a chair twice her size, clearly not standard county-issue."

When I read this, I nearly doubled over laughing. You'd think he was talking about some spike-heeled dame from a film noir. That "brown leather executive chair," as a matter of fact, was just a ratty old armchair that I'd found some years earlier sitting in a hallway. Some departing Grade 3 had apparently discarded it. It *was* huge. It was so huge, in fact, that I could actually curl up in it and catch a few winks. Unfortunately, it was infested with termites, and every time I shifted my weight, it emitted a cloud of sawdust—which probably accounts for the haze Chris saw hanging over me that morning in July.

Finally he looked at me.

"I thought you should know the *L.A. Times* has filed a public records request on Fuhrman." He slid a file across my desk.

The case was old, 1987. It involved a robbery suspect named Joseph Britton who was fleeing an automated teller machine when he was shot by a couple of police officers. One of them was Mark Fuhrman. Britton sued the city, claiming that one of the two officers had called him a "nigger" and then planted evidence on him.

The problems with Fuhrman just kept on coming. I'd gotten the documents from that disability case Mark had filed against the city in August 1983. It appeared to me that he'd put on quite a show for his psychiatrists. He'd claimed to be suffering from stress growing out of his service in Vietnam (though he hadn't seen any action), as well as his years going head-to-head with gang bangers. All of this, it appeared, was exacerbated by the strains of his divorce. Yet his job ratings were generally high. No way, I thought, was any judge going to let a cop's psychiatric reports into the record. But we'd surely have to litigate it. I knew the defense would pull out all the stops trying to get them in.

Now a lawsuit?

"We checked it out," Chris reassured me. "Rejected for prosecution."

That was acceptable damage. Every officer has complaints in his file. If he's out there in the neighborhood making arrests, somebody's going to try and sue to get the city to fork over a few bucks in a settlement. If SID had investigated and rejected the complaint, that was good enough for me.

"And the public records request?" I asked him.

"The *L.A. Times* has a right to get the file in ten days. I'll probably give it to them on day nine and a half."

Totally on top of things. I really liked this guy.

I knew that Chris had solid ties to the 'hood. He also knew Downtown juries. I wanted his opinion on Fuhrman.

"Everybody's going nuts on this planting thing," I told him. "What do you think?"

Chris was silent for a moment.

"Well, people in the 'hood think he [Simpson] was framed," he said finally.

"Well, what do *you* think?"

"I doubt it," came his reply.

Chris knew cops. He investigated them on a regular basis. He could tell a legitimate complaint from a fairy tale. The kind of elaborate evidence-planting and conspiracy that the defense was suggesting just didn't ring true.

"Black people won't want to convict Simpson," Chris warned me. "But if you've got the evidence, you can overcome that. You'll make it."

I found that reassuring.

After he'd left my office, it dawned on me. "My God . . . *Chris!* Why didn't I think of it before? He'd be perfect to handle Cowlings."

Since the day after the Bronco chase, we'd had A. C. Cowlings under charges for aiding and abetting a fugitive. Gil and the brass had talked it over and decided the best way to investigate him would be through a separate grand jury. This would have to be handled with great sensitivity because the law strictly prohibits the district attorney from using evidence gathered from one grand jury to assist in the investigation of a case already filed. It's called "commingling."

There were other complications. Whoever took the assignment would have to be prepared to subpoena Simpson's own attorneys, at least two of whom had been present in the house from which he'd escaped. It meant we had to give Cowlings to someone who was strong enough to push through an investigation in the face of monumental stonewalling.

Chris would be perfect. He was tough and tenacious and he seemed eager for the action. We knew, even at this point, that the Simpson case was shaping up to be the biggest one ever tried by our office. You couldn't blame a deputy for wanting to be part of it. The beauty of Cowlings, from Chris's perspective, was that it was a limited engagement. He could be a member of the team in an important but low-profile part of the case. And as soon as it was over, he'd get his life back.

And so, in late July 1994, Chris took over the Cowlings investigation, which, as I had predicted, turned out to be the ultimate dead end. Cooperative witnesses were almost impossible to find. Simpson's personal assistant, Cathy Randa, had shredded documents pertaining to domestic violence. She sure as hell wasn't talkin'. Paula Barbieri appeared before the grand jury wearing a prim, high-buttoned shirt with a cross dangling from her neck, and wouldn't even own up to being Simpson's girlfriend. Robert Kardashian, Simpson's wealthy pal, who hadn't practiced law for years, ducked each of Chris's queries about Simpson's departure from his house with a smug "That's privileged." O. J. Simpson's cadre of loyalists had closed ranks tightly around him.

When it became clear that we weren't going to have enough evidence to indict, we thanked the jury and sent them home. I was left with a clear conscience. Chris and the D.A. investigators had gone to extraordinary lengths pursuing leads. Later, Chris regaled us with tales of these exploits. His favorite concerned a trip he and two investigators had made to the Bahamas in search of the *Miss Turnbury*. She was a yacht that supposedly figured in one of the Simpson escape scenarios. What Chris had hoped would be an exotic trek to paradise turned into the junket from hell. Mosquitoes the size of bats, inflated tourist prices, five bucks for a bottle of beer, a hundred bucks for dinner. And, of course, nothing but dead ends on the investigation. Each time he told that story it got funnier: the mosquitoes got larger, the price of beer rose to ten dollars a bottle. Chris made me laugh until the tears ran down my cheeks. I hated the idea of letting him go.

Bill and I had been talking about bringing on another attorney as a special "case manager." Someone to coordinate the work of the law clerks and junior deputies who were being assigned to do research for us. Even before we dismissed the charges against Cowlings in early November, I called Chris into my office to make him a proposition.

"Bill and I are so balled up arguing these stupid motions that we don't have any time to do any of the organization," I told him. "We don't have the time to do any creative thinking. I guess what I'm saying is that I'd like you to be part of the first string."

He looked down. Then he looked away. There were a few beats. I knew—or at least I thought I knew—what he was thinking: *They need some color at that Clorox-white counsel table.*

"I'd be honored," he told me. It was a strangely formal reply. But Chris had a chivalrous streak, and I found that endearing.

It's been said that we recruited Chris because he was black. But that isn't true. At the time he popped his head in my door, we had no scouts out beating the bushes for minority talent. A good lawyer presented himself. I knew him. I trusted him. He happened to be black. Now, did I think his race would help us with a predominantly black jury? Possibly. But there was also a risk that those jurors might reject him as an Uncle Tom. At the very least, the D.A.'s office would almost certainly be charged with race pandering. Sure enough, a day or so after Chris's appointment was made public, Johnnie Cochran went around telling reporters that we'd hired ourselves a token black man. Even after the dirty tricks I'd seen him pull during the voir dire, I would still have believed Johnnie had more class than that.

To me, Chris's race was a wash. My only thought was *He's strong. He's smart. Can he handle the beating we're gonna take?* And I knew the answer: *Yeah, he can.*

I found Chris a cubicle in the middle of the Planning and Training Unit. I also handed him a big chunk of the case, a part that needed a lot of catch-up work.

Nicole and O. J. Simpson's private life was still a mystery to me. We had police reports, but these were encoded in cop-speak, a militaristic argot that imparts no warmth, no human dimension to the events recounted. It seemed that no one could supply the key to the code. That is, until the publication of Faye Resnick's book. I had let Faye slip through my fingers in the first go-round. Not this time. I told Chris to reel her in. No excuses. The evidence she'd been withholding was motive for murder.

I'm not sure what kind of tactics Chris used to flush Faye out of hiding in Vermont or wherever the hell she was holed up. I know he talked to her lawyer, who claimed that she was spooked over the sensation the book had caused. If we wanted her to come in to see us, he said, we'd have to assign her a security detail. I found this a little dramatic, particularly in light of the fact she'd invited her former boyfriend—an O.J. loyalist who was probably in contact with the Simpson camp—to her hotel room for a visit. What was the point of telling the enemy where you were and then asking for security?

Chris finally prevailed personally upon her publisher, Michael Viner, to bring Resnick in out of the cold. Viner's motives, I suspected, were not solely to advance the interests of justice. Every time a witness marched out of the Criminal Courts Building, it was a big news day. That meant publicity for the book, the author, and the publisher. But I was willing to play this game if it would advance our cause.

They made quite a pair, Resnick and Viner. He was a pale, almost rabbinical-looking man. Faye, to my surprise, had metamorphosed from the trembling, fetal creature who'd visited my office three months earlier into a burnished vamp whose months in New England seemed actually to have enhanced her tan. She bore right down on me, all hugs and kisses, far more expansive and relaxed than during our first meeting. Maybe it was because she felt having her book out there before the public was, as I had suggested, a sort of insurance policy. If Faye got knocked off, I guess we'd pretty much know where to start looking.

The first time we'd met, we'd both been relatively anonymous. Now, for the moment at least, we were two of the most visible women in America. Maybe in Faye's peculiar worldview, this created some kind of bond between us. Whatever the reason, this time around, she was full of stories. She told how she and Nicole had met in 1990 but did not hit it off until one day at a sunbathing party where they discovered that they had both banged the same guy, Joseph Perulli. Joseph had apparently broken off his relationship with Nicole, and Faye was trying to give her tips on how to win him back.

"I liked her immediately once . . . once she wasn't seeing him anymore," Faye whispered, in her sultry contralto. "But now I want to help her, right?"

"Go figure," I interjected dryly.

Faye claimed she did not know about O.J.'s New Year's Eve attack until she and Nicole went into group therapy in February 1993. The therapist asked Nicole to tell the story, and she ran from the room crying. Afterward, Faye engaged in a little Tough Love; she told Nicole, "If you can't confront any questions at all, you're never going to make headway." "Nicole wanted to get rid of all that bad stuff but she was afraid to," Faye told us. "O.J. would get so mad at her that she would be frightened to do it."

Nicole made so much "progress" in her therapy that she decided to beg O.J. to come back so that they could mend their marriage. In retrospect, a terrible mistake. In early May 1994, Nicole was supposedly still talking about reconciliation with O.J., but she also told Faye that she was having an affair with Marcus Allen (which Allen later denied).

Faye looked at me solemnly and said, "I believe that Nicole thought she was going to die, and I think she was doing some really wild things. I think she was out of control. Nicole had done some strange things in the last month of her life."

"Like?"

"Telling our friend Cora Fischman about her and I being together. I thought that was strange, which she promised me she wouldn't tell anybody. Because I'm not bisexual, neither is she. And it was something that just happened one night and she promised me she would never tell anybody about it. And for her to tell, I couldn't imagine Nicole doing that. For her to see Marcus, I couldn't imagine Nicole doing that. Those two things, I—I can't—I can only see that they're desperate, they're an act of a desperate woman thinking she's going to die."

Faye also confirmed one of my earlier hunches: that the IRS letter had made Nicole furious enough to walk out for good. "She realized that he didn't care about the kids," Faye told me. "The children meant nothing to him. [Nicole] said, 'If he's going to kill me, let him get it over with.' "

Faye herself had apparently fallen upon hard times and was living at Nicole's condo. She told me how she'd gotten increasingly freaked by O.J.'s behavior. He'd called Faye one day in April demanding to know why Nicole wasn't returning his calls. "If you don't tell me why she's not calling," he said, "I don't know what I'm going to do." She believed his words were a death threat to Nicole.

It turns out that Faye was doing a lot of coke and Valium about then. Nicole organized an intervention to get her into a rehab clinic in Marina del Rey. Faye checked in on June 9. Three days later, at nine o'clock on June 12, she called Nicole from a pay phone at the clinic, asking her how the recital had gone.

"That was the best mood I have ever heard her in. She sounded so resolved and so clear and so strong, felt so good about what she had done. She felt good about the fact that her family was behind her at this time."

Her parents' support meant a lot to Nicole, Faye said. Nicole confided in her that "the only reason she stayed with O.J. after that [the New Year's Eve incident] was because of her family. They needed his support financially. And when she told them that she wanted to leave him, they made her feel so—so bad about it, and they basically did not accept her leaving him. And to me that was one of the biggest secrets of all. I mean, I was devastated by that. It's like their daughter is a throwaway daughter."

Chris and I both believed that Faye was telling the truth about Simpson's abuse of Nicole. He hit the trail and checked out various sources, all of whom ended up confirming her accounts. A nurse at the rehab clinic confirmed that Faye really had called Nicole the night of the murders. Various members of the Brentwood crowd—Candace Garvey, Bruce and Kris Jenner—also verified Faye's account of O. J. Simpson's obsessive, abusive relationship with his wife.

Chris had several follow-up interviews with Faye. She flirted outrageously with him. Her pet name for him was "D'Artagnan." A Musketeer? Go figure. She would leave throaty messages on his answering machine: "D'Artagnan, I need to speak with you." He'd play them for me when he got to work.

Anyway, Chris liked her. He was all for putting her on the witness stand. But I held back. As I've said before, Faye had a very serious downside. There was her drug problem, for starters. On top of that we'd heard that Robert Shapiro professed to have witnesses to an ongoing lesbian relationship between Faye and Nicole. These "witnesses" could supposedly describe the lovemaking positions both women had assumed during these encounters. Moreover, while on her

book tour, Faye had drawn fire from black women in the audience of a national talk show. To them, she was just one more white bitch trying to bring down O. J. Simpson. If the jury had it in for *me*, you can imagine how'd they'd respond to her.

In the end, I prevailed. We didn't call Faye, and I'm sure that it didn't break her heart. Faye's information supplied the connective material to turn our collection of isolated police reports about Nicole's deeply troubled marriage into a coherent history. It gave us a badly needed boost.

And now, I thought, if we could just reach the Browns.

This is the part that gets weird for me. It wasn't for lack of desire, but I was never able to get as close to the victims' families in this case as I would have liked. I felt enormous sympathy for the Browns and the Goldmans. And I felt a special rapport with Kim Goldman. Her grief, never far from the surface, simply broke my heart. A brother murdered! I thought of my own brother, Jon, the person closest in the world to me. I couldn't imagine what it would be like to lose him.

Whenever I called the Goldmans' home, whoever answered the phone, usually Fred or Patti, would tell the other to pick up the extension and we'd all talk. I'd fill them in on the latest news and check to see how they were holding up. Patti never failed to ask about my health and my children. Same for Fred. I found that remarkable, especially in light of the loss of their own child. Such incredibly wonderful people.

But the awkward fact remained, the victims' families and I enjoyed nothing approaching the close, comfortable relationship I'd had with Rebecca Schaeffer's mother. Danna and I had exchanged notes and phone calls during a whole year of pretrial motions. But once Simpson had invoked his right to a speedy trial, the accelerated schedule, along with the unbelievable pressures of TFC, made the kind of relationships that mature and deepen with time close to impossible.

Whenever we seemed to be on the point of establishing a closer rapport, the media pulled the families in another direction. As a practical matter, I couldn't order them not to talk to reporters. But in the past, I had found that victims' families were usually willing to be guided by me. After all, the articles and television segments could affect the prosecution, and our shared goal was presumably to see justice done. Danna Schaeffer had been conscientious about consulting me each time she was called by a reporter. Her cooperation helped me exert some kind of damage control over publicity the defense would claim was prejudicial to their client. In the Simpson case, all bets were off.

I liked Fred Goldman a lot, and I know he did his best to help us. But he really felt he had to be out there, making statements and expressing his outrage, to make sure that a media obsessed with the melodrama of Nicole and O.J. didn't neglect his own son's memory. (Privately I applauded him. Fred and his family, I felt, served as the very conscience of this case.) Fred, at least, would give me a heads-up before he gave an interview to Geraldo. Not so, the Browns. I wouldn't hear of their forays until I picked up the paper or passed a television set.

Early on, Denise and Dominique Brown had appeared on *Good Morning America*, where they'd seemed to me neutral, almost supportive of their brother-in-law. This was especially strange, I remember thinking, in light of Denise's comment to Tom Lange the morning he called to tell her of her sister's murder: "I knew the son of a bitch was going to do it," she'd told him. Nothing equivocal about that. And then, in November, for reasons unknown to me (she certainly didn't consult me about it), Denise Brown came out swinging. She announced publicly that she'd known O.J. was the killer from the moment she heard about Nicole's death. She also claimed that Nicole had predicted Simpson would kill her and get away with it.

The defense team went absolutely crazy over this. Johnnie Cochran got up in court and fulminated about how awful it was for the Browns and Goldmans to be doing this to the defendant before trial. Denise's television appearances also prompted a sanctimonious announcement from Shapiro that he "forgives" the family. When I heard that, I just thought, *Fuck you, you patronizing asshole.*

The absurd thing about it all was that the defense, the press, and perhaps the public all assumed that the District Attorney's office had sent the victims' families out on a campaign to spin public opinion. But nothing could have been further from the truth. The Goldmans and the Browns were simply beyond our control.

Of all the families of victims I've had contact with over the years, the Browns were by far the strangest. I'd known families who were indifferent and others who were overinvolved. This was something else.

On the surface they appeared warm enough. Lou Brown would come into court saying, "Where's my hug?" and then hug me. I let him hug me because I couldn't think of any tactful way to deflect it. But I wasn't comfortable with it, in part because of something I saw during one of my visits to the Browns' home at Dana Point. Lou had shown me into his study. On a table covered with photos—almost none of Nicole—there was a picture of Dominique—the family called her Mini—dressed in a teensy-weensy bikini, in what struck me as a provocative pose. There was also a shot of some magazine pinup, totally nude.

It was also clear to me early on that Lou Brown was a patriarch of the old order. According to Tanya, Lou had been delighted with his famous son-in-law and he'd been completely opposed to his daughter's divorce. When Nicole first walked out on O. J. Simpson, her father would not speak to her or even help her move.

Juditha was a handsome, middle-aged woman of German birth; to me, she seemed sweet and well-meaning but utterly passive. She was well aware of Nicole's domestic problems. Every time Nicole and O.J. fought, she told us, O.J. would take Juditha's picture off the wall and throw it out a window. It became a running joke: "Oh, am I on the front lawn again?" Juditha seemed to have downplayed in her own mind what should have been a red flag, not—I believe—because she didn't care about Nicole, but because she just couldn't bring herself to deal with the trauma that would have resulted from confronting her *own* husband and her own emotions. Juditha was mildly supportive when Nicole left O.J., but was all too willing to let her go back on the occasions when she tried to reconcile. It must have been difficult for Juditha to look back on those events and reckon with them. But she never talked to me about that.

The Brown sisters all seemed clued into O. J. Simpson's true nature. Denise had taken photos to document Nicole's injuries after the New Year's Eve incident. Dominique, who seemed to me the coolest of the lot and a real straight shooter, also seemed to have the most pent-up rage. She told me how, when Nicole was pregnant,

Simpson called her sister a "fat pig," and about how uncaring he was as a father. How he liked to show the kids off, but he really wasn't around for them.

The Browns gave me a document, written by Nicole, dated Sunday, January 10, 1988. I found this particularly harrowing. Nicole had taken Sydney, along with her mother and Mini, to see "Disney on Ice." When they all got back to Rockingham, Simpson was there with Al Cowlings. Nicole could tell something was wrong. A.C. looked tense.

> [O.J.] followed Mini and Mom out to the car, rattling 100 mph about what a liar I am. He never stopped. He followed Sydney and I around the house. "Please don't yell and scream in front of Sydney." So A.C. grabbed her. And I tried to get away from her so she wouldn't have to hear it.

Here was Nicole, two months pregnant at the time. He tells her he wants her to get an abortion. He orders her out of the house, saying, "I have a gun in my hand right now. Get the fuck out of here."

She grabbed her baby, the cats, the diaper bag, and a bottle. Then she "got the heck" outta there.

Given the circumstances, I found Nicole's account strangely dispassionate, as if she were separated by habit from her own feelings. And yet as I read between the lines, I could sense her mounting panic as she tried to protect her child. I could just imagine what Sydney must have seen and heard. That poor little girl. Forced to watch and listen as her father humiliated her mother. Kicked out onto the street. And I'm thinking, *This guy abuses his pregnant wife, demanding she abort their baby, and now he moans to the world that the worst part of being incarcerated is the separation from his children?*

The Browns also gave us a journal in which Nicole had chronicled more of her husband's systematic neglect of his children. When I first glanced through it, I did not recognize it for what it really was. Nicole's lawyers would later explain to me what these notations meant. They'd instructed her to write everything down in case of future litigation on custody or child support. When the father failed to show, missed days, came late, she was to document it in writing. And she had done as they'd instructed.

As I read through those entries, I saw and heard a Nicole who was becoming increasingly agitated. The angrier she got, the more she wrote. Beyond the simple recording of dates, she had started describing how her ex-husband acted, what he'd said to the kids. In the strictest sense, what we had from Nicole was not really a diary. And yet it was the essential diary.

Nicole began making entries in early 1992, after leaving her husband for the first time to set up housekeeping at her new condo on Gretna Green in Brentwood. "Home," she wrote on Sunday, February 23. "Moving in." Most of her entries were spare; one of the longest was for Monday, June 29, 1992.

> O.J. called about 7:00 or 7:30. Justin kept wanting to talk. Asked if he can sleep there. Such a need for Daddy . . . Sad!! So he came at about 8:15. Justin is in heaven. I stayed home w/Sydney. It's been 2 weeks since Justin spent the nite & saw OJ. 3 weeks since Sydney spent the nite and saw OJ. . . .

During the early part of 1993, Nicole was clearly considering reconciliation. "O.J. & I got back together April 12 93," she wrote. By spring of the following year, however, they were on the skids again. Nicole had bought her condo on Bundy. She seemed to be shuttling between Bundy and Rockingham, unsure of where to call home. O.J. was a chronic no-show as a father. By May 1994, Nicole had apparently had enough. "We've officially split," she announced to her journal. "I told OJ we're going back to every other weekend. . . . I need the rest & O.J.'s gone so much—he needs time alone with [the kids] 'til he leaves again."

On June 3, when she had little more than a week to live, Nicole documented another violent outburst. O.J. had come by the condo to pick up the kids; when he discovered they'd made other plans, he lit into Nicole for some perceived slight of the day before.

"You hang up [*sic*] on me last nite, you're gonna pay for this, bitch!" he shouted at her. "You're holding money from the IRS—you're going to jail you fucking cunt! . . . I've already talked to my lawyers about this," he continued. "They'll get you for tax evasion, bitch. . . . You're not gonna have a fucking dime left."

He continued his tirade even as Sydney's little girlfriend arrived for a sleepover. "I'm not sure if they heard all or any of it," Nicole agonized. "I just turned around & walked away."

As I picked my way through a spotty trail of journal entries and documents, I could see how, over the next five days, the hostilities escalated. Simpson's letter threatening to report her to the IRS flung kerosene on the flames. That letter had apparently gone through a few drafts. When we subpoenaed it from O. J. Simpson's divorce attorney, Skip Taft, we also recovered a note from the lawyer saying that he had made the changes O.J. wanted but did not get "revengeful." Two days later, Simpson sent Nicole a nasty follow-up to the IRS letter, informing her that while he welcomed the children at Rockingham, "Gigi [his housekeeper] is not an emergency cook, baby-sitter or errand running [*sic*] for you! She is an employee of mine and I expect you to respect that—now, and in the future."

Four days later, Nicole was dead.

I knew there had to be more to document this downward spiraling relationship. Correspondence, a daybook, photos. I wanted to find just one shot of the Simpsons standing side by side—one in which Nicole was not wearing heels—to show the disparity in their sizes. I was sure her family could give us what we needed, but every time we went to them with a request, we had to wheedle and beg, and often came away empty-handed.

(For the time, when they were stalling on giving us the journals, Chris and I actually discussed the possibility of serving Lou with a search warrant. Talk about unprecedented. A search warrant on a victim's family? Would we ever have looked like heartless bastards! Fortunately, the Browns turned them over before this became necessary.)

Unlike most victims' relatives, who desperately try to move your case forward—"What can we do? What information can we offer to put this animal behind bars?"—Lou Brown played things very close to the vest. Lou had cleaned out the condo after Nicole's death and reportedly stored her belongings. Chris and I asked him repeatedly to produce those boxes; he kept dodging us. It was "I'll get it for you. . . . I'll look for it, I'll look for it." He never came up with them.

As to why, I can only speculate. Perhaps he felt that our probing violated his privacy. Believe me, I could relate to that, since my own secrets had become a tabloid commodity. But what completely floored me was then learning that the Browns had cooperated with Sheila Weller, author of a soon-to-be-published book called *Raging Heart*, and that they had given her information they'd never given us. That book, I'd learn, was pretty hard on O. J. Simpson. I couldn't figure out why they were being so reticent with the D.A.'s office. After all, we were the people who had a shot at putting him away.

Faye Resnick seemed to be right: O. J. Simpson had given the Browns considerable financial help over the years. We discovered a deed to their house that seemed to indicate that Simpson had taken over the mortgage. I wondered if Lou's reluctance came from feeling beholden to his son-in-law. Or was he afraid of him? Or both?

Early in December we got a call from Nicole's bank. She'd been renting a safe-deposit box, bank officials told us. Her father was now trying to get into it. We knew that the box might contain crucial evidence. Given Lou's prior recalcitrance, we thought it was better just to go and get it ourselves. So Chris sent a couple of D.A.'s investigators down to the bank with a warrant and instructions to drill that box.

The contents were more disturbing to me than anything I had seen to date. There were three Polaroid pictures of Nicole. The first looked like it was taken when she was very young, early in her relationship with Simpson, when she was still a teenager. Her hair was wrapped up in a towel. Her eye was blackened, her face puffed up and reddened. I studied the shot, looked at Chris, and just shook my head.

The box also contained several letters, one written by Nicole to O.J. very early in their relationship, complaining that he neglected her. There were three others from him to her, apologizing for having abused her and taking responsibility for having gone crazy. Implicitly acknowledged in one of those letters is the fact that he beat her because she refused to have sex with him.

Why would a woman keep those things in a lockbox? There was only one explanation. Even as she was trying to break free of O.J., part of Nicole accepted that she would never really escape, that O. J. Simpson might murder her. The message in the box was clear: *in the event of my death, look for this guy.*

I kept coming back to her eyes. She was so young at the time those pictures were taken that her eyes still reflected authentic emotion. I compared the photos mentally to those hanging by the stairs at Rockingham. A decade or more had passed between those two shots. The pain in her eyes had gelled into a glassy, deadened stare. Seventeen years of denying terror and clinging to hope, only to have that hope destroyed time and time again.

On Sunday afternoon, December 18, Chris and I drove out to Dana Point to confront the Browns. Phil and Tom went with us, although they were not real happy to be there. For starters, they were ticked off at Chris and me because we had used D.A. investigators, not the LAPD, to drill the box. But I'm sure they were also dreading the encounter with Lou, who by now had learned that we'd done an end run around him.

As always, Juditha Brown was gracious. She laid out a plate of pasta for us. I sat across from Lou. He didn't appear angry, but there were tears in his eyes.

"Why didn't you just ask me?" he said.

Tom and Phil were only too happy to let someone else answer. I was trying to come up with a reply when Chris stepped into the breach. He could be very good under pressure. He mumbled something plausible: "We weren't sure that you could get into it legally. We could. We just felt it would be better for everyone if we went ahead and did it."

That diplomatic fiction seemed to ease the tension. Juditha sat down with us for a long taped interview. I pressed her for specifics on the battering incidents we were trying to document. By her own admission, Juditha had no head for dates. And she had no memory at all of that harrowing incident following "Disney on Ice" when her son-in-law had called the pregnant Nicole a "liar" and a "fat pig." I showed her Nicole's letter to refresh her memory. Nicole had been clear about the fact that her mother and Mini had been there when O.J. flew off the handle, "rattling 100 mph."

"I don't remember anything about that at all," Juditha told me.

I was flabbergasted.

"You were there," I reminded her. "And he was calling her a fat liar."

"Yes," Juditha acknowledged, "but, you see—the problem with all these things is that all this stuff happened so many times, it . . . didn't mean anything anymore after a while."

It didn't mean anything?

The thing that seemed to upset Juditha most was her son-in-law's treatment of his children. After Nicole and O.J. fought, she would go often to a beach house they owned. "That was always her refuge," Juditha explained. "And then when she left him, that was the first lock that he changed. So she couldn't go down to the beach house anymore. That's how much he loves his kids. You know, all this circus about 'I love my kids.' That was their favorite place!"

Juditha was warming to the subject. It seemed curious to me that she could work up more outrage over the ill-treatment of her grandchildren than over the very obvious abuse of her own daughter.

"And another thing that upset me about him was, when she once said she cannot afford the school anymore, it's just so much money. And he says, 'Then put 'em in regular school. Other kids survive.' So there was no consideration to the kids as long as he could get to her. This is something I hold against him, and I always have. Just out to hurt Nicole. If Nicole didn't do how O.J wanted, it was always money and it was how to get to her then."

After the murder, the Browns received a call from Simpson's lawyer. "Don't expect Nicole's alimony check," Juditha recalled hearing, "because the children just have to get used to a lower lifestyle."

This would have appalled me if I had not already formed an opinion as to what a selfish, unfeeling creep Orenthal James Simpson really was.

Lou promised to give Phil and Tom permission to search the storage facility where he had put the contents of Nicole's condo. Before we left, I showed him one of the photos taken from the lockbox. As he looked at it, his expression did not change.

"What do you think?" I asked him.

"Well, they'd had a fight," he replied.

Inside I was screaming: *Why didn't you encourage her to leave? Why didn't you say to her, "Baby, you shouldn't be with this monster?"* But I didn't. I'm sure in his own way, Lou Brown was suffering terribly. Maybe he was saying those same things to himself. Maybe. But I had to keep my mouth shut. You cannot afford to alienate a witness.

CAR TAPE. *December 16, 1994. We have to go out and see the Browns again this Sunday. This case is kicking all my personal issues. . . . That little girl, Nicole, never had a chance. What a tortured life she led. I don't think she ever had much peace.*

I can't talk about this anymore. . . .

I was dashing around Glendale trying to run a month's worth of errands in two hours and log a few minutes of car tape in the process, when the earth seemed to give way under me. I felt queer and shaky. I had to pull into a parking lot.

That little girl, Nicole, never had a chance. . . . I shut off the tape and rested my head on the steering wheel. I really *couldn't* talk about it anymore.

The case was taking its toll on me. The stress. The long hours. That's the punishment you expect as a prosecutor. But the type of battering this case was giving me was of a more hurtful, insidious order. It had come to the point where the mention of Nicole's name caused me pain.

On the face of things, there were not many points of similarity between Nicole and me. She'd been a WASP goddess in a white Ferrari. I was a scrappy Jewish civil servant with a swamp for a bedroom. What are the odds that two such dissimilar women could experience anything close to the same kind of misery? And yet, so many details from her brief and tormented life seemed to resonate with my own.

In early December, Nicole's divorce lawyers at had messengered us a packet of documents. These included a deposition Nicole had given Simpson's attorneys in the interest of establishing her own inability to support herself. Within its pages, Nicole's true helplessness showed through with painful clarity.

She told how she'd tried her hand at interior decorating, but her only "clients" had been her husband and his friends. She'd thought about going into the restaurant business or starting up a coffee bar with Faye Resnick. You could see her turning over and over in her mind the alternatives that would reduce her dependence upon O. J. Simpson's money. She was looking not only for a job, but for a career—one that would support her and give a sense of purpose to her life.

"I'm sure I'll get a goal someday," she'd told them. That plaintive line struck me to the heart.

Nicole had the right instincts. She knew the way to save herself was to find a career. She just couldn't connect, somehow. Lack of talent? Lack of drive? I don't know. When all is said and done, not enough of Nicole was revealed in these documents to answer those questions. Whenever I was tempted to fault her for having stayed in that awful relationship for fifteen years—seventeen if you count the fitful two years after the divorce—I took stock and realized that my own first marriage had lasted for five, eight if you count the time Gaby and I lived together. What tricks do we play on ourselves, to linger so long in hell?

These were not thoughts I shared with anyone at the office. At least not directly. Whenever I met with our domestic violence experts, Lydia Bodin and Scott Gordon, I'd ply them with questions.

"Why the hell didn't she cut and run?" I'd ask Scott.

"Minimizing" was what he called it. He told me, "Women who are in abusive relationships downplay the seriousness of their own circumstances. They deny it to themselves. They present a brave front to others, trying to hold things together. It's a coping mechanism."

Minimizing. That certainly hit me where I lived. *Nothing's wrong here. I can get this thing back under control. Just don't admit that there's a problem.*

Scott, of course, was delighted by my newfound interest in DV. Since the beginning, he'd been arguing to me and anyone else who'd listen that domestic violence was the cornerstone of this case. I'd remained aloof, but through sheer persistence, he'd picked up advocates. When, in early October, I finally assigned Chris Darden to this detail, the domestic violence movement within our office gained even more momentum.

Chris, Scott, Lydia, and Hank Goldberg, a fellow D.A. who was terrific at writing motions, worked like Trojans to document incidences of O. J. Simpson's brutality toward Nicole. This was not easy to do. As I've said, an abuser does not normally hit his victim in the presence of others. So, as a starting point, they turned to an inventory Nicole had compiled at the suggestion of her divorce lawyers. According to this document, she'd gotten her first beating right after she started to live with O. J. Simpson. A year or so later, while they were staying at the Sherry Netherland in New York City, Simpson beat Nicole for hours as she crawled for the door. From her diaries we had Nicole's own description of how he "hit me while he fucked me." How he called her mother a "whore." These violent episodes continued throughout the eighties.

Chris, it turned out, had an excellent way with the domestic violence witnesses. He was calm, reassuring, patient. He managed to get Denise Brown to recall an upsetting episode. The scene was Rockingham, where Denise and her date were hanging out after an evening with O.J. and Nicole. Everybody was drunk. Denise blurted that she thought O.J. took Nicole for granted—and Simpson blew. He grabbed his guests and his wife and flung them, one by one, onto the lawn.

Chris also turned up a woman named Connie Good, whose boyfriend had lived next door to Nicole's apartment in 1977 or 1978. She told how on one evening in particular, while she was visiting, she'd heard screaming from Nicole's apartment. She'd also heard thuds.

"Sounded like it was either on the floor or against the wall," she recalled. Simpson was shouting, "Fucking bitch!" Later, Good ran into Nicole in the elevator; the girl had two black eyes.

The DV dragnet turned up something else especially heartbreaking. Sojourn, a battered-women's hotline out of Santa Monica, reported taking a call five days before the murder from a woman in West L.A. Her name was Nicole. She had two children and she was frightened because her ex-husband was stalking her. She'd called the cops more than eight times. Their response? "Nothing much ever done."

As the evidence mounted, Chris and Scott put more pressure on me to give domestic violence a bigger role in the case.

"This is not some murder that incidentally involved domestic violence," Scott would tell me. "It's a domestic violence case that ended in murder."

I had to admit that this approach afforded us a solid legal advantage. If we identified this as a domestic violence case that ended in murder, we could argue that the incidents of abuse that led up to the crime should be admissible. Being able to present those attacks in open court might have two beneficial effects: one, to strip the jury of their rosy illusions about the defendant; two, to give us the opportunity to present a compelling motive for murder.

Scott was pressing me to meet with a couple of domestic violence experts he'd brought in from out of town, Angela Brown and Dr. Donald Dutton. I kept putting him off. Finally, we'd run out of time. I remember very clearly one afternoon in mid-December when both experts had been hanging around all day to meet with me and Chris. Dr. Dutton had to get back to British Columbia. I looked at my watch. God—it was 8:30. They'd been waiting for me for more than five hours. I felt horribly embarrassed.

I grabbed my notebooks and ran to Scott's cubicle. There, I found Donald, in his tweedy jacket and sensible shoes, and Angela, in her long, flowing skirt and silk drape blouse, sitting on the floor in Scott's cubicle, surrounded by their binders and notes. I threw myself on their mercy.

"Do you have another hour or so of energy to talk to me?" I asked.

"I think we're kind of bushed, to tell you the truth, Marcia," Don replied. "But if you want to join us, we could probably continue our discussion for a bit over cocktails, hey?"

We went over to the Inter-Continental Hotel, where Chris joined us. There, we ended up engaging in one of the liveliest and most perceptive discussions any of us had ever had about the case.

The question pressing most heavily on my mind was whether, given all we knew of the Simpsons' relationship and the events leading up to June 12, the experts would have predicted that Simpson was about to erupt into a homicidal rage. Was this murder the result of a long-standing plan, or one formulated on the night it was committed?

The critical variable, Don Dutton explained, was "estrangement." When Nicole didn't invite Simpson to sit with her at Sydney's dance recital, when she declined to invite him to join them at Mezzaluna, she made a public declaration of her independence and embarrassed him in front of friends and family.

"A rebuff equals incitement to murder?" I asked, still incredulous. A month ago I would have had a hard time buying this proposition. But Don now made a cogent argument for how O. J. Simpson would have overreacted to rejection. His overweening ego and controlling behavior masked a fundamentally flawed, insecure, and extremely immature personality. To such an unstable man, violence would seem a justifiable means of reestablishing control.

Still, I wondered silently, why would *these* snubs, *this* evening, have proved so incendiary? Two years earlier, Nicole had divorced him, a development that he appeared to take with comparative equanimity. I suspected that there had to have been something else that incited him—and that it had to do with a string of calls made from the cell phone in his Bronco that night to Paula Barbieri. Paula, of course, was continuing to elude us, so I didn't know for sure what had gone down. But my guess was that Simpson's frustration over his inability to reach her that night had spilled over in rage against Nicole. The first time Nicole dumped him, he'd had Paula to catch him. The second time, he went into free fall.

Months later, of course, this hunch would prove correct. In a deposition given at the civil trial, Paula would testify that she had left a "Dear John" message on Simpson's machine the afternoon before the murders. It was *clearly* the emotional trigger. We certainly could have used it at the criminal trial.

Thanks loads, Paula.

After that night of conversation, the domestic violence advocates finally won me over. I felt they should be allowed to take their best shot. So I gave them my blessing to draft a motion asking the court to allow into evidence all the incidents of domestic violence they had worked so hard to unearth.

The Dream Team, of course, fought tooth and nail to keep that motion under seal. Up to that point, they'd more or less succeeded in advancing the fiction that Simpson was a decent guy who had just hit a rough patch in his marriage. Now, he was about to be unmasked as a sadist.

The defense managed to get the hearing delayed for a month, until the jurors were safely sequestered at the Inter-Continental Hotel. For now, domestic violence was temporarily on hold.

While Chris and crew were planning their DV offensive, I'd remained on the sidelines of the action. I'd been up to my ears preparing the physical evidence, which was turning out to be a monumentally complicated task. All along, I'd expected Barry Scheck to object to the admissibility of the DNA test results. That meant we could look forward to a set of what are called *Kelly-Frye* hearings that would take us well past the first of the year. Suddenly, without warning, they changed their game plan.

I heard about it one Sunday morning, after a late night of work capped off by a game of pool and a shot of Glenlivet. Suzanne called to say that Art Harris at CNN was trying to get in touch with me. I had played phone tag with him the day before, but figured he had just wanted some inside skinny. As it turned out, he had something to tell me: the Simpson team was going to withdraw their challenge to the DNA evidence. On one level, this shouldn't have surprised me. We'd known all along that they wanted to rush us into trial as quickly as possible—and cut our preparation time as much as possible. It also kept Simpson's public image as a celebrity fresh in the public's mind—the longer he sat in jail, the more like a criminal he would seem.

Even so, on hearing the news, I went into shock. I'd been planning on taking a lot of the physical-evidence witnesses, like Dennis Fung and Greg Matheson, myself. But the chunk of time I was counting on to prepare that part of the case—and maybe even have a day or two at home over Christmas—would now be gone. I am such an anal-retentive overpreparer by nature that this news from Art conjured up my personal vision of hell. I would have to pedal twice as fast just to finish everything I had to get done on my own part of the case as well as keeping an eye on the work of others.

It was at that point, I think, that I realized the impossibility of adequately preparing for the trial, now set to start in mid- to late January. The stress was getting to me. Most of the time, I felt ill. I suffered from respiratory ailments, head colds, aching joints. And these disturbing new illnesses were compounded by bouts of bone-crushing fatigue. I had enough self-awareness to realize where this was leading me. And I didn't want to go there.

Not again.

When I was very new at this job, I had an experience that left me badly shaken. I'd been a D.A. only about six months when I prosecuted my first rape case. The victim asked that she be assigned a woman prosecutor. I was the only one available.

I met the victim outside the courtroom before the preliminary hearing. She was a light-skinned black woman with close-cropped hair and wire-rimmed glasses. She looked about my age—mid-twenties—and had an average build. She'd been waiting forever for a bus, and she was late for work. Out of nowhere a man pulled up in a car and offered to give her a ride. She hesitated but she wasn't going very far and he seemed okay, so she agreed. He pulled into an alley—and raped her. She'd been able to escape from the car and made her way to an emergency room, where the police were called. They caught the guy the same day.

I was impressed by this woman. She was calm, articulate, conservatively dressed. She was going to make a terrific witness. Since it was my first rape case, I remember taking what seemed to me awkward steps to reassure her.

"You only have to look at him once to identify him for the judge," I told her. "Other than that, you can look at me, and when his lawyer's asking you questions, you can look at the lawyer. If you need a break, say so. I'll make sure it happens. . . . You're to be treated with respect, and I'm here to make sure of it."

How do you comfort someone like that when you haven't been in her shoes? I squeezed her hand and gave her my phone number.

She smiled and thanked me.

I went back to work. An hour later my head was throbbing. My bones ached. My skin hurt. Down in the courtroom, I could barely stand up to handle a motion for a continuance. The defense attorney actually looked over at me and said, "Go home. It's making me hurt just to look at you."

I did go home. And when I got there I crawled right into bed. I was burning with fever. Then freezing. Then burning again. I took my temperature: 103 degrees. As I lay there shivering, I wondered how this could have come on so suddenly. I'd felt perfectly fine that morning. All the way up until the interview. What was it about the interview? Slowly, as though curtains of gauze were parting in my head, I saw unfold a series of events that had occurred almost ten years earlier.

*   *   *

I was almost seventeen and I'd just finished high school. As a graduation gift, my parents sent me on a Jewish youth group tour to Europe. I was one of about thirty girls in a group that ranged in age from sixteen to twenty-five. I think I was the only one from California; the rest of them were from around New York. When we landed in Europe, we were bused to a resort and parceled off in groups of four into a cluster of little huts.

We went to dinner that night in the hotel dining room, where we occupied one long table. We were attended by two waiters, young men in their twenties, who were clearly delighted at having exclusive access to a group of young American tourists. One of the waiters, a stocky dark man, spent a lot of time leaning over my shoulder and brushing against me. After dinner, he and his buddy invited the entire group to join them at a nearby restaurant-bar. Everyone agreed, except me. I was tired and didn't like to party in large groups. But the waiter who'd been dogging me was persistent.

"Come with us," he urged me. "You'll have fun. You can't just sit in a room by yourself."

Once again, I refused.

The others left. I went back to the hut. It was empty and I enjoyed the first few moments of solitude I'd been able to steal since leaving the States. I flopped down on the hard bed and fell asleep.

It seemed only a few minutes later when I felt a weight on the edge of my bed. I opened my eyes and saw to my shock the waiter who'd been coming on to me at dinner. I was paralyzed with fright. I remember that he was trying to talk to me and then he started to stroke my hair. I pulled away and asked him to leave. He said he wouldn't until I came with him. I knew I had to get him out of that room.

I found myself walking around the grounds of the resort with a man who had broken into my room. I simply did not know how to get free from him. I suppose I could have run, but I was held there by some inexplicable imperative not to offend him. *Pretend everything is all right,* I told myself, *and it will be.*

It was so strange. His manner was uncomfortably intimate, yet somehow respectful. I let him lead me into a "club." It wasn't a bar in the usual sense. There was no hard liquor, just beer and wine. There was a jukebox that played local hits, and everyone was eating watermelon and dancing. I spotted some of my friends from the tour, and that put me more at ease. My companion guided me to a table near the window, left me for a moment, then returned with a couple of plates of watermelon. I ordered a Coke.

Pretty soon we were talking easily. I'd begun to doubt my own senses. Had I not awakened in terror only a couple of hours earlier to find this man sitting on my bed? Had I dreamed that? No, of course not. I wouldn't even be here now, sharing a bright comfortable space, with my friends all around me, if he hadn't broken into my room.

My "companion" had launched into a long narrative about himself. Waiting tables was just a temporary thing. It gave him quick money until he could figure out what to do with his life. When a stranger shares his aspirations with you, it somehow inspires confidence. Perhaps I'd been spooked too easily.

After an hour or so we left the club to take a walk. I noticed that it was getting harder and harder to hear him. A strong, hot wind had kicked up and it was whistling past my ears, carrying his words away. I had to ask him to repeat himself over and over again, even though he was only about a foot away. He suggested that we sit on the steps of the hotel restaurant where we'd had dinner earlier, so we could hear each another.

"I have a bunch of records in my room," he told me. "Why don't you come over and I'll play them for you?"

I loved music and the idea of being out of this eerie wind listening to R&B seemed comforting just then. Still . . . He sensed my indecision and put a hand on my arm.

"Look, I feel so close to you. I feel like a brother to you. You're almost ten years younger than me. I know you'll like the music. We'll listen to a few records, and then I'll walk you back to your room."

As we walked toward his room, I tried to get my bearings. Where was my hut? Out here in the dark they all looked alike.

His room was bare. It contained only a chest of drawers and a nightstand. A small record player, the kind that's obsolete nowadays, sat on the top of the dresser. There were no chairs, so I perched primly on the edge of the bed—legs crossed, back hunched, my arms around my knees—while he selected a record.

Fever

247

Within moments he was seated next to me, whispering in my ear how pretty I was and how much he liked me. I pulled away, confused and betrayed.

"What are you doing?" I complained.

He leaped over to the door and threw the bolt. When I tried to follow he turned and fixed me with a hard, determined look.

"Don't make me hurt you," he said.

I began to scream, but no one came.

"No one can hear you," he hissed. "Not over the winds tonight."

I began to gag on my own tears as he straddled me, ripped open my light cotton pants, and raped me.

It was over in seconds. As I lay there sobbing, he took my face in his hands and said, "Now, you will never tell anyone about this. And when you leave tomorrow you will say good-bye to me sweetly or I'll make you sorry. Do you hear?"

Too terrified to object, I nodded.

"Good," he said. "Now I will walk you back to your room. Fix your pants."

I looked down at my pants. The zipper was completely ripped out. I held them together at the waist as I stumbled out the door behind him. I know he spoke to me as we walked back to my hut, but I couldn't hear what he was saying because the winds were still strong and I was lost in a world of pain.

After he left me at the door, I waited for him to be gone before I looked inside the room. I prayed that no one would be there. I couldn't stand the idea of being seen by anyone. I felt dirty, worthless.

The hut was empty. I hurried inside, yanked off my pants, balled them up, and hid them. Then, carefully, I put on a new pair and sat on the floor, unable to think of any way to make the pain to go away. And then I remembered the sea.

The hut was near the beach. I walked out to the shore until the waves came up over my bare ankles. The water was warm, somehow reassuring. I waded in up to my knees. It was very shallow near the shore. I had to go out quite a ways before the water reached my shoulders. I let myself be lifted and lowered by the gentle waves. In that numbed state it would have been so easy for me just to drift away.

I watched the shimmer of lights across the dark expanse of water to the north. They were lovely. And when I found myself admiring their beauty I became aware of myself again. In an instant, the numbness gave way to anger. *What am I doing? I should destroy myself for what he did to me?* I was up to my nose in brine, when I just exploded in rage. "No!" I screamed. And I began to swim back to shore.

The next morning when we boarded the bus, my attacker smiled at me, waiting for his big good-bye. I stared right through him.

Over the next few days my group leader noticed my withdrawal and took me aside.

"Just a mood," I told her. "I'll get over it."

And I did. I willed myself to. I buried that memory good and deep. Ten years later it came hurtling up through layers of defenses in a blazing fever.

I knew how to minimize. Boy, did I ever. And as a result, I'd learned the power of memories denied. In December 1994, I saw my own memories reemerge. Nicole Simpson had awakened them. I found myself flashing on old arguments, screaming matches, shoving matches, and tearful reunions. Events that had seemed only bizarre at the time replayed themselves now in a more sinister light.

One episode in particular haunted me. During one of my many separations from Gaby, I was staying in a girlfriend's apartment. A neighbor called the police to report a prowler. In fact, it had been Gaby lurking around my patio. I didn't know about any of this until he called me from jail, frantic. They'd taken his shoes and belt and he was confined to a small cell.

"Get me out of here," he demanded. "Now!"

I didn't have any money, so I ran around that night collecting bail money from various "contacts." Then I raced down to the police station.

I'd never been in a jail before. I was relieved to find the watch commander a cheerful, matter-of-fact guy who stared in disbelief when I told him I was there to bail out Gaby. It was a "What are you doing with an asshole like that?" sort of look. As I paid out the money, I could see Gaby pacing his cell like a cat. I thought he'd be furious, but he was just so relieved to be sprung he grabbed me and kissed me. I lived with him for two more years.

At the time, I accepted these events as normal. Only now did I finally get it. I was being *stalked*, for God's sake. Not only had I been stalked, but I went to the jail to bail out my stalker! The parallels with Nicole Brown Simpson's life were chilling.

Memories. Once you unleash them, you have to be prepared to reckon with them. In the interest of self-preservation, I made a decision to suppress certain ugly realities about my life with Gaby.

As I look back on it, I can see that others about me were doing the same thing. What I had seen in the Browns as disengagement was, I realize now, an attempt to protect themselves from the ravages of memory. Not that I wasn't angered by their stonewalling, but as the New Year dawned, I felt infinitely more compassion for their plight. Denial is sometimes the only comfort you can offer yourself. Because once you let yourself feel, the misery is endless.

The Empty Chair

CAR TAPE. *It's now January sixth. Fifth. Something like that. It's Thursday after New Year's Eve. We worked all through New Year's Eve, New Year's Day. Finally took Monday off.*

We mapped out our whole trial strategy. Bill wasn't there Saturday and we finished the whole thing. Me and Hank and Chris got through the whole map of the case, which was wonderful. Bill came in on Sunday. . . . Having Chris in there—he's tough, he's a fighter, he's smart and when he gets in to do something I know he's gonna do it perfectly.

By New Year's, just three weeks before opening statements were set to begin, Bill Hodgman was fading before my eyes. He grew thinner and more haggard with each passing day. He wouldn't talk to me about what was bothering him. All he would say was that he wasn't sleeping well.

That was clear. His eyes were always bloodshot. His face was etched with fatigue. He was trying to hang in there with all the strength he could muster; I could see him struggling to get through the inhuman workload we labored under every day. But after his scuffle with the seventy-one-year-old black juror back in October, he had been out sick with the flu, or some mysterious stomach ailment, almost constantly. Bill was clearly wrestling with his own demons. Believe me, I could sympathize. Yet neither of us felt comfortable confiding our personal problems to the other. So I could only guess at what was eating him.

Bill just didn't seem prepared to do what was required in this case: get in there and kick the shit out of the defense. Shortly after that weird episode with the juror, he got sucked into another bullshit controversy.

O. J. Simpson had been receiving jailhouse visits from Roosevelt Grier, a former NFL defensive lineman who was purportedly now a minister. Grier and the defendant met regularly in a visiting room, where they sat on either side of a glass partition. They spoke to each other by telephone. On December 14, a sheriff's deputy who had been manning the control booth supposedly heard Simpson slam down the receiver and blurt out something that could have been interpreted as a confession. (The *National Enquirer* would later report an unidentified source at the jail as saying that Simpson, who was holding a Bible at the time, had exclaimed, "I did it.")

But when all this came down, no one in the D.A.'s office had a clue as to what Simpson had actually said. Ito had ordered the sheriffs not to say anything, and they were so scared of bad press they wouldn't even tell us on the QT. The deputies filed a report with the court, but it was kept under seal. And so we found ourselves in a ridiculous position: the Sheriff's Department, the judge, and the defense team all knew what Simpson had said—but we didn't. Roosevelt Grier, of course, knew, but he wasn't telling. He claimed that Simpson's outburst was protected by clergyman-penitent privilege.

We took the position that it was not. For all we knew, Grier had gotten his credentials through a diploma mill. So we filed a motion compelling him to testify. Bill and I huddled to decide who should take him. I'd handled most of the motions so far. "It should be you," I told him. I expected that this would be the sort of civilized exchange to which Bill was well suited. Grier had a reputation as a decent, principled guy. I thought he might actually welcome the opportunity to offer his testimony in a neutral and forthright manner.

My hopes quickly faded once we got to the courtroom. As Grier hulked to the witness stand, I could see that he was going to be a real handful. He carried a Bible, which he clutched as tightly as a fumbled football recovered from the twenty-yard line. He made no bones about which side he favored. He glared at Bill angrily and gave evasive, curt answers. He described his visits to Simpson as "Bible-reading sessions." Bill had to bob and weave through Johnnie Cochran's objections, as the Dream Team continued to insist that nothing from the so-called Bible-reading sessions could be admissible—that even a discussion of the Rams' chances against the 49ers was covered by privilege.

Simpson beamed as Ito let them have that one. Bill tried another tack. Under oath, the deputies had described Simpson as "upset . . . very loud, in a raised voice . . . yelling." Bill suggested that because Simpson was shouting so loudly, he'd waived confidentiality. Did Simpson indeed raise his voice over normal speaking levels? Bill asked Grier.

"No, sir," he snapped, icily.

Bill was really rattled. When he returned to the counsel table I leaned over and whispered, "That was a tough one. You did good, partner."

As usual, this wrangling came to no satisfactory conclusion. Ito issued another incomprehensible ruling. He agreed that Simpson had indeed shouted loudly enough for bystanders to hear him and thus had technically waived his privilege. But he—Ito—was the one who had instructed the Sheriff's Department to set up a private receiving room for Simpson's visitors. Now, he reasoned, these special accommodations (which, incidentally, did not include soundproofing and required the presence of a guard) had lulled Simpson into mistakenly believing that his conversations could not be overheard. In accordance with this Alice-in-Wonderland logic, he gave the decision to the defense.

Once again, Bill and I just looked at each other and shook our heads in angry amazement. We'd just been denied a possible admission of guilt.

And the episode turned out to be a disaster for Bill. Right after Grier's appearance, a local newspaper columnist, Bill Boyarsky, scolded Bill in print for referring to the witness as "Mr." rather than

"Reverend." This was idiotic. First of all, as one etiquette specialist later pointed out, referring to a man of the cloth as "Mr." is perfectly respectful. But even that is beside the point. One of the very issues we were there to determine was whether Grier really *was* a minister! Even so, Boyarsky's was the kind of criticism that should roll right off your back. But Bill took it to heart. The morning after the Grier episode, he called in sick again. Hank Goldberg and I had to scramble to put on the rest of the witnesses.

It is difficult for an outsider to imagine the pressures upon Bill Hodgman. All of us felt them. Beyond the usual rub of egos between attorneys and judge, we had those goddamned media commentators weighing in on a daily basis with win-loss tallies. That kind of scrutiny created a petty, puerile competition for media attention among the lawyers. I had long since resolved not to read or watch the press accounts of the trial—it was just too painful to see everything we did twisted, mangled, and misunderstood over and over again.

Nonetheless, I felt their impact in court. Every motion became an opportunity to grab headlines or sound bites that would run on the six o'clock news. Every time the defense gained a tiny, often insignificant, advantage, Bob and Johnnie would race each other to the lectern to give an interminable, meaningless oration. I would lean over to Chris and ask, "What the hell is he talking about?" And Chris would reply, "Man, don't you watch TV?"

That was the great thing about Chris. He could put a setback into perspective with a quip. I found myself turning to him more and more for advice and support.

Since October, when I'd appointed him case manager, his cubicle had become the center of a beehive of activity. The cheap metal partitions had been rearranged to convert it to what Bill Hodgman liked to call the War Room. (Prosecutors love military talk. I, like many of my fellow deputies in Special Trials, had a big old metal cart that I'd load with briefs and haul down to court. Everyone called it the War Wagon.)

Chris's cubicle was a little bigger than the others and it was the only one of the bunch with its own access to the hallway: the cubicle dweller's equivalent of a corner office. In one corner stood a three-foot-high Bart Simpson doll someone had given Chris as a joke. There was also a photograph of him hugging it. We all started calling his cubicle the Roy Pod, a reference to the habit Chris and his two investigators had of referring to each another as "Roy." Some weird inside joke. He loved the nickname so much that he ordered up special team hats with "ROY" stitched on them. He tried to give me one that read "ROY TOY."

"In your dreams, buster," I told him.

Chris hired five very talented law clerks. He had also brought on several Grade 1—entry-level—D.A.s. These "babycakes," as he called them, were outstanding—eager, bright, dedicated, and willing to do anything asked of them, no matter how menial.

I was used to trying my cases alone: researching, writing, interviewing, and investigating. Everyone in Special Trials did that. So it was awkward for me at first, adjusting to the idea of clerks doing my drudge work. But during the pretrial months it became clear to me I couldn't afford my usual approach. I was overseeing virtually every aspect of the case; when anyone had a question about *anything* they came to me. My bosom buddy and fellow D.A., Cheri Lewis, once threw her body across the door to block access to all comers until I had signed a document she had thrust under my nose. And of course, the defense was still bombarding us with spurious and time-consuming motions. The hours I would normally have had free for holing up in my office to work were being spent in court arguing. For the first time in my life, I *had* to delegate responsibility.

Chris had no trouble delegating. It used to crack me up. I'd pass the Roy Pod and find him reclining far back in his chair gazing at the ceiling. He'd be surrounded by babycakes who were either taking dictation, listening to him ruminate upon strategy, or just paying homage. I took to calling him "King Chris." As time went on, Chris came to believe that the Pod was not a suitably impressive headquarters for a case manager. So he demanded and got an office next to mine.

Chris could be that way: jealous of his prerogatives and sullen when he didn't get what he wanted. He was competitive. He didn't seem to like Rockne Harmon and George "Woody" Clarke, two deputies we'd brought in from outside the county to handle DNA. Chris considered them interlopers and potential rivals. No question, Chris could be a pain in the ass—but he was a creative, battle-hardened trial lawyer. And he brought a lot of life and humor to the place. I needed him.

On Tuesday and Thursday nights, we'd go out after work. The group usually included me; Cheri Lewis; Chris; my clerk, Dana Escobar; Chris's clerk, David Wooden; and Lisa Kahn's clerk, Diana Martinez, who was so tough we referred to her as "the President of All the Women." We'd truck on over to the Saratoga, a tiny bar and grill about a mile from the courthouse. It was owned by a Yugoslavian family who just loved us. They'd open the kitchen and cook us dinner. Their specialties were steak and fish, which were a little heavy for me at that hour. Although they didn't normally serve salads, they'd indulge me with a plate of sliced cucumbers and tomatoes.

We'd always sit in the Booth, a table for eight at the back of the restaurant. One of the two TVs mounted at either end of the bar was easily visible from this spot, and on a good night they'd let us control the remote. The cops and firemen who hung off the bar stools were always buying us rounds. I don't think I ever paid for a drink at the Saratoga. I felt safe there.

These times were especially sweet when we had some small victory to celebrate. Like when each new blood-evidence result came in, pointing the finger of guilt at no one but the defendant. "Man," someone would say, "we got the motherfucker cold. Even the *jury* has to see it." And we'd laugh. Chris and I knew what this brave talk was: whistling past the graveyard. You had to rattle sabers to ward off despair. The veterans at the table realized that. The clerks didn't: they took the victory talk at face value. I worried about them. They had so little life experience to fall back on. How, I wondered, would they handle a bitter defeat?

On January 11, the twelve jurors and twelve alternates were formally sequestered at the Inter-Continental Hotel. Now that they were theoretically safe from the polluting effects of the media, Lance Ito finally gave us the go-ahead to argue our domestic violence motion, the conduit for getting the battering incidents into evidence.

On the defense side, Gerry Uelmen, former dean at Santa Clara

University School of Law, had been assigned to damage control. His first request was to ask that the victims' families be excluded from the courtroom. I'm frankly surprised that he had the nerve to try this. The Dream Team must have dreaded the idea of tears and outbursts—sure to underscore the fact that their client was not such a nice guy. But taking on the victims' families was a risky public relations move.

"I'm offended by it," Chris Darden objected. "And I'm sure the victims' families are offended by the request."

Ito let the families stay.

Uelmen then pointed a finger at the prosecution, accusing us of slapping the "label" of domestic violence upon this case to prejudice the public against the defendant. Statistically speaking, he explained, fewer than one percent of all cases of domestic violence end in murder.

"When we look at what was obviously a bumpy marriage," he assured the court, "I think it is quite remarkable that it was resolved in as amicable a way as it was."

What the defense had done was turn logic on its head. It fell to Scott Gordon to correct the misimpression. If you looked at studies of women killed by a husband or boyfriend, he explained, fully *90 percent* of the victims had reported at least one prior act of abuse. Furthermore, the murder of Nicole Brown Simpson fit the profile of a domestic violence murder: the killer usually bludgeons, strangles, or stabs his victim, or slashes her throat.

Lydia Bodin then went methodically through the time line of terror. She cited over *sixty* incidents beginning in 1977, when Connie Good saw Nicole Brown in the elevator with two black eyes, bringing the court up through the IRS letter and the events on the afternoon of June 12. And all the while, O. J. Simpson rolled his eyes, looked disgusted, laughed, and joked with his attorneys. His behavior would have been scandalous even if he were innocent of these crimes. What did he feel he could gain, I wondered, by appearing so callous?

Within the week, Lance Ito handed down his ruling. The jury could hear about the 1989 New Year's Eve beating. They could hear about the incident in 1985 where Simpson broke the windshield of his car with a baseball bat. They could hear about the 1993 call to 911 when Simpson broke Nicole's door. They could hear evidence from Keith Zlomsowitch and others about how the defendant had stalked Nicole. And finally we got in that IRS letter.

That decision was hailed as a victory for our side. But I could manage only a feeble hurrah. For one thing, there was a lot of important stuff that didn't make it in: Nicole's journals (though privately I'd known all along this was a long shot). And there was the testimony of the witness named Nancy Ney, who'd answered Nicole's call for help on the Sojourn hotline. These items were ruled hearsay and therefore inadmissible. But they weren't the omissions that concerned me most.

Back in December the defense had complained that we'd given them the domestic violence stuff so late that they could not respond to it. In fact, Chris and his team pulled it together as quickly as they possibly could. It was just an enormously time-consuming effort—complicated by the fact that Faye Resnick, the one person who could help us with real leads, did not cooperate with us until October, after her book was published. To sanction us for this supposed tardiness, Ito split the testimony in half, forcing us to hold off revealing the older episodes of abuse—including Connie Good's 1977 testimony, until later in the trial. Unfortunately, the power of these episodes was cumulative. You had to start from the beginning in order to see the pattern of pathological sadism. Lance had, once again, made a misguided attempt at compromise, and in doing so, he'd crippled our domestic violence case from its infancy.

On the evening the ruling came down, I joined my colleagues at the Saratoga to celebrate. Yet, as I slid into the Booth, shoulder to shoulder with my ebullient trench buddies, I felt miles apart from them. Chris, Scott, Lydia, and their adherents were right, of course. This *was* a case of domestic violence that ended in murder. But I knew from experience, both personal and professional, that the very mention of the words "domestic violence" aroused volatile emotions in people. There was no telling what kind of response they might elicit from our jury. The fact that most of our jurors were women was no comfort to me: female jurors often view victims of domestic violence with uncomprehending disdain. On top of this, we had the complications of race and celebrity. This did not mean that our female jurors couldn't be brought around, but we would have to proceed cautiously.

If it appeared that the domestic violence evidence was alienating our jury, someone would have to make the strategic call to stand down. It would not be a popular move, certainly not within our office. But somewhere down the line a tough decision might have to be made. And even as I lifted a glass to victory, I realized the person to make it would have to be me.

It was barely ten days before opening arguments were set to begin. For several weeks now, I'd been channeling work away from Bill onto Chris's desk. I knew that Bill was not feeling well, and I didn't want to overtax him. Chris was worried that Bill would feel we were pushing him out.

"No," I told him. "We just have to take some of the weight off of him for a while."

Late one night in mid-January, Chris and I met in his office for an informal strategy session.

"Hey, G," he greeted me, "pull up a chair." Chris had started calling me G, for "gangster," an expression of friendship and respect in his old neighborhood.

We were the only ones around. Out of his desk drawer he pulled two bottles: tequila for himself, Glenlivet for me. He poured us each a drink.

I ran down a list of witnesses in the order I envisioned presenting them. Chris would open with the domestic violence witnesses. Then I would be up with the next twenty or so witnesses, including Kato and Allan Park, whose testimony was going to be extremely complex. By now they'd both given so many statements, the task of collating them was daunting. Plus, I had to coordinate all the diagrams, charts, and photographs. It was like completing a giant Rubik's Cube, where all the squares on each side had to match. Everyone else could compart-mentalize, but I had to keep my eye on our overall strategy.

I'd given Bill the coroner, Dr. Irwin Golden, whose testimony promised to be a real can of worms. Hank Goldberg had agreed to take the criminalists, Dennis Fung and Andrea Mazzola, which was equally unenviable duty. Woody Clarke and Rock Harmon would do DNA. Chris wanted to pick up some of the physical evidence—which really was the heart of the case. But he had no special expertise in DNA, blood, or hair and trace; it would have taken too long to get him up to speed. That left him with nothing but domestic violence witnesses. These would go quickly. If he didn't pick up some additional turf now, he would be effectively out of the case after the first week of trial. Chris didn't want that; I didn't either.

That left Fuhrman.

By now Fuhrman's file was even fatter than when I'd first reviewed it, and infinitely more depressing. In addition to the psychiatrists' evaluations of 1981 and 1982, there was now the witness statement from a realtor named Kathleen Bell, who had told defense investigators that five years earlier she had met Fuhrman at a marine recruiting station in Redondo Beach. He'd supposedly told her that if he saw a black man driving in a car with a white woman, he would pull them over. If he didn't have a good reason, he said, he'd "find one." Fuhrman, according to Bell's account, went on to say that if he had his way he'd see all "niggers" gathered together and burned or bombed.

When I read that, I felt I might be sick.

In the months since the trial, some Monday-morning quarterbacks have claimed that I was arrogant for using Mark Fuhrman, knowing his downside. Exactly what was I to do? Close my eyes, click my heels three times, and will him to disappear? From the day of the murders, the defense had access to the police reports identifying Mark as the officer who found the bloody glove. If we hadn't called him, they certainly would have. And in doing so they would certainly have explored his dark side. We would have been left looking like we were trying to hide him. As I saw it, we had no choice but to brass it out.

Chris and I had talked all the way through this one. Fuhrman's racial views were not pertinent here. How he'd performed as a detective on the Simpson investigation was all that counted. The idea that he had planted the glove was utterly fantastic. Cops who arrived on the crime scene before Fuhrman had seen only one glove—not two—lying between the victims. What were the Dream Teamers planning to suggest—that Mark had slipped out to Bloomingdale's to buy a mate?

Still, taking on Fuhrman stood to be extremely stressful.

"It can't be Bill who takes him," I told Chris. "It's gotta be you or me. If you don't want to touch him, I understand. This one is going to be a bitch."

Chris was quiet for a moment, his shaved head buried in his hands. Then he looked me in the eye. No matter where we went with this, there was danger ahead. He knew I wouldn't ask him to do anything that I wouldn't do. He also knew I was carrying the entire weight of this case on my shoulders.

"I'll take him," he told me quietly. "But I'm telling you, that motherfucker better tell me everything, and I mean *everything*. I don't want any surprises."

I was praying for a miracle: namely, that Chris and Mark would hit it off. No such luck. They hated each other on sight. I wasn't there for their first meeting, which was held in Chris's office during the first or second week of January. But afterward, Chris came to me complaining that Fuhrman was arrogant. Mark, in turn, complained to Cheri that Chris was hostile and insensitive to his situation. I gotta hand it to Chris, though: he did not bail on me. He hung right in to argue a very unpleasant motion.

We knew that Johnnie and the Dream Team were angling to introduce Fuhrman's disability file, and the Bell statement, which would allow them to argue that Mark's "racial animus" drove him to frame Simpson by planting the glove at Rockingham.

I favored a preemptive strike. I wanted to get Ito to make a decisive call right up front that would foreclose this race strategy before opening statements—when I knew Johnnie would be trying to play that card for all it was worth.

It should have been an easy call. Other cops who'd arrived at Bundy before Fuhrman saw only one glove. There was *never* a second glove that Fuhrman could have picked up and transported to Simpson's house! There was no evidence to show that Fuhrman had ever planted *any* evidence or done anything improper in the case at all. Unless the defense could come up with an offer of proof to show how he could have planted that glove, Fuhrman's racial views, whatever they were, were completely irrelevant.

With Lance, our oral arguments never seemed to carry much weight. I knew our best shot was to get down on paper a motion that was persuasive and compelling enough that he'd convince himself of its wisdom *before* he got to court. So Cheri and I wrote and rewrote that motion.

I knew that it was good. The law was clearly on our side. The drafters of the state evidence code knew that jurors might not be able to resist a strong and irrational emotional reaction to something as inflammatory as a racial slur, even if it had no relevance. It was the very reason the code excluded evidence that was more prejudicial than useful in determining the truth.

There was no question that the lawyer who could most effectively argue the inflammatory effects of racial epithets—particularly the N-word—was Chris Darden.

Chris attacked this mission with righteous conviction. But the night before he was to argue it, he got a case of nerves. He came to my office, his eyes wide and apologetic, and asked for my help. I gave him what I myself would have used: a straight, rather formal, legal argument about how allowing in racial epithets would simply prejudice the jury and obscure the truth.

Then he totally threw out what I had written for him. And when he rose to the lectern on the morning of January 13, he spoke from the heart.

"There is no legal purpose," he said, his voice rich with conviction, "there is no valid or legitimate purpose. But Mr. Cochran and the defense, they have a purpose in going to that area and the purpose is to inflame the passions of the jury and to ask them to pick sides, not on the basis of the evidence in this case. . . . The evidence in this case against this defendant is overwhelming. But when you mention that word to this jury or to any African American, it blinds people. It will blind this jury. It will blind them to the truth. It will cause extreme prejudice to the prosecution's case."

I sucked in my breath. Chris was taking on the race-baiters full in the teeth.

"I remember the first time I was ever called that word," he continued. "I'm sure Mr. Cochran remembers the first time. And whenever I reflect back on that experience, I find it extremely upsetting and I probably appear to be getting a little upset right now. It is probably the most negative experience I have ever had in my life."

I glanced over at Johnnie Cochran. Gone was the easy posture. He was tensed up, like a testy weasel. The chemistry between Chris and Johnnie, I thought, was becoming one of the uglier dynamics in this courtroom. Chris had respected Johnnie so much. But Johnnie didn't respect him back. He couldn't handle another smart and vital black male in the courtroom. Johnnie had played this bullshit race card at scores of other trials where nobody, certainly no white guys, had the *huevos* to call him on it. Now Chris was hitting him where he lived.

Johnnie rose to reply.

"I have a funeral to attend today," he told the court. "But I would be remiss if I were not at this time to take this opportunity to respond to my good friend, Mr. Chris Darden."

His "politesse" was tinged with sarcasm.

"His remarks this morning are perhaps the most incredible remarks I've heard in a court of law in the thirty-two years I've been practicing law. His remarks are demeaning to African Americans as a group. And so I want to apologize to African Americans all over the country."

Apologize for Chris! I couldn't believe what I was hearing. *What are you saying, Johnnie, that people can hear themselves slandered and feel nothing? If I heard that a witness had referred to women as bitches or cunts, do you think that wouldn't affect me?* Now was the time for Judge Lance Ito to shut this travesty down. Any judge with the most rudimentary control of his courtroom would have said, "Don't waste the time of this court, Mr. Cochran. Come up with a proffer to show how it was even possible for Detective Fuhrman to plant that glove. Until you do, we're not talking about race in this case. O. J. Simpson didn't kill her because she was white, and he did not get arrested because he's black."

But Ito let Johnnie flame on. The groundwork had been set for the defense to present for the jury a fantasy that had no place in a court of law.

Chris Darden appeared stricken. And what made things worse was the painful, public nature of his humiliation. The nakedness of it. With the whole nation—indeed, much of the world—watching, Johnnie Cochran accused a brother of selling out his race. What a despicable piece of shit!

I reached for the notepad and scribbled a note to Chris. "You were beautiful," I wrote him. "You were great."

To my deep astonishment, Ito did the right thing. In a ruling that was legally and logically sound, he stated that the defense would not be able to introduce evidence of racial animus unless they made an offer of proof showing how Fuhrman could have planted the glove. He even gave them a deadline: three days. If they could not come up with a proffer by nine A.M., Monday, January 23, there would be no N-words uttered in that courtroom.

I could practically hear the cheers from the eighteenth floor. Now, I thought, we really have a fighting chance.

On Monday morning—put-up-or-shut-up day—Lee Bailey stood and, without so much as a by-your-leave, reopened debate on the subject of racial animus. That he was allowed to do so was completely improper. The ruling had been made! Yet Ito allowed Bailey to rave on, unchecked, about how the N-word went to Fuhrman's credibility.

"I cannot imagine a clearer case," Bailey blustered, "of the defense having an absolute and inalienable, indelible, irrevocable right to smash into any person so low-life as to make those utterances and then to proceed to the witness stand and attempt to incriminate for murder through these defalcations and sporulation a member of the African American race. . . . We're not trying to prove that he planted anything because we don't have to."

(Bailey's testimony sent me reaching for my Webster's, which defines "defalcation" as "embezzlement" and "sporulation" as "the division of spores." He may have been aiming for "spoliation," which I see is defined as "the act of plundering.")

In the face of this thunderous barrage of verbiage, Ito caved—and reversed himself. The defense could present witnesses who claimed to have heard Mark Fuhrman use the N-word within the past ten years.

I have never seen a man with so little spine.

If I had to point to the single most serious error that Ito made during this misbegotten spectacle, I would have to say that it was this inexcusable Fuhrman ruling. Race had no place in this trial. Once Ito had permitted the injection of racial venom, a conviction was remote, if not impossible. There would be at least one juror whose raw feelings would cloud his or her reason. From this point on, I sincerely believe, the best we could ever have hoped for was a hung jury.

I was both furious and demoralized. What we should do, I told myself angrily, was appeal the ruling to a higher court. It's called taking a writ. But this was likely to be an exercise in futility. The Court of Appeals never likes to get involved in evidentiary decisions during the trial. In fact, I'd never heard of the prosecution's winning one of those puppies. Besides, the real danger, of course, was that if I tried to get Ito reversed, he'd be so infuriated that he'd take it out on us for the rest of the case. Just what we needed—to alienate him hopelessly before we even reached opening arguments.

Looking back on this in the clear light of hindsight, though, I can see my reluctance for what it really was—a failure of nerve. I thought that if we could appease Ito and stay in his good graces, he would treat us fairly in front of the jury. If I'd known then what I know now—how he'd swat us around like stepchildren all throughout the trial—I would have taken that writ in the blink of an eye.

I didn't realize that I had nothing to lose. I should have given it my best shot and taken the only opportunity I had to keep the defense from playing the race card.

I didn't. And to this day it remains my most painful regret.

I was exhausted, feeling overwhelmed. Every night, I'd work till midnight, just shut the door and work. One afternoon I took a couple of hours off to get my hair done and I felt like a truant. Of course, I lugged along my law books to make the downtime count.

The next morning, I found myself mired in traffic. The rain was pouring down. I was totally frazzled. At home, my bedroom was leaking, my bed was soaked, and I kept getting sick. At court, they were about to hear a motion, but I was bumper-to-bumper in metal on the freeway. Ito was going to scream at me for being late, I knew it.

Everywhere I turned, I seemed to bang into a wall. There was Ito, increasingly cryptic and vain. He was starting to remind me of Marlon Brando in *Apocalypse Now*. There was Mark Fuhrman, either a bigot or a liar. There was the Brown family, avoiding us, but ladling out facts to a quickie biographer, and I'm thinking that the whole damned publishing world knows more about my case than I do. It was the most ridiculous situation I'd ever seen, and there I was stuck on the fucking Five, and every single thing I was seeing about human nature in this case was making me sick. I just wanted to cut out to an island somewhere, where I didn't have to deal with anyone else.

For a while, I had been telling myself that once the opening statements were over, I could have some semblance of my family life back. But who was I kidding? Once the trial was under way, things would only get worse. Networks were going to devote their whole day's programming to it. It was a goddamned industry. Without my having any say in the matter, I'd been turned into a symbol of Working Mother, Successful Professional, Voice of the People, Stand-in for Justice Itself. I took these things to heart and didn't want to let anyone down. But, God, I was so tired.

On Saturday night, a little more than a week before trial, we were all bunkered into our offices, working. Bill came in to talk. He was unhappy. He confided that he felt he should retire as much as possible from the case; he felt very uncomfortable, he couldn't relate to anyone or anything. "I don't fit in," he said, and I knew what he meant.

It was true. In one sense it was a woman's case, it was a woman's issue. In another sense, the defense had made it a race issue. Bill felt the jury would see him as a representative of the white male establishment, with no connection to the strong emotional issues of the case.

Chris felt he was in an ethical bind. He called me late one evening at home to fret about the Hodgman dilemma. We called each other more and more of an evening. I'd often talk to him while burning off tension on my exercise bike.

"We've got to give Hodgman some witnesses in the beginning of the case," he'd insist.

Then I'd say, "No, don't bother Bill. He doesn't need it." We just kept going round and round on this.

Right up to the last moment, the press and public assumed that Bill would make an opening statement. But it seemed awkward as well as cumbersome to divide the opening among three prosecutors. The way I envisioned it, Chris would lead off with the *why* of the crime, the motive: domestic violence. And I would follow with the *how.* A clean one-two punch.

There *was* work for Bill to do—and it wasn't fun. It would be his job to question the coroner, Dr. Golden, whose reports were so flawed we didn't want to flaunt them in the opening. The autopsies were also complex and difficult to summarize. In the meantime, we assigned to Bill the task of riding herd on Johnnie. Bill, sitting with us at counsel's table, could register the objections whenever His Smoothness strayed out of line. That way, the jury wouldn't become annoyed at Chris or me. Bill accepted this assignment with his usual grace.

The evening before opening statements, Chris and I went down to the courtroom for a practice run in front of Bill and a handful of others. I'd rarely seen the place empty like this: just a sterile cube of plywood paneling. It appeared to have been designed by a clerk, not an architect. Someone who had in mind a system for the shuffling of papers, but no grander vision of justice.

Within ten hours, the room would be the center of the world's attention. Those empty counsel tables would be piled high with the notes and briefs of at least twenty noisy, combative attorneys. Each side would be scrambling to seize the advantage. Who would impose upon this unruly contest the ideals of morality and fairness? I looked to the bench and saw an empty chair. And I thought sadly how it always looked empty. Even when Lance was sitting in it.

My technical assistant, Jonathan Fairtlough, had set up the laser disc that projected both stills and moving images onto a large screen. I usually get up there with my charts, diagrams, and photos mounted on poster board. But Jonathan, bless his heart, led me by the hand into the modern age.

I wanted the jurors to feel physically drawn into the crime scene. I wanted them to travel up the walkway at Bundy. To see how the killer approached his victims from the bushes. I wanted them to see Nicole lying on her left side, feet wedged up under the gate. I wanted them to see her slashed throat. I wanted them to understand the physical reality of the space in which Ron Goldman had been trapped. He had been backed into a cage.

Then I'd let them see the detective's-eye view at Rockingham. Entering the property; visiting the guest houses; discovering the brown leather glove. We would go straight up to the foot of O. J. Simpson's bed, ending with a photo of the rumpled socks.

Originally, we wanted to have video footage interspliced with still shots, so that you'd be coming up the walkway at Bundy; then you'd see stills of her body, and then his body, and then the blood drops. It didn't work; it was too jarring to come out from the video into the stills. When we strung together all the stills it was very powerful. But it had to be perfectly choreographed. Jonathan not only had to show each image at the appropriate moment, but had to segue from my voice into the picture. It was an elaborate little dance.

I had worked and reworked the presentation of the hair and fiber evidence. It was the sort of stuff that could be deadly dull or power-fully compelling. Finally, I got some rhythm going. I'd start with a straight presentation of the evidence, then I'd pause and highlight it with a challenge to reason. For example, "Nylon carpet fiber like that found in the defendant's Bronco. *Stop* and *think* for a minute," I'd say to the jury. "How could that fiber from the defendant's Bronco get on the cap?" Then I'd hit it again with "The head hairs like those of the defendant were found at the Bundy crime scene. *Stop. Think*—how could head hairs like the defendant's get on that cap?" Then I'd men-tion Ron Goldman, and note that the shirt he was wearing also had head hair on it like the defendant's. *"Think,"* I'd implore them. "How did the defendant's hair get on Ronald Goldman's shirt?"

"It cannot be denied," I would tell the jury, "that there will be a temptation to treat this evidence differently because of the image the media [have] created of Mr. Simpson—but we all know that what we see on TV is not evidence. Winning is not what this is about; this is *not* a game; this is about justice and seeing that justice is done. Two people have been brutally murdered—and the evidence points to the guilt of only one person as their murderer, Orenthal James Simpson."

It was strong. I knew it was strong. Bill, Chris, and Jonathan—the whole team—were really jazzed.

January 23, 1995 . . . opening day.

I can't believe I really said that. Opening day! After a while I just got sucked into sports-speak like everyone else. I can't remember what

I wore, so don't even ask. Before an opening statement, I trip into hyperfocus. The details of the goings-on around me don't even register. What I do recall is that the team was extra thoughtful of me. Even the reporters in the hallway gave me ceremonious berth.

The courtroom was jammed, the atmosphere incredibly tense. It was the first time we had all been together: judge, prosecutors, defense counsel, media, spectators, and jury. Not to mention the millions out there watching the live feed. I tried to make eye contact with the jury. But my God, what a scary bunch. The Great Stone Faces, I came to call them.

Chris was eager, ready to go. But then we got bogged down in motions that dragged on through the morning and into the afternoon. A major bummer. His opening was held over until the next day. I prayed it wouldn't throw him off stride.

The next day when he rose to speak, I knew he was nervous. Was he picking up negative vibes from the jury box? Was he making eye contact? *Make eye contact, Chris.* Until now, I hadn't heard Chris's opening in its entirety. It struck me now as eloquent, almost musical, as he described the love that was really a sickness:

"It is not the actor who is on trial here today, ladies and gentlemen, it is not that public face. It is his other face. Like many men in public [life], they have a . . . private side. . . . A private face. And that is the face we will expose to you in this trial. The other side of O. J. Simpson . . . We will expose . . . the face he wore behind the locks and the gates and the walls at Rockingham; that other face, the one that Nicole Brown encountered almost every day of her adult life . . .

"The evidence will show that the face you see . . . is the face of a batterer, a wife beater, an abuser, a controller," he told the jury. "He didn't hate Nicole. He didn't kill her because he didn't love her any more. He killed for a reason almost as old as mankind itself. He killed her out of jealousy. He killed her to control her. He killed Ron Goldman because he got in the way."

If I had any criticism of Chris's opening, it would be his insistence upon including Keith Zlomsowitch and several other domestic violence witnesses whom I wasn't certain we would ever bring to the stand. "Always promise less than you deliver," I'd told Chris. But he was headstrong. He didn't always listen.

When it came my turn at the lectern, I paused. For a moment I just stared into those faces. Eight blacks. Two Hispanics, one man who professed to be half Native American, and a single white. *Will this thing really come down to race?* I wondered. *Are the impassive faces of the six black women on this panel hiding their resentment of me? Can I find some common ground here? Call a truce?* Coming on like gangbusters didn't seem the ticket. In our strategy sessions up on the eighteenth floor, we'd all agreed that a calm, measured, rational approach was what was called for. Any hint of stridency would feed the perception of these jurors that we were out to lynch the defendant.

"You have now heard the *why.* Why would Orenthal Simpson, a man who seemingly had it all, commit such heinous crimes?" I began quietly. "The one simple truth about the evidence described by Mr. Darden is that it shows that Mr. Simpson is a man—not a stereo-type—but flesh and blood who can do both good and evil. Being wealthy, being famous cannot change one simple truth: he is a person, and people have good sides and bad sides. Whether you see both sides or not, both sides are always there."

Jonathan and I led the jurors through Bundy and Rockingham. The trip was flawless.

"It is going to be up to you, ladies and gentlemen. You are going to have to be ever vigilant in acting as the judges in this case. Each one of you is a judge. Each one of you is a trier of fact. You have to examine all the evidence very carefully and ask . . . 'Is this reasonable?' 'Is this logical?' 'Does this make sense?' . . ."

"Your Honor," Johnnie interrupted. "She is starting to argue now."

"Sounds like argument to me," Lance agreed.

The objection annoyed me, but I pressed on.

"My job is to seek justice," I continued. ". . . You will have to remember what this case is about: justice for all. Ladies and gentlemen, if those words are to mean anything, we must all be equal in the eyes of the law and we cannot use a sliding scale to judge guilt or innocence based on a defendant or a victim's popularity. We live in very, very strange times . . ."

Once again Johnnie broke in, "Your Honor, she is arguing."

"Counsel," Ito addressed me impatiently. "This has all been argu-ment for the last five minutes."

Now this may not sound like any big deal to you. But, believe me, it was a *very* big deal. In opening statements all that we lawyers are allowed to do is to lay out the facts, not attempt to persuade. The distinction, however, is often blurred. As a practical matter a judge will allow both sides considerable latitude in their openings. I felt my remarks were well within bounds. Johnnie was just prodding to see how easily he could shut me down—and, more important, if Lance would let him.

Lance did. He sustained the objection in such a cutesy, condescending way as to make it clear that he and Johnnie were on exactly the same page.

I tried to continue.

"We cannot succumb to the temptation to thwart justice and throw truth out the window."

"I'm going to have to stop you right here," Lance announced. And he dragged me over to sidebar—in full view of the jury—and scolded me for ignoring his admonishments.

Now, I'll tell you what's bad about that. It sends a message to the jury that the judge has no great respect for the prosecutor. And that's a real unfair message to send—especially on the very first day, when the jurors have their antennae up, looking for clues as to whom to believe. Lance's attitude toward me had a lot to do with his own ego. As an ex-prosecutor, he felt compelled to show us, "I used to do what you do and I did it better." Whenever Johnnie rose to speak, however, Lance's whole demeanor changed. He was beneficent. He was indulgent. It seemed to me Lance Ito just loved the idea of being Johnnie's friend.

Lance still had me at sidebar. And now he was ordering me to "say 'thank you, ladies and gentlemen,' and wrap it up."

I was seething. Nevertheless, I returned to the podium, smile pasted on my face, and delivered my parting line as gracefully as I could.

"Ladies and gentlemen. I want to thank you very much for your kind attention in this matter. . . . We all know it is difficult and we appreciate all of your dedication to duty and service in this case. Thank you very much."

After I sat down, there was a minor hullaballoo. Court TV's cameraman had inadvertently photographed an alternate juror. Ito went ballistic and threatened to pull the cameras from the courtroom.

So much time was pissed away resolving this fracas that Johnnie did not get to begin his own opening that afternoon. There was much wailing and gnashing of teeth on the defense side about how unfair it was to the poor defendant to let the jurors go back to their rooms and dwell on the prosecution's allegations overnight.

The fussing was just a smoke screen. In fact, we were about to be ambushed—but good.

Ito had ordered both sides to produce any exhibits they intended to use within forty-eight hours of opening statements. Our graphics people had worked into the wee hours of the morning to make that deadline. The defense guy in charge of discovery, Carl Douglas, had led me to believe his side was similarly squeezed. It wasn't until the evening before Johnnie was to give his opening that Carl handed me some eight-and-a-half-by-eleven reproductions of the display they intended to use. Most were too smudged to be legible.

"You call this discovery, Carl?" I asked him, incredulous. After I showed him one particularly muddy page, he agreed to go over the particulars with me. "Just because I like you, my sister."

Before we broke for the night, Carl mentioned that there might be "a few more . . . nothing major." I was sympathetic to the problem of having to produce everything so quickly, so I asked him to let me see what he had first thing in the morning. He agreed.

Next morning, when I walked into court, I saw *fifteen boards* stacked against Deirdre Robertson's desk. What the hell was this? There were about twice as many exhibits as Carl had shown me the night before. As I got close enough to read them, I was horrified. One entire display was devoted to the results of serologist Greg Matheson's analysis of the evidence. This included the socks found at the foot of Simpson's bed. Under a column labeled "Testing," there was an entry that read "Blood search. [None obvious.]"

The quote was taken from Greg's own notes. He made them in June 1994 after examining the dark socks for blood under natural light. He'd found "none obvious." But then he scheduled the socks for a blood search. Several weeks later, after blood was found, conventional serology testing confirmed the blood markers belonged to Nicole. The defense display board juxtaposed the June finding of "none obvious" with the later results showing Nicole's blood on the socks.

Now, why was this such a big deal? Because it played right into the defense's conspiracy theory. If they could get the jurors to believe that there was no blood on the socks as of June, then the blood tested later had to have been planted. At my angry insistence, Ito made them change the labels on the board to reflect the truth. But he gave us only fifteen minutes to study the remaining exhibits. There was simply no way we could uncover and correct all the deceptions.

The imbroglio over the displays, it turned out, was just the warm-up number. When it came time for his opening, Johnnie launched into a flame that was one part sermon, three parts argument. It, like the exhibits, was shot through with misrepresentations. He called the jury's attention to a report that showed that blood found under Nicole's fingernails was type B. That was not her type; nor was it Ron Goldman's or O. J. Simpson's. Logical inference? The blood under Nicole's nails must belong to the "real killer." What Johnnie failed to share with the jury was the very next line in the report: "Nicole cannot be excluded as a source of blood if . . . type B observed on the items were degraded from BA [Nicole's blood type] to . . . type B."

Further DNA testing revealed that it was, indeed, her blood.

Johnnie rambled on and on, tossing out the names of witnesses who had never been introduced in discovery. This was strictly illegal. During the pretrial hearings, Judge Ito had sanctioned the prosecution for two-week delays between taking witness statements and turning them over to the defense. But the defense had been sitting on some of these statements for over seven months, seven months!! And they were introducing these witnesses only *now*—during Johnnie's opening.

One of these lamers was Mary Anne Gerchas, who, Johnnie promised the jury, would testify that she saw four men—two Hispanic and two white—running from Nicole's condo the night of the murders. Johnnie also promised that a mystery witness—a maid of one of Simpson's neighbors—would tell how she saw Simpson's Bronco parked on Rockingham right around the time of the murders. And then, of course, there was Dr. Lenore Walker, the so-called mother of the battered women's syndrome, who would supposedly testify that O. J. Simpson's abuse of Nicole was not the sort of violence that normally precedes a homicide. From the moment I heard that, I vowed to take the cross of Dr. Walker on myself. Of course, she evaporated, like so many of the phantoms Johnnie invoked during his opening.

Lance just let Johnnie run on. Chris and I were sitting at counsel table hissing to Bill. "Object! Object! Bill, are you going to object?"

At first Bill was reluctant to take off the white gloves. To Bill's way of thinking, he and Johnnie were old buddies, going back to their days together in the D.A.'s office. He thought civility would prevail. I knew better. Johnnie had nothing but contempt for Bill. He loved to see Bill walk into court. He made no bones about it. He'd grin at me and go, "Oh, good, you're gonna let Hodgman do it? Good! Good to see you, Bill! Good to see you!" And Bill thought it was because Johnnie liked him. I'm saying to myself, *No, Bill, it's because he thinks you're easy pickins.* It was a painful thing for me to watch.

As Johnnie's claims became more and more outrageous, even Bill finally began to burn. "I can't believe this," he would mutter over and over. "This is unbelievable!" Then, at last, he leaped to his feet and shouted "Objection!" with such conviction that we were all electrified. He really got up and fought for a change; it was wonderful to see. Bill kept objecting. Before Johnnie finished his outrageous tirade, Bill Hodgman had objected a total of twenty times.

Lance, the dunderhead, knew what was going on. If we had tried to pull even a tenth of what the defense pulled here, he'd have had us locked up. But he would not overrule Cochran. He just sat up there on the bench rolling his eyes at me like, "Can you believe it?" As if it were some big joke when the People get screwed. I wanted to scream at him, "You're not some idle bystander here, buddy. You can actually stop this circus!" But how can you expect a clown to stop a circus?

Bill was seething when he left the courtroom. I stayed close to him all the way to the eighteenth floor. He had me very worried. He looked like he'd been through a shredder. His speech was incoherent—he was having trouble putting sentences together, and his breathing was very shallow. He couldn't seem to sit still. He was ultrahyper, and Bill Hodgman has never been hyper. Gil had called an emergency meeting in the conference room. But no sooner had Bill walked in the door than he rasped, "I gotta go. I've got to take a walk," and left.

Okay, he just needs a breather, I told myself. *He'll be fine.* Moments later I heard someone in the hall shout, "Down here, in Cheri's office."

Bill was lying on the rug. Cheri had made him lie down, he was so short of breath. Patti Jo was on the phone to the hospital.

I just stood there watching him and feeling guilty. *Oh, God,* I thought. *We shouldn't have pushed him. Oh, God. I should've seen it coming. Oh, God, you know, this case is gonna kill him. This sweet, lovely man. I can't stand this stupid fucking case!*

Fortunately, one of those in our company was Dr. Mark Goulston, a physician friend of Gil's who'd been hanging out with us since the case began. He was kind of the camp mascot. We called him Dr. Mark. I knew he had also been talking to Bill about the pressures on him. I pulled him aside to get a reading on Bill's condition. Goulston told me that he had been giving Bill a very mild sedative to help him sleep. Today's episode had been brought on by stress. Whether there would be lasting damage to his health, no one knew. Later, we would find out that Bill had a mild heart condition that, had it not been flushed out by this incident, might have killed him.

God, I thought. *This job chews up strong men and spits out their bones.*

Don't think I wasn't tempted to throw in the towel myself. To go in to Gil and say, "I can't do this anymore. Give it to . . . God, I don't know who, just give it to someone else." But I caught myself. How would I ever explain to my children why I walked out on the biggest case of my life? How could I ever look them in the eye and explain the necessity of seeing a job through to the end? What would I be teaching them? "Cut your losses, boys. Pick only those battles you can win." That was not what I wanted to leave them. I wanted them to realize that sometimes honor demands fighting even to an almost certain defeat.

And how would I explain it to the Browns, to the Goldmans, who were expecting justice?

"Forgive me for doing this, Dr. Mark," I said, turning once again to Goulston. "But I'm watching Bill, and I'm thinking, 'I don't want to go there.' Could you give me a prescription for Xanax?"

I'd do anything I had to do; zonk myself into a coma if necessary. But I intended to stay in the goddamned ring.

Exposure

After Bill's gurney disappeared down the hallway, all of us, deputies and law clerks alike, milled around the War Room, stunned. I stood for a moment, as confused as any of them. Then I pulled myself together, marched back to my office, and shut the door. Cheri Lewis slipped in behind me. She thought I might want some company, but I was beyond talk. I paced for a while. Then, in direct violation of county rules, I lit up a Dunhill.

Cheri arched her eyebrows.

"So what are they going to do?" I snapped as I blew smoke toward the ceiling. "Send me Downtown and make me try the Simpson case?"

A knock on the door.

"Who is it."

Gil poked his head in. I quickly stubbed out the cigarette.

Here was the man who'd told me to "lay back," to "lighten up" a little. "Don't be so tough," he'd said. "Humor the judge." But there was nothing conciliatory in Gil Garcetti's expression now.

"Fuck him," he said tersely. "Take the gloves off."

No problem, Chief.

The defense's misconduct had made Ito look like a stooge for

Simpson. Right after the hearing the public flooded our office—and presumably Ito's as well—with faxes and telegrams venting their outrage at how badly we'd been treated. This kind of reproof wounded Ito's pride and often caused him to veer wildly in the opposite direction. I figured he'd be pretty sympathetic to whatever we suggested in the way of sanctions.

If I'd wanted to play hardball, I could have demanded that every witness for which the Scheme Team had not provided discovery be excluded from testifying. Bye-bye to Mary Anne Gerchas, Howard Weitzman, and Skip Taft, among others. Exclusion is the most serious penalty—short of contempt—that can be imposed upon attorneys who have deliberately hidden witnesses to gain tactical advantage.

Tempting as this was, such a demand would have been counterproductive. For one thing, exclusion posed an appellate risk. Preventing witnesses who might offer material evidence from testifying is arguably an infringement of a defendant's Sixth Amendment right to a fair trial. All things considered, I felt that it was more equitable to let the disputed witnesses come to the stand—provided we be allowed to let the jury know how they'd been illegally hidden from them. This way they could make up their own minds about these folks' credibility.

I figured Lance would give us that much. But I wanted more. I intended to request that he allow me to reopen my statement: do a second opening! This would let me expose at least some of Johnnie's misrepresentations—that this was a drug murder, that the defense had proof of a second assailant, that Simpson was at home during the time of the murders. But I had no idea if there was any legal precedent for this. Never in my fourteen years of practice had I heard of it happening.

I buzzed my law clerk, Dana Escobar.

"Dana," I told him, "I've got a tricky one for you."

"No problem, boss." He and a handful of other clerks set to work. Amazingly, within the hour, they had pulled up a 1964 civil case in which the court had allowed the reopening of the statement. Cheri and Hank commandeered a corner of the War Room and began drafting a motion to reopen.

Our investigators had also picked up a paper trail on Mary Anne

Gerchas, who'd supposedly seen the four men in watch caps running from Nicole's condo.

"Looks like she stayed at a Marriott for about four months and stiffed them on the bill," one investigator told me. "She owes thousands."

I whistled softly. "No wonder they wanted to hide discovery on her."

Our investigators had also turned up an exercise video that Simpson had taped only two weeks before the murders. It showed Simpson, at a trim 212 pounds, doing push-ups and throwing jabs and uppercuts. The video would refute the defense's claim more vividly than words ever could; no way was this guy the feeble cripple described by Johnnie in his opening statement. Simpson was also running on at the mouth—an infuriating trait his fans seemed to perceive as charm.

"I'm tellin' you," he joked, throwing out his right arm as if delivering a punch. "You just gotta get your *space* in if you're workin' out with the wife, if you know what I mean. You could always blame it on workin' out."

It was incredible. Here was the defendant making light of wife-beating. I wanted the jury to hear that; I would push for both the video and audio portions of the tape to be entered into evidence. And then I worried, *Will this jury even get it?*

For two days in court, we haggled over what punishment the defense should receive. Ito, clearly chastened by Bill's collapse, gave us a receptive ear. But when it came right down to sanctions, as usual he split the baby.

I could reopen my statement, *but* I'd only get ten minutes. We could show the exercise video, *but* we couldn't run the sound, which, of course, meant losing the wife-beating remark. And most disappointing, he denied us the chance to correct the impression that Nicole had the blood of some unknown suspect under her fingernails. His reason? *We hadn't lodged an objection at the moment Johnnie made the statement.* Those jurors needed to know that Johnnie had misled them. Maybe I could live with the damage, I told myself, as long as Ito dressed down the defense in front of the jury. Ito had us half believing that he would do this. He also promised to make sure the jury realized that the trial had been delayed for two days because of the defense's misconduct. But at the last moment, Lance lost his nerve.

"All right, ladies and gentlemen," he told the jurors after they had settled into the box on the morning of Monday, January 30. "I need to advise you of certain things."

His voice was so soft, it was scarcely audible. This was how he intended to censure Johnnie Cochran?

"I need . . . to explain to you some of the reasons for the delay that we have had over the past two days. . . . During the course of the opening statements, defense counsel mentioned witnesses who had not previously been disclosed to the prosecution. . . . This was a violation of the law. And one of the causes of the two-day delay, including the absence of Mr. Hodgman."

The absence of Mr. Hodgman! I couldn't believe it. Listening to this castrated admonishment, the jury could reasonably infer that the delay was *Bill's* fault.

If anyone was going to repair the damage, it would have to be me. And I would have to do it with a surgical strike. When it came time to do what would be called my "historic" reopening, I walked very slowly to the lectern. I paused. This was not to be an angry scatter blast of rebuttal. I would be calm and deliberate. I would limit myself to three points—each of them a promise to definitively refute Johnnie's reckless assertions. When we delivered, and the defense failed to back up their claims, the jurors would know which side was credible and which side depended on lies.

Item: That on the night of June 12, O. J. Simpson was physically unfit to commit murder.

"You will see him doing push-ups," I told the jury. "You will see him stretching, reaching, throwing jabs and uppercuts. . . . You will see him doing trunk twists. . . . We are going to show you that tape during the course of this trial."

Item: That the LAPD refused to allow O. J. Simpson to have an attorney present when he gave his statement to police.

"In fact, what the evidence will show is that the detectives asked Mr. Weitzman to stay for the interview, but that he declined to do so, stating that he would prefer to go out to lunch. . . . Mr. Simpson . . . said, 'Go ahead.'. . ."

Item: That we'd deliberately hidden from the jury the existence of Mary Anne Gerchas. We hadn't told them about her, I explained, because we didn't know about her.

"You'll be hearing a lot more about Ms. Gerchas along the course of the trial," I told them. "But right now, I'll address a few points that Mr. Cochran didn't tell you about. For example, she spoke to [a friend] the day after the murders . . . [and told her] that she was not even at Bundy on the night of the murders. [The friend] will tell you [that] Ms. Gerchas is one of these people who comes out of the woodwork in high-profile cases. . . . [She] was obsessed with this case and she talked as if she knew the defendant personally. . . . The evidence will show that Mary Anne Gerchas is a known liar and a Simpson case groupie."

I spoke for only seven of the ten minutes allotted to me. I didn't want to take a chance of running over and having Lance bawl me out in front of the jury.

CAR TAPE. *It's Wednesday, February first. I reopened our opening statement yesterday very briefly just to tell them about some of [the defense's] lies, but I don't know if it's enough to bring them around. If it was an ordinary jury I'd just be sitting there laughing because no reasonable mind could possibly buy the garbage they're feeding them. But with a jury where people don't want to believe the evidence, they'll seize on anything. We may all be playing to the second jury, assuming this one hangs up and doesn't acquit. What a lovely frame of mind.*

A common procedure in murder cases is to call the coroner as the first witness. It's easy to understand why prosecutors do this. Calling the coroner places the victims' bodies squarely in the jury's line of sight. You can't say it any more bluntly: "Two people have been murdered, folks. That's why we're here." If ever a jury needed a reminder of that, it was in this case, where so much of the attention had been riveted upon the defendant.

But this wasn't a standard case. We simply could not afford to lead with Dr. Golden.

Even before preliminary hearings back in July, we'd realized that the deputy medical examiner's report was riddled with errors. Some of the victims' wounds, which could be clearly seen in the coroner's photos, hadn't been documented at all. Worse, the tissue samples removed from Nicole's brain showed evidence of a brain contusion, but Golden's report had made no mention of it. The problem with the omission was that now we couldn't determine which side of the head had been struck—and not knowing this seriously hampered any reconstruction of the attack upon Nicole.

The contusion was critical because it lent support to other findings that Nicole had been attacked, but left alive and unconscious for at least a minute or two before the coup de grâce to her throat. This indicated that Simpson had stuck around after the first attack on Nicole. Now, why would a man who had just committed murder hang around to risk getting caught, not to mention missing his alibi flight to Chicago? The crucial minutes of Nicole's unconsciousness were clearly Simpson's window of opportunity to kill Ron.

How could we salvage this fiasco? Bill had a good idea. Why not get a reputable M.E. from outside Los Angeles to examine all the data, and testify either in addition to or in place of Dr. Golden? He suggested Dr. Werner Spitz, former chief medical examiner of Wayne County, Michigan. Spitz had written a key textbook in the field, and had consulted on other high-profile cases. Gil had heard that he was a "good man" and told us to give him a call.

It occurred to me that Spitz might not like the idea of having to second-guess another pathologist's work. But I thought that he might be sympathetic to our dire circumstances and agree to lend a hand. Bill and Dr. Spitz exchanged phone calls for about a week, but in the end, he never testified for us.

I should point out here that Werner Spitz became the expert witness who testified on behalf of the plaintiffs in the Simpson civil case. He was extremely helpful to them, describing how the cuts on O. J. Simpson's hands had probably been made by the victims' fingernails. He also proclaimed in unequivocal terms that the murders took only a minute and a half. It was damning stuff, and I wish to heck we'd had it. But we couldn't get the good doctor to our courtroom. Looking back on it, I think that he and a lot of other potentially compelling witnesses might have been scared off by the frenzy surrounding the criminal trial and the gratuitous abuse they were likely to suffer at the hands of the defense. Bill ended up spending at least a hundred hours on the phone trying to enlist a reputable medical examiner. Not one would agree to help us.

So we went to our fallback position. We had Golden's report redone under the direction of his boss, the chief medical examiner, Dr. Lakshmanan Sathyavagiswaran. Dr. Lucky, as we called him, would have to use Golden's memory and the police photos to splice together some description of the wounds. But at the time, the redone report was a work in progress. Dr. Lucky wasn't ready to go to the top of the lineup. He wouldn't have the original report completely redone; we'd have to start our case by admitting a whole lot of Golden's original mistakes. Not a strong opening gambit.

Another possibility was leading with our most compelling evidence, the DNA. But that meant opening with Dennis Fung. More mistakes. More egg on our face. And besides, it was such technical stuff that the jury would have been asleep from the get-go. No, thank you.

Chris and Scott were pushing to open with domestic violence. As usual, I hung back. I knew the risks. We were dealing with ambiguous and volatile testimony. It's difficult to convince jurors of either sex, of any race, that spousal abuse is a crime. And yet, opening with the New Year's beating incident offered us a substantial logistical advantage as well. It would enable us to tell, in roughly chronological order, the tortured, complicated story of how O. J. Simpson's obsession brought him to Bundy on the night of June 12, 1994. That tipped the scale. We'd open *People v. Orenthal James Simpson* with domestic violence.

"Mr. Darden," Ito asked Chris, "who is your first witness?"

"Sharyn Gilbert, Your Honor," he replied.

Gilbert, a neatly dressed black woman in her late thirties, raised her hand and took the oath.

"Ms. Gilbert," Chris said, "were you a 911 operator and dispatcher [for the LAPD] on January [1], 1989?"

"Yes, I was," she replied.

Gilbert explained that she had been at her console at 3:58 A.M. on New Year's morning when she received a "drop in." A distress call. At first, Gilbert couldn't make out a voice on the other end. She made a note in her log: "trouble unknown." A few moments later, however, she heard someone being hit.

Chris played the tape to a quiet courtroom. At first you could hear only the incongruous hiss of an empty line—then came a woman's screams. In the distance blows were struck and there was more screaming. And then the line went dead. I stole a glance at the jury box. Glum stares. No evidence of thoughtful contemplation. No hint of emotion.

Gilbert told how she'd picked up the caller's address off the computer and dispatched a cruiser to 360 North Rockingham. Detective John Edwards took the call. He was our next witness. Under Chris's deliberate questioning, Edwards told how he'd driven into the hills on Rockingham. There was a thick mist that morning. It had been raining. He buzzed the security gate. A half-nude, mud-caked Nicole stumbled out of the bushes. When she managed to get the gate open she flung herself on him and clung tightly.

"She was wet," Edwards recalled. "She was shivering, she was cold. I could feel her bones and she was real cold. And she was beat up."

Nicole was also crying, "He's going to kill me."

Edwards's testimony was very damaging to O. J. Simpson. He'd seen a one-inch-long cut on Nicole's left upper lip. Her right forehead was swollen. One of her eyes was starting to blacken. Her cheek was puffy and she had a handprint on her neck. Moreover, Edward saw that Nicole Brown Simpson seemed genuinely terrified of her husband.

To my way of thinking, a smart defense attorney would want to get this guy off the stand as quickly as possible. Not Johnnie. He trotted Edwards back through the details of the incident, sniping at him for not going into the house to interview the maid. (Please keep in mind, this officer had an injured victim in his car!) Johnnie wanted to position Nicole as the provocateur and Simpson as the reasonable one. But that backfired. Asked to describe Simpson's demeanor, Edwards replied, "He had veins . . . popping out right here [he gestured to his own temple] on the upper part of his head, along the side of his head.

The veins were pulsing and popping out, and I'd never seen that before on television or anywhere."

"So you associated that with anger?" Johnnie persisted.

Duh.

I have to believe that left to his own devices Johnnie would have been more effective with Edwards. He could have taken the tack, "Did you ever have the occasion to go out to Rockingham again, Officer Edwards?". . . ."No, I did not, sir." That would have suggested to the jury that his client was reformed and repentant. I suspected that he did not do this because his client was pressuring him to take Edwards down. Still galled by the New Year's Eve incident, Simpson was looking for any opportunity to rewrite history. (This perverse impulse, in fact, persisted into the civil trial, when, in the face of a mountain of evidence to the contrary, he continued to insist that he'd never struck Nicole. Never!) Unfortunately for Simpson, kicking Officer Edwards around was not his ticket to rehabilitation. It only served to repeat the facts of a crime to which he ultimately had pled "no contest."

"Amateurish," I scribbled on a Post-it to Chris. He rolled his eyes in agreement.

I wondered if the jury was taking all this in.

The 911 dispatchers and Detective Edwards had laid a credible foundation for our next witness, Ron Shipp. Chris and I were pinning a lot of our hopes on Ron. Of all of our domestic violence witnesses, he was potentially the most damaging to the defendant. His testimony was also the hardest won.

Back in July, the cops passed me a tip about Ron. A former LAPD officer, he'd suffered from a drinking problem and left the force about five years earlier. Since then, he'd apparently tried his hand at acting, without much success. The really interesting thing about him was that he'd been a longtime friend of O. J. Simpson's. He'd even worked security details for O. J.—and, in fact, had had some contact with him after the murders. The cops suspected that Shipp knew "something very important." I sent out the word that I wanted to speak with him.

Shipp showed up at the CCB on Thursday, July 28, in the company of his attorney, Bob McNeil—as it happened, a law school buddy of mine. Shipp was a compact black man, a few years younger than O. J. Simpson. His honest, open face, strewn generously with freckles, radiated decency.

I motioned them to an office down the hall from mine. Phil Vannatter joined us. He and Ron went back a long way on the force; I let him do the questioning.

"You know why we're here, Ron," Phil said. "We're here to talk about O. J. Simpson and Nicole. . . . And what I would like you to do . . . is just tell me what you know about their relationship. What was going on between them."

Ron hesitated.

"I met Nicole before they were married and were living together . . . fifteen years [ago]. . . . As far as I was concerned . . . they had a great marriage. A great relationship."

So far, no good.

Shipp explained that he'd known Simpson for twenty-six years. When he was working patrol, he'd bring his cop friends over to play tennis at Simpson's house. Ron insisted he hadn't known about any problems in the Simpson marriage before the New Year's Eve incident. A couple of days after that happened, Nicole had telephoned him for help. Ron, she knew, taught classes at the Police Academy dealing with spousal abuse. She wanted him to talk to her husband. Ron came over to the house with some lesson plans from the class, including a profile of the victim and the batterer.

"And she sat there and she pointed out hers and what she thought was his [profile]," Ron told us. At this point, he stopped. He was clearly uncomfortable.

"You would feel better if you know that you've told the truth," I said gently. "You could not have prevented what happened . . . no matter how hard you tried. . . . The only thing that you can do now . . . is to tell the truth."

Ron took a deep breath. "I told her before she let him back in the house to get counseling," he said.

At Nicole's request, he arranged to talk to Simpson and show him the batterer's profile. "When he first saw it," Ron recalled, "he says, 'It's not me.' " Then Simpson backed up to admit he saw a "little bit" of himself in the category of "pathological jealousy."

Simpson was terrified that bad publicity from the New Year's battering would ruin his career. Ron suggested that he make a bold move. Simpson should go public with his problem. If he did that, Shipp predicted, women's groups would rally behind him.

"He acted like it sounded good to him," Ron recalled. "The next day, I don't know who he talked to, but he was advised by someone . . . not to touch it with a ten-foot pole. And that was that."

We asked Shipp what happened after Nicole and Simpson split up. Ron said, "She had this thing about who was going to be her friend." Most of the couple's mutual friends, he said, threw their loyalties to the Juice. But even at the risk of offending his hero, Ron would check in on Nicole from time to time to see how she was. This I found touching. I could see that Ron Shipp was a man of integrity and courage.

Phil asked whether he had any opinion about Simpson's guilt or innocence. It was obviously a tough question. Ron paused.

"Whoever did this did a heck of a job of framing him," he finally replied.

There were tears in his eyes.

I knew even then that there was way more that Shipp could tell us. I told Phil to stay on top of him. Months passed. Meetings were set; meetings were canceled. But Shipp, it turned out, hadn't been so elusive with everyone.

Suzanne, Patti Jo, the law clerks, everyone was constantly dropping must-reads on my desk. In December one of them had deposited Sheila Weller's *Raging Heart.* My first impulse was to dismiss it as sensationalism. But things had reached the point where, in order to keep up with the latest developments in this case, I had to check out the best-seller list. So late one night, as I was doing a turn on my exercise bike, I propped the book on the handlebars and started skimming.

I hadn't gotten ten pages into it before a passage leaped out at me. It concerned a man named "Leo" who'd spent time with Simpson at Rockingham the evening after the murder. Leo was identified as a man with a "good working knowledge of criminal forensics." Simpson had asked to speak to him privately that night in his bedroom.

"How long does it take for DNA to come back?" Simpson had supposedly asked him. Leo thought it took a couple of months.

Simpson then told him that the police had asked him to take a poly-graph but that he'd refused, " 'Cause I *have* had some dreams about killing her.' "

I read this account with dawning amazement. *Leo was Ron Shipp!* Ron had told us he'd been to Rockingham that night to pay his respects to O.J. and his family. But he certainly hadn't passed along any conversation that he might have had while alone with Simpson in his bedroom. And he certainly hadn't mentioned the dream.

The following day, I had Chris bring Shipp in. This time we got the full story—the one he had told Weller. After hearing about the murders on June 13, Shipp had driven to Rockingham. At first, he was turned away at the gate, but later, around six o'clock, he'd managed to get in.

The house was full of people—Arnelle and Jason; Simpson's sisters and their husbands; Simpson's personal assistant of many years, Cathy Randa; Bob Kardashian. At one point Simpson said he wanted to go to bed. He asked Ron to come upstairs with him. Shipp told us how Simpson took off his shirt and pants and folded them carefully. Simpson was apparently meticulous about his clothes. As he was undressing he'd asked Ron about polygraph tests. How reliable were those things?

"Very reliable," Ron had told him.

And Simpson had replied with a chuckle, "To be honest, Shipp, I've had some dreams of killing her."

Had Ron taken any money from Sheila Weller? Chris asked. Ron insisted he hadn't. He'd told Weller about Simpson's dream because he wanted to unburden his conscience. He wanted the information to get out, but he didn't want to be fingered for it. Weller had promised him anonymity.

So much for anonymity. We intended to put Ron Shipp on the stand.

Actually, there were pros and cons involved in Shipp's testimony. It looked pretty bad that he'd originally withheld the information from us. But it was also apparent that he was telling the truth. The "dream" conversation had allegedly occurred on Monday night—the same day that Vannatter and Lange, in the course of taking Simpson's original statement, had asked him if he'd consent to a lie-detector test.

Remember, Simpson had told them, "I'm sure eventually I'll do it. But it's like I've got some weird thoughts now. . . . You know, when you've been with a person for seventeen years, you think everything. I've got to understand what this thing is. If it's true blue, I don't mind."

The "dream" mentioned to Shipp obviously fell into that "weird thoughts" category. What he wanted, no doubt, was to argue that his angry thoughts about Nicole aroused such internal turmoil that it might make a polygraph needle jerk. Even then, the son of a bitch was working up an alibi in the event he failed the lie-detector test.

The defense lawyers, of course, had access to our interview with Shipp, and the prospect of this "dream" evidence clearly agitated them. Out of the presence of the jury, Carl Douglas argued strenuously that it shouldn't be admitted because dreams could not "predict behavior." Of course, we were never suggesting that they could.

What we wanted to show was Simpson's general mind-set on the day after the murders. Here you have him suggesting to Tom and Phil in the police statement that he and Nicole were totally cool about their failed reconciliation. A few hours later he's telling Ron Shipp that he's had dreams of *killing* her. That day, Ito rejected Douglas's arguments, allowing us to present Shipp's testimony. Lance caught flak for that ruling among the talking heads and eventually he wimped out and instructed the jurors to ignore the dream comments. Too bad—he got it right the first time.

I ran into Ron moments before his testimony. He was sitting in the little foyer outside the War Room. He looked like he hadn't been sleeping well. I went up to him and gave him a hug.

"We're behind you," I assured him. "And we can party when you're done."

He laughed, but I could tell he was heartsick. I really felt for the guy. He was not just an admiring fan about to bring down his hero. He was a black man testifying against another black man. Ron knew—we all knew—that he'd catch some hell for turning on Simpson. But none of us had any idea how much he'd end up paying.

When Ron took the stand, Chris laid a brilliant foundation for his long, adulatory history with Simpson.

"And do you and the defendant remain friends today?" Chris asked him.

"I still love the guy. But—um . . . This is a weird situation," Ron allowed.

Leading up to the dream episode, Chris asked Ron, "Did he [Simpson] ask you any questions about the investigation that night?"

"After he told me about what they found at his house," Ron replied, "he asked me, 'How long does it take DNA to come back?' "

"And at that time, did you know the correct answer to that question?"

"I just off-the-cuff said two months."

"And what did he say in response?"

"He kind of jokingly just said, you know, 'To be honest, Shipp . . . I've had some dreams of killing her.' "

I winced a little. The defendant's dream comments had originally been made in the context of his having been asked to take a lie-detector test. But that couldn't be said in court, because testimony relating to polygraphs is inadmissible under California law. So while the jury heard that Simpson had dreamed of killing his ex-wife, that comment now seemed to come out of nowhere. They couldn't be told that it was part of a scheme to give himself an excuse for failing a lie-detector test.

What followed was one of the meanest cross-examinations I've ever seen. It was intended, I think, to send a message that no traitors from the Simpson camp would be tolerated; the defense was determined to destroy Shipp. Johnnie, it came out, was related in some distant way to Ron, and he couldn't bring himself to make the kill. Carl Douglas was the designated hit man.

First, Carl tried to establish that Shipp didn't know the defendant as well as he'd claimed. After all, they never double-dated with their wives. O.J. had never played a single game of tennis with him.

"I guess you can say," Ron said slowly, "I was like everybody else, one of his servants."

Far from compromising himself, Ron's reply served to make him appear both humble and self-aware.

Carl hammered away at Shipp, trying to get him to admit that the dream story was nothing more than an attempt to call attention to himself and advance his own acting career.

"I'm doing this for my conscience and my peace of mind," Ron replied calmly. "I will not have the blood of Nicole on Ron Shipp. I can sleep at night, unlike a lot of others."

As Ron looked better and better, Carl's jabs got meaner.

"Isn't it true that you were never alone with O. J. Simpson that night at Rockingham? Isn't it true that the defendant's sister, Shirley, was the one who accompanied him upstairs alone that night?" Carl even offered a veiled hint that Ron might have been in on the police conspiracy to plant evidence.

Ron looked right past Carl, straight into the face of his former hero.

"This is sad, O.J. . . . This is really sad."

Then Carl Douglas sank to a new low, even for the Dream Team. First he brought up Ron's old drinking problem. We objected, of course—what was the relevance of a condition that ended years ago? Overruled.

Wasn't it true, he asked, that a few days before the murders Ron brought a tall blond woman to Rockingham and asked to use the Jacuzzi? *Objection, irrelevant. Overruled.* Ron tried to explain that he *and* his wife were friends of hers. Didn't matter. The message Carl intended to send to those five black women on the jury was perfectly clear:

Black man steps out on his black wife with a white bitch. Are you going to tolerate this, my sisters?

It was horrible.

I was unprepared for the reports that came back to me following Ron's testimony. Black journalists in the newsroom below us were branding him a liar and a traitor. The next issue of the city's black-owned newspaper, the *Sentinel,* ran a banner headline proclaiming Shipp a "drunk" and accusing him of joining "O.J.'s Cast of 'Addicts, Liars.' " For weeks thereafter, Ron received death threats against himself, his wife, and his children.

I had been aware, of course, of the deep racial schism in this case. But I'd held out some hope that a man of such obvious integrity as Ron Shipp might somehow bridge the divide. When I saw the trouble he'd bought upon himself and his family by speaking the truth, I felt both my ideals and my confidence crumbling. If Ron Shipp's testimony could be flung away so cavalierly, there would never be enough evidence in this world to prove O. J. Simpson's guilt.

Denise Brown was pretty much a law unto herself. And I had no illusions about how she would be received. She was the white girl's white sister.

During the pretrial motions, she'd taken the defense to task on camera asking why, if they were trying so hard to find the truth, they were trying to get the evidence suppressed. On a personal level, I dug her gutsy style, but as a prosecutor I wasn't thrilled with her penchant for publicity. One ill-considered remark to the press, I knew, could render her worthless as a witness. On top of it, Denise had had her own problems with alcohol. Shapiro was threatening a blistering cross in which he would exploit whatever information he had to taint her credibility.

"You'd better clamp down on her," I told Chris. We needed to keep the testimony tidy and circumscribed. Understated sincerity. Easy on the tears. That was the ticket for this witness. Ito had ruled that we couldn't bring up any violent incidents that occurred before 1981, so we had to be especially careful.

But Denise was not so easily reined in. On the morning of her testimony, she showed up in a black pantsuit with a large gold cross hanging from her neck. It was very stylish, but way too hip to make points with this jury.

During her first few minutes on the stand, Denise seemed in control of herself. Chris handled her well, leading her carefully through the early days of her sister's relationship with O. J. Simpson.

"When did you first meet the defendant?" he asked her.

"Back in 1977," she replied. "He was playing football for Buffalo."

Nicole had invited Denise and Dominique out East for a game. While they were sitting in the stands, a friend of O.J.'s came over to say hello to Nicole. She kissed him on both cheeks.

"And after the game, did you go to the defendant's house?" Chris asked.

What! I thought. *Why is Chris giving her this opening? She's not supposed to discuss anything that happened in 1977.*

"You returned to the defendant's home after the game, right?"

Yes, they did.

"Anything unusual happen then?"

Denise began to vent.

"O.J. got real upset and he started screaming at Nicole."

Shapiro objected and asked for a sidebar. I couldn't blame him. Ito dressed Chris down for letting his witness mention an incident that occurred before the ten-year time limit.

"You are to disregard the last . . . answer," Ito told the jury. "Treat it as though you never heard it."

Things got worse. Denise told about the night she and her boyfriend Dino had double-dated with Nicole and O.J. at a watering hole in Santa Ana. They were throwing back shots of tequila when Simpson grabbed Nicole's crotch and proclaimed, "This is where babies come from and this belongs to me."

"And Nicole just sort of wrote it off like it was nothing," Denise said. "Like she was used to that kind of treatment."

A quiver had crept into her voice. *Oh no,* I thought, *no tears!*

For some reason, Chris then asked Denise whether Simpson shied away when people came up to ask him for autographs. Denise, contempt in her voice, said, "Oh, no, not at all. He loves the attention. He loves it. He's got a big ego. It feeds his ego."

Another objection. Another sidebar. This time Ito directly instructed the witness to stick to relevant issues.

Denise then described that other double date after which they'd all returned to Rockingham, a little drunk on margaritas. They were sitting at the bar when she was moved to tell O.J. that she thought he "took Nicole for granted." He "blew up," she said, and started throwing things around: pictures; photos—then Nicole and the other guests. "She ended up . . . falling," Denise said of her sister. "She ended up on her elbows and on her butt."

At that point, Denise rested, forehead in hand, and wept.

"It's just so hard," she whimpered.

There was no doubt in my mind that she was sincerely overcome. But I cringed at how this would play to the Twelve Stone Faces. "No tears," I'd warned Chris. But when you put on a grieving relative, you take your chances. I glanced at the jury box. Sure enough, I saw not compassion but scowls of disbelief.

I knew this icy reaction to Denise's testimony was sounding the death knell to our domestic violence case. We'd put the brutal facts right in front of this jury, and they were quite visibly rejecting them. It couldn't have been more clear if they'd actually given the thumbs-down.

Right then and there I made a quiet decision to cut our losses. Chris would not accept this without a fight. He and Scott were so personally invested in DV that they would want to pick up the thread again later on in the trial, when Ito had said we could present the B-string battering incidents. I knew I could not let this happen. Introducing the abuse witnesses so late in the case would seem out of context—certainly a step backward. It would also seem like a desperate effort at character assassination, the kind of move you make if you've failed to prove your case. The witnesses would seem like afterthoughts, and the jury would have been furious at hearing them then. I held the veto and I would use it.

On February 3, the day of Denise's testimony, we had proof positive that this jury was too besotted by the fame of the defendant to hear the cries of his victims. No one else knew it for sure. But I knew Denise Brown would be the last domestic violence witness in the case of *People v. Orenthal James Simpson.*

CAR TAPE. *It's February 6, Monday. Came to work and saw the* National Enquirer's *two-page inside spread of me. . . . I use the word with great intent. I'm just plastered all over the place. [It's] just so disgusting. I felt so humiliated. . . .*

This would never happen to a man. The world is so far more sexist than anybody ever dreamed. I feel so sick, I can barely see straight.

After Denise's breakdown on the stand that Friday afternoon, Ito dismissed us early. In a way I was relieved that the rest of her testimony would be held over until Monday. It would buy me some time. I was due to put on the dog-bark witnesses immediately after Chris wrapped up domestic violence. Now I had an unbroken block of weekend hours to polish my questions.

When I arrived at my office on Monday morning, I was feeling pretty squared away. There was a knock on my door. Suzanne appeared, looking very uncomfortable.

"What's up?" I asked her, trying to arrange foldersful of witness outlines in chronological order.

"Um . . . Marcia . . ." she stammered. "I don't know how to tell you this . . ."

That stopped me cold. Whenever Suzanne opened a conversation this way, it usually meant fresh hell from the "newses"—her quaint expression for the broadcast media. I kept expecting those guys to lose interest in me. Each new offensive left me more bewildered than the last. I felt like I was chained to a breakwater. The waves would batter me into the pilings. They'd subside for a while and then swell and pound me again. There was nothing I could do about it.

"It's really not that bad," Suzanne continued in her best effort to soothe. "It's just that your ex-mother-in-law . . ."

Huh?

"Well, she sold some pictures of you to the *Enquirer* . . . Did you ever visit a nude beach in Europe?"

Nude beach? At first, it didn't register. And then my befuddled thoughts settled on an image of that carefree afternoon more than twenty years ago when I was kicking loose after the bar exam. In my mind's eye, I could see Gaby and me and our Italian train-conductor friend. We were playful and giddy. I'd shed my top. It was so innocent. And such a long time ago, and in another world.

I'd never been on real close terms with Gaby's mother, Clara. After Gaby's accident, she'd taken him back to Israel to live with her. I hadn't spoken to her for at least fourteen years, but I could imagine she was pretty bitter about the way things turned out. And I'm sure she held me responsible, however unfairly, for Gaby's misfortunes. But to sell a personal photo of me to a tabloid? I later learned that a private eye, hoping to curry favor with the Dream Team, had tracked her down in Israel and put her in touch with the *Enquirer.*

I tried to speak but I couldn't get any words out.

"I can bring it to you if you want," Suzanne offered, breaking the long silence.

I knew if I looked at those photos, realizing that they were being sold by the millions at checkout counters around America, I'd fall to fucking pieces. The only comfort, however slight, came from the knowledge that my jury was sequestered. Even if news of them were tracked into the Inter-Continental by visiting spouses, at least the jurors wouldn't be able to see them. But wouldn't just the knowledge of those photos affect my credibility? And what about my peers? I'd have to walk down the halls of my own office knowing everyone had seen me bare-breasted. And what about the defense? *The defense.* I'm sure those low-dealing bastards were laughing up their sleeves about now.

"Thanks for the heads-up," I finally managed to get out. "Maybe I'll come by later and take a look."

It was a lame attempt at bravado. But better, I guess, than self-pity.

I packed up my books and notepads and flattered myself that I could shut the whole incident out of my head. During the morning session, I felt as if I did manage to concentrate on Denise's testimony. By the mid-morning break, I was finally feeling strong enough to assess the damage. I asked Scott Gordon to come with me for moral support.

We ran into Suzanne's secretary at the door.

"Maria," I whispered to her. "Before I take the gut shot, tell me, what do you think?"

"I tell you, girlfriend," she whispered back, "you got nothin' to be ashamed of."

The *Enquirer* was lying on Suzanne's desk. I flipped to the spread. There I was, wearing a "sunny smile" and a striped bikini bottom. And nothing on top. A black bar had been superimposed over my nipples. But it did nothing to mitigate the tawdry effect. Here I was, a professional woman in the middle of prosecuting a major criminal trial, suddenly exposed naked in a supermarket tabloid. I was so lost in my own humiliation that I couldn't hear the words of comfort my co-workers were trying to offer me.

I should never have tried to make it back to court that day. I guess

I wanted to prove that I was tough enough to keep my head up and keep on working. I overestimated my own strength. No sooner had I taken my seat at the counsel table beside Scott than I felt the tears welling up in my eyes.

Oh, God, no, I told myself. *You can't lose it now.*

Way off in the distance, I heard Chris's voice as he conducted his redirect of Denise. He turned in my direction and beckoned me to sidebar. I could tell that he needed me immediately.

It didn't matter. I felt myself slipping further and further into pain. The tears were rolling down my cheeks. I wiped them away and leaned into Scott's shoulder to hide my humiliation from the defense, the jury, the press.

The redirect ended quickly, and Lance must have caught my distress, because, in a singular act of compassion, he quickly managed to recess court for the day.

I holed up in my office, trying to regain my composure. I couldn't stop beating myself up for crying in court. Chris walked in without knocking and, with his usual lack of ceremony, dropped into a chair.

"I'm sorry I let you down today," I apologized. "It won't happen again."

He shrugged.

"Don't let them get you down, G," he said. "In a week no one will remember it."

He was right. Or at least I wanted to think he was right.

"Besides," he continued, "I thought you looked real good in those pictures."

"You really think so?"

"Sure."

"You didn't think I looked fat?"

He laughed.

"No way, man. It gave me a woody."

I took a minute to get it. By that time Chris was grinning.

I laughed. Then we both started to laugh. And we laughed and continued laughing until we were actually howling. With a single bawdy quip, Chris had managed to restore my perspective. *How,* I asked myself, *does he manage to do that?*

Me Recuerdo

My first witnesses were not flashy, but they were rock-solid.

Pablo Fenjves and Nicole's other neighbors were all emphatic in their testimony: they'd heard a dog start to bark at 10:15 to 10:20 P.M. By that time the killer was most likely on the premises. The murders were most likely in progress. In fact, Ron and Nicole were probably dead.

During the months after the trial a bleating throng of pundits would try to suggest that I declined to put on certain witnesses because they didn't fit into my "time line." That is absolute rubbish. At no time did I or any other member of the prosecution team lock ourselves in to 10:15 as the time of the murder. From the very start of this case, the window of opportunity we were looking at was 10:15 to 10:40. Even the later time would have given O. J. Simpson twelve to fourteen minutes to dash back to Rockingham in time to be seen by Allan Park.

Johnnie couldn't put a ding in the dog-bark witnesses. Nor did he score any points on the employees of Mezzaluna. In fact, the defense seemed to be holding back. I knew they were saving their salvos for the cops.

Although we couldn't make out any coherent strategy coming from the Simpson camp, we knew they would hammer away at two related themes: The cops messed up the scene. And Mark Fuhrman moved evidence. Our first LAPD witness, Officer Robert Riske, went a long way toward debunking both claims.

Riske, a muscular man with close-cropped sandy hair, had been the first officer to arrive at the scene. He described how he and all the cops after him had taken particular care to avoid tracking through the pools of blood. Most important, when Riske arrived at Bundy, *there had been only one glove at the scene. That was a full two hours before Mark Fuhrman arrived.*

Let's think through this again: the defense lives and dies on the premise that Mark Fuhrman pocketed one of the murder gloves and carried it to Rockingham. But it couldn't have happened. *There wasn't a second glove to steal.*

I thought Riske made a superb witness. He didn't embellish; he didn't minimize. Johnnie, however, tried to make Riske out to be an inexperienced klutz.

The officer had found Nicole's bathtub full of water. Had he tested the temperature?

No.

The officer and his partner had found a cup of Ben & Jerry's ice cream sitting on a banister inside the house. Did they have it photographed?

No.

Sounds bad, huh?

Well, it isn't. In fact, it wasn't within the scope of their responsibilities to do *any* of those things. Riske and his partner were responsible for calling their superiors and securing the crime scene. Period. I made sure to establish this on redirect.

Johnnie then called Officer Riske's attention to two photos. The first showed the knit hat, the envelope, and the glove in one position; the second showed them at slightly different angles to each other. Johnnie contended that this showed that evidence had been moved while Mark Fuhrman was in the "same general area."

I leaped in with an objection.

"This is the same thing Mr. Cochran has been doing throughout this trial," I complained to Ito. "This is another distortion; this is another deception."

Here's what I was talking about: between the time the first and second photos were taken, the bodies had been removed from the scene. In one photo, in fact, you could see the toe of Ron Goldman's boot; in the second, you could not. The simple act of moving the bodies caused the area around them to be disturbed. That's *why* we take "before and after" photos.

Johnnie was also angling to play a laser disc with isolated segments of a crime-scene video.

Chris tried to block that kick. "We have never been provided a copy of this video," he told the court. And, indeed, we hadn't. The tape showed the back of an unidentified cop traipsing straight through a pool of blood on the Bundy walk. An image that, of course, shot to hell our contention that the cops had taken precautions to keep the crime scene intact.

Chris and I argued that there was no way of telling when this video had been taken. It hadn't been shot by police, so there was no time stamped anywhere on it. You could tell from the sun line that it had to be sometime in the afternoon. And that was all. But, once again, Lance waffled. He disallowed the video, but permitted the defense to show Riske the photo of the unidentified cop to see if he could ID him. Of course, he couldn't. Riske left the crime scene at 7:15 A.M., and the photo had been taken well after that.

That photo business really galled me. In the lower left-hand corner there was a gray square where something had been blocked out. A TV show's logo? I beckoned one of our law clerks.

"Get this photo to Suzanne, ASAP," I whispered. "I need to know who took it and whether it was before or after the crime scene was released. Go now!"

The clerk shot out of the courtroom. By the break, Suzanne had located the source: Darryl Smith, a freelance photographer on assignment for *Inside Edition*. Smith was a very cool guy, about six and a half feet tall. Suzanne arranged for him to come to my office and look at the video.

"Yep," he said, "that's mine."

We watched the original footage, which preceded the shot offered by the defense. It showed the officers taking down the yellow tape and rolling it up. The Bundy crime scene had been broken down! After that, the cops could walk anywhere they pleased. I put Darryl himself on the stand to confirm that the officers were in the clear. Man, was that satisfying.

How, I wondered, did Johnnie think he could get away with a trick like that? Giving your client a vigorous defense is one thing. Deliberate deception is another. But then—did this jury realize that the defense was selling them snake oil, deceiving them with these "before and after" photos? They should have taken that as an insult to their intelligence. Did they realize how cynically the defense was trying to manipulate them? Did they care?

It seemed to me that the boys over at the defense table had whipped each other up into such a macho frenzy that they had totally jettisoned the ethics of our profession. Each was trying to outdo the others with feats of chicanery, which some collective hallucination had allowed them to believe constituted intrepid lawyering. Even refined former law school dean Gerald Uelmen had been sucked into slapping high fives with the guys.

We could not let our guard down. Not for one minute.

My alarm went off at five A.M. It was Sunday, February 12. It was still dark. I was still on duty.

This was the day we were scheduled to take the jury out to see Bundy and Rockingham. Oh, shit. As I stumbled to the shower, I wondered if there was any way to call this thing off.

Believe it or not, the "walk-through" was originally my idea. Taking the jury to the crime scene usually works to a prosecutor's advantage. Taking murder out of the courtroom and onto the killing grounds makes it less of an abstraction. It gives us an opportunity to turn the jury's attention back to the victims.

What had started out as a potential blessing for our side went sour once we got down to thrashing out the terms for this field trip. Once again, Lance Ito let us down.

The logical time for our viewing was at night, when, of course, the murders occurred. But Ito made us do it in broad daylight, when Bundy would seem like Main Street USA. Thus the jurors would get no sense of the danger Nicole was in as she descended that small flight of steps into darkness.

The only way Ito would allow us the Bundy visit was if we allowed the defense their "fair share"—which meant taking the jurors to Rockingham. I emphatically did not want the jury to visit O. J. Simpson's estate. What was the point? The only areas of possible significance at Rockingham were Kato's room and the south pathway where the glove had been found. I allowed that it might also be marginally useful for the jury to see the layout of the exterior from Allan Park's point of view. But there was absolutely _no_ reason for them go inside the house. The jury—especially _this_ jury—would be so dazzled by Simpson's wealth that it was certain to erect yet another barrier to their ever imagining him a killer.

But the defense argued that an on-scene viewing of the master bedroom was necessary because the bloody socks had been found at the foot of Simpson's bed. And so, Ito decreed that the itinerary would include Rockingham as well.

Lance Ito's magical mystery tour began that morning under the Criminal Courts Building, in the lot where the sheriffs bring in the prisoners. It's a dreary, cavernous place that has always reminded me of Hieronymus Bosch's vision of hell. A fitting starting point for this junket. Chris, Hank, Scott, Cheri, and our investigators were waiting for me. We all took one van. The defense followed in another. The defendant himself was loaded into one of the sheriff's cars. The jurors brought up the rear in a bus.

Lance appeared to be having the time of his life. He was ordering deputies around and conferring imperiously with the troops. He'd taken great pains to arrange the security precautions for this outing. But I had no idea what lengths he'd gone to until our little caravan neared the freeway. I'd curled up across a couple of empty seats, trying to catch a few more winks, when I heard Scott Gordon murmur, "Geez!"

I raised my head to an amazing scene. The Ten West was totally empty! In fact, it appeared to have been cleared for miles ahead. Once again, O. J. Simpson had managed to sweep the traffic from the Los Angeles freeways. I swore under my breath. Ito's sense of pomp and overweening self-importance had turned this into a Spielberg production.

We cruised past Mezzaluna. I was disappointed we didn't have a chance to stop there. The deputies hadn't thought to pack us anything to drink, and I'd hoped for a little break to duck into the nearby Starbucks for a cup of coffee. Now I saw that was out of the question anyway. The sidewalks were packed ten deep with spectators straining to get a glimpse of us.

Finally, we arrived at Bundy, where the jurors were issued their instructions. They were to view the site in perfect silence—no questions. Fine. But Ito hadn't allowed us to make the walk-through clear enough to eliminate the need for questions. We'd asked the court for permission to attach photos of the bodies and evidence on the spots where they had been found; Ito had refused. So we just had to hope that those images were searing enough that even *these* jurors couldn't fail to remember them now.

What, I wondered, would they see when they looked at this narrow lot, its cement walkway long since scrubbed clean of carnage? For one thing, they had to be struck by how small the place was. Everyone seeing Bundy for the first time remarks upon that. The enclosure where the bodies were found was incredibly tiny. It was difficult to imagine one killer and two victims scuffling in that space. Forget the possibility of *two* killers. It couldn't happen.

As usual, the jurors' faces were devoid of expression. Certainly no signs of mental lightbulbs popping. Only one juror, a white man named Tracy Kennedy, was madly scribbling notes. One young black man, Michael Knox, wore a cap and a jacket that read "San Francisco 49ers." Simpson, of course, hails from that city and once played for the Niners.

Tell us, Mr. Knox. Could you telegraph your sympathies any more clearly?

The jurors were taken in groups of four and five through Nicole's condo. One lawyer was allowed to tag along with each group. I hadn't been there since the week of July 4. Now, as I walked in the door, I was shocked. The place was totally bare.

The Brown family, in their haste to put the past behind them, had stripped it to the walls. There was nothing to remind these jurors that a warm, vital woman had once lived here. This played into the defense's hands very nicely. It's so much easier to acquit someone of murder when you have no feeling for the victim as a real person. Nicole Brown had been erased from her own home.

It got worse. I'd wanted the jurors to see what a short drive it was between Bundy and Rockingham, to reinforce our contention that Simpson could have made the trip home within five minutes.

No dice. For "security" reasons, we had to take a circuitous detour. I could scarcely contain my fury. The point of this kind of field trip is to allow the jury to see the pertinent scenes under conditions as close as possible to those at the time of the murders. But here, *nothing* was the same. Not the condo, not the route, not the time of day—and certainly not Rockingham.

The defense, of course, was looking forward to showing off that mansion, hoping the jurors would ask themselves, *Why would a guy throw all this away over a woman?* Over our objections the defense had also arranged to have the jury go through Simpson's trophy room. Ito's justification? That Ron Shipp had testified to "the magnetism of this particular room." So now the jurors would have a chance to be equally awed by the symbols of the defendant's victories on the gridiron.

My only consolation was the thought that the jury would be filing past that wall of photos: Simpson with white fat-cat CEOs, Simpson with white celebrities, Simpson with his white golfing buddies, and, above all, a picture of Nicole on the ski slopes with their children. Those images, at least, would serve as a reminder of how completely the defendant had checked out on the black community.

At Nicole's condo, O. J. Simpson had managed to keep a surprisingly low profile. By law, a defendant can't be excluded from a jury view. The Browns had objected so strenuously to the idea of his walking through Nicole's condo, however, that he'd agreed to stay in the cruiser, out of sight of the jury.

When we reached Rockingham, however, Simpson played the lord come home to the manor. He was supposed to be shackled at the wrists or ankles. This is standard procedure. In fact, a smart defense attorney will often advise his client not to go out on the walk-through for this very reason. You don't want him paraded before the jury dragging his chains like Marley's ghost. But in this case, someone had apparently prevailed upon the Sheriff's Department to leave the cuffs off. As Simpson strolled the grounds with Robert Kardashian, the deputies walked a few respectful paces behind him.

Simpson was so full of swagger that he ventured inside the garage and lifted the tarp that covered his red Ferrari. He turned to a deputy and smirked, "Do you know what TestaRossa means?"

There was sniggering all around. And I thought to myself, *Right. Anything O. J. Simpson wants to do is fine, as long as the guys think it's funny.*

Lance let the lawyers do the first walk-through. I'd gotten no farther than the foyer when I realized something was very wrong here. On my previous visits, the house had struck me as neglected and lifeless. Now it looked like a squadron of fairies had scrubbed it with Q-Tips. It was gleaming. In the living room, a fire was blazing. Fresh-cut flowers had been artfully arranged in a vase on the side table. But the most dramatic transformation was that collection of photographs.

The Wall of the Fat Cats had been cleansed of Caucasians. Gone were the golfing buddies and shots of Nicole in Aspen. Every single shot contained a black face. Simpson's mother, his sister, their husbands, their kids. Upstairs, there was even a Norman Rockwell reproduction: the little black girl going to school accompanied by federal marshals. In the bathroom, there was a poster made by Simpson's children; *that* had not been there on June 13. But the pièce de résistance was the master bedroom. On the mantel above the fireplace sat books on philosophy and religion. On the nightstand, next to a Holy Bible, stood a photo of the defendant's mother, Eunice.

But these distortions were merely cosmetic compared to the more material misrepresentation I discovered when my little tour party took its turn down the path behind Kato's room.

Seven months earlier, during the preliminary hearings, Robert Shapiro had tried to argue that if Simpson had been on the south pathway, he wouldn't have had to walk around to the front door to get back into the house. This was because two other doors along the south pathway led inside. I'd made a note to myself to check that out.

What I'd discovered in examining the photos and talking to Kato was that neither of those doors was operable. One of them, which led into the garage, had been blocked from the inside by a large dresser that supported a television set. The other, which led into the laundry room, was kept bolted from the inside and blocked by a stepladder and a laundry basket.

Today, however, the laundry-room door, free of obstacles, was standing wide open.

They'd altered the conditions. The defense team had deliberately changed things, both to pander to the jury's racial prejudices and to obscure the facts in the case. I turned to Chris. "We have got to have them put this place back to the way it was, or else cancel the whole damned viewing," I said.

Chris predicted that this would not sit well with the Little Prince, his pet name for Ito. I knew he was right, but we had to try.

When I demanded that Lance call a hearing right then and there to consider my motion, he was visibly irritated. He'd orchestrated this sound-and-light show down to the last detail and he didn't want to change the program. He also knew that if he canceled the viewing, the defense would go nuts. Never mind that the Bundy condo had been rendered a lifeless husk. Forget that Rockingham had been transformed into a soundstage for *Leave It to Beaver*. Lance still seemed to be worried about pissing Johnnie off.

Under protest, however, Ito convened a hearing on the front lawn. Both sets of attorneys stood in a semicircle around the court reporter while I argued, ticking off the items, that the scene had been materially altered.

"This is a sympathy play on their part. That's all it is," I concluded. "There's no evidentiary value to it."

Ito allowed that he was a little worried about the photographs. He asked Johnnie about them. Cochran's response was interesting in light of what was later documented in Larry Schiller's *American Tragedy*. Schiller, appointed scribe of O. J. Simpson, writes that the defense team had supervised every step of this extraordinary effort to tamper with the jury view. Cochran himself is quoted as demanding that the white faces be replaced with black ones—in fact, the Norman Rockwell print came from his office!

Now, put on the spot, Johnnie equivocated.

"As to the photographs, Mr. Douglas is in charge of that," Johnnie said. "I don't want to respond to the argument. . . . This is preposterous." Then he turned the question over to Carl Douglas, whose response was equally evasive: "I was not here on June the thirteenth, so I am unable to adequately respond specifically to what pictures were up and where they where. I don't know for a fact."

"Your Honor," I put in, "I *was* here on the thirteenth, and I know—"

Johnnie cut me off. "I would not ask Miss Clark to tell you anything," he said to the judge. "Gigi the housekeeper, she would be the one to tell you."

Rising to the bait, Lance turned to the housekeeper and asked if anything had been changed.

"Just add his mother picture there," she said in broken English.

"She's not a detective," I protested, "she's a *housekeeper!*"

Of course, Ito refused to cancel the viewing. In the end, the only thing he was willing to do was to order the defense to take down the photo of Mama Simpson and to put out the fires.

"Nice try, guys," he told them.

"Nice try?" That's a reprimand? You've got to grab these guys by the collar and demand respect, Lance. They're only lawyers.

The result of all my objections? Lance climbed onto the jurors' bus and told them to "ignore anything you see in the photographs that are inside the residence."

Great. Like "Ignore the pink elephant in the living room."

Ito ordered the deputies to escort the jurors as they went through the trophy room, so that they wouldn't linger over the mementos of the defendant's glory days. Of course no warning issuing from the lips of Lance Ito could keep them from gawking. And they did. Openly. Michael Knox, the guy in the 49ers gear, all but pressed his nose against the photographs.

It was the only sign of animation I saw in our jury all day.

CAR TAPE. *February 15. I haven't had a day off, not even one day off, in about a month. I'm so exhausted right now I can't even think. . . . Bailey took on this cop yesterday, a really mild-mannered guy that was only there to make sure the crime-scene tape was up properly. And he starts thumping him about all this stuff that's got nothing to do with him. About when to notify the coroner. And instead of sustaining my objections, the judge lets him go running wild with it. . . .*

His sexism, their sexism, has gotten so irritating. It's funny, you know. I never, never used to cry sexism. But this case is rampant with it. The judge makes these cute little corrections to me about "personpower" instead of "manpower." That's just a change of a word, Judge. How about your fucking attitude? And Cochran is so condescending and patronizing. We got to sidebar and I'm arguing against him and he starts calling me "hysterical." I mean, Jesus. I've never seen anything like this. It's absolutely frightening. I mean . . . I don't think we have come a very long way, baby.

Ito continued to let the defense bash away at the first cops on the scene: Riske, Rossi, and Phillips. And then they kept Tom Lange on the stand for four painful days of cross-examination.

I had entertained the possibility of not even calling Tom. We really didn't need him for anything except to identify the crime-scene photos and key pieces of evidence, and that could be done by others. Still, it's customary to call your lead investigator; my colleagues pointed out that it would look kind of odd if we didn't.

Tom's upside, to my way of thinking, was that he didn't have much of a downside. Since the Fuhrman business surfaced, we'd had to ask each and every cop, "Do you have a package at Internal Affairs?" "Do you have a package at SID?" We'd had to run background checks on our officers—a process formerly reserved for shady witnesses and known ex-felons.

Tom came out squeaky clean. His only *possible* error in judgment at the crime scene was the blanket he'd use to cover Nicole on the scene. Nicole had lain uncovered in full public view for more than three hours. In a gesture of decency, Tom had found a blanket in a closet to spread over her. Now, of course, the defense was going to argue that the incriminating trace evidence found on Ron's body and the knit cap—hair and fibers that matched Simpson's—had somehow come from that blanket. Unfortunately, the LAPD had disposed of the blanket after the coroner arrived. Still, I felt we could defuse this by pointing out that neither Ron nor the knit cap had ever come in contact with the blanket.

Tom and I got through direct in about one day. I used the opportunity to put on some real evidence, like the glove and the knit cap. It was the first time the jury had really gotten a good look at this stuff.

Johnnie's cross was scattershot. He accused Lange and his colleagues of the routine imperfections of any investigation: for instance, why was it, he asked, that a key drop of blood evidence—found on the Bundy rear gate—wasn't discovered until July 3? That was a reasonable question. Others were totally bogus. Like demanding to know why Lange hadn't insisted that a rape test be performed on Nicole.

"Sex was the last thing on the mind of this attacker," said Lange. "It was an overkill . . . there's no evidence of rape."

Come on, Johnnie, how many rapists put their victim's panties *back on?*

Then Johnnie lit into him for the blanket. He took Lange to task for not picking up a piece of bloody paper that lay between the victims. Tom had felt it had no evidentiary value. Which it didn't—it was obviously just a scrap of trash that happened to be lying there.

And then Johnnie flipped a race card into the mix. At one point, he rolled Lange back to the moment he first got called to the murder scene, at three A.M. on June 13.

"And then you drove from your home in *Simi Valley* down to the location, is that right?"

"Yes."

"And how long did it take you to get from *Simi Valley* to the location in Brentwood?"

Simi Valley, of course, is Whitetown, the suburb where the Rodney King jurors acquitted the cops caught beating a black man on videotape. It's code for "racist frame-up."

But Johnnie couldn't leave it at that. He opened a line of questions concerning a pair of Reeboks Tom took from Simpson's closet and stowed in his trunk overnight. It was inappropriate for Tom to do this, and *would* have led to trouble if the shoes had turned out to be importance evidence. But those shoes led to nothing; they were a total red herring. To Johnnie, it was another opportunity for a jab at the detective's race.

"You took those shoes home to *Simi Valley* with you?"

Underhanded son of a bitch!

But Johnnie had still another item on his agenda. He was itching for the jury to hear about Faye Resnick's drug habit, and what the defense would imply was her hypnotic influence over Nicole. Johnnie wanted to plant the notion that the real killer lay somewhere in Faye's circle of associates—a drug dealer to whom she owed money, perhaps. He surmised correctly, however—that Chris and I were not going to call Faye to testify. Johnnie could have called her himself, but she was a double-edged blade. If the defense got her up on the stand, she would doubtless end up telling the jury about O.J.'s brutality to Nicole.

So he decided to use Lange to introduce the totally unsupported idea that this was a drug killing. Johnnie asked Tom if he'd ever heard of something called a "Colombian necklace."

"I believe so," Tom replied.

"And it's true, is it not, that a Colombian necklace is a situation where drug dealers will slice the neck of a victim, including the carotid artery, in order to . . . instill fear and send a message to others who have not paid for their drugs or been informing to the police. . . ."

Tom said he'd heard that.

Tom was driving me up a wall. He just wouldn't stand up for himself. Every time Johnnie threw out some preposterous theory, he'd answer with, "Yes, that's possible." He was hoping to come across as cool and unbiased, but he ended up conceding things that could not possibly have been true: that the murders could have been a drug hit or a Mafia contract killing. What he should have been saying was, "No, Counsel. I disagree with you. This didn't look anything like a drug hit to me. And here's why. Drug dealers, Mafia hit men, will off their victims with a bullet to the brain. They don't leave behind physical evidence smeared from pole to pole. *This* was a rage killing."

During the break I pulled him aside and said, "Tom, what are you doing, man?"

"Well"—he shrugged—"you can clean up on redirect."

"Baby," I told him, "by the time I get back to you on redirect, that jury's gonna be off thinking about Colombian cartels. You gotta take your shot now!"

Redirect is never as impressive as cross. On cross, jurors are listening carefully to see whether the witness is backing down from the assertions made on direct. By the time we do redirect, the jury tunes out because they expect the witness to clean up his testimony under friendly questioning. You've got to hold your own on cross! But Tom didn't seem to get that.

During the break, however, someone slipped Tom the word that Johnnie had bungled his drug-lord argot. The "necklace" was actually a "necktie." So when Tom got back on the stand, he triumphantly gave the actual definition of "necklace"—a South African political killing, in which assassins place a burning tire around the victim's neck, a modus operandi that had absolutely nothing to do with our case. I was glad to see Tom finally showing some spunk. But I'll tell you, it was a rare moment.

I have since seen him stick up for himself admirably. During the civil trial, when Simpson's attorney, Robert Baker, showed him the photo of some smudge he claimed was an unidentified footprint, Baker tried to trap him by asking, "There had to have been a second assailant . . . isn't that true?"

"No," Tom shot back. "I don't know that that is a shoe print. . . . If there were a shoe print, you'd expect to find others around it, and there weren't."

During the criminal trial, however, Cochran danced Lange all over the lot. He held Tom to account for all the deficiencies of the coroner: why there weren't plastic bags over the victims' hands, why the contents of the stomachs were discarded, and so on. Question after question went beyond the scope of the witness's expertise. I objected until I was hoarse. The witness is not a medical examiner! But Ito allowed all of it.

Even now, when I read the transcript of Tom Lange's testimony my stomach twists into knots. That cross-examination should have been handled in the space of an afternoon. It took four days.

Ito's timidity played havoc with our trial strategy. Normally you can prepare your direct testimony with an eye to limiting what can be brought out in cross-examination. (The rules of evidence state that cross is limited to the subjects raised on direct.) But since Ito let the defense go anywhere during cross, that tack was useless. Instead, we had to fix things afterward, which meant we were having to spend hours and hours of preparation on lengthy redirect.

After the verdict, when pundits started using Chris and me as their personal punching bags, they would point to the expeditious pace of O. J. Simpson's civil trial and ask, "Why is it that in the civil trial, these people can go straight from A to B? Why did you guys wander all over the map?" The answer is very simple. Judge Hiroshi Fujisaki routinely cut off Simpson's attorneys with the message, "If you want to grill these witnesses, you'll have to call them on your own, and not waste our time in cross."

Lance Ito didn't have the strength to do that.

I've thought a lot, since, about how I would have handled that courtroom if it had been me sitting on the bench. I know for sure I would have limited the scope of cross-examination. If direct went "1, 2, 3," I wouldn't let cross go "1, 2, 3 . . . 3½." I would have allowed no speaking objections. You know, the kind where the attorneys try to elaborate their objections with rhetoric. "Objection, Your Honor. Ms. Clark is trying to mislead the court. . . ." It's "Objection"—*period.* I would have ruled from the bench and taken no sidebars on the matter. "You stay there, Mr. Bailey. I've ruled!" If a lawyer repeatedly asks improper questions, I'd object on my own: "Don't do it again, Mr. Cochran. If you do, we're gonna talk contempt here." Flout my orders and you get reamed in front of the jury. I'm going to make it hurt, and hurt bad. Pretty soon lawyers get it through their head that it's not worth their while to pull a fast one. I'd be one of those judges everyone might hate, but I'd treat everyone the same.

At any rate, the Lange cross was incredibly frustrating for me. And even more so for Chris. The frustration, in fact, led him to do something really stupid.

One day after court, Chris dropped by my office and said, almost offhandedly, "I just thought I should let you know that I was talking to Geraldo."

You what?

"I just told him I'd like the officers to be more aggressive."

I couldn't believe it. The whole team had a pact that we wouldn't speak to the press. It went without saying that a prosecutor shouldn't be calling a talk-show host to vent.

"Chris," I said quietly. "Please tell me you didn't. That's all we need, for the cops to hear you complaining about them on national TV."

Chris normally showed much better judgment. This slip had me a

Simpson's home, through the Rockingham gate.

*Simpson's study,
where the divorce file and
the letter threatening Nicole
with an IRS investigation
were found on June 28.*

*The trophy room.
Jurors gaped in
awe during the
walk-through.*

*Inscription in the
Rockingham driveway.*

Photos of Nicole and white fat cats hang on the wall by the stairs at Rockingham on June 13. They were later replaced with shots of black friends and family for the jury walk-through.

ABOVE: *Ron Goldman's jeans.*
INSET: *Ron's canvas boot.*

When the Bronco was reexamined at the defense's request, we found blood that had earlier gone uncollected by the criminalist Dennis Fung.

LOS ANGELES POLICE DEPARTMENT
SCIENTIFIC INVESTIGATION DIV.
PHOTOGRAPHIC SECTION

15

Blood on the rear gate at Bundy, left uncollected for nearly three weeks. Thank you, Dennis Fung.

LEFT: *The famous Rockingham glove, as it was found—not planted.*
BELOW: *At my request, a photo was taken of the Bundy and Rockingham gloves together—again.*

For a week Barry Scheck grilled Dennis Fung in one of the most painful attacks I'd ever seen.

T.B. OWEN/BLACK STAR

Lee Bailey at his best: his cross-examination of Mark Fuhrman.

GLOBE PHOTOS

GILLES MINGASSON/GAMMA LIAISON

Kato Kaelin, sycophant to the stars. Questioning Kato was an exercise in frustration.

Though we agreed on little and locked horns often, I generally enjoyed sparring with Johnnie. That was before the race card turned ugly.

Chris whispered one-liners that caused me to turn away from the cameras to hide my laughter.

Day of the verdict. Chris and I struggled to find words of encouragement for our team.

little worried. I thought maybe the strain of taking on Johnnie was getting to him. Cochran never missed an opportunity to jerk his chain, and Chris just couldn't let it slide. He'd managed to keep his temper in check until, during Johnnie's cross of Tom Lange, Cochran insisted on slipping in innuendos about Faye Resnick.

"Did you learn," he asked Tom, "whether or not Faye Resnick moved in with Nicole Brown Simpson on Friday, June 3, 1994?"

I objected: this was hearsay. Ito agreed.

But Johnnie kept pushing. "Did you ever ascertain whether or not Miss Nicole Brown Simpson had anyone who lived with her in the month before June 12 other than the children?"

"Yes."

I objected again. Ito sustained the objection once more, but Johnnie rode right over him.

"Did you find out at some point . . . that Faye Resnick moved in with Nicole Brown Simpson on or about June 3, 1994—"

"Same objection," I interjected. "Hearsay."

This time, for reasons known only to Lance, I was overruled.

"This is what I had heard, yes," Tom replied.

Johnnie was about to pursue this when Lance took the initiative and called us to a sidebar.

"Is this a disputed fact?" Ito asked me.

I was so furious I could hardly speak. But I managed. "It doesn't matter whether it is a disputed fact or not," I said. "We have all kind of slop in the record now that has been thrown in front of this jury through counsel's method of cross-examination by saying, 'Have you heard this?' 'Do you know about that?' . . ."

Johnnie certainly knew he was on shaky legal ground. So he tried a diversionary tactic: attacking us personally.

"They obviously haven't tried any cases in a long time," he said, referring to Chris and me, "and obviously don't know how, but *this* is cross-examination."

Chris blew up.

"*Who* is he talking about, doesn't know how to try [a] case?" His voice was soft but the undercurrent of fury was palpable.

"Wait, Mr. Darden," Lance warned. He'd made a rule that only one lawyer per side could speak to an issue.

Chris didn't pay any attention to him.

"Is he the only lawyer who knows how to try [a] case?"

Lance had heard enough. "I'm going to hold you in contempt," he said.

"I *should* be held in contempt," Chris threw back at him. "I have sat here and listened to—"

"Mr. Darden, I'm warning you right now."

"This *cross-examination* is out of order," Chris continued.

Ito excused the jury. Then he turned to Chris again.

"Mr. Darden, let me give you a piece of advice. Take about three deep breaths, as I am going to do, and then contemplate what you are going to say next. Do you want to take a recess now for a moment?"

"I don't require a recess," Chris replied.

". . . I have cited you. Do you have any response?"

"I would like counsel, Your Honor." Meaning: I need a lawyer.

Ito told him he could have it. I figured I'd better step in here.

"I would like to be heard in Mr. Darden's behalf," I said. Lance asked if that meant I was representing him, and I said it did.

"What we are all concerned about here, Your Honor," I explained, "is that there is a method of cross-examination that is being conducted by Mr. Cochran that has—"

But Lance cut me off. "That's not what I'm interested in, Mrs. Clark." Ito was fixated on one thing: bringing Chris to heel with an apology. "When I invite counsel to take three deep breaths and think carefully about what they are going to say to the court next," he said, "that's an opportunity to say 'Gee, I'm sorry. I lost my head there. I apologize to the court. I apologize to counsel.' When you get that response, then we move on. Do you want to fight with the court some more? You are welcome to do so."

He declared a ten-minute recess and told us to think things over.

Back at counsel table, Chris and I huddled. One look at him and I knew that taking deep breaths and apologizing was the furthest thing from his mind. Chris needed real representation now. I told him I could have the office call county counsel. "In the meantime," I said, "shall I act as your attorney?"

He thought for a moment, then nodded.

"Just don't get me arrested," he said.

When Ito reconvened the court, I asked for a continuance, so Chris could get a county lawyer and a fair hearing.

Denied.

"This is civil contempt, Counsel. It has to be adjudicated immediately, unless you want to make it a criminal contempt and have a jury trial . . ." he informed me.

"Can we use the same jury, Your Honor?" I quipped lamely.

Lance was not amused. "I've offered you now three times an opportunity to end this right now."

I had to think fast. If I let Ito believe I had advised Chris to apologize and he had refused, Chris would be in the hot seat alone. I could not do that to my partner. The only other way I saw was to take the heat myself.

You want to play, Lance? Let's play.

Very calmly—at least I was hoping it looked calm—I began removing my jewelry. First a gold bangle bracelet, which I slid down my wrist and laid unobtrusively on the table. Then my Citizen watch. I flashed momentarily on that night so many years ago when I was collared by the narc in the Ban-Lon shirt. Well, here it was: my belated bust. On national television.

I was just as scared now as I had been then. Would we be spending the night in a holding cell? I wondered. The deputies would certainly find accommodations away from the general population. Wouldn't they? I'd need to make arrangements at home. But I couldn't say where I was. *"Mommy's in jail"?* I felt that sickening anxiety brought on by a fall from grace.

Lance knew very well what I was doing, and I'm sure he was panicking as he realized this was no bluff. Still, we were acting like a bunch of cranky children. How far would this go?

From somewhere out in the audience someone called out, "Jesus Christ!"

It was Gerry Spence, the Wyoming defense attorney whose frontier-philosopher routine had made him a regular on the talk-show circuit.

"Now *there's* a candidate for contempt," I muttered under my breath.

Lance found himself in a game of chicken, and I think he knew he'd blink before I would. He began to ease his foot off the accelerator. "Miss Clark," he said, "all levity aside, I've offered you now three times an opportunity to end this right now. This is very simple. And perhaps if Mr. Darden had the opportunity to review the transcript that I have before me, he would see the wisdom of that."

Seeing the transcript would not only help us assess our chances if we challenged the contempt order, but, much more important, it might give us a half-respectable way out of this mess.

"Why don't we review the transcript, Your Honor?" I agreed.

We went to sidebar. Bailey joined us there. "Apologize, Chris," he advised him sincerely. "It's not worth your bar ticket."

I had to agree. I was looking over the transcript and I didn't like our chances. We had taken this far enough.

"It ain't worth it, G," I told him.

I think by this time Chris's anger had cooled. He seemed grateful for a way out.

"It appears that the court is correct, that perhaps my comments may have been or are somewhat inappropriate," he told Ito. "I apologize to the court. I meant no disrespect. . . ."

When Ito returned the apology, I was relieved, but also a little disgusted. After all, it was Johnnie who'd behaved outrageously. But it was Chris who'd had to fall on his sword.

On my way home that night, I paged Chris from my car phone. A few minutes later he called me back.

"Clark, what do you want?" he yelled. I could hear the noise of the freeway behind him. He was on his car phone, too.

"Hey, is that any way to talk to your attorney?" I joked.

"Well, my attorney sold me down the river, remember? Have I told you you're fired?"

"Well, you can't fire me—I quit! Besides, you haven't paid me. That's the last time I take on a criminal defendant without a retainer."

"Pay you? *Pay you?* I'll pay you, Clark. You'll find a bag of 'Snack Ems' on your chair in the morning. Consider yourself overpaid."

By now we were both convulsed with laughter. Then Chris sobered up and in a sweet, almost childlike way asked, "Did you really mean that?"

"Mean what?"

"Taking off your jewelry and all that?"

"Of course I did," I told him. "You know I got your back, G."

Johnnie was still hammering away at Tom Lange when the defense team dropped another bombshell on us. Rosa Lopez, the mystery alibi witness to whom Johnnie had alluded several times in his opening statement, was about to flee the country. He had to get her into court. Now!

The first we'd heard of this shadowy figure was a two-page statement the defense had given us only minutes before Johnnie's opening. Lopez's statement was, to be sure, short on details. She was a Salvadoran maid who worked for Simpson's neighbors. Rosa claimed to have been out walking her employers' dog at around ten, and reported seeing Simpson's Bronco parked by the curb at 10:15. Since that was about the time the dog started barking at Bundy, her story, if true, would blow a big hole in our case.

But was her story true? We strongly suspected that it was not. First tip-off: Lopez had not offered this information to police, who canvassed the neighborhood immediately after the murders. Then we did a little digging into Lopez and discovered that she had been friendly with Simpson's Israeli housekeeper, Michelle.

Michelle was, by all accounts, fanatically loyal to the defendant. And she'd had a rocky history with Nicole. When the cops were called to the Simpson house the night of the New Year's Eve argument, it was Michelle who'd tried at first to persuade them to go away. Then she'd actually come out to the police cruiser, where Nicole had taken refuge, and tried to pull her back into the house.

Later on, Michelle had locked horns with Nicole in an incident involving the kids. Sydney and Justin had tracked dirt into the house. Michelle scolded them, and that provoked an argument with Nicole—who slapped her. So there was no question as to where Michelle's loyalties lay.

According to the story the defense was handing out, Rosa had told Michelle about seeing the Bronco at the curb, and Michelle insisted that she get in touch with Simpson's attorneys. Think about this for a moment. Lopez's statement comes in suspiciously late. It includes exactly *one* firm detail—which just happens to be a key exoneration point for the defendant. The witness is friendly with the defendant's devoted maid. This had all the earmarks of a defense plant.

Lopez's testimony wasn't scheduled to come up until the defense put on its case; we thought we'd have several months to do some more checking on her. Now, her supposed threat to leave the country spiked that plan: Johnnie wanted to call her in to preserve her testimony.

We saw the timing as one more low trick. The defense suspected that Rosa was a serious flake and they were afraid of how she would play as a witness. Rather than take a chance with her during their case-in-chief—and giving us the opportunity to investigate her and prepare our cross—they wanted to do a dress rehearsal in what is called a conditional exam, which is done outside the presence of the jury. If Lopez didn't come across well here, she'd be buried in the middle of our case. If she was persuasive, however, they could bring her back later. And if she fled in the meantime, they could enter her earlier testimony into the record. For the defense it was a no-lose proposition.

For us, it was lose all around. Interjecting Rosa into the middle of the People's case would not only break our momentum, but get the jury thinking about alibis. We had to stop it.

Lance ruled that we would examine Lopez out of the jury's presence, so he could decide whether she truly posed a flight risk. That Friday, she took the stand. She was a sunken, peculiar little woman, wearing what appeared to be a purple velour jogging suit. She didn't look particularly happy to be there. She'd come with an attorney. *Where,* I thought, *does a down-at-the-heels character like this one get the bucks to hire a lawyer?*

Under Johnnie's questioning, Lopez contended that because of her involvement in the case, she had lost her job and had to move out— and was about to return to her homeland. "The reporters wouldn't leave me alone," Lopez told the court in Spanish, through an interpreter. "I'm tired of looking at them. They have been harassing me."

Harassing? Even allowing for the translation, this smacked of coaching.

She began to weep. Someone gave her a Kleenex.

"Do you have any present plans to return to El Salvador?" Johnnie asked her.

"I would like to go tomorrow."

Since I was on witness fifteen and counting, Chris had agreed to question Rosa. "You made [a reservation] today?" he asked her. ". . . Prior to coming to court this morning?"

"Sí," she assured him.

He asked her whether anyone had told her to do so. No, she said, she had decided to do it. She would stay away for a long time.

I passed a note to Chris:

"Ask her what airline and under what name."

He did. She replied that her reservation was booked under her own name. And then he asked her the airline.

"Taca. Taca International. T-A-C-A."

Cheri ran out to check. What a surprise: Rosa had no reservation.

Chris bored into her: "Miss Lopez, we just called the airline. They don't have a reservation for you. Can you explain to the court why it is that you just told us you have a reservation?"

"Because I am going to reserve it, sir. As soon as I reserve it, I will buy my ticket and I will leave. If you want to, the cameras can follow me."

Rosa was not as dull-witted as she seemed.

But Chris had nailed her. Wasn't it true that she told us she had actually made the reservation? he wanted to know. She avoided the question, but finally had to answer.

"No," she said.

Not only was she lying, but now she was lying *about lying.*

To me, the issue seemed clear-cut. Lopez had no reservation; there was no immediate threat that she'd flee. Ergo, no need for a conditional exam. Johnnie, however, argued that this woman was a salt-o'-the-earth heroine who was risking her personal safety by even showing up. It would be an insult to every citizen who comes forward in a trial, he explained, if we were going to doubt this fine woman's word that she was about to leave.

Chris was astounded. "Are we talking about the same Rosa Lopez?"

But Ito was simply not willing to take the chance that she would skip the country—in that case, he reasoned, Simpson would be denied an important witness. The only question that remained was whether the hearing would be held in the presence of the jury or recorded on videotape. We were pushing for the latter. From what I'd seen of Rosa, there was an excellent chance that she would self-destruct so spectacularly that the defense wouldn't dare introduce the tape.

It was our understanding that Ito wouldn't make his final determination until Monday and I'd told everyone—including the judge—that I had to leave early that day. Late that Friday, Chris, Frank, and I were in a conference upstairs—I was about to leave, in fact—when a law clerk delivered the news. Ito was calling in the jury! He intended to start the hearing immediately. He would keep court in session until midnight if he had to.

The news nearly sent me into a panic. I'd given Lance notice at least twice that I couldn't stay any later than four o'clock. He assured me in chambers that it wouldn't be a problem; we should be done by noon. Now, it was already getting near six.

I raced downstairs and asked to be heard.

"I have informed the court I cannot be present tonight because I do have to take care of my children . . ." I said. "And I do not want proceedings to go before a jury when I can't be here."

I reminded Lance that we had talked about this earlier. As I spoke I began feeling self-conscious and very alone. I looked Lance in the eye. "I can't be here, Your Honor."

My voice was quavering. Oh, God. I was like a six-year-old whose daddy had backed down on a promise to take her to the park. "But you promised me, Daddy!"

Get a grip!

"Miss Clark," Lance replied, "I'm sorry. I apologize to you. I had forgotten that problem." He explained to the court that he had made "adjustments" for my children problems. "I just plain forgot," he apologized.

Johnnie saw an opportunity here and he grabbed it. *Let's do it without Marcia!*

"This is Mr. Darden's witness," he said. "As the court has seen, Mr. Darden is absolutely capable of conducting this examination. . . . It seems to me we should be able to proceed ahead."

Johnnie, I knew, would be delighted to do Lopez without me. He could push Chris's buttons in a way he couldn't push mine.

Ito cut him off, reminding him that I was the lead prosecutor, and that if it were Johnnie who'd requested an early departure, he'd call a recess for him as well. He would call the jury back in and tell them we were through for the weekend.

Over the next four court days, Chris annihilated Rosa Lopez. The D.A. investigators had turned up Sylvia Guerra, a maid who worked for neighbors of Rosa's employers. Sylvia told how Rosa had approached her and offered her $5,000 to corroborate the Bronco story. She'd also tried to sell her tale to the *National Enquirer,* but even that purveyor of grotesqueries wouldn't go for it.

We also discovered that there was a tape recording that a defense investigator named Bill Pavelic had done with Rosa. The defense-team investigator told Chris that he'd "forgotten" all about it. Ito ordered him to bring the tape and notes to court. "I shall do my best to get those items," Pavelic answered.

For once, Ito was firm. "No, don't do your best," Lance boomed. "Have them here tomorrow!"

The next morning, Chris, Johnnie, Carl, and I met in Lance's chambers to listen to the tape. No wonder the defense had tried to conceal it from us—it was an absolute joke. When Rosa said she heard someone walking outside her window at nine, Pavelic quickly corrected her, adjusting the time to "nine-thirty or nine-forty-five." When it came to the critical time when she spotted the Bronco, there was a long pause accompanied by a rustling of papers. Then Rosa comes back with a firm "Ten-twenty. Ten-fifteen, I'm takin' my dog for a walk."

It was clear to me that she'd been coached to within an inch of her life.

Afterward, during Chris's cross, Rosa withdrew further and further from her original claims, repeatedly chanting *"No me recuerdo." I don't remember.* Johnnie wouldn't leave it alone. He tried to float an explanation that in El Salvador "I don't remember" is a colloquial expression for "I don't know." It was ridiculous. He was making a fool of himself over a witness who had taken a steep skid from defense linchpin to laughingstock.

In the end, even Lance Ito could not ignore the defense's serious misconduct in deliberately hiding discovery for this witness and others. Ruling that Johnny had made "untrue representations" to the court in "reckless disregard of the truth," Lance fined Johnnie and Carl Douglas a mere $950 each. (If Ito had made the fine $1,000, the sanction, by law, would have been reported to the state bar, and Lance Ito did not want to be the one to put a blot on Johnnie Cochran's record.) The judge also promised to tell the jury that this was a violation of law and that they could consider the delay in disclosure when assessing the credibility of the witness. Of course, this was academic, since the defense prudently dropped Lopez from their witness list.

Days of court time wasted, the jury detained for no good reason, the People's case disrupted—all because the defense wanted to float a trial balloon for a phony witness. In the end Rosa Lopez didn't amount to a hill of beans. But I'll always remember her for those humiliating moments when I was forced to tell the judge, on national television, that I had to leave to go home.

It turned out, that was only the beginning of my nightmare. To my utter dismay, my personal life was about to become a national issue.

Back in court Monday morning, I was arguing the motion to keep Rosa Lopez's testimony from the jury, and Johnnie got ticked off at me. So he launched into a surprise attack. He accused me of using child care as a "ploy" to buy time. It was an outrageous allegation. I wasn't going to let it pass.

"I'm offended as a woman, as a single parent, and as a prosecutor and an officer of the court to hear an argument posed by counsel like that of Mr. Cochran today," I said. "Some of us have child-care issues, and they are serious and they are paramount. Obviously, Mr. Cochran cannot understand that, but he should not come before this court and impugn the integrity of someone who does have those considerations."

At the moment when I loosed this little salvo, I was still under the impression that this child-care thing was a limited skirmish being waged between Johnnie and me, albeit in front of a national audience. The following day, however, when I was on my way back to my office during recess, Suzanne drew me aside in the foyer of the War Room. The expression on her face was pained, so I knew she was going to tell me something horrible. Well, what else was new?

"I can't let you go back down to court without warning you," she told me.

"Go ahead," I told her. "I won't shoot."

"Gordon has filed for primary custody. His declaration is being carried all over the newses."

I'd been bracing for another Simpson setback. This blow hit me like a two-by-four. My knees got wobbly. My throat grabbed up.

"Oh, my God, no. Oh no." It was all I could say. I sank into a chair and put my face in my hands.

Suzanne broke into my misery. "They're running excerpts from his declaration on all of the channels."

"What is he saying?" I asked weakly.

She beckoned me to her office. There, all nine of her television screens were on. The talking heads on every single one were all covering the same thing: Gordon's request for custody.

"How does this happen?" I asked Suzanne, incredulous. "How does the media get hold of a motion before *I* know it even exists?"

I had been a street fighter all my life, but this kind of warfare was all new to me. My divorce from Gaby had been uncontested. I hadn't asked for anything except my freedom. And back then there was nothing to get from me. Now I was faced with the loss of my children. And because I was locked into this trial, I didn't even have the freedom to devote the 110 percent I needed so badly to put into the fight.

I needed time to think what to do. I needed time to talk to a lawyer, I needed time to absorb the shock, but the demands of this case afforded me none. Clearly, especially after Johnnie's attack, no one would understand if I asked Ito for a few days off to handle this personal crisis. Instead I'd probably be crucified both in court and in the press, and the stories would all have the same punch line: "See what happens when you let a girl do a man's job?"

Would a judge really take my children away? Here I was with my life in overdrive. Never enough sleep. Constantly under the gun to do in one week what a prosecutor normally required six months to do. I'd been proud of the fact that I'd been able to meet *all* my commitments. That had meant putting in a full workday, rushing home, then, at the end of the evening, putting in another five hours of work before collapsing in an exhausted heap among my pillows.

I'd promised myself almost daily that once I got through with this damned trial, I'd never think about touching a high-profile case again. To paraphrase Jim Morrison, my ballroom days were over, baby. I wanted to try nothing but nice anonymous little cases where no camera would care to go. A year ago, when I'd come back to Special Trials, I'd planned to try one or two more big cases. Of course, when I thought "big," I hadn't foreseen the Simpson case. Nothing in my experience, or anyone else's, could have prepared me for that.

Two months into the Simpson case, these ambitions had already lost their appeal. The total immersion I'd not only enjoyed but needed in years past was no longer attractive to me. When I'd been doing run-of-the-mill cases, work and home were not in constant conflict. But Simpson had rewritten the rulebook.

I couldn't stop staring at the TV screens. My divorce was being treated like the news of a military coup or the latest election results. I felt that weird, disembodied sensation I'd suffered so many times throughout this case when I'd seen myself on television or in newspapers and magazines. Who was that woman? She looked like me, all right, but I had no sense of connection to her.

Suzanne's phones were ringing off their hooks. The media wanted my response to the allegations. "We want to give you a chance to tell your side," they said.

"No," I told Suzanne. "Ms. Clark does not care to make a response."

I didn't need anyone to advise me on this one. You don't wash your laundry, dirty or otherwise, in public.

That night, after everyone was asleep, I went into my own bedroom. From the top shelf of the closet I pulled out a photo album and I opened the embossed maroon cover. The very first photo was of Matt the day he was born. Why *do* all newborns look like Yoda? I was in my hospital gown, preparing to nurse him for the first time. I looked exhausted but happy. Very happy.

I'd always wanted to have children. But I didn't want to do it until I'd set my life up well enough to give them a good home and a sense of permanence. That meant waiting until I was a Grade 4. During the seventies and eighties, it was an unspoken fact at the D.A.'s office that if a woman took maternity leave, it could derail her efforts to advance. People just took you a lot less seriously when they saw you going off to make babies. The office is much better about that now, but back when I was a young deputy, it was a reality.

When I made Grade 4, I was thirty-five and pushing the edge of the maternity envelope. Hanging over me was my childhood premonition that I would die young. I really never expected to live beyond the age of forty-five. I suppose that some subrational part of my brain believed that if I had children I might get an extension on the deadline. A continuance, so to speak. It made sense to me that nature has an interest in keeping a mother alive, at least until her children are grown. And if I had children, I would *want* to live. I would fight to live. You don't think about having kids unless you're hungry for life.

I remember thinking that getting pregnant would be as easy as quitting birth control. But it wasn't. After a year of no birth control and no baby, I'd consulted my gynecologist. He gave me a few shots, then a few pills. Then a more powerful fertility pill. Two months later, I was expecting. I was thrilled beyond words. But I was afraid to tell anyone at work. I wasn't a teenager. Miscarriages at my age were not uncommon. And what if the amniocentesis showed my baby wasn't okay? I couldn't even bear to think about that. I decided to keep the news to myself.

I bought a few drop-waisted jumpers to camouflage my growing belly and silently endured the ribbing I took about my change in style from tailored suits to Laura Ashley. For court appearances I found I could get away with leaving my skirt unbuttoned and keeping my jacket closed—at least for the first five months or so.

Secretly, I was elated. Every day I'd look in the mirror and lightly move my hand over my belly. Had it grown? Unlikely, since I'd checked it just hours ago. It was a thrill unlike any other I'd known to see the baby in the sonogram. My little boy was real! I could *see* his heartbeat. After amnio showed the baby was healthy, I was so happy I felt drunk.

During that time, I caught the Bardo case. I was still hiding my pregnancy, and I knew there was a very good chance I'd be in trial by the time I went into labor. (As it turned out, that case took so long to get to court that I'd long since given birth to Matthew.) But I still kept mum about the pregnancy well into my sixth month. I didn't want to be treated as an invalid. (In hindsight I suppose my camouflage efforts fooled no one. But they let me act out the charade.) I felt great, at least most of the time. I'd ridden out the morning-sickness phase by sneaking animal crackers in court. They were the only thing that seemed to settle my queasy stomach. But morning sickness passed, and things were good for me.

Come month six, however, I had to tell my supervisor, an impersonal, imperious man, about my condition.

"I just wanted you to know that I'm pregnant." It came tumbling out. "I'm not going to take any time off before the birth. And I won't take a lot of maternity leave after I have the baby." I braced myself for his reaction.

"No problem," he said, barely looking up. "Ride that horse till it drops."

During the preliminary hearings for Bardo, I was almost nine months pregnant. The press had been allowed to park a camera in the jury box, which meant they got a side view that made me look like Shamu. I joked with the cameraman that if he ever aired that shot, I'd move to have the press excluded. But the fact of the matter is, I loved it. I was really a mommy. My swollen silhouette proved it. What my friends couldn't believe was how I always talked about this baby. And what I'd do for the next one.

"How can you even think about *another* baby?" they'd ask. "You haven't even had this one yet."

But, you see, I never considered having only one child. It would be two or none. I remembered all too well the six years of loneliness I'd felt until my brother was born. I wanted to make sure that my children were born as close together as my health and strength would allow. Then they would always have each other for company.

And so, I found myself pregnant again. This time, trying a double homicide. I was worried about being able to finish the case before I went into labor. But the judge ran a tight ship, and I figured things would move quickly.

Right in the middle of jury selection, however, the Rodney King verdict had come in. The riots shut us down for a few days. During that time, I fretted. Would our jury, which was shaping up to be largely African-American, take out their anger on me? It wasn't a great time to be trying a case. Fortunately, the defendants thought so too. They moved for a mistrial, and the judge granted it.

That left me at loose ends, and still very pregnant. I got lucky. One of my friends in the Special Trials Unit, John Zajec, was getting ready to go to trial on another double homicide. For the past few months, whenever we met in the strip of hallway between our offices, John and I had been batting around the various legal and strategic issues on his case. When my case got bumped to the back burner, I'd go down to his office and hustle up some conversation. I was such a junkie, if I couldn't have a case of my own, I'd glom onto someone else's.

Over lunch, I'd come up with an idea. Maybe I could be his second chair.

"If you don't like the idea, just tell me so," I told him slyly. "But maybe having a pregnant chick next to you will get some jury sympathy. And I'll put on all the boring stuff."

"Sounds great," he told me.

And that's how I wound up arguing for the imposition of the death penalty exactly one week before giving birth to Tyler. My spirits were high, but my body wasn't exactly cooperating. Although I was in good shape physically, my pelvic bones had loosened up, a natural occurrence that prepares women for birthing. I found that if I stood up too fast after I'd been sitting for a while, my legs felt like they'd come out of their sockets and I'd have to kind of shake them back into place.

I could hide most of that business sitting at counsel table. The awkward part came when I'd been standing at the lectern examining a witness. I'd just asked him if he'd like to refresh his memory by looking at the text of his statement. Yes, he told me, he would. I took a step, or rather tried to, when I realized that my leg wouldn't go back where it belonged. I was struggling to coax it back into place when the judge, puzzled by the pause, asked, "Ms. Clark, would you like to approach the witness?"

"Yes . . . well . . . I'd like to, Your Honor."

I was having to smother laughter. This was like a Buster Keaton routine. Finally, I shook the sucker back into joint and glided to the witness stand. Later when I told John what had happened, he just shook his head and said, "You women! I don't know how you do it."

The jurors returned a verdict of guilty. They later confided in me that they'd been taking bets as to whether I'd make it to the end.

I could never have imagined that motherhood would be so all-consuming. You spend the first thirty-six years of your life as a free agent—and pow. You're responsible for the survival of a totally help-less humanoid. Colic! Life for the first four months is like one long wail. You're frantic to ease the pain. Must be something you're eating, right? So you add vegetables. Then you eliminate vegetables, cut out spices, reduce dairy intake.

Only time takes care of the problem.

My friends all warned me about what to expect when I went back to work. You think you'll be glad to get out of the house, they said. But when the time comes, you'll yearn to get back. You'll actually find yourself calling home during the day just to hear the baby cry. They were right. Those same friends would later reassure me that it's pos-sible to love a second baby as much as the first. It's true. I don't know how that works, I guess the heart just expands.

Mothering, of course, complicated life exponentially. Suddenly, a trip to the grocery store became a major logistical ordeal. If I took a baby, or two of them, I'd have to bring a stroller or backpack carrier, a diaper bag, a bottle, and at least one toy. I'd reach in my purse for a pen and come up with a toy airplane or a G.I. Joe. Or I'd be sitting in court trying a case, and my beeper would go off with a call from home.

My colleagues were sympathetic. Even during the Simpson case, when we were all in the throes of monstrous stress, my teammates were all so sweet and considerate. It wasn't unusual for our meetings to be interrupted by a phone call from the domestic front and Hank and Scott would riff on my transformation from Darth Vader to Mother Goose. Not until this Monday morning in February, when Johnnie hit me with his accusations that I had used my children—*used* them—had I come face-to-face with reality: not all the world loves a working mother.

I turned to the last page of the photo album and was mortified to realize that I hadn't inserted any of the pictures taken over the last eight months. They were still up on the shelf in their plastic covers. When the trial was over, I'd get the album up-to-date, I promised myself.

I wanted to lock myself into the bathroom and scream, to pound on the walls. I wanted to mount an offensive that would lay waste to three countries. But I couldn't do that. I couldn't afford self-indulgence. I had to call a lawyer immediately to get the ball rolling.

Next morning, I slunk into work like a dog expecting to be hit. When I opened the door to my office I was overwhelmed by the sight and scent of flowers. There were red roses, yellow roses, white roses. There were stalks of gladiolus and eucalyptus, birds-of-paradise, pink and lavender freesias, knots of sweet William and violets. My dank bureaucratic lair had been transformed into a hothouse in full riot. I read the cards on the first three or four bouquets to see who my well-wishers were. No one I knew—just strangers, from Texas, Connecticut, Washington, D.C. All over. They were sending me sympathy and wishing me luck.

Well, I'll be dipped.

For months before this, supporters had been sending the team jewelry, cosmetics, clothing, and other trinkets. When the bottlers of Evian water saw that Chris and I kept Crystal Geyser on the counsel table, they air-freighted us cases of their own stuff. Someone even sent Chris an expensive leather flight jacket. Chris thought it was hilarious. He started calling this bounty "free shit," FS for short.

But the FS we'd gotten to date was nothing compared to the avalanche that poured in during those days after Gordon's custody filing. Scott dubbed the new influx "more free shit." MFS! Before, I'd gotten flowers only from women; now I got them from men as well. And everybody wanted to know how they could help me out.

Amid this outpouring of goodwill there was a touching solicitude for me personally. A Holocaust survivor sent me a book on coping. My haggard appearance caused others to send cough medicine and vitamins. I got a lot of books on stress. I received angels of every kind. Ceramic, wood, papier-mâché. I kept them all.

I think what touched me most was a letter sent by a convent of Dominican nuns. This wonderful missive urged courage and fortitude;

it was sort of the Dominican version of "Go, girlfriend." I taped it to the wall next to my desk and turned to it several times a day for comfort.

Sisters, if you're reading this, please accept my gratitude. The next few weeks would be the most trying of my life. Through it all, your prayers preserved my sanity.

And FS restored my faith in my fellow man.

_M_arine to Marine

CAR TAPE. _February 28. I'd like to trade lives with just about anybody right now. "County jail inmate" sounds good._

During the days before Mark Fuhrman took the stand, he was a pain in the ass. He'd hulk into the office in the company of three beefy bodyguards lent to him by the Metro Division. Chris was supposed to be looking after him, but instead went out of his way to stay clear of the scene. So Cheri Lewis usually drew the short straw and had to baby-sit. Once he settled into Cheri's office, Mark would spend his hours sulking, throwing tantrums, or wailing about how the defense had ruined his life.

Not that I wasn't sympathetic. At a personal level my heart went out to him. Publicity seekers, hucksters, disaffected cops and county workers, and wackos of every stripe were streaming out of the wood-work to recall supposed locker-room boasts that he'd had an affair with Nicole Brown or had painted swastikas on the lockers of fellow officers. IAD had looked into the allegations. They all turned out to be bullshit.

Mark was clearly the object of a witch-hunt. But I felt that we were spending entirely too many hours mollycoddling one witness. Mark Fuhrman just wasn't that important. He'd found a single piece of evidence in a case that involved dozens of equally inculpatory findings. He'd had nothing at all to do with the blood at Bundy, the blood in the Bronco, the hair and fibers on Ron Goldman and on the knit cap, the blood and fibers on Simpson's socks. Under normal circumstances, any one of these would have been enough to nail a defendant.

Fuhrman was a big deal only because the defense required a bogeyman to distract the jury from the devastating evidence against their client.

Almost every day, the defense made some attempt to inject race into the courtroom. It seemed to me the height of immorality—cynically exploiting a serious social issue for the benefit of a murderer who'd never lifted a damned finger to advance the cause of civil rights. O. J. Simpson wasn't "rousted" by a band of racist cops—the *evidence* demanded that he be arrested and tried. You can call the cops sloppy, you can call me and my colleagues inept, but the facts showed that Simpson was guilty. The deliberate twisting of reality to distort this horrific murder into a racial cause was the biggest lie told in the entire case.

And by the time Mark Fuhrman hit the stand, the Big Lie had done its damage. It was even beginning to affect our own thinking. We spent way too much time playing defense. Every so often I had to shake myself back to reality. This case was about rage and control. It was about compelling and overwhelming circumstantial evidence pointing to the guilt of one man and one man alone. To the extent that we allowed ourselves to be distracted by false issues, we failed to fulfill our duty to the People.

As for our whining detective, the only question on the table, as far as I was concerned, was "Did Mark Fuhrman plant evidence?" The answer was an obvious "No." We'd established beyond doubt that there was only one glove at Bundy when the first officers arrived. There was still only one glove there when Mark arrived two hours later. He couldn't have planted evidence even if he'd wanted to. The issue of whether he was a racist was completely irrelevant. Or, at least, it should have been.

Lance Ito screwed us on that one.

Back in January, you'll recall, we'd argued against allowing the defense to introduce evidence that Mark Fuhrman had ever uttered the word "nigger." It would serve no purpose, we warned, but to antagonize the jury. Ito originally agreed with us, but then, as usual, reversed himself. Of the many errors Ito made during this trial, that one was the most blindly destructive. It was also the most far-reaching. Once he'd allowed the N-word in, he was forced to make a series of bad decisions all the way down the line. In the aggregate, they assured a miscarriage of justice.

The N-word ruling hung around our necks like an eight-hundred-pound albatross. We should have been able to have Mark Fuhrman testify to the very limited area of the case of which he had knowledge. Now, by putting him on the stand, we risked provoking a riot in the jury box.

So why didn't we just refuse to call Fuhrman as a witness? Simple. Leaving him out would have been worse.

What would have happened if we hadn't called him? It's not as if he'd have disappeared from the case. The defense would ask every witness, at every opportunity, why Mark Fuhrman wasn't at this trial. "Is he beyond subpoena power? Is he refusing to testify? No? I see." Net result? We'd look like we were hiding him. Why would we do that? Because we *had* something to hide. And then, this theme would be sure to reach its crescendo during closing arguments, where the law explicitly permits either side to comment on the failure of the other to call a logical witness. The defense would blow us away.

Or, even worse, they might have called Fuhrman themselves! Gerald Uelmen had already announced their intention to do precisely that. Back in January, he'd made a not-so-veiled threat: if we didn't present Fuhrman, "he will make another appearance in this case, being called as a hostile witness by the defense." If that happened, they could really go crazy on us.

"Did the prosecution ever subpoena you?" they'd ask him. "Did they tell you why they didn't? You found the glove at Rockingham, right? Would you agree that was a pretty important piece of evidence? Isn't it true the prosecution didn't call you because you'd be forced to admit that you planted that glove?"

Of course, we'd object. And our objections might have been sustained. But the damage would have been done.

Look, if I could have thwarted the race card by not calling Fuhrman, I would have crossed him off the witness list in a heartbeat. But failure to produce him would simply have aggravated the controversy. The only course open to us was to call Fuhrman and try to block the kicks.

I was guardedly optimistic about the possibilities for damage control. We had in our possession only three pieces of evidence to suggest that Mark had ever used the N-word: the Joseph Britton civil case against the city; the statements Fuhrman had made as part of his disability claim against the city; and, of course, the letter from Kathleen Bell. Only one of those three had a chance of getting admitted into court, and even that one had some pretty big credibility problems.

Britton, you'll recall, was the African-American robbery suspect who'd been shot leaving an automated teller machine back in 1987. He'd claimed that the cop who shot him then planted a weapon at his feet to justify the shooting. On top of it all, the cop supposedly shouted, "You stupid nigger. Why did you run?" Fuhrman was one of the policemen who had apprehended Britton. Now the defense wanted to present Britton as a witness, apparently to finger Fuhrman as his tormentor. But once we checked them out, those allegations fell apart. In a deposition after the fact, he'd described the officer who'd shot him as having "red hair and a mustache." Not our Fuhrman. And in an interview with CBS News in October 1994, Britton was asked point-blank if Fuhrman had said anything racial to him.

"At this point—no," he replied. "I can't say that he did."

What the heck does that mean? At some point in the future, you'll decide that he did?

Ito found the value of Britton's testimony to be "highly speculative" and dismissed it out of hand.

Fuhrman's disability claim was more complicated. There seemed to be no question that Mark had popped off to his shrinks about "Mexicans and niggers," but even the doctors who examined him concluded that he was exaggerating, perhaps lying outright, about the degree of racial hostility he felt. The suit was dismissed after the examiners concluded that Mark was faking.

I could believe this. It is no secret around law enforcement that cops will tell whoppers to get an early pension. A pension can be quite a windfall. What troubled me was the nature of the lie. Why had he chosen to portray himself as a raving racist? I knew Mark had been assigned to some pretty rough neighborhoods. Gangs, dope, poverty—in South-Central and East L.A., all conspired to produce one of the highest rates of violence in the nation. A cop who butts heads with hoods day after day after day can suffer a nasty case of burnout. But Mark's anger seemed directed at criminals in general—not minorities in particular.

Back in July, after I'd gotten the lowdown on Mark's disability claim, I'd placed a confidential call to Ron Phillips to get his reading on Fuhrman. Ron wasn't a close friend of Mark's, but he'd supervised him. Ron told me that at the time Mark had made those statements to the shrinks, his first marriage had just fallen apart and he'd gone into an emotional tailspin. When Ron started working with Mark a few years later, he found him a hot dog: arrogant, mouthy, easily provoked to anger.

But over the next few years, Ron explained to me, Mark went through a sea change. The hostility subsided. His performance improved. Making detective gave him a world of confidence. His new marriage also seemed to stabilize him. Ron felt Mark Fuhrman had matured a good deal and had turned out to be not only a decent guy but one damned fine cop.

That opinion was shared by other officers, even black ones. When the charges of evidence-planting first surfaced, several black cops called our office to put in a good word for him. We got a memo from one guy from the West L.A. Division who told how he and other African Americans played early-morning basketball with Mark. "At no time," he wrote, "have I heard him disrespect me or any other African American. Not even in jest."

Prosecutors who'd had the opportunity to work with Mark in the past were also favorably impressed. Hank could vouch for the fact that Mark never pushed questionable filings. Any case he brought was well investigated and carefully prepared. My friend and fellow D.A. Lynn Reed, who worked in the West L.A. office, recalled how thoughtful Fuhrman had always been to her black rape victims. Once he'd gone to bat for a black suspect who, on the basis of witness reports and other evidence, seemed to have committed murder. Mark was the lead investigator; he could easily have ignored the suspect's claims of innocence. But he was willing to check out the guy's story, and after putting in some decent overtime, he wound up clearing him of all charges. These were hardly the actions of a dedicated racist.

Fuhrman also had an enthusiastic supporter in Danette Meyers, the African-American deputy D.A. he'd worked with in West L.A. During my brief turn in management I'd been her supervisor, and I admired the hell out of her. She was tough and hard-hitting—a trial junkie like me. She and Fuhrman often went out to lunch and dinner together. Danette had even baby-sat for Mark's kids.

After the *New Yorker* piece appeared, I'd given her a call for a character reading on Fuhrman.

"Mark's a good cop," Danette told me. "He wouldn't frame anyone." She paused for a moment. "Don't let them get you down, girl."

Coming from Danette, this endorsement carried a lot of weight. It reinforced my own conviction that Mark, if he had ever had been a racist, had reformed. People do change.

In any case, the statements Fuhrman had made to the shrinks weren't going to find their way into court. Ito did not find "a direct link between comments made in approximately 1980 and credibility in 1994."

Another bullet whizzing past our ears.

That left Kathleen Bell.

Back in July, shortly after the *New Yorker* article appeared, someone dropped a facsimile of a letter on my desk. It was one page, typed all in caps.

"DEAR MR. COCHRAN . . ." it began. "OFFICER FERMAN [*sic*] WAS A MAN THAT I HAD THE MISFORTUNE OF MEETING. . . . MR. FERMAN MAY BE MORE OF A RACIST THAN YOU COULD EVEN IMAGINE."

The writer, Kathleen Bell, went on to explain how, between 1985 and 1986, she'd worked in a real estate agency located above a marine recruiting station near Mark's neighborhood in Redondo Beach. She'd drop down to say hi to the marines working there. On a couple of occasions she'd seen Mark Fuhrman. She'd remembered him "distinctly" because of his height and build.

"OFFICER FERMAN SAID THAT WHEN HE SEES A 'NIGGER' (AS HE CALLED IT) DRIVING WITH A WHITE WOMAN, HE WOULD PULL THEM OVER," Bell wrote. "BUT I ASKED WOULD [*sic*] IF HE DIDN'T HAVE A REASON. AND HE SAID THAT HE WOULD FIND ONE." Fuhrman, Bell went on to say, would like nothing more than to see all niggers gathered together and killed. She was "almost certain" that she'd called the LAPD to complain about "Ferman" even though she did not know his last name at that time.

A couple of weeks after writing this letter Bell gave a longer statement to the defense, claiming that Fuhrman had told her, "If I had my way, they would take all the niggers, put them in a big group, and burn them."

Kathleen Bell's allegations struck me unlikely. First off, the comments about the black man and white woman in the car fit too neatly into the defense's case. That is, Fuhrman is enraged when he sees Simpson with a Caucasian wife, so when he gets the chance he plants evidence to frame him. But the slurs Bell attributed to Fuhrman were mighty improbable, especially in the mid-eighties. A racist cop might talk trash in a locker room, but you would never hear that kind of bald, incendiary stuff in a public place—for the very reason Bell's letter suggests. Somebody might call in a complaint, triggering an investigation by Internal Affairs. She seemed to recall Fuhrman's remarks with suspicious particularity, given that they were ten years old.

We got wind that Bell would be putting in an appearance on *Larry King Live*. We asked Mark to watch it on the off chance he might say, "Yeah. I remember her." Afterward, he called me to say, "Look, I may have met her. But she doesn't look familiar. I really can't say that I did."

I assigned Cheri and an investigator to scope out the scene in Redondo Beach and get the lowdown on Bell. One of the marines described her as a "pudgy" woman who would come down to the recruiting station to flirt and invite marines out to lunch. Sometime during 1985 or 1986, Mark Fuhrman had visited the recruiting station to inquire about going into the reserves. A former marine pilot,

Joseph Foss, recalled standing in front of the office with Fuhrman when Bell approached them. Foss introduced them. Then, he claimed, Bell apparently hit on Fuhrman, but he rebuffed her advances with what Foss described as a "gracious" rejection. Foss said he never heard Fuhrman make racially charged comments to Kathleen Bell or anyone else.

Two other marines assigned to the recruiting station had also been around when Fuhrman came in. One of them, a black man named Maximo Cordoba, was questioned by a private eye working for Mark. Neither marine ever saw him with Kathleen Bell—but we hadn't heard the last of Max Cordoba.

We tried repeatedly to reach Kathleen Bell, but she'd gotten herself a lawyer and he was refusing our requests to speak with her. He charged that we were just trying to dig up something to impeach her with. So? This woman writes a letter to Johnnie Cochran of her own free will. Now, when no one else can corroborate her story, she doesn't want to be questioned?

I'd suspected from the outset that Bell wasn't motivated by a good citizen's desire to blow the whistle on racism. We received a package of discovery material that lent weight to those suspicions. It contained a memo dated August 31, 1994, in which a defense investigator recounts a conversation with Ms. Bell's lawyer:

> I was contacted today by . . . an attorney who is representing Kathleen Bell. . . . He told me that Ms. Bell has talked to the tabloids but no deal has been struck. He went on to say that he has known Ms. Bell a long time and that she is a credible and truthful person. However, she is "not a wealthy woman" and if a large sum of money was offered, she would consider it. . . .

Could the message be any clearer? It sounded to me like she was saying, "I'll go to the highest bidder." We would have loved to use this material to impeach her when she appeared at trial. (And we knew she would; Ito had ruled that the Redondo Beach incidents were not too remote in time to be ruled inadmissible.) Unfortunately, we were in a bind. The more evidence we used to discredit Bell, the more latitude the defense would be given to introduce *other* evidence of the N-word in order to shore up Bell's credibility. In the end, we had to cut our losses and go easy on Kathleen Bell.

In the frenzy of Monday-morning quarterbacking that followed the trial, pundits would soberly characterize Bell as a credible witness with no ax to grind. Give me a break. This woman was looking for a payday and, very possibly, for payback. What more satisfying revenge could you take on a man who has rejected you than to humiliate him before an entire nation? The supreme irony was that Mark Fuhrman didn't even remember her. But we'd all have to deal with her in court, when Kathleen Bell would have a chance to savor her few minutes of fame.

The relationship between Chris and Mark continued to deteriorate. Chris would not spend more than five minutes in Mark's company if he could help it. And Chris made it clear that he intended to treat Mark as a hostile witness. He didn't intend to object to anything the defense said on cross. *Just great,* I thought. *If it looks like we despise Fuhrman, the jury will not only feel free to hate him, but will conclude that* we *don't believe him, and that we think he planted evidence.*

The Sunday of Presidents' Day weekend, I'd come into the office to fine-tune my direct of Kato Kaelin. I was plowing through a mountain of binders, on my fifth cigarette of the day, when Cheri knocked on the door.

"What's up?" I asked her, grateful for a break. I leaned back and put my feet on the desk. I was wearing my usual weekend uniform: leggings, sneakers, and a sweatshirt. Cheri looked worried.

"I don't know if you know what's going on," she said. "But Chris had Mark down in the grand jury room. There were about ten other deputies and law clerks firing questions at him."

I shot forward in my chair and slammed my feet onto the floor. Why the grand jury room? Why the cast of thousands? If you want to act out a cross realistically, only one person should be doing the questioning.

Alan Yochelson, one of our deputies who was a good bud of Chris's, stuck his head in the door.

"What the fuck is going on down there?" I demanded.

"They were firing questions at him and he denied using racial slurs," Alan reported. "I don't know if Chris expected this setup would get him to admit it, or what. But whatever he expected, Mark hasn't admitted to anything."

"Where are they now?" I asked.

"I don't know, it broke up a few minutes ago," said Cheri. "I'm not sure where Chris is, maybe in with Terry."

I was furious. This was just so typical of Chris. He loved to be the center of attention. He'd never do anything quietly if he could turn it into a sound-and-light show. That's the problem with the team approach to prosecution. You can't stay on top of what other members of the team are doing all the time; you have to give them a certain amount of autonomy. But if they're willful, they're likely to do ill-considered things. I kept my temper in check until the end of the day, when Chris himself finally thought to pay me a visit.

"Quite a spectacle," I drawled sarcastically. "Who's writing the screenplay?"

He came back defensively. "Hey, there wasn't any air conditioning in my office, so I got Terry to open up the grand jury room for us. There were people hanging around. They wanted to give us ideas." His voice trailed off. His back was half turned to me as he fiddled with the collection of ceramic mugs on my little refrigerator.

Finally, he turned. His previous bravado was gone. "Look, Marcia," he said, "I can't deal with that motherfucker. I don't think I can do him."

"You're dumping him on me *now?*" I wailed. "You know I'm buried."

It was true. I had a ton of work to do with Kato, plus at least two more days' worth of interviewing with Allan Park. I was still searching for a use-of-force expert to explain how one man could quickly dispatch two victims with a knife. And I hadn't even started on the hair and trace evidence.

Chris shrugged. "Let Hank do it."

"Hank's got his hands full with Dennis Fung."

The only other alternative was a special prosecutor, but I dismissed that idea out of hand. It would send the wrong message to the jury.

"Well, I'm sorry, but I just can't do it."

I leaned forward and rested my head on my hands. There was no way around it. I would have to take Mark.

This would double my load over the next two weeks. Chris had not done much actual prep work with Fuhrman, which meant I would have to organize his testimony from scratch. I'd have to weave in all the reasons why he couldn't and wouldn't have planted evidence—but if I spent too much time talking about how he'd done nothing wrong, we'd look defensive. Spend too little and we'd leave holes for the defense to fill in with sinister fantasies. It would be yet another tightrope walk.

Damn. I only wished Chris had dumped him earlier.

"Chris?" I lifted my head but he was gone.

Was I pissed? I sure was. For about a hour. And then my anger softened. Chris was under pressure, too. Some of it I could only guess at. I reminded myself that home for him was a black working-class community where the prevailing sentiment was that Simpson had been framed. Chris had to worry about whether his best friends considered him an Uncle Tom. He'd been spat on. He'd been flipped off. Every day of the week he had to walk out his door prepared to take it on the chin.

I remembered one ugly incident when he and I had made a trip out to the offices of Nicole's divorce attorneys in West L.A. As he entered the elevator, a young white woman beside us glanced up at Chris. Then she pulled her purse closer to her body. I'll never forget the look on his face. One minute you're an attorney, a civil servant, a full partner. The next minute you're a suspected mugger. Chris had managed to keep his dignity in a dangerous, miserable, unfair world, and his courage often moved me. Beyond that, he had the greatness of soul to think beyond himself and his race and take up the cudgel for battered women. He'd gone to bat for DV—which, deep down, I knew lay at the center of this case. He'd picked up that burden when I'd felt too weak to carry it. He took on my demon issue.

The least I could do was take on his.

Early the following week, I'd polished off a bag of the pretzels I always nibble on and was scouting the office for more goodies. People were always sending us care packages. I'd nicknamed the War Room the Snack Vortex. I'd spotted a gift basket and was about to plunder a tin of pâté when Scott Gordon put his hand on my arm.

"Someone leaked the mock cross to *Newsweek*," he whispered. His eyes were darting over my shoulder. He was clearly afraid of being overheard.

"Mark denied everything," I whispered back. "What's newsworthy about that?"

"Well, that's not how the article reads."

The way it read, apparently, was that Detective Fuhrman had "admitted that he'd made racial slurs in the past."

Oh, man. Could they hit us any lower? How could someone on our own team have gabbed to the press—and leaked lies to boot?

I caught up with Chris in Suzanne's office. He was pacing furiously. Obviously, he'd heard the news.

"I want every single person on this team to take a polygraph!" he was saying. "Everyone! Right fucking now. I'm going to get to the bottom of this!"

I tried to lighten him up.

"You know, I think everyone in the world should take polygraphs," I said. Chris, however, was in no mood for jokes. He meant it.

Gil thought Chris's polygraph idea was risky. "If the source is someone on the team," he mused aloud, "don't you think that person will leak the fact that we gave everyone a polygraph?"

I could see both sides. Sure, we needed to identify and isolate the culprit. Still, giving everyone polygraphs was just the kind of sensational, nasty development that was bound to get out. And if it did, we'd look like a bunch of paranoid jerks. I don't think Gil was seriously considering it, but was trying to let Chris down gently.

Gil called a staff meeting in the conference room.

"I'm asking whoever it is to come forward and make a clean breast of it," he said. "It can be done confidentially." He spoke mildly, yet his words conveyed such sadness and disappointment I thought they might actually tweak a guilty conscience. When it was his turn to speak, though, Chris rejected the conciliatory approach.

"We're going to have an investigation," he ranted. "And I promise you, we're going to find out which scumbag did this."

I looked around the table. No one wore what I would call a guilty expression. But, then, what good attorney doesn't have a poker face?

The leak and the suspicion that followed in its wake took their toll on the whole team. Speculation would settle on one person, and he'd be given the cold shoulder for a day or so. Then the onus would shift to another suspect. Chris just wouldn't let the matter drop. Without consulting me, he'd engaged the informal assistance of Anthony Pellicano, the private eye who'd been volunteering his services to Fuhrman. He'd instructed Tony to "look for somebody close to Mark." Which was dumb, because the last person who'd be the rat-fink was a friend of Mark's. Far more likely, it was someone who held some grudge against Mark, or someone who was on the periphery of the case and wanted more of the limelight.

Not long afterward, Mark talked with Cheri Lewis. "Do you know Chris suspects you might be the leak?" he asked.

"Based on what?" she protested.

"I don't know. That's just what Chris told Pellicano."

Cheri found Chris and confronted him head-on.

"I didn't exactly say that," Chris hedged. "I just told Tony to look at people who are close to Mark."

"But that includes me," Cheri complained. "Why on earth would you include me?"

"Well," Chris replied with a sideways glance, "because I think you're sleeping with him."

"Are you out of your *mind?*" she gasped. "Why the hell would I jeopardize my career—with a married cop, no less? I demand to be given a polygraph!"

What a mess. Two of my closest friends, the people I most depended on to see this case through, were at each other's throat. If the defense could see this, they'd be trading high fives for a solid hour. Maybe even Chris realized how out of control this thing had gotten, because he backed off. Eventually he and Cheri patched things up. But it was sickening to see deputy turn on deputy.

This may shock my critics, but I'm proud of the job I did with Mark Fuhrman—in spite of what would later reveal itself to be a time bomb ticking in my ear. I was under tremendous pressure; the structure of his direct had to be intricate and subtle. It required me to take him step-by-step through his role in the case, carefully layering beneath that superficial narrative the information that made it clear he couldn't have framed Simpson. And I had to decide whether to bring out the Kathleen Bell allegations on direct. If I fronted them, we'd have to figure out a way to let the jury see that she wasn't credible. And that would have to be done in a way that wouldn't set *Mark* off. Fuhrman now had found ample grounds to mistrust everyone in the D.A.'s office and was edgier than ever. A big part of my job became soothing him so that he wouldn't flip out on the witness stand.

Chris's disastrous mock cross complicated things considerably. I knew that Bailey would want to bring it up. I surely would, if I were him. It was also a fair bet that Ito would allow it. The problem was, I didn't know for sure what had happened in the grand jury room; there was no transcript. At least, not a formal one. It was always possible that someone surreptitiously took notes and then, heaven shield us from horrors, slipped them to the defense. During a hearing after the *Newsweek* article appeared, Bailey had brought up the names of several deputies who I hadn't even realized had been there. How he got that information, I don't know. But it was one more indication that we had a traitor in our midst.

I called Chris into my office for a thorough debriefing. "So what exactly did you ask Fuhrman?" I said. But all Chris could remember for sure was that when he'd asked Fuhrman whether he'd used the slur in the past ten years, Fuhrman had denied it.

"No equivocation? Maybe he just couldn't remember?" I asked hopefully.

"Nope," Chris assured me. "He denied it completely and will not budge."

I found it hard to believe that Mark had never uttered that word. Not after what I'd seen in the disability file. I *did* believe that he'd never said it to an African American, face-to-face. But *never?* Not over a beer? Not to his buddies? Not in private? That seemed unlikely to me. Could I get him to admit it? Judging from Chris's experience with him, probably not. Perhaps I could get him to soften his denial to "I don't remember." But a witness can be pushed only so far.

A prosecutor is in a tough position when she doesn't fully believe her own witness. As I girded up for the encounter with Mark Fuhrman, I made a pact with myself: If I couldn't shake him off his denial about the N-word, then I had an obligation to tell the jury that I had doubts about it. But I'd contrast it with that part of the testimony I was perfectly certain of: that he didn't plant evidence.

At my request, Mark drew up a list of other cops on the scene who could help shore up his credibility. He'd looked over the Bundy crime-scene log and given us a few names, among them his partner, Brad Roberts. When I saw that name, I just shook my head and said to myself, *He doesn't get it.*

Brad was a real good guy and a fine cop, but he couldn't speak to the important issues of credibility. Brad had arrived at Bundy *after* Mark had, so he was in no position to attest to the fact that there had been only one glove between the bodies. Other cops who had been on the scene in advance of Fuhrman had already done that. Nor had Brad been with Mark when he'd found the glove at Rockingham.

About all Brad could say was that he, too, had seen what appeared to be a fingerprint on the gate at Bundy—not a good gambit since that putative print had never turned up. There was nothing he could offer our case, except to attest to his buddy's being a straight-up guy. Just what we needed for this jury—a character reference from another white cop.

In preparation for his testimony, Mark showed up for our pretrial interview in the company of one of the most imposing men I'd ever seen in my life. Lieutenant Chuck Higbee, formerly of the LAPD, looked to be in his mid-fifties. He wore his hair in a buzz cut and stood about six-one. His T-shirt strained to cover his enormous shoulders and biceps. Higbee was a legend on the force, owing partly to his toughness but more to his willingness to lend a hand to cops in trouble. The LAPD had attached him to Fuhrman's regular detail in the belief that he might exert a calming influence.

I extended my hand, and it was swallowed up by Higbee's huge paw.

"Pleasure to meet you," he said. The voice was smooth, his manner buoyant, in contrast to his stolid appearance. Could I count on him as an ally?

Mark hung back a bit until I offered him a seat.

"Guess it's me and you," I said, pulling out a yellow pad.

Mark wasn't shy about telling me that he was glad I'd taken over. "Chris and I just couldn't get along," he told me. "I'd wait around for hours, then he'd come in and ask me some race questions and walk out."

At the mention of "race questions," his tone became hurt and angry.

"Okay," I said. "I want to begin with where you were the day of the twelfth. Let's account for all your movements from that point forward."

"I was down in Palm Springs for an officers' party," he began. "I left there at about seven or eight P.M. Then I went home and got to bed about ten or eleven."

I took him through the whole case. We worked for two hours straight before taking a break. Once again, I was reminded of why I'd been so impressed with Mark at the outset. This guy was really on top of the facts. I had a copy of his testimony from the preliminary hearing handy in case he needed to refresh his memory. But he never did. He had almost total recall.

Higbee was a champ. Whenever Mark ran on too long with an answer, he'd interrupt with a gentle "Hold on, Mark. Just answer the question. If you start volunteering, the defense will object and that will interrupt your testimony." Higbee obviously knew his way around a courtroom.

During a break, Mark went into the hall to stretch. I took the opportunity to broach the race question with Higbee. Particularly Fuhrman's insistence that he had never uttered the N-word in the past decade.

"It would really help if we could soften that denial a little," I told him. "Is there anything we can do about it?"

Higbee thought for a moment. "If you want my advice, just leave it alone," he finally said. "The more you push it, the worse he'll get."

"But don't you agree it would be better to front the issue? Take it on first, and soften it with some kind of admission?"

"All you'll do is alienate him," Higbee warned. "Then he'll take the stand in a hostile frame of mind. If you guys can just maintain a decent rapport, I'm sure it'll all go smoothly."

When Mark returned, we spent another hour going through the questions I intended to weave through his direct.

"When you stepped out of the house to go down the south pathway, did you know whether Kato had already gone down that pathway?"

"No."

"Did you know whether Simpson had an alibi for the time of the murders?"

"No."

"Did you know whether there was an eyewitness to the murders?"

"No."

"Were you the first officer on the Bundy scene?"

"No."

"How many officers were there by the time you arrived?"

"On the scene itself? About ten, I guess."

"Did you know whether they'd examined the evidence and been all through the crime scene before you got there?"

"No."

For an officer in this position to have planted evidence would have been an act of insanity. With no information about Simpson's whereabouts—for all he knew, Simpson could have had an airtight alibi for the time of the murders—Fuhrman could have exposed himself to a major felony rap by monkeying with the evidence. It just didn't make sense.

"Okay," I pushed on. "Let's talk about the 1985 baseball-bat-through-the-windshield thing. You could have arrested Simpson that day, couldn't you?"

"Well, not at that time," he explained. "Back then, we still needed the victim to cooperate to make an arrest. . ."

"What could you have done?"

"I could have written up a field identification card on the incident. I could have issued him a warning. I could have recommended a filing [of charges] to the city attorney," he said.

"Did you do any of those things?" I asked.

"No."

"Why not?"

"I thought the situation looked under control," Mark explained. "He was calm and polite. She looked very upset, but she didn't want to cooperate. I couldn't see any reason to aggravate the situation any further."

Certainly a jury could not fail to grasp the point. If this guy was such a flaming racist—if he was the sort to go bonkers at the sight of a black man with a white woman—why hadn't he seized this opportunity to hold O. J. Simpson's feet to the fire? If anything, the baseball bat incident suggested that he was so in awe of Simpson that he had turned a blind eye to an incident of spousal abuse, just like the succession of cops before him.

After Mark and Higbee left, I curled up in my chair and stared out the window at the smoggy sunset. What should I do? Heed Higbee's warning and stay away from race? Some of my own colleagues were warning me to keep Kathleen Bell's allegations out of my direct examination. But if I did, the defense would play it as though I'd deliberately tried to hide that evidence from the jury. Still, if I pressed Mark about Bell, would he turn on me in court? The question troubled me.

The night before Mark was scheduled to begin testimony, I was tossing in bed when an inspiration came to me. What if I feathered Bell's statements right into the testimony about the 1985 baseball bat incident? We'd intercut her comments about Mark's shaking down interracial couples with the details of Mark's 911 call to Rockingham, where'd he'd gone out of his way not to hassle O. J. Simpson. It could be a powerful juxtaposition.

As I drove into work the next morning, March 9, 1995, I played out the succession of questions in my head. Mark was waiting in my office. He looked a lot less assured than other times I'd seen him. I shut the door. Speaking as brightly and matter-of-factly as I could, I laid out the Bell strategy to him. I didn't ask him; I simply told him what I intended to do. He just smiled and nodded his head in acquiescence. As I headed for court, I just prayed he'd stay calm and show the jury a human being instead of a race-baiting freak.

The courtroom was so thick with tension that you could practically feel the molecules bouncing off your skin. There was an unnatural quiet, like the pall of dead air before a storm. I had to find a way to relieve some of the pressure on Mark. I approached him easily and smiled.

"Detective Fuhrman," I said. "Can you tell us how you feel about testifying today?"

"Nervous," he replied. "Reluctant."

"Can you tell us why?"

"Since June thirteenth, it seems that I've seen a lot of the evidence ignored, a lot of personal issues come to the forefront. I think it's too bad."

"Heard a lot about yourself in the press, have you?"

"Daily."

"You've indicated you feel nervous about testifying. Have you gone over your testimony in the presence of several district attorneys in order to prepare yourself [for court] and the allegations you may hear from the defense?"

He indicated that he had.

I directed his attention to the year 1985, when he was a young patrolman.

"Did you respond to a radio call which led you to the location of 360 North Rockingham in Brentwood?"

Mark told how he and his partner had arrived to find O. J. Simpson and a woman who was leaning on the hood of a Mercedes-Benz. "She had her hands to her face," he said. "And she was sobbing."

Mark moved smoothly through the incident, ending with the confession that he'd done nothing to pursue the case against Simpson, although he could have.

Time to feather. Deftly. Not too heavy-handed.

"Now, back in 1985 and 1986, sir," I asked him, "can you tell us whether you knew someone or met someone by the name of Kathleen Bell?"

"Yes. I can tell you. I did not."

Jonathan flashed Bell's faxed letter to Cochran on the screen. I couldn't present it any other way, to tell you the truth. The words were so offensive. Especially the genocidal remarks about burning. Maybe it's being Jewish myself, or maybe it's just being human, but I couldn't bring myself to speak them aloud.

"Did the conversation Kathleen Bell describes in this letter occur?" I asked him.

"No, it did not."

Mark sailed confidently through the rest of direct. He was smooth and relaxed. The irritability and childish petulance of the past few months had vanished. No one watching him on the stand today would ever believe all the hand-holding sessions that had led to this moment.

Throughout Mark's testimony, opposing counsel was unexpectedly quiet. Lee Bailey was in charge of Fuhrman's cross; he voiced no objections and he took no notes. I found that interesting. Now, it's true that the prosecution's witnesses seldom deviate from their written statements, which we hand over to the defense during discovery. But no one ever says the same thing in exactly the same way. Sometimes those variations are significant. If an attorney's not taking notes, he'll have a hard time remembering the distinctions when it's time for cross.

Bailey's failure to take notes told me one of two things. Either he had a hell of a memory—or he'd already prepared a cross-examination from which he would not deviate. I didn't think it could be the first. At sidebar, his hands trembled so badly that he could barely read the papers he was holding. If the problem was alcohol, as rumor had it, then his memory couldn't be all that great. The second scenario seemed more likely. If he truly did have a preset program, then it was likely to shake Bailey up a bit if I threw in something a little obscure. Something he might have overlooked.

That led me to a mistake. Mark had told me about a large plastic bag he'd found in the rear of the Bronco. It was his theory that Simpson might have intended to use it to carry Nicole's body away from the murder site. I figured I'd throw it out to see what old Bailey made of it. So late on Friday afternoon, March 10, I ticked off an inventory of evidence from the Bronco, including a shovel "about five feet long" and a large piece of "heavy-gauge plastic" that had been tucked into a side pocket in the cargo area. Mark identified these items as the ones he'd seen when he looked through the window of the Bronco the morning of the thirteenth. Let the jurors draw their own conclusions.

It is an understatement to say that things didn't work out as I'd planned. I was getting ready to end my direct when Ito decided to break for the day. That left Bailey with the entire weekend to figure out how to counter the bag business.

It turned out to be a no-brainer. That weekend, owners of Ford

4×4s all over America flooded our phone lines to report that the plastic bag was standard-issue in Broncos.

Man, did I want to hide under a bed.

On Monday morning, with Mark back on the stand, I swallowed hard and asked him about the plastic bag again. "Do you happen to know whether it belongs in a Bronco?"

"Well, now I do," he said.

"And what is it?" I asked, setting up the punch line for which I was the joke.

"It is the spare-tire bag," Mark said.

I vowed to swear off cute tricks for all eternity.

Much of the civilized world tuned in to catch the opening day of Bailey's cross-examination of Mark Fuhrman. That's just what Bailey had hoped for. For weeks now he'd been pounding his chest and blustering to the media how he would do the most "annihilating, character-assassinating" cross-examination ever. Now millions of viewers were dangling over the walls of the virtual Colosseum in eager anticipation of a bloodbath.

When Bailey approached the witness, he couldn't resist jabbing the bamboo under our nails.

"Can you tell us when it was that you were enlightened to the fact the plastic you saw in Mr. Simpson's Bronco comes with the car?"

"I believe it was Saturday," Mark replied.

"So after nine months of investigation, you discovered on Saturday that this important piece of evidence was perfectly innocuous. Is that right?"

Ouch.

I have to say that I found myself admiring Bailey's style. Unlike every other member of the Dream Team, who tended to meander and become mired in meaningless detail, Bailey kept his cross on course. I enjoyed watching him as I had enjoyed watching no other member of that defense. There was a glimmer of real lawyering here.

As he steered the cross to Kathleen Bell, I held my breath. I would have to practice a judicious restraint. I didn't want to object unless I absolutely had to. We didn't want to appear to have something to hide. Above all, I didn't want to object and have Ito overrule us. That would make it look as if we were trying to "cover up a racist." But I would have to be ready to jump in if the cross turned into a mêlée.

"Detective Fuhrman," Bailey exhorted, "would you take a look at this photograph of a blond woman and tell me whether or not that is the person that was being interviewed on Larry King when you watched the show at the request of the prosecution?"

Bell's photo was flashed on the screen. Mark turned to look at it.

"I do not recall ever meeting this woman in the recruiting station or anywhere else."

"Ever had any contact with any relative or possible relative of Kathleen Bell in your capacity as a policeman?"

"I would have no way of knowing that," Mark replied. "The name Ms. Bell does not ring a—"

"The name Bell doesn't ring a bell, is that what you were trying to say," Bailey said, finishing his sentence.

Chuckles rattled through the audience. Even a few of the jurors grinned.

Good, I thought to myself. A soft denial. That left room for the possibility that he could have met her, but had simply forgotten.

Mark was holding his own. He didn't let Bailey push him into any categorical denials. That was good. And in the hours that followed, Fuhrman kept his cool under the questioning of the old warrior.

As we went on to day three, I thought I could detect a hint of desperation in Bailey's voice. So far, he'd failed to deliver his Perry Mason moment. Now he locked in on the subject that he hoped would deliver a knockout blow.

He started by bringing up, as I'd dreaded, Chris's misguided grand jury room session with Mark. During our arguments before Fuhrman's testimony began, Bailey had displayed a great deal of knowledge about that mock session. He knew that the Bell letter had come up, and now he asked Mark about the racial epithets Bell had described.

"Did any of the questions [in the mock cross] require you to say whether or not language of that sort was part of your vocabulary?" asked Bailey.

"I might have offered that," said Mark.

"Ah," said Bailey. "Tell us please, what was it you offered these lawyers in that room about your vocabulary, Detective Fuhrman?"

I objected, claiming that it was irrelevant. It was, but Ito had already committed himself to allowing this filth. Overruled.

"Would you answer?" Bailey persisted.

"Yes," said Fuhrman. "That I don't use any type of language to describe people of any race such as what is alleged by Kathleen Bell."

Bailey was circling in for the kill, and I couldn't do a damned thing about it except hope that Mark would give himself some wiggle room. As Bailey began to ask Fuhrman the questions that would deny him that space, I objected, and though Ito sustained a couple of my objections because Bailey's phrasing was vague, I knew I was only staving off the inevitable.

Bailey would not be denied. "Do you use the word 'nigger' in describing people?" he spat.

I had no choice. "Same objection," I interjected again.

"Overruled."

"No, sir," Mark answered.

"Have you used that word in the past ten years?"

"Object," Chris hissed at me. This was the guy who was going to treat Fuhrman as a hostile witness, right? Now he's pushing me to run interference. But I couldn't object again. I knew that very question had been asked of Mark by *our* side in the grand jury room session. If so, Bailey could make a fool of me if I spoke up: "Why would Miss Clark object to the very question that *the prosecution* themselves posed to Detective Fuhrman?" My objection would make me look like a liar and a racist myself—like I was trying to hide whatever offensive remarks Fuhrman had given to us.

A quick glance at the jury told me we couldn't afford to be over-ruled on any more objections about race. They were glaring at me with hatred. They wanted to hear Fuhrman's answers.

"Not that I recall, no," Mark answered.

Mark's competitive instincts, which he'd managed to hold in check until now, were finally rearing their head. What was it? A more prominent jutting of the chin? Was he leaning forward instead of back? I couldn't put my finger on it. But I felt the shift.

"You mean if you called someone a nigger you have forgotten it?"

"I'm not sure I can answer the question the way you phrased it, sir."

"Are you therefore saying that you have not used that word in the past ten years, Detective Fuhrman?"

"Yes," Mark answered. "That is what I'm saying."

"And you say under oath that you have not addressed any black person as nigger or spoken about black people as niggers in the past ten years, Detective Fuhrman?"

"That's what I'm saying."

Please, Mark, I was begging silently, *how about something like, "I don't know. Ten years is a long time. Ten years ago? I might have."*

But Mark Fuhrman was enjoying watching his adversary squirm. Bailey had failed to deliver on his boastful claims that he would "annihilate" him. Now that victory, as Mark saw it, was within reach, he wasn't giving an inch.

"So that anyone who comes to this court and quotes you as using that word in dealing with African Americans would be a liar, would they not, Detective Fuhrman?"

"Yes, they would."

"All of them, correct?"

"All of them."

Mark had left himself no out. But that wasn't the worst of it. He compounded his folly with arrogance. Bailey returned to the very first moments of Mark's testimony, when Fuhrman mentioned the accusations being hurled against him. These, of course, included making racial slurs and planting evidence. But when Bailey asked Mark, "What were you thinking of when you talked of those problems?" Mark said, "Being accused of committing a felony in a capital crime."

"Was that the only accusation that was troubling you as you took the witness stand?"

"That," Mark blurted out, "is the only one I care about."

Bailey saw his opportunity.

"The other one, the [accusation] that you used racial epithets, you don't care about at all, is that correct?"

"I didn't say them," Mark insisted. "I don't care about them."

I was so mortified I felt as if my skin were on fire. *You don't care about that fucked-up statement? Don't care! How can you not care?*

Someone just accused you of advocating genocide, for Christ's sake. That at least has to offend you. How can you say you don't care?

How could I deal with this? If, on redirect, I asked Mark to try and explain the comment, it could get a lot worse:

"What did you mean when you said you don't care?"

"I don't care because it isn't true."

"Yet the accusation that you'd planted evidence wasn't true either, and you were upset by that. . . ." And so on.

Even worse, he could ramble on in the spirit of "Well, I didn't really mean I don't care, I just mean . . ."

There was no coming back from it. And no chance that the jury had missed it, either.

Meanwhile, in sessions held out of the jury's presence, Bailey and I were going at it tooth and nail. The defense was demanding that Ito let them call witnesses who could supposedly corroborate Kathleen Bell's accusations of Fuhrman. One of these was Maximo Cordoba.

Cordoba, you'll recall, was the black marine stationed at the recruiting station in Redondo Beach. We had originally considered calling him as a prosecution witness. But he was a real piece of work. He'd been interviewed several times by the LAPD as well as by Mark's private investigator, Anthony Pellicano. In a taped interview with Pellicano on September 16, 1994, Cordoba couldn't recall ever hearing Mark make the racially charged statements attributed to him by Kathleen Bell. In fact, he made no mention of hearing Mark use *any* racial slurs. In a telephone interview with a detective from the LAPD on January 17, 1995, Cordoba said he couldn't recall ever seeing Mark and Kathleen Bell at the recruiting office at the same time. And again, no mention of racial slurs.

Three days later, Max came to our office, where he was interviewed by Cheri and Chris. Once again he insisted he'd never seen Mark and Bell together. Now, however, he seemed to remember that Fuhrman—or perhaps it was one of the marines, he couldn't be sure—had called him "boy." This witness's "memory" was troubling. And it became increasingly dubious several months down the line when he told a reporter that the "boy" episode had come back to him *in a dream.* Max's record was so riddled with inconsistent statements, we couldn't possibly call him as a prosecution witness. The defense, however, did not feel similarly constrained.

On the second day of Fuhrman's cross-examination, Bailey asked to address the court before the jury came in. Hoping to use it in his cross, he came up with yet another Max Cordoba story. According to this tale, Max had been in the station when Mark came in to hand him an application to join a reserve unit. Cordoba said he didn't know anything about it and called to a fellow marine, "Hey, Roher. Your boy is here." At this, Fuhrman turned on Cordoba saying, "Let's get something straight. The only boy here is you, nigger." Then, as Bailey told it, Fuhrman followed Cordoba into the parking lot to repeat the epithet.

Was this all Bailey hyperbole, or had Cordoba come up with yet another, more sensational version of the bullshit statement he'd given us in January? I stood up.

"These allegations get more outrageous by the minute," I said. "He never made such a statement, and he never alleged that Mark Fuhrman had made such a statement."

I demanded that Ito exclude any cross-examination on such a highly suspect statement. At the very least we should be allowed to call Cordoba to the witness stand outside the presence of the jury so that Ito could see for himself just how incredible this witness was before the jury heard his latest unfounded accusation. As a parting shot, I predicted that Cordoba would not, in fact, testify to the version given by Bailey.

"That," I said, referring to the story Bailey told, "is something that is never going to be delivered on and the court will have allowed the jury to be inflamed by something that will evaporate in thin air."

That goaded Lee into his big mistake. He jumped to his feet and proclaimed, "Your Honor, I have spoken to him on the phone personally, marine to marine. I haven't the slightest doubt that he will march up to that witness stand and tell the world what Fuhrman called him, on no provocation whatsoever."

Ito ruled that Bailey could ask Fuhrman about Cordoba only after we'd had another shot at interviewing him in light of this new allegation. But the need for another interview would soon be rendered moot.

*   *   *

That evening I agreed to meet the team for dinner at the Saratoga. Chris, Cheri, and a bunch of the law clerks were already there when I arrived. They slid down the booth to make room for me.

My head ached, I was kinked up with tension. I ordered a Scotch. Probably a bad idea, but I needed to relax. Scott Gordon joined us. So did a couple of young lawyers from media relations. We thought we might get some work done, but everybody was just too tired and beat up with the stress of having Fuhrman on the stand. So we cut loose. As the evening wore on, the subject of Maximo Cordoba seemed funnier and funnier. "Next time around he'll probably remember that he was married to Kathleen Bell," Cheri groused. We split our sides laughing. All anyone had to do was puff out his chest and grunt, "Marine to marine," and we'd collapse in hysterics. Every team needs a good blowout.

That night, when I'd headed home and was preparing to drop into bed, Chris called me and told me to tune into *Dateline*. Quick. I switched on the TV in my bedroom and there was old Max Cordoba talking to Jane Pauley. He was denying ever having spoken to F. Lee Bailey. Not marine to marine. Not any other way.

Thank you, God.

The next morning, I awoke feeling as if trolls in knuckle studs had worked over my cerebral cortex. Mark Fuhrman was still on the stand. I groaned and pulled the covers tight over my head.

Now I accept it as a fundamental fact of survival that when one gets up in the morning, one must be prepared to do battle before the day is through. Not today. I couldn't face it. I dragged myself into court intending to dump Bailey on Chris. But Chris would have none of it.

"C'mon, baby, *you've* got to do it." He grinned. "Get in there and break off a piece for Daddy."

I turned to Jonathan Fairtlough, who'd brought a copy of the *Dateline* tape.

"Cued up?" I asked him. My head was still pounding.

"All set, boss. You just say when."

"No matter what you hear or see," I instructed him, "when I tell you to play the tape, just do it."

The point I rose to make that morning was a serious one indeed. An attorney for the defense had willfully misled the court. He'd claimed that he'd spoken to a witness when, in fact, he had not. It was this kind of fast-and-loose gamesmanship that in any other court would get a lawyer held in contempt.

"This is the kind of nonsense that gives lawyers a bad name, Your Honor," I said. "He was intending to convey to the court that he had personal knowledge of what this man said because this man said it to him personally—'marine to marine.' . . . That is nonsense."

I asked Jonathan to roll the tape. Bailey saw what I was up to and began to yell at the top of his lungs that this was "outrageous."

"Mr. Bailey—you can see how agitated he is—has been caught in a lie," I observed to the court, "and you know something? Not in this case. You don't get away with that. There are just too many people watching."

Poor Jonathan looked like a deer caught in the headlights. But I calmly repeated, "Jonathan, roll the tape."

Bailey continued screaming, but for once Ito wasn't listening. He'd turned to watch as Cordoba, now blown up larger than life on the big screen, denied ever having spoken to Bailey. It was amazing. Only by seeing the events in his own courtroom *on television* could Lance understand what had happened! He asked me what sanction I felt should be imposed on the defense.

"I think that the witness should be precluded from testifying," I said. "I think that Mr. Bailey should be cited for contempt and fined substantially. As an officer of the court, he has lied to this court."

Bailey put his hand on the podium, trying to edge me out, but I wouldn't budge.

"Excuse me, Mr. Bailey," I told him. "Stand up and speak when it's your turn."

In a sidelong glance, I caught the hatred in his eyes. Bailey was an old-school lawyer. He was used to being able to bluster and bully his way through everything. He wasn't prepared for a woman to take him on that way.

Lance looked thunderstruck. I could see he knew he'd been played for a fool. It was clear that Bailey would not be able to use his crazy Cordoba story in the Fuhrman cross, but I was really hoping Lance would also make Bailey pay for his deception. I was wrong. Bailey claimed he'd spoken to Cordoba *through an investigator* and how Cordoba had just forgotten that Bailey himself had come on the line to talk with him for a few moments.

Bottom line, Ito hated fighting more than he hated being duped. All he wanted to do was end the hostilities. He called Lee and me to apologize to each other and bury the hatchet.

I'm sure the look on my face said, *Yeah, I'll bury the hatchet—in his head,* because when Lance saw it, he knew I was neither repentant nor inclined to fake it. He turned to Chris and asked him to try and reason with me.

"I don't want to apologize," I said under my breath. "I have nothing to apologize for. He lied and now he's covering it up."

But Chris didn't listen to me. He turned to the bench and announced, "I'll apologize for my warrior if you'll apologize on behalf of yours."

"You motherfucker," I mouthed to Chris. He'd just rolled me out like a Persian rug. When he returned to the table, I lit into him. "This is payback for the contempt thing. You're still pissed about that, aren't you?" His expression was perfectly straight, but his shoulders shook with laughter. I couldn't blame him. Lawyer gets caught lying on national TV. Judge won't do a goddamned thing. What can you do but laugh?

The truce between Lee Bailey and me lasted about two seconds. Once again he was up on his feet, asking to address the court out of the presence of the jury. He'd brought along some props: a plastic bag and a pair of brown leather gloves. He wanted permission to show Mark the plastic bag. He wanted to put the gloves inside the bag and demonstrate how the witness could have secreted the package in his sock—which, he claimed, was a habit of old marines. Of course, he had not one scintilla of evidence to prove that Mark had ever done such a thing. The defense had been discomfited by the revelation that Mark rarely wore a jacket. I'd introduced this fact during the cops' testimony, through photos taken at the crime scene. So if he had no jacket, how the hell could he hide the glove until he could plant it? Now

Bailey wanted to give the jury a fallback scenario: that Mark stuffed the glove in his sock.

By the way, this proposed stunt was strictly improper. The law stipulates that any experiment or attempt to re-create an event must duplicate the original circumstances as nearly as possible. The standard is "substantial similarity." It doesn't take a legal wizard to see that there were no "original circumstances" here. There was absolutely no evidence that anything like this had ever happened. The experiment proposed by Bailey would be substantially similar to—what? A non-occurrence? What it had, however, was tons of graphic prejudicial value.

As Bailey continued to outline his proposal, I thought, *I shouldn't even have to respond to this, it's so ludicrous.* But I knew that if I held my peace, Ito might well allow it.

So I argued to the court that you couldn't justify an experiment when there's not only *no* evidence to support that the event occurred, but there *is* evidence to prove that it *never* occurred. No one ever said they saw a plastic bag in anyone's possession that night. Not to mention that there was no second glove available at Bundy to go into that bag.

The gloves were lying on the defense table. I picked them up to study them. They were size small—not extra large, like the gloves in evidence. The defense was obviously afraid that if it used gloves of actual size, either they wouldn't fit in the bag or the bag would make a conspicuous bulge in the sock.

"This is ridiculous," I told the court. "There is no connection to this case. A leather glove of a different size, a different color, a different make, a different style, that has no relevance to this case. . . . This is a fantasy concocted by the defense for which there is no evidentiary basis, no logical or factual connection to this case."

Ito tried to sort this out for himself. There was a disparity between the sizes of the two sets of gloves. . . .

"They are out of extra large, Your Honor," Bailey explained lamely.

"Not only that," I continued, turning the gloves over in my hands. "but the glove in issue is an Aris. . . . I can't even tell if [this] is a man's or a woman's glove." Then some mischief came to me. "Size small," I noted. "I guess it is Mr. Bailey's."

Talk about a cheap shot. No sooner did the words slip from my lips than I regretted them. Guess you can't take the street out of the girl.

To be honest, Ito would have been within his rights to sanction me. Instead, he just looked at me and shook his head. He knew that everyone's nerves were strained to the breaking point. Besides, the cold fact was, he hadn't held Bailey in contempt for outright lying to the court; so how was he going to justify sending me to the slammer for one gibe, uh, below the belt?

Ito, thank God, did not punish me by allowing the defense to perform Bailey's specious experiment. He shut Bailey down cold.

You want to know the funny thing about my tasteless jab? Bailey never got it. He would walk around saying to anyone who would listen, "Look. Anyone can see my hands are at least a medium, if not a large." He'd spread his hands out for viewing. On the day we called Richard Rubin, our glove expert, Bailey raced over to him to get an expert opinion on the size of his hands. After Rubin confirmed that they did, indeed, appear to be a size large, Bailey looked at me as if to say, "You see?"

I nearly lost it.

CAR TAPE. *March 15. Mark Fuhrman's been on the stand for almost a week now, but he's holding his own pretty well. We may have gotten to the end of cross, and I think right now Chris and I are at odds about whether or not to do redirect. I wanted to not do any, which would really kind of send a nice message that he hasn't been hurt. I'm really torn about this. . . .*

In the meantime, I get all these outrageous offers to be on all these television shows. I think I'll just quit the case and do it. Oh, God. I really hate this. I feel so alone. I feel like I have three feet of vacuum around me everywhere I go. I don't feel like anybody can penetrate it.

When Mark Fuhrman finally stepped down after six days on the stand, he was almost universally hailed as the victor in a grudge match against Bailey. The press showered him with praise. Cops and civilians alike sent him flowers, gifts, and baskets of food. The LAPD ordered up a cake for him and they celebrated alongside the deputies and the law clerks in the War Room.

I was in no mood for rejoicing. The last place I wanted to be was at a party for Mark Fuhrman.

I sent my regrets. Mark Fuhrman's testimony had taken its toll on my spirits. I'd always prided myself on my clinical focus. Even as I waded hip-deep through the mud and blood, I could count on my discipline and detachment to serve as barriers against the ugliness. But sitting for days in that courtroom hearing Bailey bellow "nigger" had driven my morale to an all-time low. Chris had been right when he argued against the admissibility of the N-word back in January. No decent person can hear that word without feeling a shock down the spine. If it inspired revulsion in me, I could only imagine what it inspired in the jury.

My mind ached. My muscles ached. Most of all, my heart ached. I realized, I guess we all did, that we were taking this battering in the service of a lost cause. I do believe it takes a special kind of courage to drag yourself up to the front day after day to fight a losing battle. I wanted to think I had that kind of courage. Every day I made a point of considering the plight of the Goldmans and the Browns, who had suffered the worst loss possible. I owed them. If this ordeal proved too much for me, if I allowed myself to collapse under the strain, I knew I would spend the rest of my life in a limbo of self-loathing. When the bell rang at the end of fifteen rounds, the decision might not go my way, but I wanted to be standing. Bloody, staggering, puking, maybe. But still standing.

Across the room, of course, the lawyers on the Dream Team were bright-eyed, starched, and perky. The defense had a policy of alternating cross-examination so that no single lawyer took on more than two or three witnesses in a row. That was a very good strategy to avoid burning out any one lawyer, but it simply wasn't an option for us. For the first part of the case, at least, we didn't want the jurors to see the People's advocates as a blurred succession of suits. We wanted them to become familiar with Chris and me as human beings, and bond with us, if they could.

It fell to me to carry the burden of this strategy. After Chris's opening volley with the domestic violence witnesses, I had twenty-five witnesses straight. It was an agonizing grind. At the conclusion of Fuhrman, I would have given my eyeteeth to be able to sit down and rest for a bit. But I had three more witnesses to go before our physical-evidence guys—Woody Clarke, Rock Harmon, Brian Kelberg, and Hank Goldberg—relieved me. It doesn't sound like so much. But one of those three remaining witnesses was Kato Kaelin.

Kato was driving me to an early grave. I knew that he had a lot he could tell me about the brutality of O. J. Simpson. He'd been an eyewitness to the door-smashing incident of 1993, when the 911 tape revealed Simpson going after Nicole like a madman. But the only thing Kato would admit to seeing was "maybe an argument." Kaelin's insistence on minimizing stood to make his testimony more damaging than helpful to us.

It both amused and infuriated me when, after the trial was over, Kato tried to float the story that he would have been happy to cooperate with me if only I hadn't intimidated him. Give me a break, Junior. I spent over thirty hours with that guy—wheedling, cajoling, talking dude-speak. I'd done everything but offer him rent-free lodging in my toolshed to induce him to come out with the truth.

Kato was holding back because he couldn't tell which way the wind was blowing. He was obviously afraid that dumping on O. J. Simpson might hurt his so-called career. I would have been at a loss to unlock the riddle that was Kato if it hadn't been for Kato's old friend Grant Cramer, an actor with whom Kato crashed during the days after the murder. Grant was a man of good character and conscience who came forward and confided in us with a candor Kato could never manage.

The best we'd been able to get out of Kato was that during the trip to McDonald's on the night of the murders, O. J. Simpson had seemed "tired" and "rushed." But Kaelin was much more forthcoming with Grant in the murder's aftermath. Grant told us that after arriving at his pad the afternoon of June 13, an agitated Kato said that on that Sunday evening Simpson seemed "frazzled and out of breath." He certainly had not looked like he'd just awakened from sleep when the limo driver arrived.

While still at Cramer's house, Kato began receiving calls from the Simpson camp: Howard Weitzman, Simpson's assistant, Cathy

Randa, and even Simpson himself. All of them wanted to know what he'd told the cops. After the third call, Kato asked Grant to drive him over to Rockingham. Grant pleaded with his friend not to go, but Kato wouldn't listen. Grant didn't see Kato for three days.

When Kato turned up again, he was distraught. He told Cramer that Simpson's family and friends were at the residence, along with some attorneys. Kato said that the defendant had hugged him. "Thank God you were here," Simpson said, "and you can say I was at home when this thing happened."

"No, O.J., I can't," Kato replied. "I didn't see you after we got back. When I walked back to my room you were still standing by the Bentley." And that was the last Simpson had spoken to Kato, although Kato remained in the house, sometimes sleeping on the floor, for three days.

Not once in all our interview had Kato mentioned going back to Rockingham. When I confronted him with Grant's information, he suddenly "remembered" it.

When I heard this, it clicked into place why Kato felt he'd needed to bring his attorney along to the grand jury way back when. Simpson was making what was, most likely, a ham-handed attempt to manipulate his testimony. Kato must have felt himself caught between a rock and a hard place. Clearly, he still felt that way, because I had to struggle for every shred of information from him. He never volunteered anything, and when I forced him to describe something, he'd give the sketchiest possible rendition, always skewed toward protecting his friend. It was like interviewing a defense witness.

Which, of course, he was.

And that meant I had to develop a strategy for handling him on the witness stand.

First, I figured, I would get all I could the nice way. I wouldn't alienate him before extracting everything he'd give me without a fight. Then I'd see how he did on cross. If he screwed up—tried to backpedal—it would actually make his direct testimony look more credible, because the jury would see how much he loved the defense. Then, on redirect, I'd hit him with the hard stuff. And I had an idea for how to do just that.

Kato Kaelin took the stand the morning of March 21, wearing a

fashionable blazer and black jeans. His direct testimony was every bit
the struggle I'd anticipated. Every time I asked Kato how Simpson had
behaved, looked, or spoken, Kato, running his hands through his hair
and chopping up his sentences like a sushi chef, went out of his way to
describe it as the picture of normalcy. Simpson was "tired, "rushed."
Perhaps a little "upset," because Nicole hadn't let him see Sydney. But
never "frazzled" or "angry."

One of the facts that Kato had let slip during our pretrial interviews was that Simpson and Paula Barbieri had had a blowup on the
night before the murders. Paula wanted to attend Sydney's dance
recital the following day as a show of good faith on Simpson's part.
She apparently wanted him to announce to Nicole and his ex-in-laws
that she was his woman now. Paula was stung at Simpson's refusal,
and she ended up skipping to Las Vegas, where she checked into the
Mirage Hotel as one of a party on a reservation guaranteed by singer
Michael Bolton. But if Simpson attended the recital unaccompanied,
hoping to patch things up with Nicole, his own hopes were dashed.
Nicole wouldn't have him. To make it worse, she dissed him in front
of everyone by pointedly excluding him from the family celebration at
Mezzaluna.

When he returned home to Rockingham in the wake of that disappointment, he said something disparaging to Kato about the sexy
little black dress Nicole wore to the recital. Kato recalled the remark to
me as something like, "Man, I see Nicole and her friends in those little
tight-ass dresses and I wonder what they're going to do when they're
grandmas." At the grand jury, however, Kato said Simpson had simply
appeared to be "joking" about the dress.

Now, on the stand, Kato once again did his best to downplay the
implications of Simpson's remark. The matter came up late, after his
halting direct testimony, and, as I suspected, a cross-exam where Bob
Shapiro cuddled up to him like a buddy.

It was now my redirect, and I was ready. "Your Honor," I said
to Ito, "I am going to ask the Court to take this witness as a hostile
witness."

There were several advantages in doing this. For one thing, it
would underscore that Kato was a *defense* witness. That would give the
jury notice that any evidence he gave to incriminate Simpson was the

real goods. But even more important, once a witness is declared to be hostile, you get to ask leading questions. Ordinarily, when a lawyer calls a witness, he has to ask open-ended questions that don't suggest the answer—that's what distinguishes direct examination from cross-exam. With a hostile witness, in effect, you get to cross-examine your own witness.

Only then, with the freedom to ask leading questions, did I get Kato to concede that Simpson's comment about Nicole's little black dress was spoken with a certain degree of "upsetness."

"Now, is it your testimony today that he was more upset about [Nicole not letting him see] Sydney than he was about Nicole wearing the tight dresses?" I bore into him.

"Yes."

"But that was not your testimony before, was it, Mr. Kaelin?"

"No."

"Earlier you had testified that he was 'relaxed' and 'nonchalant' when he spoke about Sydney and the recital?"

"That's what I remember."

"Isn't it also true that you testified previously in this trial that he was more upset about Nicole wearing the tight dresses than he was about not being able to see Sydney, is that right?"

"Yes."

"Now you are changing that testimony; is that what you are doing, sir?"

"Yes."

After the verdict, when it became clear that Simpson's acquittal would not restore his former status, Kato lost the surfer-boy stutter, bought a pair of specs and a blazer, and experienced a spell of enhanced memory. For the benefit of the plaintiffs in the Browns' and Goldmans' civil suits against Simpson, Kato could suddenly recall that Simpson had been upset and unsettled about Nicole since the day before the murders, when he'd watched *The World According to Garp*. The film's oral-sex scene had reminded him of Nicole's tryst on the couch with Keith Zlomsowitch. He'd been upset with Nicole at the recital and accused her of playing "hardball" by not letting him see Sydney. Kato Kaelin certainly wasn't the only one to remember the truth by the time the civil trial came around. But he typified the appalling, self-absorbed popularity junkies with no moral compass who came creeping out of the woodwork to offer information that they'd shamefully refused to give *us*.

The weird thing about Kato's trial appearance was that, despite all the pulled punches, his essential testimony would have been devastating to the defense if a thoughtful jury had listened. Take, for instance, his account of the trip to McDonald's. Something about that whole business had struck me as phony from day one. Simpson comes to Kato's room saying he needs to borrow five dollars to pay the skycap? All he's got is hundred-dollar bills. In the next breath he's saying that he's going out to get something to eat. Common sense compels one to ask, "If he's going out, can't he get change himself?"

Kato then gives him a twenty but when it comes time to pay for the food at the drive-in window, Kato pays again. And Simpson gives him back all the change. By now, Simpson has had *two* opportunities to get change, but he bypassed them both. Why?

Because he intended all along to set Kato up as an alibi.

When Simpson went out back to the guest house to ask Kato for change, it was solely for the purpose of having Kato notice he was at home, and to give his McDonald's outing as an explanation for his impending absence. But then Kato invited himself along and screwed up the plan. I had to chuckle privately at Simpson's predicament. He thinks he's home free when Kato—that perennial wad of gum stuck to the Bruno Magli loafer—crashes the dinner party. He can't refuse to take Kato. That would look worse than not having spoken to him at all.

"You invited yourself to go with him?" I had asked Kaelin while still on direct. "He seemed real excited to have you come?"

Kaelin paused for a moment. "Wouldn't you?"

Laughter rippled through the courtroom. But Kato had succeeded in sidestepping an important point. The moment was lost. I could have choked the little creep.

The fact is, Kato's tagging along uninvited tightened the schedule that Simpson had given himself for committing murder. That explained why Simpson ate his burger while driving instead of taking it into the house, as Kato had. It would also explain why, when they returned to Rockingham and Kato began walking toward the front door, Simpson hung back at the Bentley. When Kato finally got the hint that Simpson had no intention of spending any more time with him, he returned to his room in the guest quarters.

Before he lost sight of Simpson standing by the Bentley, watching him, Kato noticed that he was wearing "blue, dark blue or black" sweats. I had him describe those clothes in some detail. The reason would become apparent later: they were the source of the blue-black fibers that our FBI expert, Doug Deedrick, found on Ron Goldman's shirt, the Rockingham glove, and Simpson's bloody socks.

Simpson's setup had backfired. *Not only did Kato fail to give him an alibi, but he was the one who established conclusively that Simpson's whereabouts were unknown from approximately 9:36 P.M. until 10:53 P.M.* (precise times established through phone records). No two ways about it. O. J. Simpson had a window of seventy-two to seventy-seven minutes to commit murder.

All in all, Kato's testimony gave lie to nearly every single one of the defense theories.

Defense Theory Number 1: The cops went over to Simpson's house because they considered Simpson a suspect.

Kato: They interrogated me. They examined my eyes, searched my room, checked the bottoms of my shoes for blood. They treated me like a suspect. I never saw any of the detectives search the house or the grounds.

(In other words, even after jumping the fence at Rockingham, the cops had their options open. They weren't doing any of the things they should have been doing if they'd already concluded that Simpson was the murderer; instead, they treated the houseguest as a suspect.)

Defense Theory Number 2: The cops planted Simpson's blood at Rockingham.

Kato: I saw blood in the foyer of Rockingham at seven-thirty A.M., after the cops woke me.

(That was before Simpson even left Chicago. Which meant they didn't even have his blood to plant when Kato saw those drops—nor would they for another eight hours, when Simpson yielded a blood sample.)

Defense Theory Number 3: Mark Fuhrman planted a glove on the south pathway.

Kato: I heard the thumps on the wall between ten-forty and ten-forty-five.

(Someone was bumping behind Kato's room a good six hours or so before Mark Fuhrman even arrived at Rockingham and found the glove there on the other side of Kato's wall.)

Defense Theory Number 4: Fuhrman got into the Bronco and smeared the bloody glove around the console and tracked blood onto the floormat.

Kato: Detective Vannatter asked me if I knew where to find a key to the Bronco. I looked but never could find one.

(How could Fuhrman have done this dirty work? The Bronco was locked and the cops couldn't get into it until it was hauled to the impound lot.)

When you look at that testimony—given by a witness desperate to assist the defense!—you can see that it confirmed to the jury that the detectives—not only Fuhrman, but Vannatter and Lange as well—told them the truth on every major point. There was, indeed, no conspiracy. To persist in believing the space-invader theories, you would have to reject Kato's testimony out of hand.

But, of course, a jury hell-bent on acquittal could do just that.

CAR TAPE. *Monday, March 27. Coming up, Allan Park. That's gonna be a knock-down-drag-out. Johnnie's gonna take that witness, unfortunately. Kinda wouldn't mind seeing Bailey at work again. He did good cross on Fuhrman. Boy, was that a painful time.*

If ever there was an antidote to the despicable, mendacious opportunism of Kato Kaelin, it could be found in our limo-driver witness, Allan Park. Even the Dream Team, I learned later, privately referred to him as Young Abe Lincoln.

Early on in the investigation, Allan had gotten burned by the defense. On June 14 he'd spoken to Bob Shapiro, telling him what had happened at Rockingham two nights earlier. Unbeknownst to Park, Shapiro was taping their phone conversation. We didn't learn about this until we made a discovery request to the defense at the preliminary hearing in July. Shapiro had to turn over the tape. I should point out that it's illegal in the state of California to tape a phone conversation without the knowledge of both parties.

Shapiro had inadvertently left the tape running after the interview with Park was finished. The last thing Allan had told him was that on the way to the airport, Simpson had complained repeatedly of being hot, even though the night was cool and there was air-conditioning on in the limo. After Allan hung up, Shapiro turned to Skip Taft and said, "Hmm, does he always run hot after a shower?"

I just looked at the tape recorder. "No, you dolt," I said, out loud. "He always runs hot after murdering two people."

Allan did not find the taping episode amusing, to say the least. After that, he brought his mother with him whenever he was called in on case-related business. This was not as strange as it sounds, since his mother was a criminal defense attorney. After some initial wariness, Mrs. Park, a small, direct woman with very large eyes, warmed to me. By the time the case came to trial, we'd all gotten pretty close. She confided in me that Lee Bailey had called Allan to try to persuade him to participate in an "experiment." They wanted him literally to re-create his trip to Rockingham. To drive the limo up to the gate and listen for car sounds to see if he could have heard a Bronco. Then they'd have someone walk where Allan said he saw Simpson, and they'd ask him to describe what he saw. Mrs. Park told Bailey that she wouldn't mind as long as the prosecution could be present to observe the "experiment" as well. After that, they'd gotten hinky on her, setting up meetings, canceling at the last minute. When she asked if they'd notified us about this outing, they evaded the question. Finally, she put the kibosh on the whole idea.

During one of our office interviews, Allan, his mother, and I ended up going through a blow-by-blow description of the evening of June 12, beginning with his boss giving him the assignment to pick up Simpson. He'd used the cell phone in the limo, which meant we could use the phone records to confirm the timing of each event. When we got to the point where Allan was driving up Rockingham, I asked him how he was able to locate Simpson's house.

"I was looking at addresses," he replied.

At that point his mother jumped in.

"You mean on the curb? The numbers on the curb?" she asked.

She and I just looked at each other.

"So did you see Simpson's address on the Rockingham curb?" I asked.

"Yes, I saw it," Allan replied slowly. "I remember I had to stop and back up to make sure. It was painted on the curb: 360."

When the police arrived at Rockingham in the early-morning hours of the thirteenth, the Bronco had been parked a few feet north of the street number. If Allan saw the address painted on the curb, he couldn't have missed noticing the Bronco if it had, indeed, been parked there.

"Do you remember what time it was when you first pulled up to Rockingham and saw the address on the curb?"

"I looked at the clock, just to make sure I was on time, and I was early. It was ten-twenty-two."

Man, oh man, I thought. *Is Johnnie going to go crazy over this one.*

Again, at about 10:35, Allan decided to drive over to the Rockingham gate to see if that entrance would be easier to pull into than the Ashford gate. He drove down Rockingham and pulled parallel to the gate to look inside. In that position, he would have been right next to the Bronco if it had been there.

"Was it?"

"No."

The Bronco was not there at 10:22. It was not there at 10:35. So much for Rosa Lopez.

The rest of Allan's times dovetailed perfectly with Kato's testimony. Kato said he'd left his guest cottage a couple of minutes after hearing the "thumps." He was spotted by Park around 10:53 or 10:54. This was only seconds before Allan saw the six-foot, two-hundred-pound black person dressed in dark clothing stride quickly into the house. (Working backward from Park's cell-phone records, we managed to establish that Kato had heard the thumps at about 10:51 or 10:52.) Then, the lights went on and O. J. Simpson answered the buzzer. "I overslept," he said. "I just got out of the shower. I'll be down in a minute."

The one-two punch of Kaelin and Park pretty much clinched it. If you believed their accounts, you would have no choice but to conclude that O. J. Simpson was lying about his whereabouts on the night of the murders. And if he was lying, you'd have to ask yourself why.

When I called Allan to the witness stand on Tuesday, March 28, he laid out the facts with the sturdy decency that was his hallmark. He was simply a citizen coming forward with evidence about a crime. No book deal, no TV shows. He wouldn't surmise anything. He gave precisely what he'd heard and seen. Nothing more; nothing less.

At one point I asked Simpson to stand. "Can you tell us if that appears to be the size of the person you saw enter the front entrance of the house at Rockingham?" I asked Park, pointing to Simpson. Johnnie objected, but Lance overruled him.

Simpson, who'd been fidgeting nervously, now stooped, trying to make himself less imposing.

"Yes, around the size," Allan answered.

To me that was the defining moment of the case. If you believe Allan Park, you have Simpson walking into his house and then answering the intercom. It all unravels from there. He was not at home asleep. He was lying to Park. And he was lying because he was covering up the fact that he had just returned from murdering Nicole Brown and Ron Goldman.

I felt great about Allan's testimony. The only place he tripped up was in his recollection of the number of cars in the driveway when he'd pulled in. There were two, he thought. One was the Bentley. The other, parked right behind it, was a small dark car, possibly a Saab. I knew he was wrong about that. Arnelle's car was a black Saab, but it hadn't been there at eleven o'clock, because she'd been out at the movies with friends. She didn't return until about 1:30 A.M. Photos taken later on the thirteenth showed her car parked behind the Bentley. Perhaps Allan had seen those photos so many times he'd come to believe that he'd seen the car that night, upon his arrival.

It was an inconsequential point. Even Johnnie, who mounted a spirited assault upon Allan during cross, chuckled when he came to this one. The issue of the second car was so meaningless that no one even mentioned it during closing arguments. Yet Park's recollection of a second car would come back to haunt us in ways we could never have imagined.

*   *   *

My streak of witnesses ended strongly with James Williams, the skycap from LAX. The direct was short and sweet. James, who'd checked Simpson's bags through to Chicago, never saw the small, dark bag that both Kato and Park had seen lying on the lawn at Rockingham.

"Is there a trash can anywhere near the stand where you work?" I asked him.

"Yes, just to the left of it," he replied.

The implication I'd wanted to produce, of course, was that Simpson could have disposed of the knife—and perhaps the black bag—right then and there. And in doing so, I'd laid a trap for the defense. On cross-examination Carl Douglas tumbled right into it. In fact, he made the worst error that a lawyer can ever make on cross: asking a question he doesn't have the answer to.

"Mr. Williams," he said with a sneer. "You don't recall ever seeing Mr. Simpson anywhere near that trash can on June the twelfth, do you, sir?"

"Yes," James replied ingenuously. "He was standing near the trash can."

I had to put my hand against my face to keep the jury from seeing how hard I was laughing.

I had to get away from this case. I also needed to get away from my life. The pressures were killing me.

During the frenzy surrounding Mark Fuhrman's testimony, I was constantly getting beeped, finding myself called in to the civil courthouse for my own case. Even though the civil court was virtually across the street from the CCB, I couldn't just walk there—dozens of reporters would follow. Instead, Lieutenant Gary Schram and his men would escort me to the underground parking lot of the CCB, where they'd put me in a car and drive through a connecting tunnel to the underground lot of the civil courthouse. There, they would turn me over to sheriff's deputies. The deputies would then take me up in the service elevator and through a labyrinth of corridors to the courtroom.

I had a new lawyer, Judy Forman. She was not only a decent person—she would become one of my closest friends and confidantes—but also one tough cookie. Judy was trying to make sure that certain issues presented in the divorce case were kept confidential.

Chris knew the stress I was under and he offered to go with me to family court. I always declined. I didn't want to burden him with my problems. He had his own share of sorrow. His brother, Michael, was dying of AIDs. As I listened to Chris describe Michael's skull-like face and impossibly shrunken body, I knew this deathwatch was sheer agony for him. I vowed to myself that I wouldn't ask for help unless I was desperate.

As the custody case progressed, though, desperate was exactly what I became. Gordon's lawyers were demanding to take my deposition. That process could run on for days, during which time I would be subjected to intense personal questioning, about my private life . . . everything. Depositions in custody matters are harrowing under the most ordinary circumstances. These were not ordinary.

I was under the worst pressure I'd ever experienced. I was in the middle of this incredible trial. I was exhausted. One afternoon the thought of doing the deposition simply overwhelmed me. I sat at my desk staring dumbly at the documents in front of me, unable to focus.

I looked up to see Chris standing at the door. His expression was concerned. He knew what was going down.

"I'll go with you," he said quietly.

"You're kidding, right?"

"No, I'm not. I'll go with you. You know I got your back, G."

Chris did go with me. I can't tell you what went down at the deposition. The custody case file has been sealed at my request, in the interests of protecting my children. It severely limits what I myself can say. But I can tell you this. Being able to exchange supportive glances with my *compadre* and joke with him during the breaks made a huge difference to me. I'll never forget it.

Come the last week in March, Chris was taking a trip to the Bay Area to visit his family. He also wanted to spend some time with his teenaged daughter, Jenee. It was sweet to hear him talk about her. He was a tender, doting father. Of course, San Francisco was my old stamping ground; I said wistfully that I missed the place.

"Wanna join me?" he asked.

It was a weekend when the boys would be with their father. So I thought about it. The Bay. Long walks. Irish coffees. A world that had nothing to do with this craziness.

"I sure as hell would."

We made the five-hour drive in Chris's Toyota Camry. I was so paranoid about being spotted that when we stopped at a gas station, I pulled the hood of my parka over my face. But the farther north we got, the more relaxed I felt. We could talk for once without running the risk of being overheard. We vented about Fuhrman, Johnnie, Ito, the goddamned media. TFC, TFC, This Fucking Case.

"When this is over," I told him, "I'm gonna take about a year off and do nothing but read murder mysteries and play with my kids."

"Man, I'll tell you what," he replied. "When this case is over, I'm gonna take about a year off and do nothing but kick it in my crib, drink beer, and watch the games."

Is it me, or do men seem to lack imagination?

That weekend I was in a state of absolute euphoria. Chris and I checked into the Fairmont—taking separate rooms, for those of you keeping score. He introduced me to his family. One night his sisters and I went out to a place near the wharf. People recognized us—hell, all that airtime had made us the two most recognizable civil servants in the country—but they kept their distance. I felt lighter, more hopeful than I had in months. It seemed possible that someday life might return to normal.

On the trip home I remained enveloped in this euphoria, until we stopped at a fast-food joint. I ran inside to pick up a quick dinner. I hadn't been standing in line but a few seconds when I felt it. People were staring. We must be getting close to L.A. I fumbled for my wallet, grabbed the bags, and ran back to the car.

The weekend had been an illusion. Nothing had changed. I was still a featured player in a freak show. There was nothing I could do to keep back the tears.

Chris, who was about to pull out of the lot, caught me in a side-long glance and said, "Hey, what's up with you?"

Last he knew, we were having a pretty good time.

"I can't face it," I whispered, tears now streaming freely down my cheeks. "I want it all to be over."

"Yeah, me too," Chris said quietly. "But look at the bright side.

People all over the world are naming their baby girls Marcia. *Marcia, Marcia, Marcia.* They'll probably come out with Marcia dolls. They'll argue with everyone and accuse them of wearing gloves in size small."

A few seconds into this riff I was doubled over with laughter and coming back with my own ideas for a Chris doll. It would say "Mmm, ummm, hummm" after everything and get held in contempt.

We laughed the rest of the way home. Once again, Chris had snatched me back from the brink of despair.

There's been a lot of speculation about whether Chris and I were lovers. And if there's any one of you out there with lingering curiosity on this point, I'm truly sorry. The question is irrelevant. Fact of the matter is, Chris Darden and I were closer than lovers. And unless you've been through what we went through, you can't possibly know what that means.

The Big Picture

CAR TAPE. *April 18. I haven't been talking much because my life is so painful I don't want to talk about it. I just want to pretend it's not there. Everything seems like it's getting a lot crazier on my personal front. . . . Thank God . . . I can sit down and let others stand up and talk to the witnesses. The problem is that I still have to be there to prompt and give ideas and kind of guide things. So I've never really got my hand out of it. It would sure be nice to get out of court for a week or so and just kind of chill out. But I can see now that's probably never gonna happen. I've got to be there. I have the big picture . . . me and Chris are really the only ones who do.*

By early April, we'd penetrated to the very heart of our case. The physical evidence.

Now, normally I love that stuff, and if I'd had my way—plus eight spare months to prepare—I would have handled it all myself. But here, that simply wasn't possible. I'd had to delegate. So I kept the hair and trace evidence for myself, and gave the glove, which was a pretty straightforward assignment, to Chris. Then I'd divided the remainder of the science witnesses among Rockne Harmon, Woody Clarke, Brian Kelberg, and Hank Goldberg. Rock and Woody got DNA. Brian, the coroner. Hank caught the criminalists, including Dennis Fung.

Talk about drawing the short straw. What *was* it with that guy Fung?

Dennis's scattered performance before the grand jury boded ill, but I had no idea how bad things really were until a few days after the preliminary hearings. Back in August I was holed up in my office, poring over the photos of Rockingham. I spend a lot of time looking at police photos. Every time you return to them, you see something else. Kind of an Antonioni thing.

I was studying a picture of Dennis crouched near the laundry hamper in Simpson's master bathroom. He was holding something dark in his hand. I looked closer. Could it be? It had to be. Jesus! It was the dark sweatshirt Kato had described Simpson wearing when they drove to McDonald's! Why hadn't anyone told me about this? Those sweats had to be tested for blood immediately. Unless, of course, they were never seized.

Please, God.

Tom Lange was in the War Room with Patti Jo. I sent for him and handed him the photo.

"Look at this carefully and tell me what you see in the hamper."

"Dark sweats," he replied. He looked like he might have to sit down.

"Is it possible they were taken and Fung forgot to write it up?" Maybe there was one brown bag that had been overlooked in the booking process.

"I know there was nothing seized that wasn't booked," he said with grim finality.

"I want to see Fung right fucking now," I snapped. Tom got him over in just one phone call.

Dennis strolled in wearing jeans, sneakers, and a windbreaker.

"Do have a seat," I told him.

I like to get my bad news as soon as possible.

"Do you remember going through Simpson's hamper when you were at Rockingham on June thirteenth?"

"I think so," Dennis replied in his usual fog of distraction.

I handed him the eight-by-ten.

"Tell me if you collected the clothing you're holding in that picture."

"I know I didn't book any clothing out of the bathroom," he replied. "Why?" But I could see awareness dawning.

"You must have known that clothing in the hamper was likely to have been worn recently by the defendant. In a knife killing there's bound to be some trace evidence, if not the blood of the victims. So why didn't you take the sweats?"

I was pissed off. But I was also truly curious.

"Well, I looked to see if there was blood on them. I figured if they'd been used in the murder the blood would be big and obvious. I didn't see any, so I put them back." He shrugged dejectedly.

"But if the killer stood behind his victims," I pressed, "he might get only a fine spray on him, if that. You can't see a fine spray of blood on black clothing. Not in normal light."

You shouldn't have to tell a criminalist this.

Dennis passed his hand over his face and stared at the ground. He'd screwed up big-time. What could I say? There was no use belaboring the point or making Dennis feel any worse. The damage was done.

The hard, ugly fact was that Fung's oversights would hobble us at every turn.

On his first pass at Bundy on June 13, Fung hadn't picked up the bloodstains on the rear gate. This, after Tom Lange had specifically instructed him to do so. Fung's property reports from that date show that he'd collected a stain from the rear driveway, then gone up front to collect a stain from the front gate, then returned to the rear driveway to collect another stain. The guy was painfully disorganized. He didn't get around to picking up the stains from the rear gate until three weeks later.

Same with the Bronco. For reasons known only to Fung, he'd taken only a "representative sample" of the blood smears from inside the vehicle on June 14, which meant he hadn't collected all of the blood on the console. That blood would be a devastating blow to the defense: DNA results from that stain showed Ron Goldman's blood mixed with that of the defendant. There could be no innocent expla-nation for this except the truth: that Simpson had tracked the blood of his victims into the Bronco.

During a re-exam of the Bronco on September 1 we ended up col-lecting a considerable amount of blood that Dennis left behind on the first sweep. (Ironically, that re-exam was done at the request of the defense. Had it not been for their demand to see the Bronco, Ron Goldman's blood might never have been found.)

Both of Fung's oversights—the rear gate and the Bronco con-sole—left us vulnerable. They gave the defense an opening to argue that blood on both the console and the rear gate had been "planted," presumably using blood drawn from Simpson the day he was ques-tioned by police. Both of these charges were easily refuted. We had in our possession police photos taken of the Bronco on both the morning of June 14 and again on September 1. They showed stains on the console in exactly the same places. Ron Goldman's blood had been there during the first sweep; but because of Fung, it had been left behind.

Same with the blood on the rear gate. Lange noticed it the morning after the murders. So did at least two other officers. Three weeks before Dennis took the stand, Hank and Woody—during one of their many late-night work sessions—came across a police photo of the inside of the gate taken from about fifteen feet away. In this "per-spective shot," as such photos are called, one of the bloodstains was clearly visible under magnification.

The real stumbling block for the defense remained those blood droplets leading up the walkway at Bundy, away from the bodies. No way could they have been planted. They'd been collected during the early-morning hours of June 13, before Simpson had been questioned, let alone had his blood drawn. Where would Mark Fuhrman, Phil Vannatter, or anyone else in this alleged conspiracy have gotten hold of any of O. J. Simpson's blood, even if they'd had a mind to plant it?

The only path open to the defense was to claim that the Bundy blood trail was either so degraded or so contaminated by the LAPD's sloppy collection work that the results had gone haywire.

We suspected the Dream Team was planning to make its contami-nation case upon the crushed bones of Dennis Fung. And so Hank spent days and days preparing him. He reported back to me that he thought Dennis would be "okay." Dennis's "tentative demeanor," as Hank put it with characteristic delicacy, might actually be endearing to the jury.

On April 3, Dennis Fung took the stand.

Hank did a very smart thing. But since it was a quiet and intelligent thing, it went largely unnoticed by the press. He led Dennis step-by-step through the process of evidence collection, leading up to the subject of "substrate controls."

Now, please. Hang tough while I explain. Substrate control is a fancy term for a very simple concept. Once you understand it, it should help you see why the contamination theories put forward by the defense were such utter nonsense.

What happens is this. A criminalist goes into a room and sees blood on, say, the carpet. He lifts a sample from the bloody spot and smears it on one little square of cotton cloth. That's the "evidence sample." Then he goes just a little beyond the stain to what looks like clean carpet, and he tests that. He puts this on another cotton cloth, to make what scientists call the "control."

So, you test the control. If it shows traces of another blood type, that tells you that there may be contamination. But if the control comes up clean—*formidable!* You can safely infer that the DNA profile on the evidence sample is valid. It tells you that the criminalist did his job right. If Dennis's procedures were so sloppy that the bloodstains he collected had become contaminated, then the controls—collected under identical circumstances—would have been contaminated in an identical fashion. In fact, every one of Fung's controls came up clean as a whistle.

The controls should have rendered moot any further argument about the validity of the sample. But they did not. Barry Scheck kept Fung on the stand for seven days over the course of two weeks. The entire time Scheck slashed away at him in his nasal, nails-on-chalkboard voice for things like storing the samples in a hot truck, and accusing him of handling evidence without gloves and not using a fresh set of tweezers for each swatch.

Red herrings all. Later in the trial we would bring on Gary Sims of the California Department of Justice, who set the record straight. DNA is a much tougher material than the defense would have you believe. Gary described tests run by the FBI in which agents had done about every stupid thing you could think of to contaminate evidence. They'd used the same pair of scissors to cut different swatches without cleaning them in between. One analyst had sweated on samples before testing them. One agent coughed on samples for a solid minute. The testers even shook dandruff on their samples. In each case, the contaminants had no effect on the DNA profile. Even the defense's own expert witness, Henry Lee, would later testify that a cop could track blood from the crime scene or the heel of his shoe, and that blood could produce a valid test result. As for degradation, DNA gives valid results on body parts found out in the jungle after days of exposure to hot sun, dampness, insect infestation, and animal scavenging. You're going to destroy it during a few hours in a warm truck?

The bigger point, however, was this: under no circumstances could either contamination or degradation yield a set of flawed results all pointing to a single suspect. And yet, this was the very premise upon which Scheck sought to discredit Fung.

I found little to admire in Barry Scheck. Here was a man who was an expert in the science of DNA. He believed in it. He'd staked his reputation on it. He and his partner, Peter Neufeld, had founded an organization called the Innocence Project, which routinely used DNA testing to exonerate defendants falsely convicted of crimes. He knew what contamination and degradation could and could not do to a sample.

Now, you could argue, "He's a defense attorney. A defense attorney knows what the truth is and he argues counter to it all the time." But when a lawyer who's an authority in science gets up and puts forward a defense based on what he knows to be scientifically incorrect, you're talking about something far worse than professional sophistry.

Not only did I find Scheck's performance intellectually dishonest, I considered him by far the most obnoxious lawyer in that courtroom.

And that's saying a lot. Scheck's treatment of Dennis Fung was deplorable. Even Lee Bailey had displayed a fundamental courtesy to Mark Fuhrman while dueling to the death with him on cross.

Not Scheck. He knew he was going up against a witness who was easy pickings, someone from whom he could have extracted every concession he wanted, with kindness. And yet he set upon Fung like a common bully, jabbing a stubby finger in his face and screaming "Liar!"

Dennis, who wanted only to please, buckled in the first ten minutes.

Scheck would pose to him absurd hypotheticals. Remember the blanket Tom Lange had found inside the condo and spread over Nicole's dead body? It was back to haunt us. Barry contended that when Tom performed this act of decency he had "contaminated" the crime scene. O. J. Simpson had visited this residence, Scheck observed. He might have "sat or laid" on that blanket and shed his own hair on it.

"Could that, in your expert opinion," he asked Dennis, "be a source of secondary transfer of his hairs to the crime scene?"

Hank and Chris and I cringed. We knew what was coming.

"It's possible" was the reply.

". . . Are you with me so far?" Barry queried.

"It's kind of hard to follow," Dennis replied. "But yes."

"And if a dog . . . Kato the dog . . . were lying on this blanket . . . dog hairs can be transferred to the blanket?"

"Yes."

"And the dog itself may have hairs and fibers from other people with whom it has been in contact?"

What Dennis could have said, and should have said, was this: "Counselor, if you're asking me if that blanket could transport dog hairs that were carrying Mr. Simpson's hairs that subsequently found their way to the inside of the knit cap, I'd have to say this scenario is too ludicrous to warrant serious consideration."

Instead, Dennis replied, "Yes, there's a chance."

Scheck hoped to use Fung to advance the theory that the blood on the back gate at Bundy had been planted sometime later than June 13. He got Fung to say that he had not seen the blood himself that morning. Fung also testified that he'd not heard Tom Lange ask him to collect the stains on the morning of the first search.

Scheck pulled out one of the photographs of the back gate taken at such an angle that the blood spots were not apparent.

"Let's look back at the picture of the gate on June thirteenth."

The photo was displayed on the Elmo. No blood to be seen.

Scheck turned to Dennis and in a tone as contemptuous as it was shrill, inquired, "Where isss ittttt, Misterrrr Fung?"

That line, of course, became the sound bite du jour. But it was revealed for the empty histrionics it was when we introduced our own shot of the gate—which showed that at least one of the stains was clearly visible.

Scheck moved on to another tack, building to what he no doubt expected would be a boffo climax. He'd hoped to establish that Phil Vannatter had kept custody of Simpson's reference vial long enough to plant the blood to frame him. Fung had testified that Phil had brought it to Rockingham in the late afternoon of June 13 and personally handed it over at about 5:20 P.M. But there was no written record of that exchange. Scheck produced a series of video clips from a local station, KABC. They showed Fung and Andrea Mazzola leaving the house, putting various items into the crime-scene truck. But a gray envelope carrying the blood vial was not among them.

Scheck tried to cast Dennis in the role of a conspirator by suggesting that he'd lied about ever receiving the blood from Vannatter. In an attempt to establish this, he produced a crime-scene checklist filled out by Fung and Mazzola and turned over to the defense during discovery. Page 4 of this document was different from the others. It was not an original; it was a photocopy. You could tell that because there were no staple holes, just black hen scratches where the holes should have been.

Scheck intended to use this to suggest that the original page would have shown Dennis's actual log-cut time, which, he speculated, was 5:15 P.M. (This was based upon nothing, as far as I can tell, but Scheck's fevered imagination.) Since Vannatter arrived at 5:20, that would mean the two had missed each other.

"If there were something filled in there that said five-fifteen as to the time leaving the scene," Scheck charged, "that would be inconsistent with what you wrote [5:20 P.M.] on the gray envelope you received from Detective Vannatter?"

Hank objected. He was overruled.

"If there was that time there," Dennis said meekly. "Yes, it would."

Scheck acted as though he'd cornered the kidnapper of the Lindbergh baby.

"And that is why you *destroyed* the original page four, Mr. Fung?"

At the break we noticed that Dennis happened to be holding his case notebook.

"Dennis," Hank asked him, "could I take a look at that?"

Hank quickly flipped through the binder. And from a pocket on the inside cover, he withdrew the original of the infamous page 4. It was *identical* to the photocopy. No mention of 5:15 P.M. or any other time. We decided that we would not share this development with Scheck. He had, after all, ambushed us with the copy; let him find out about the original the hard way.

The timing was perfect, because after the break Hank started redirect.

"During the recess, sir," he asked the witness, "did you have an opportunity to look in your notebook and find the original of page four?"

Yes, he did. Dennis produced the form.

Scheck predictably screamed "discovery violation," but this time Ito tuned him out and let Hank pass the original of the disputed page 4 among the jurors.

Live by the sword, die by the sword, buddy.

Still, lodged in the jurors' recent memory were those snippets of videotape that Scheck had introduced, showing Dennis and Andrea purportedly leaving Rockingham without the vial of Simpson's blood. These, he'd intimated, showed that Dennis had deceived the court when he'd testified about receiving the blood vial from Vannatter.

Now, Dennis Fung might be a dope, but he was not a liar. We knew the truncated footage did not tell the whole story.

Hank and Bill Hodgman were quietly negotiating with KABC for the portion of their videotape that had not aired. Normally, broadcasters are reluctant to release unaired material. Maybe the execs over at the station felt Fung deserved a break, I don't know. Anyway, on Easter Sunday, Hank was in the office, working with Fung on upcoming redirect, when the unedited footage arrived.

There is a wonderful account of this in Hank's own book, *The Prosecution Responds.* He tells how he and Dennis sat over bagels and lox and ran the outtakes. Sure enough, at 5:17 P.M. by the time counter, there was Phil Vannatter strolling up the Rockingham walk. "He was carrying a leather attaché case," Hank recalled, "the way a schoolboy would carry a notebook against the side of his body. A gray piece of paper sat on top of the attaché case. A gust of wind blew back the top of the paper, allowing us to see the reverse side. We could clearly observe the flap and metal clasp, showing that it was the back of an envelope."

The envelope carrying the blood vial. Dennis could identify it by the form printed on the face of the envelope.

"We could see a long shot of the front door at Rockingham," Hank writes. "Just inside the foyer, we could see Dennis. In one hand he had the plastic garbage bag. In the other, he had what could only have been the evidence envelope containing the vial."

Dennis jumped up for joy, screaming, "Yes! Yes! Yes!"

First thing on Monday, Hank played that tape for the jury. Barry was forced to eat crow.

"Your Honor," he said with uncharacteristic humility, "we have viewed the . . . tape. It is certainly enlightening."

The defense ended up stipulating to the time on KABC's footage. And Hank went on to do a beautiful job on redirect.

Dennis stepped down on April 18. He'd been on the witness stand over two interminable weeks. Most of this time had been pissed away on Scheck's cross. As Dennis tried to make his escape from the courtroom, he was intercepted by a jubilant defense team, who shook his hand and greeted him like a long-lost relative. I was baffled. For starters, why were attorneys for the defense displaying public affection for a man who, they'd just claimed, helped frame their client? And why on earth was Fung allowing himself to be fawned over by these hypocrites? When Hank asked him about it later, Dennis replied that he'd been "somewhat in a daze" after leaving the witness stand. And knowing Dennis, that answer rings true.

It is that curious image of him fraternizing with his tormentors that lingers in the memory of the public. Seared with equal clarity into the American consciousness are those shrill invectives of Barry Scheck. What amazed me was that he drew such favorable reviews for his performance.

No question, Fung turned in a sorry performance. But in the end, Scheck bluffed, Hank called him on it. And Barry had to fold.

CAR TAPE. *April 18. Just heard that some idiot out there's come out with an unauthorized biography on me. The weird thing is to see the change in the judge's attitude. . . . It's like, the more famous I get the more he's willing to pay deference, to be nicer to me. . . . Ito is really somebody who is very affected by the media stuff, by popularity, you know? When Johnnie was the most famous one . . . he was very deferential, to the point of idiocy. But I think having the press call him on his deference to Johnnie and then maybe hearing the jurors say that Johnnie was in control of the courtroom perhaps set him back a bit. But I think what set [Ito] back even more is seeing my getting famous. It's all of a sudden somebody else whose favor he needs to curry. Very weird. Very, very weird.*

CAR TAPE. *April 27. Constantly sick. I can't seem to recover. Finally, my teammates pushed me in to the doctor. . . . I just need rest. With all this stress, I mean, it's impossible. I can't just go home and lie down. There's just no corner. I really hope something gives somewhere. This is just too much. Fortunately, it's not my witness who's up right now, and I can afford the luxury of concentrating on the custody case for a little bit.*

I needed more time. I always felt breathless, my chest constricted with fatigue. I woke up each morning in a state of dread, knowing that before the day was through some new crisis was sure to break. To make things worse, by the time Dennis Fung got off the stand, it looked like we might be headed for a mistrial.

We were losing jurors at the rate of about two a month. The judge, of course, was worried that we wouldn't have enough alternates to last the trial, which now looked like it would be going well into the summer. Lawyers on both sides of the room kept an anxious eye on the shifting composition of the jury.

In January we lost a middle-aged female juror whom we'd pegged as pro-prosecution. She'd stated right up front on her questionnaire that she'd had to get a restraining order against her abusive ex-boyfriend. How the defense had dropped its guard long enough to let her slip through, I don't know.

But now they were looking to rectify their error. It turned out that the ex-boyfriend had called the court claiming that she shouldn't be on the case because she'd had problems with black co-workers. The charges were investigated; they were bunk. What was happening is that the son of a bitch was harassing her even as she sat behind a veil of sequestration. The thing I found so sad about this is that, in managing to be get herself on this jury, the woman had found herself a temporary haven.

The defense filed a motion to have her booted. We objected, and lost.

Defense: 1. The People: 0.

The same day, January 18, Ito dismissed a black man who had formerly worked for Hertz. Critics of the prosecution have asked us how we ever let this guy onto the jury in the first place. That's a fair question. When his employment history came out during voir dire, I wanted to boot him. Bill, however, argued persuasively that this guy was a follower who would do neither harm nor good. The juror himself assured us that he'd never had any personal contact with Simpson.

After he was seated, though, we began receiving a string of tips from other Hertz employees to the effect that not only had Juror Number 228 met Simpson, but they'd seen him shaking hands with Simpson at a celebrity affair that *the juror himself* had helped organize! When we reported this to Ito, we learned that the judge already had this information and had, for some inexplicable reason, been sitting on it. Why, I'm not sure. As far as I could tell, there was no nefarious motive for his foot-dragging. I think he was just disorganized. Yet he actually seemed pissed off at us for bringing it to his attention. Only the court, he admonished us, is allowed to do juror investigations! Still, the facts were undeniable. This juror had lied.

I'd noticed throughout the trial that Simpson would sometimes smirk when looking at the jury box. Now I realized the reason. He had Hertz-man as the ace up his sleeve. Not anymore. Bye-bye, Hertz guy.

Defense: 1. The People: 1.

For a couple of weeks, it seemed like the jury situation had stabilized. Then, in early February, rumors began to circulate that we might lose an elderly white female juror, Number 2017, who we felt was favorable to us.

Another juror, a stout black woman held generally to be a darling of the defense, claimed that this feeble little white woman had "pushed" her during an evening walk. Even Ito had to see that this was a put-up job. But to keep the peace he ended up excusing 2017 on the hollow pretext that she'd been treated for arthritis by the same doctor who'd treated O. J. Simpson.

Defense: 2. The People: 1.

During March, two more jurors bit the dust. The first was Michael Knox, the black man who'd worn the 49ers cap and jacket to the jury walk. Knox later wrote a book, *The Private Diary of an O.J. Juror*, in which he explained that the only reason he'd flown the 49ers' colors was that his brother was a public relations flak for the team and the cap was a freebie. (That, of course, did not explain why he had deliberately flouted the judge's order to ignore memorabilia on the walls of the defendant's home.) The Dream Team was desperate to keep this guy. But the knockout punch came when the court discovered that Knox had failed to report that he'd been arrested for kidnapping a former girlfriend. Gone. History.

Defense: 2. The People: 2.

A little over two weeks later, Ito kicked Tracy Kennedy, the white guy who professed to be part American Indian. Kennedy was well-educated and a part-time high school teacher, a prosecution juror if ever there was one. Since October, Shapiro had seemed to be obsessed with this guy. He complained that Kennedy was often seen "staring out into space." It turned out, however, that Kennedy had been paying a great deal of attention to the goings-on around him. The sheriff's deputies seized a laptop computer on which Kennedy had been keeping notes on his fellow jurors. These musings seemed to be preparation for writing a book.

He'd been caught red-handed with the goods; nothing we could do.

Defense: 3. The People: 2.

For about a month, during the early part of our physical-evidence testimony, there were no more dismissals. But those of us on the prosecution side, at least, knew that this was only an appearance of calm. While Dennis Fung was still on the witness stand, Ito was investigating Juror Number 462, Jeanette Harris. The court had received an anonymous tip that she'd once sought a restraining order against her husband.

Harris was definitely someone we'd have been delighted to kick. She was part of a bloc we called the Clique of Four. That bunch included another middle-aged black woman named Sheila Woods, an impressionable young black woman named Tracy Hampton, and an ill-tempered black man named Willie Cravin—all of whom we believed to have a strong pro-defense bias.

Harris, at least, had been honest enough to lay out her feelings about the defendant during jury selection. She felt sympathy for him. During voir dire she'd been asked about the Bronco chase. "My family," she answered, "is comprised mostly of males, so I know that females have this real desire, you know, to protect their young men." Her "heart went out" to Simpson, she'd said. I wanted to kick her. Bill wasn't crazy about her either, but she managed to win us over. During voir dire she had made it a point to be pleasant to me. She made good eye contact, gave intelligent answers, and seemed to indicate that she could render an impartial verdict. All in all, she was impressive enough to make it very difficult for us to overcome a *Wheeler* objection if the defense tried to claim we were targeting her because she was black.

Almost immediately after the jury was sequestered in the Inter-Continental, we began to get reports back from the deputies that Jeanette was a troublemaker. She didn't like any of the white jurors, who, she felt, didn't want to sit with the blacks. This ran contrary to the intelligence we were receiving—which was that Harris and her friends didn't want to sit with the whites.

Anyway, after we got the tip concerning Harris's domestic problems, Ito pulled her file from the civil courthouse. She had, indeed, filed for a restraining order against her husband on grounds of abuse. When Ito brought her in and confronted her with it, she tried to minimize, but she couldn't deny it. The defense fought to keep her, but it was over. They'd gotten one of our jurors booted on a domestic violence issue. Harris had to go.

After she was booted from the jury, Harris gave a set of wideranging interviews to station KCAL in which she claimed, among other things, that she thought Denise Brown was "acting." This made me sick at heart. It still does. I think the thing that bothers me most is how Harris's grandstanding and her apparent callousness seemed to confirm the social theories of Don Vinson, among others, who had pronounced with smug certainty that black women don't take domestic violence seriously.

You cannot make these reckless generalizations about people. Experience had shown me that black female jurors are perfectly capable of convicting a black man who brutalizes his wife or girlfriend. As I've said before—and I'll say it as many times as I have to—*the Simpson case was an anomaly.* What was perceived here as apathy on the part of black women jurors toward Nicole's suffering seemed to me rather a deliberate form of denial. I truly believe that our black female jurors knew in their hearts that O. J. Simpson was no better than the average asshole who gets drunk on Friday nights and throws his woman against a wall. But I think they felt they couldn't afford to act on that knowledge. Too few black men succeed in penetrating the ranks of upper-class white society for them to allow one to be taken out in such an ignominious way. Looking back on it, I think I'd have to say that blacks of both sexes were moved to breathtaking feats of denial in order to keep the Juice from going down.

With the departure of Jeanette Harris, the Clique of Four lost its center of gravity. Little Tracy Hampton claimed to have awakened one night to find a white female deputy standing at the foot of her bed. She went running to Ito, claiming that the deputies were "spying" on her, that they were going in and out of her room when she wasn't there.

Now, during jury selection Hampton had come across as an okay sort. She was unusually quiet, but not someone we particularly had to worry about hanging the jury. During the early days of sequestration, however, she'd been drawn into the gravitational pull of the stronger personalities in the Clique and had gotten way off into the race thing.

Now we had to figure out what to make of her allegations. Ito talked to the deputies, who denied her charges. The defense, obviously, wanted to keep this juror, so they were all for rotating the deputies to another post. Chris, for once, agreed with the defense. He was afraid of the bad press it would generate if we cut Hampton loose and she spouted off to reporters about "spying" and "racial discrimination."

I was scandalized. These deputies were doing a difficult job and doing it admirably. They'd done everything for these jurors. When a couple of jurors had deaths in the family, the deputies had accompanied them to the funerals and quite literally given them a shoulder to cry on. Now we were going to let their reputations be sacrificed for the sake of expediency? I felt it was just flat-out wrong to punish those deputies based upon the word of a juror who, in my opinion, wasn't wrapped too tight.

But Ito thought he could hose Hampton down by removing the deputies. So that's what he did.

Whenever I hear the pundits wringing their hands over the racial tensions on the jury, I defy them to explain what happened next. After little Tracy got the white deputies rotated out, most of the remaining jurors were so angry and upset that they demanded to see the judge to discuss the matter. One by one they professed affection for the deputies and sorrow at the shabby treatment they'd received. Through it all, Johnnie looked confused and worried. I could just about tell what was going through his head: *Oh, my God. They're identifying with law enforcement.*

Only by promising the jurors that the deputies would not have black marks on their records did Ito get them to agree to return to the jury box. Thirteen of them wore black in support of the deputies. Two of the Clique of Four—Tracy Hampton and Sheila Woods—wore bright colors to express their opposition.

The irony, of course, is that Ito's appeasement strategy didn't work. Within days, Tracy was back in chambers whining that she was being ostracized. "I can't take it anymore," she pleaded. This time, Ito showed the good sense to cut her loose.

Two of the Clique had bitten the dust.

Defense: 3. The People: 4.

In late May, the court received an anonymous letter purporting to be from a "receptionist in a literary agency." The letter writer claimed to have knowledge that Francine Florio-Bunten—a thirty-eight-year-old white woman we considered one of ours—was circulating a proposal for a book to be entitled *Standing Alone—A Vote for Nicole*.

When I read that letter in Ito's chambers, I looked straight at Johnnie. This was a setup. I had no doubt of it then, and I have no doubt now. The defense had been itching to kick Florio-Bunten.

Ito, however, felt this source was reliable, largely because the writer had "confidential" knowledge that the jurors were staying at the Inter-Continental Hotel. (The issue of confidentiality was nonsense, of course, since the fact had already been published in a British newspaper and had long since made its way Stateside.)

Once again, Ito questioned jurors individually. The last of these, a young black woman who, I believe, was an alternate at the time, told us she'd seen Farron Chavarria, a young Hispanic woman who was friendly with Florio-Bunten, write something on a newspaper and pass it to Florio-Bunten. Francine reportedly read it and then threw it in the trash. Ito immediately dispatched a deputy to get the newspaper. Sure enough, there was a note saying, in effect, "They want to know if someone's writing a book." The words had been scribbled over, as though someone had tried to obscure what was written.

Farron was called first. She admitted writing the note—although, she said, she hadn't meant to disobey the judge's order. Then he called in Francine, who denied seeing the note, even after Ito showed it to her.

Lance had no choice. Florio-Bunten might have been lying about reading the note, and that alone was grounds for dismissal. What galled me was my certainty that Florio-Bunten had been set up. Our investigators scoured the city of Los Angeles trying to locate this supposed "literary agency." They found nothing matching the one in the letter. To this day, Florio-Bunten maintains that the letter was a fraud. And I believe her.

But what really floored me was that after her dismissal, Florio-Bunten took to the airwaves proclaiming that the prosecution's case was "too circumstantial," that the blood drops at Bundy could have been left by Simpson at an earlier time. And this was supposed to be one of *our* jurors!

Defense: 4. The People: 4.

The departure of Florio-Bunten made it inevitable that the other shoe would drop. Days later, Lance booted Chavarria for passing the note, then not leveling with him about it. And that left us down in the standings.

When the defense made its move to kick Chavarria, I leaped up and moved immediately to kick Number 1489.

Number 1489 was Willie Cravin, an African American and one of the two remaining members of the Clique of Four. Willie was a big dude with a mug so fierce that one of the reporters dubbed him the Easter Island Statue. He was a hanger for sure. He was also an irascible bully. From the outset he'd gone out of his way to be nasty to Florio-Bunten and Chavarria. He'd pushed Chavarria in the elevator as they were coming to court. And once, while they were all watching a movie, Florio-Bunten was swinging her leg and happened to tap the back of his seat. He turned and said, "Don't you ever do that to me. How dare you."

During previous in camera discussions with the jurors, we discovered that Cravin was viewed as a bully by many on the jury. He was definitely a problem.

I'd been watching and waiting, wondering when I should make my pitch. The passing of Chavarria was my cue. I suspected that I'd find Lance in a receptive frame of mind. He could keep a scorecard as well as any of us. He'd just booted two pro-prosecution jurors in succession. Now, he'd feel he'd have to give us one. I also knew that after the Tracy Hampton incident and the revolt that followed in its wake, he was keen upon promoting harmony at all costs.

"Here's a man," I told Ito, "who has systematically harassed and intimidated other jurors. Is this the kind of person [who] can actually deliberate with other jurors in a meaningful and adult fashion?"

Lance caught my drift and gave Willie the boot.

The defense was so stunned by this development that they didn't realize what had happened to them. Half an hour later, when the reality of losing Cravin finally dawned on them, they ran back into court, saying, "We want to take a writ. Have him reinstated." There was no provision in the law for that. But they tried anyway and were summarily shot down.

Defense: 5. The People: 5.

That was a fine day. I was so happy I actually skipped out of court. A lapse in decorum to be sure, but understandable given the circumstances. We'd broken the back of the Clique of Four. The composition of the jury had changed radically. Depending on who filled the spot left by Willie Cravin, we might actually hope for a level playing field. I was hoping like hell we wouldn't draw Alternate Number 165, an elderly black man who'd regaled fellow jurors with tales of racism from his Southern youth.

Of course, a hard look at the jury that day would have revealed only two votes we really felt we could count on. That of Anise Aschenbach, a sixty-one-year-old white woman who'd gone to college for a year. And Annie Backman, a twenty-three-year-old white insurance claims adjuster, who I felt might—just might—have the mathematical acumen to grasp the scientific testimony. The rest were ciphers or hard sells, including forty-four-year-old Lon Cryer, a black man whom we'd begun to suspect was a militant, and who had confided to Ito during the latest round of juror interviews that he didn't trust cops. There was also a young Hispanic deliveryman who'd been on the case since the beginning. We still had no idea where he stood. And then there were those (seven) black women. Two of them seemed fairly bright. They'd also happened to have some college education. Perhaps they could be reached. Perhaps they could persuade the rest.

That's what I was thinking on the day Willie Cravin got his walking papers. I was so high on hope, not even common sense could bring me down.

After Fung, we really picked up speed. Andrea Mazzola, Dennis's assistant, might have been a rookie in the field but on the stand she came on like a real pro. She didn't take guff from Peter Neufeld, and her clear, confident answers went a long way toward bolstering Dennis Fung's credibility.

Then on May 1, Greg Matheson, the foursquare forensic chemist I'd brought in from SID to sub for Fung at the preliminary hearings, took the stand.

In Hank's skillful hands, Greg helped us to do some serious debunking.

Defense contention: Nicole's blood had been planted on the socks found at the foot of Simpson's bed.

Debunked: Greg explained that his notation concerning the blood, "none obvious," meant just that—no blood observable *under ordinary light* on June 29. It didn't, as Johnnie had tried to suggest in his opening statement, mean that Nicole's blood wasn't on the socks as of that date, leaving open the possibility that it had been planted later. The blood just wasn't detected until Collin did his presumptive test a few weeks later.

(There's an interesting aside to this story: The cops just assumed the blood belonged to O. J. Simpson. I was the one who pushed the crime lab to take it one test further and do conventional testing, which, to everyone's utter amazement, showed that the blood on O. J. Simpson's sock belonged to Nicole.)

Defense contention: "Missing blood." Thano Peratis, the LAPD nurse who'd drawn Simpson's reference sample of blood, had testified at the preliminary hearings that he'd drawn 8 milliliters. In poring over records, Barry Scheck noticed the actual amount was 6.5 milliliters. A discrepancy of about 1.5 milliliters. Do you have any idea how little that is? About a quarter of a tablespoon. As near as I could figure it, the defense was contending that this minuscule volume of "missing" reference blood had multiplied miraculously—to be slathered generously by "conspirators" over gateposts, socks, and other incriminating pieces of evidence.

Debunked: When Thano heard that the defense was making hay with his measurements, he called us to correct the record. He really didn't know how much he'd drawn. He was just estimating. It could have been as much as 7 milliliters or as little as 6. Since the vials themselves have no hatch marks, it's impossible to know exactly how much blood was in them to begin with. Even if you assumed the scenario most favorable to the defense—that he'd drawn 7 milliliters—that left only 0.5 milliliter unaccounted for.

In his sensible, careful testimony, Greg went on to account for it. Small amounts of blood, he explained, are routinely lost in testing as a natural consequence of the opening and closing of the vial.

So much for missing blood.

Defense Contention: Contamination.

Debunked: Greg's most powerful testimony went to a single blood spot, Sample Number 49, found on the walkway at Bundy. Forget DNA testing for a moment. The very basic conventional serology tests Greg did on that single stain showed that it matched Simpson's blood. And that only 0.5 percent of the population had that blood type. This was a bigger deal than we knew at the time: the basic tests, it turns out, aren't sensitive enough to be affected by contamination even if there *was* any. We extracted that concession from one of the defense's own witnesses, Dr. John Gerdes. Throughout the trial, the results on that drop linking O. J. Simpson to the crime scene remained unrefuted.

The star of our DNA case was Dr. Robin Cotton, a petite woman with short blond hair and wire-rimmed glasses. She was the director of Cellmark Diagnostics, the largest private DNA lab in the country. I'd presented her as a witness in the first DNA case I ever tried, and I'd been mightily impressed. She was indubitably honest, and her explanations of the very complicated procedures of DNA testing were as simple as one could humanly make them.

Woody Clarke, a slender, sweet-faced man who was one of California's leading attorney-experts in DNA evidence, had the difficult job of leading Cotton through this potential quagmire. He elevated the discussion above the technicalities to drive home three essential points.

Would the method of collection and packaging cause the evidence to change from one person's type to another? he asked her.

It would not.

What if it degraded totally?

Then it would produce no result, she explained; not a change in type. What will happen is that a dirty surface will eat up DNA faster than a clean nonporous surface, which was why the blood on the rear gate was in better shape than the droplets on the cement walkway.

"So this process of degradation," Woody continued, "can it change my DNA into looking like your DNA?"

"No."

"Or [the DNA of] any members of the jury or the audience?"

"No."

Bottom line: *Neither sloppy collection nor degradation can change one person's blood into another's!* It was a point we would hammer home again, and again, and again.

Dr. Cotton gave us something else. An incredible set of statistics. One blood drop on the driveway behind Nicole's condo was good enough for RFLP, the most sensitive DNA test that can be performed. Only one in 170 million people had blood that would match that drop—and it matched Simpson's. Even more compelling, the blood on the rear gate also matched the defendant's. And it was in better shape, so we'd been able to do more extensive tests that narrowed the field even further. Only one in 57 billion people had that DNA type. There are only 5 billion people on the planet. Odds like this are called "identification." It's probably the closest thing you can get to a perfect match.

Robin's results were verified by Gary Sims, of the California Department of Justice, who testified after her. Gary had done the RFLP testing on some of the same stains, but using different probes. The results of both labs combined to produce the most powerful matches and most reliable conclusions that anyone had been able to introduce into a court of law.

As Gary was testifying, I glanced over at the jury. They appeared despondent. I had a painful, dawning insight. The stronger, the more compelling our evidence became, the more they hated us.

We were all a little nervous on the morning of May 24, when Collin Yamauchi took the witness stand. Collin had done the first PCR testing at the LAPD lab—the lab the defense had taken to calling the "cesspool of contamination." The defense would try to claim that he'd contaminated the samples *before* they got to Cellmark and the Department of Justice, so it wouldn't matter what Robin or Gary had found. Garbage in; garbage out.

During his first appearance before the grand jury, Collin had been solid, but unpolished. This time he'd really gotten his act together. Under Rock's direct, Collin calmly explained how he'd begun his testing by opening the vial of Simpson's blood and placing a small drop of the blood on what is called a Fitzco card. This is a small package containing filter paper. In the process of opening it, he'd gotten a bit of blood on his gloves, but he'd promptly stripped them, discarded them, and put on new ones before moving over to the evidence swatches. Collin went carefully over the procedure he'd followed in dealing with those samples. He'd even used a fresh knife after cutting each swatch. Pretty damned careful.

Barry Scheck, of course, seized upon the "spilled" blood, arguing that it had somehow contaminated the evidence samples. But as usual, he was blowing smoke. Collin had been standing over fifteen feet away from the evidence swatches, which were sealed inside little paper envelopes, which had been placed inside coin envelopes, which were taped shut. How could the blood have reached them?

Gary Sims of the California Department of Justice had already testified that DNA does not "jump," nor does it "fly." It does not waft across the room as an aerosol and penetrate two layers of packaging. And even if you assumed for one mad moment that this was possible, how did this itinerant DNA manage to come to rest *only* on the evidence swatches, and not on the control swatches?

(Later on, one defense expert theorized gamely that the control swatches *were* contaminated, but in amounts so small you couldn't measure them. Now think about this for a minute. A scientist knows, if anyone does, that if you can't measure something, you can't really say it's there, now can you? We're not talking about quarks here. This is blood, a substance which is quantifiable even in trace amounts. But by then, we'd tripped so far through the looking glass that an inane observation like this one could actually pass for rebuttal.)

Collin's testimony was going great. He was firm and lucid, no mean feat considering the technical detail he had to recount. The apprehension I'd felt when he took the stand was giving way to pride. Then, suddenly, things went radically wrong.

Rock asked Collin the following: "Based on what you heard in the media at the time or . . . before you did the tests in this case, did you have an expectation of what the outcome of these tests would be?"

This might seem like an odd question. But in fact, during our private conversations with Collin, he'd confided in us that he was a big fan of O. J. Simpson. We wanted to let the jury in on the fact that this man was not conspirator material. Naturally, we thought Collin would say something along the lines of how he'd admired Simpson as an athlete and how improbable he thought it was that Simpson could do something like this. The point was to demonstrate that if there was any "examiner bias," it was in the defendant's favor.

Instead, Collin blurted out, "I heard on the news that, well, yeah. He's got an airtight alibi. He's—he's in Chicago. . . . And I go, 'Oh, well, he's probably not related to the scene.' "

Ito promptly cut off the witness and ordered counsel to sidebar.

"We have a huge problem." He glowered. "We just brought in a statement by the defendant . . ."

What the hell could he be referring to? The statement Simpson gave to Lange and Vannatter in their interview on June 13? Section 356 of the California evidence code says that if one side introduces part of a writing or statement, the other side has the right to bring in the rest. But it was absurd to apply that rule here. Collin's "alibi" remark had nothing at all to do with Simpson's statement. It was simply Collin's own conjecture, based on news reports—and false ones at that.

Johnnie whispered urgently to Scheck, and Scheck nodded. I knew exactly what he was saying: "Go for it. Get that statement in!"

And Ito was going to allow it!

Here's the situation. Simpson's attorneys had been dying to get that statement into evidence so that the jury would get to hear Simpson's tape-recorded expressions of innocence *without his ever being exposed to cross-examination.* Problem was, they couldn't introduce it on their own. They had to wait for us to bring it up. Collin, supposedly, had given them an opening.

We had to close it fast.

I knew that unless I played along like this was a serious legal question, Ito's ego would be bruised and we'd pay dearly. We'd have to submit a motion to stop this thing.

I went looking for Hank and found him in the War Room.

"I'm going to need some paper quick, so I can get him to turn around without his losing face," I told him.

That fucking statement!

How many hours had Hank and Chris and I—in fact, the entire team—spent agonizing over what to do about it? We'd looked at it from every side. There were a couple of good arguments for allowing it in. Phil had gotten Simpson to admit that the last time he'd visited Bundy was five days earlier and he told detectives he had not been bleeding at that time. That made it patently absurd for the defense to argue that the blood drops had been left by Simpson on a social visit to Bundy before June 12. But on the other hand, the defense wasn't even thinking about arguing that Simpson had bled there on some other occasion, so we'd gain nothing.

At one point, Simpson had said that the last thing he did before leaving for the airport was to get his cell phone out of the Bronco. That part I liked. When you combined it with the cell phone records showing the call to Paula Barbieri at 10:03, it placed him in the Bronco just before the murders.

But the rest of the statement was a disaster for us. Not only were the cops' questions real softballs, but when Phil asked whether Nicole ever got any threatening phone calls, Simpson responded, "You—you guys haven't told me anything. I—I have no idea what happened. . . . Every time I ask you guys, you say you're going to tell me in a bit."

Nice bit of sympathy grabbing. The defense was sure to play it for maximum schmaltz: "Poor Juice. Mean old cops won't tell him anything. Is that any way to treat a grieving man who's had no sleep in the past two days? He's doing everything he can to cooperate. He's giving a statement without an attorney present—surely not the action of a guilty man. And a blood sample? Why, he'd rolled his sleeve right up. Now, I ask you, ladies and gentlemen of the jury: why would he be so cooperative if he were guilty?

The only strategy worth considering was whether we should try and get into evidence that one snippet of tape where Simpson talked about getting his car phone out of the Bronco just before he left. That short excerpt would be limited enough to prevent the defense from getting the rest of the statement in. Nothing else was needed to explain or qualify it, according to the evidence code. Of course, the downside to playing one brief segment was that the jury would naturally wonder why we didn't want them to hear the rest of the tape.

On the other hand, if we didn't play the statement, we could still put on the phone records showing that a call had been made from Simpson's cell phone to Paula at 10:03 P.M. A reasonable juror would infer that he'd been in the Bronco. The defense would have no way to counter that but to call Simpson and get him to try to explain it.

That was an idea we all liked. If we could force Simpson into the blue chair, we just might be in fat city.

It's not that I thought Simpson would be an easy mark. I never thought that. I had him pegged as a pretty cagey guy. True, he'd botched the murders, leaving a trail of evidence rimmed in neon lights all the way to Rockingham. But then, he wasn't an experienced killer. He'd managed, at least, not to get caught in the act. And by the time he'd talked to the cops, he'd clearly regained enough composure to hide the ball from two experienced homicide detectives.

But if he were to find himself being questioned by a hostile female . . . well, that might be a different story. Simpson would never be able to hold it together if he thought a woman had control over him. And when you can compel a guy to sit on the witness stand and answer questions, that's control.

Beyond that, he seemed to have a special bug up his ass about me. Every so often I'd catch him trying to make eye contact. When he'd managed to sneak in his little speech to the court during jury selection, he couldn't resist turning his head to address me, personally. Did he imagine he could charm me? What Simpson didn't realize was that I had no special feelings for him. Not even a particularly intense hatred. This may have been the Trial of the Century, but to me O. J. Simpson was a common criminal. I felt no more repulsed by him than by any of the other scumbags I'd prosecuted over the past thirteen years.

Don't get me wrong. I would have loved—believe me, *loved*—to take my shot at him. Had I gotten him on that stand, I would have kept him there for as long as it took. Because *eventually* he'd do something to hang himself. The upshot of the "alibi" episode with Collin was anticlimactic. By the time I returned to court, it had already fizzled like a damp charge. Ito had apparently come to his senses. He'd had a chance to review Simpson's statement and he ruled that Collin had not "opened the door." He denied the defense's request to introduce the statement. We kept it out for the rest of the trial.

CAR TAPE. *Let's see. It's Thursday, June 8. Yeah. June 8. And Brian Kelberg is up there doing the coroner's stuff. He's doing a fabulous job. Just a brilliant job. I find myself very jealous though, because . . . he had four months to prepare for two witnesses and I have weeks to prepare for about thirty. But . . . hey, what can you do.*

We'd decided, during our marathon mapping session back in January, that there was no way we could put the assistant coroner, Dr. Irwin Golden, on the witness stand. At least not alone. He'd been so thoroughly trashed during the preliminary hearing that we'd need to put him on in tandem with a stronger witness. Our best gambit, we felt, was to import a well-respected medical examiner from another jurisdiction—but none of them wanted to risk being torn limb from limb in the lion's den. All the while, Dr. Golden's report was being reexamined and corrected under the supervision of the L.A. County coroner, Dr. Lakshmanan Sathyavagiswaran. He concluded that the fundamental work was sound.

Dr. Lucky was a meticulous man. The only reason we hadn't drafted him right off the bat as a stand-in was the fact that he was Golden's superior and the jury might see him as having an interest in protecting one of his own people. In the end, however, we figured that Dr. Lucky's benign manner and obvious integrity would overcome any initial skepticism.

The coroner was originally Bill Hodgman's jurisdiction. But after his health difficulties in January, Bill had been working behind the scenes as case manager, a job that was itself becoming more and more demanding. I gave the coroner to Brian Kelberg instead.

Brian was the logical man for the job. Brilliant, methodical, and knowledgeable in the field of medicine. When I first brought him into the case, he'd come kicking and screaming. Brian just didn't like team prosecutions. I'd called him in to consult on several of my earlier cases when I'd had plenty of time to confer with him. Back then, things were great. He'd come in, plonk down, put his feet up, and we'd vivi-sect every minute scientific detail of the case. We both loved that. But by the time he was front and center in the Simpson case, the pace had already hit overdrive.

Before I could devote myself to preparations with Brian, I had had to put on my own twenty-five witnesses. Then I had to spend hours with Hank preparing for Fung. Hank had needed a lot of support, and I couldn't afford to look away for a moment. That frustrated and annoyed Brian. He'd complain to Bill about my inaccessibility. He left notes warning, "You'd better find some time." To make things worse, Brian and Chris absolutely hated each other. The team had begun polarizing into the Brian camp and the Chris camp. Throughout May, the infighting was reaching epic proportions. Luckily, by the time we'd moved on to the DNA testimony, things had settled down a bit. I started meeting regularly with Brian and that got us back on track.

Brian's mission was twofold: one, to lay out medical hypotheticals showing how one man could have committed both murders; and two, to demonstrate how quickly those murders could have occurred. The first point, of course, was to dispel the defense's contention that there could have been two assailants; the second point was to establish that the murders had occurred between 10:15 P.M. and 10:40 P.M.

Over the course of a week, Brian guided the coroner through a plausible death scene scenario. It went something like this: At the outset of the attack, Nicole had confronted her killer face-to-face and struggled very briefly. Then she'd turned and had been struck in the back of the head, which knocked her against a wall. That accounted for the concussion that rendered her unconscious. After her attacker delivered one vicious slash to the throat, Nicole fell or was dropped onto the second step. She remained there unconscious, moving little or not at all, bleeding profusely.

Judging by the condition of the brain at autopsy, Dr. Lucky con-cluded that Nicole had lain there for at least a minute before her assailant resumed his attack, this time pulling her head back by the hair and administering the coup de grâce.

"How did the fatal wound occur?" Brian asked the coroner.

"My opinion," replied Dr. Lucky, "is that the head was extended backwards and the knife was used to cause this incised stab wound from left to right."

The killer had apparently encountered very little resistance.

"Doctor," Brian said, ". . . if you could use me and my head and hair, would you demonstrate what is your opinion as to the manner in which that last major incised stab wound was inflicted?"

Dr. Lucky left the stand, walked over to Brian, pulled his head back by the hair, and demonstrated a throat slashing by drawing a ruler across his neck.

Among the spectators, there was a rustle of discomfort.

So what was the killer doing during the minute or so between the first and second cuts? Lakshmanan left open the possibility that he had used this interval to murder Ron Goldman. Further into his testimony, he gave a second demonstration, this time going through the motions of stabbing a "victim"—once again, Brian—to show how it was entirely possible to inflict fifteen knife wounds in as many seconds. Clearly, the killings could have happened very quickly.

Later on, critics would claim I let Brian keep Lakshmanan on the stand too long. Let me set the record straight. If Brian had been less thorough, we would have been rapped for that instead. As it happened, he took an A-bomb and disarmed it, wire by wire, before the American public. He left no stone unturned, no question unaddressed. And by the time he was through, he'd converted what could have been a devastating liability into an asset.

For the first time during the trial, we'd brought out the photos taken at Bundy by the coroner's investigators. The heads of the victims had been pulled back, exposing their neck wounds. In their own way, these photos were even more awful, more affecting than the autopsy photos. The jurors were clearly moved. Even the elderly black man from Mississippi, certainly no fan of the prosecution, wept openly. For the first time, it seemed it was getting through to the jury that this was a *murder* case. Two people had died.

And I thought I saw them opening their minds to the possibility that the defendant could have done this terrible thing.

*   *   *

It was Chris's turn up. With the gloves.

We'd unearthed evidence that in December 1990 Nicole had bought gloves exactly like those found at Bundy and Rockingham. She'd picked them up at Bloomingdale's in New York—one of the couple's favorite shopping grounds, we'd learned. The receipt showed that she'd purchased two pairs of gloves and a muffler at the same time. The gloves were cashmere-lined and cost $55. The style and price alone dramatically narrowed the pool of suspects. At least in California.

Phil Vannatter had lined up Richard Rubin, a former executive of Aris Isotoner, the company that manufactured the gloves, to establish that the pair we had in evidence were exactly the same model as those purchased by Nicole in 1990. He would testify that they were sold at only *one* store in the country. Bloomingdale's.

I found this whole business incredibly sad. It was clear to me that Nicole had bought those gloves as a Christmas gift for her husband. And he'd used them to murder her? *Oh, man, what a world.*

I fully intended that Simpson would put on the gloves: *not* the actual evidence gloves, but a duplicate pair. Since the AIDS crisis, anything bloodstained required protection. I figured the court would never let anyone try on the bloody gloves without wearing latex beneath them. Latex would screw up the fit. So we'd asked the glove manufacturer to send us duplicates of their Aris Leather Lights, extra large, just like the ones found at the crime scene, to try on Simpson when the time was right.

On June 15, however, the time was definitely *not* right.

Richard Rubin had flown in the night before his testimony was to begin. We needed some time to work out the logistics of how and when to perform the glove demonstration. Now, Simpson was not likely to cooperate with this experiment. From ongoing interviews with my FBI shoe expert, Bill Bodziak, I'd learned that a subject could contort his feet, or in this case, his hands, to make the fit appear too tight. I didn't need Bodziak to tell me this: I'd spent enough time struggling to get shoes on reluctant little boys to know it from experience.

I knew we needed to talk about laying the legal foundation for this demonstration, to plot it as carefully as the Normandy invasion. But

Chris was pumped up. The accolades Brian got for his handling of Dr. Lucky irked the hell out of Chris. He'd never liked Brian much, but now that Kelberg was being hailed as a returning hero, Chris's competitive instincts were aroused. He wanted to score a coup of his own. He wanted to do the glove demonstration at what he thought would be the most dramatic possible moment. During Rubin's testimony. Problem was, we hadn't received the duplicate gloves.

I didn't know this until the morning Rubin was scheduled to testify. This was Chris's baby, so I asked him where the duplicate gloves were. He didn't know. I called Bill to ask him if he knew.

"I'll check with Phil," he told me. "I believe he has them."

"Okay," I replied. "Have him bring them down."

I didn't want to be late to court. Chris was on a testosterone high—I didn't know exactly where that might take him. I didn't want to leave him alone too long.

When I got to the counsel table, I whispered to Chris that the duplicates were on their way.

"Cool," he said as Ito came out. We'd just taken our seats when Phil showed up with the evidence box. He passed it over to us from behind the rail. Chris peered into the box. Then he asked to approach the bench.

"I would like to lay the foundation," he told Ito, "to show that they [the reputed duplicates] are the exact same size, similar make and model, so that perhaps we can have Mr. Simpson try them on at some point."

Whoa, Chris, I thought, a little alarmed. We needed to talk to Rubin about how to make sure Simpson couldn't screw this up.

At that moment, Johnnie cut in, "We object to this, Your Honor. . . . We've had no time to deal with this. At some point, if Mr. Simpson testifies and we want to have him try the gloves on in evidence, that is one thing. . . . Are you going to allow them to have the defendant try [the duplicates] on?"

"I think it would be more appropriate for him to try the other gloves on," Ito put in. He meant, of course, the bloody gloves.

I did not like the way this was going. We had to steer the discussion back to the duplicates.

When Richard Rubin took the stand, Ito allowed Chris to question him, outside the presence of the jury, about the duplicate gloves he'd brought.

Chris reached into a cardboard box and withdrew the duplicate gloves. He strolled back up to the witness stand and placed them in front of Rubin.

"Showing you the gloves that have been marked 372-C," he said to Rubin. "Are those Aris Isotoner gloves?"

Rubin studied the flawless brown leather gloves resting on the edge of the witness stand.

"They're Aris gloves, but these are not Aris Light gloves that were like the ones we're talking about . . ."

What was going on here? Hadn't Chris checked these out when they first came in? We should have learned of this discrepancy—and gotten replacements—months ago.

Chris looked embarrassed. And disappointed. Very disappointed. His moment of glory was slipping away.

I pulled him aside for a private conference.

"What is the fucking deal here?"

"I don't know," he told me. He was shifting nervously from foot to foot. "We've got to have him put on the gloves."

"The crime-scene gloves?"

"Shapiro asked to see the [bloody] gloves this morning," Chris said urgently. "They've been practicing with them. If we don't do it, they will."

"Who cares?" I said. "Let them. The latex will fuck up the fit and we can tell the jury so. We can't do this, Chris. Let's wait and re-call Rubin when we get the right gloves."

"I'm telling you," he insisted, "we've got to do it now!"

"Let's let Phil try them on first," I urged him. Phil's hands were at least at big as Simpson's. Maybe if Chris saw the difficulty Phil was having in pulling the gloves over latex, he'd back down. Chris agreed.

Phil put on latex gloves, then pulled the crime-scene gloves over them. It wasn't easy, but he got them on. They were tight, which in and of itself was not bad. A witness named Brenda Vemich, a Bloomingdale's buyer who'd authenticated the receipt, had testified that the gloves were supposed to fit "tight and snug." Like racing gloves.

The problem, of course, was that Phil was a willing subject. He hadn't splayed his hands like a two-year-old to keep the gloves from being pulled down over his fingers. No one had come up with a way to keep Simpson from pulling those shenanigans.

I turned to Chris. "Don't do it. I'm warning you."

"We've got to do it," he insisted.

"Why won't you fucking listen to me. This is a trap!" My voice was hoarse with tension and anger.

"This is *my* witness," he snapped. "And I say we have to put those gloves on him now, before they do!"

I couldn't dissuade him.

We approached the bench.

"... We would like to have Mr. Simpson put on the original evidence items," Chris announced to Ito.

Johnnie, of course, had no objection to this—but he laid down his terms.

"First of all, I don't want him to do it without having latex gloves on."

Of course, he didn't.

Secondly, Johnnie asked Ito not to allow the court cameras to focus on Simpson. I saw Johnnie's strategy. He knew the jurors would buy his client's bullshit act, but he wasn't quite so sure the demonstration would stand up under the scrutiny of more critical observers later on.

Ito refused to allow any special camera arrangements, but he did approve the latex. The jury filed back into the courtroom.

And then it was show time.

"Your Honor," Chris said, "at this time, the People would ask that Mr. Simpson step forward and try on the glove recovered at Bundy was well as the glove recovered at Rockingham."

I could hear the discomfort in his voice. He knew he'd gone way out on a limb.

Deirdre Robertson took a box of latex gloves over to the defense table. From where I sat at counsel table, my line of vision was blocked. I couldn't see Simpson pulling on the latex. I know that Chris walked over to the defense table and handed him the left glove.

Then Johnnie and one of the sheriff's deputies escorted Simpson over to the jury box, where Simpson began pulling it on. He grimaced and mugged like Cinderella's stepsister trying to get into that glove.

He got it only part of the way up his wrist.

Chris handed him the right glove. Same performance.

Simpson smiled broadly and displayed his mitts to the jury—and to the camera—as though he were holding up the ball at the goal line. Can you believe this? Here is Simpson wearing gloves splattered with his murdered ex-wife's blood and he's grinning ear to ear. Any normal person in these circumstances would cringe.

I felt like dying. But the last thing I wanted was for the jury to see my distress. There was a rule I'd learned as a baby prosecutor: when they're sticking it to you, act like you couldn't care less. I felt my expression harden into a mask of indifference.

Chris held up valiantly. He had Simpson pick up one of the felt-tip pens on counsel's table and demonstrate how he could have held a knife. He then had Simpson make stabbing motions. It was a brave recovery. I gave him credit for that.

When the demonstration was finally over, Simpson casually snapped the gloves off. And I thought to myself, *If they were so hard to get on, why are they so easy to get off, Sparky?* At that point, he looked directly at me, as though he expected me to take them from him. I didn't move a muscle. I met his gaze without blinking. After a few seconds, he dropped the gloves on the table in front of me and moved on.

I looked down at the bloody, weathered leather, and I said to myself, *That's it. We just lost the case.*

Afterward, I went out of my way to avoid riding the elevator with Chris. I just wasn't ready to face him. Upstairs, I found Brian sitting in Bill's office. His chair was swiveled toward the television. When I walked in, he swung around to look at me. His face was filled with pity.

"You saw it?" I asked, despondent.

"What happened?" Brian asked. "Why'd he do it?"

"I don't know," I replied. "I just don't know."

I paused for a moment, then said, "I'll go talk to him now."

In his own memoir Chris would write that when he arrived upstairs that afternoon, his colleagues shunned him. Perhaps that's the way he remembered it but it wasn't so. His office was crowded with people: Richard Rubin; Phil; one of the D.A. investigators, Mike

Stevens. There was also a handful of law clerks, all offering sympathy and suggestions for how we could pull ourselves out of this nosedive. When I walked in, the conversation stopped. Chris looked down. He wouldn't meet my eyes. He was suffering too much and I found, to my dismay, that I was too drained, too devastated, to reach out to him and offer him any comfort.

CAR TAPE. *Today is June . . . what is it? June sixteenth. To me it felt like we lost the case yesterday. It was that bad. I'm not gonna say that to Chris or anybody else, but . . . I don't know if we can recover. It's so sad because we were on such a roll. I mean, for once we were really killing them. And here we are, back at square one again, [on the] fucking defensive. . . .*

I felt desperately sorry for Chris. He was so dejected after the glove incident. But I do think it served as a wake-up call for him. You've got to think out carefully every move before you make it. I don't think he fully realized the responsibility we had resting on our shoulders until June 15. He grew up a lot that day. And he came fighting back.

Chris and Richard Rubin, who turned out to be a brick throughout all of this, kept pressure on the Aris people to search their inventories until they came up with the right goddamned gloves—the ones they should have sent us in the first place. Chris recalled Rubin to the witness stand to have him authenticate the new pair. They were, at last, exact duplicates.

Richard testified that the gloves in their original condition would "easily" go over hands the size of Mr. Simpson's. When gloves have been exposed to repeated dampness and extremes of heat and cold, however, they can shrink as much as 15 percent.

While Chris continued his questioning, I went over to the phone on the bailiff's desk to call Brian.

"It looks like a 'go' to me," I told him.

"Tell him to do it," Brian said.

I passed a note to Chris, who stalled. I could see his confidence faltering.

"Come on, Chris. Do it," I whispered. "It's going to work this time."

And it did. This time, when Simpson tried on the gloves, they fit, you should pardon the expression, like a glove.

In the days and weeks that followed, we got literally thousands of faxes, phone calls, and letters with explanations of why the gloves hadn't fit. We also received a dozen photographs of Simpson wearing Aris Leather Lights. Not just the brown ones, like the ones we had in evidence, but a photo of Simpson wearing a pair of black Aris Lights that, I surmised, was the second pair that Nicole had purchased at Bloomingdale's. One photo showed Simpson wearing both the brown gloves and a muffler, which I also suspected—but could not prove— was the one Nicole had bought him for Christmas 1990.

I wanted these pictures entered into the record during our rebuttal case. But that meant that we had to check out each one of them. We couldn't risk putting on a fake. And so I interviewed each of the photographers, most of them amateurs who had just happened to snap a photo at the right moment. I wanted to showcase these photos as effectively as possible. The display shouldn't be slick, I decided; it should be spare and homespun. So instead of the glitzy graphics we'd used throughout the trial, I set a blank board on the easel. Then I called the photographers one by one to tape his or her photo to the board. Soon the board was filled with photos of Simpson's gloves. Photos taken by regular folks who'd caught Simpson's glove act—and didn't buy it. But what about those "regular folks" on the jury? Would they?

CAR TAPE. *June 29. I am feeling more rested today. I got myself to bed early, which is a first. . . . Chris and I are starting to get friendlier. Boy, things have been tense since that glove debacle. . . . I also jettisoned any more domestic violence witnesses. He was pissed off about that too. . . . It just doesn't fit anymore. All that stuff is out of context now. Chris is really pissed at me, saying I'm not consulting him anymore and cutting him out of the case. . . . [But] we need to go for the end of the case in a real strong, clean way.*

This one was my call. The way to go out, I decided, was on hard, irrefutable physical evidence. I wanted the one-two punch of our footprint and hair experts, who came packing dynamite.

Investigators at the Bundy crime scene, of course, had found a set of bloody footprints leading away from the bodies toward the back alley. The pattern left by the killer's sole was a waffle of "S"-shaped squiggles. We sent photos of the prints to the FBI lab, where they landed on the desk of Special Agent Bill Bodziak, the Bureau's footwear and tread expert. Bodziak couldn't locate the pattern in his computerized files of prints, so he went, quite literally, to the ends of the earth to identify them. He traveled to a little factory town in Italy, where he found the very mold that had made the so-called Silga sole. The Silgas had been used in a limited-edition Bruno Magli loafer. It was those rare Silgas that left the bloody prints at Bundy.

We found no Bruno Maglis among the shoes seized at Rockingham. We could never find a receipt for the purchase of any, either. And, of course, we had no photographs. It's worth mentioning here that shortly after the verdict, the first of many photos would surface showing Simpson wearing the very shoes Bodziak had identified. Later, during depositions at his civil trial, Simpson would deny ever owning a pair of those "ugly-ass shoes"—a line that summoned up an assortment of shoeshine men and sports photographers offering shots of Simpson wearing these very shoes.

Permit me one question. Where were all these civic-minded photographers with their glossies of the Juice sporting Bruno Maglis when the criminal trial was going on? Watching the Weather Channel?

We may not have had photos of the defendant in his Bruno Mags, but we did have strong circumstantial evidence suggesting that he'd owned the pair that made the bloody prints. For one thing, they were a size 12, the size that Simpson wore. This was significant, Bodziak told us, because only 9 percent of the men in North America wear a size 12. Most of them are between six feet and six feet four inches tall. Simpson was six feet two. Moreover, the shoes cost $160 a pair. Your average burglar wouldn't be wearing them to pull a caper. The price alone spoke volumes about the suspect. He's the same type of guy who wears cashmere-lined gloves. And of *those,* we had pictures.

Bodziak explained to the court how he'd examined Nicole's black dress and found an "impression" on the "center front." Then Hank directed his attention to an autopsy photo showing what appeared to be a heel print on Nicole's back. Although Bodziak couldn't positively identify the prints, he said neither was inconsistent with the Silga soles. His testimony conjured up a chilling image: Simpson planting his foot on Nicole's chest to make the first cut, then stepping on her back and pulling her head back by the hair to deliver the cut that nearly decapitated her.

Equally damning, Bodziak had determined that the bloody shoe print on the driver's side of the Bronco showed what looked like "S"-shaped squiggles—a particular characteristic of the Bruno Maglis.

We had suspicions that the defense team was scouring crime-scene photos to come up with something—anything—that could be construed as the footprint of a second killer.

"Mr. Bodziak," Hank asked, "based upon your analysis of all of the items that we've discussed today, was there any indication that more than one pair of shoes were involved in this crime?"

"No," the witness answered, "there was not."

It fell to Lee Bailey to try and rattle Bodziak on cross. But Bailey, whose abilities served him so well in cross-examining cops and law enforcement personnel, was woefully out of his depth when it came to the scientific evidence.

First, he tried to suggest that if Simpson had really dropped the glove on the south pathway at Rockingham, there should have been shoe prints in the leaves. Bill explained patiently that in all his years, at hundreds of crime scenes, he'd never been able to detect shoe prints in leaves.

Undeterred, Bailey went on to probe the outer limits of absurdity, suggesting that someone had either stolen Simpson's shoes or two killers had worn identical pairs of shoes to the crime scene.

The premise was preposterous. First of all, Bodziak pointed out, criminals simply don't think of their shoes as a possible source of incriminating evidence. That's what makes shoe-print identification so useful. Beyond that, it was unlikely that two criminals would be wearing identical pairs even of common shoes like Reeboks, let alone Bruno Maglis.

"To conjecture . . . that two people independently bought size-twelve Bruno Magli shoes . . . and just happened to come to this crime scene together is impossible for me to believe," Bodziak said firmly.

"Would it be possible," Bailey persisted, "for two people to arrange . . . to arrive at a crime scene in the same footwear . . . ?"

". . . I don't believe it happens, intentionally or otherwise."

Bailey wouldn't let it go.

"But it's possible?"

"In my opinion," Bodziak replied, "it's not even possible because it's so ridiculous."

Bailey had wanted to end with a flourish. Instead, he'd succeeded only in casting the two-killer theory in the silliest possible light.

I was madly putting the finishing touches on hair and trace. "Trace" refers to clothing fibers, carpet fibers, dandruff—in short, anything microscopic that a criminal might track onto or take away from a crime scene.

Prosecutors love trace evidence. It's almost as compelling as DNA in its ability to link a defendant to a crime scene. In some respects, it's even better than DNA because it's jury-friendly. You can blow up photomicrographs to eight-by-tens so that jurors can actually *see* the similarities between the defendant's head hair, for example, and what the killer left behind.

For about three months now, I'd remained in close telephone contact with Doug Deedrick, director of the FBI's hair and trace unit. Doug had a fantastic sense of humor and a gift for making the complex seem simple. He flew in four days before he was scheduled to begin testimony, bringing with him his blowups of the evidence.

One large poster-board display showed photos of the hairs removed from Simpson's head by the LAPD. The row above it showed several eight-by-tens of hairs removed from the blue knit cap found at Ron Goldman's feet. Doug had also prepared a board of Negroid hair samples, chosen at random from FBI files. The samples all looked very different from each other. It was obvious at first glance how Simpson's hair matched the hair from the cap.

One thing troubled me slightly. One of the file samples appeared, at least to my untutored eye, to look a lot like Simpson's. Maybe Doug could see the difference, but I sure couldn't.

"This is truly beautiful stuff," I told him. "But—this one down here . . ." I pointed to the hair. "It looks just like Simpson's. I'm just a lay person, what do I know. But don't you think the jury will think so, too?"

"Yes, I do." Doug grinned. "And there's a very good reason for that. Because that _is_ his hair."

Gotcha! I burst out laughing. We could go through the same shtick in front of the jury.

Just as there had been blood where blood shouldn't be, there was hair where hair shouldn't be.

- Simpson's hair on the knit cap, Ron's shirt, the Rockingham glove.

- Nicole's hair—"forcibly removed hairs"—on the Rockingham glove.

- Ron's hair on the Rockingham glove.

Things got even more interesting when we moved into the area of fibers. LAPD investigators had found beige fibers at both Bundy and Rockingham. They appeared to match the carpet in O. J. Simpson's Bronco. According to Doug, carpeting of that sort had been used only in Ford Broncos manufactured between June 1993 and June 1994. Simpson's, of course, was a 1994 model.

That was incredible news. Bronco fibers had been found _both_ on the knit cap at Bundy _and_ on the glove at Rockingham—potentially linking Simpson to both scenes.

On the day Doug Deedrick was scheduled to appear, the defense got a look at his poster boards and went ballistic. They claimed they'd never seen these hair photos before.

That, of course, was complete bull. So we sent one of our minions to track down the defense expert who'd examined them. Sure enough, he'd gotten those photos months ago.

While we were wrangling over this, Johnnie caught sight of Doug, sitting inside the rail, holding a binder.

"What's he got?" he whispered to me.

"I don't know," I whispered back.

So Johnnie and I went over to check it out. To my dismay, it contained the notes of a detailed investigation Doug had done on the Bronco fibers. What I thought had come from public records accessible to the defense had actually been unearthed by Doug through private sources. Doug thought it was exempt from the laws of discovery. Under California law, unfortunately, it was not.

This put me in a very bad spot. The defense was screaming about my "egregious" discovery violation. We stood to lose the extremely valuable carpet fiber evidence because of it.

I pleaded with Ito. "If the Court feels that we have been remiss, then I would urge the Court to penalize [me] personally. But please don't—please don't penalize the proof of the case."

Ito was irritated. But for once, his irritation didn't seem to be directed my way. He apparently realized—even Johnnie seemed to realize—that this report business had caught me by surprise. Besides, Ito seemed honestly fascinated by the hair and trace evidence and annoyed by having to exclude it.

Once again, we got half a loaf. He would allow us to introduce the fibers. We could tell the jury that Simpson's Bronco fibers were "consistent" with those found on the Bundy cap and the Bundy glove, but not that they were so incredibly rare.

I could live with it.

"Sir," I addressed Doug, "with respect to the nine or ten hairs that exhibited the same microscopic characteristics as those of the defendant inside the knit cap, do you have an opinion as to . . . how those hairs got there?"

There was an objection. Overruled.

"Because hats are worn on the head, it's certainly consistent and reasonable to believe that their presence indicates that they came from the wearer of the hat, yes," Doug replied.

"When individuals have contact through a violent struggle, have you in your past experience found the hairs of the attacker on the clothing of the victim?"

Objection. Overruled.

"Yes, I have. That's why . . . I look at clothing from victims of crime. . . ."

"If you were to assume the following events, sir. That the killer pulled back Nicole's head with his hand, with his left hand, in order to slit her throat with his right hand and then went over to Ron Goldman for [the] final attack, touching him in the process with the hand that held Nicole's hair by the head, could that account for the hairs that you found on Ron Goldman's shirt?"

"Yes," Doug replied. "That could account for the presence of those hairs."

I put the poster with the photos of Simpson's hair on the easel and asked Doug to step down and show which ones came from the samples taken from the defendant and which ones came from the evidence. I watched the jurors' faces. They actually looked interested.

The fibers proved equally graphic.

"Now assume further [that the killer] while wearing the Rockingham glove, stabbed Ronald Goldman—in a manner that brought his glove into contact with Ronald Goldman's shirt, say, stabbed him in the left abdomen. . . . Would that . . . be a reasonable explanation for your finding of fibers consistent with Ronald Goldman's shirt on the Rockingham glove?"

"Yeah," Doug replied. "I would expect a transfer in this instance, especially on a damp bloody glove. . . ."

"Now," I continued. "If the attacker wore these gloves during the murder, and during the struggle with Ronald Goldman one of those gloves was pulled off, would there be fibers from the lining of that left glove on his bare hand?"

"Yes," came the reply.

"And if the murderer continued to pursue [his] attack on Ronald Goldman after that glove came off his left hand, would those fibers on his hand be transferred to the body of Ronald Goldman, if there was contact?"

"Yes."

There was in fact one fiber from the glove's lining on Ron Goldman's shirt. I had made darn sure the jury knew about it. What Doug had just told them was that the glove came off during the attack, and that the attack had continued barehanded. That was how the cashmere fiber ended up on Ron's shirt.

But even more damning was the fact that identical blue-black cotton fibers were found on Ron Goldman's shirt, the Rockingham glove, and the socks Simpson left on his bedroom floor. Those telltale fibers—obviously from the clothes of the killer—linked Simpson directly to the Bundy crime scene. More particularly, to the body of Ron Goldman.

If I had been in Bailey's shoes, I would have confined my questions to a few pointed jabs about the fact that hair and fibers ain't fingerprints, and sat down. Instead, Bailey launched into a discussion of the definitions of "random," "same," and "similar" that seemed to leave everyone, including himself, confused.

For the rest of the case, hair and trace would stand unrefuted. The defense could apparently find no expert who would take the stand and argue that this evidence had been contaminated or planted.

I'd gotten the ending I wanted, clean and strong.

On July 6—after five months, 58 witnesses, 488 exhibits, and 34,500 pages of transcript—the People rested.

Chain of Fools

If Orenthal James Simpson had really hired a Dream Team, Johnnie Cochran would have stood before the judge on July 10, given one of his dramatic, world-weary sighs, and proclaimed, "The defense rests!"

Why *not* rest? Johnnie and company had been able to put some dings in our witnesses along the way. If it was true that these jurors were hell-bent on acquittal, the LAPD had logged in just enough screwups to lend credence to that loony conspiracy theory and provide them with a credible pretext for a verdict of "not guilty." The smart bet would have been to take the leap and say, "We rest"—and watch this jury hand Simpson his freedom on a silver platter.

But as often as not, the defense can't resist. They have to strut their stuff. I love it when this happens. I call it "defense to the rescue." Usually, it's at the client's insistence. After being pounded by accusers, a defendant wants his buddies up there telling everybody what a great guy he is. A smart jury with lingering reservations about the defendant's guilt will often find those doubts dispelled when they see a flimsy defense. They say, "Wait a minute. If this guy was really innocent, he would've had a better story than this."

At least, that's what happens in a normal trial. But that wasn't the case here. After all, it wasn't a Dream Team that would acquit O. J. Simpson. It was a Dream Jury.

Ironically, those hot dogs at the defense table could not leave well enough alone. Even though they had no coherent case of their own to present, Cochran and company were determined to put on a show. And as a result, they nearly blew it.

Because the evidence against their client was so strong, Johnnie was, in effect, unable to call honest, credible witnesses to the stand—their candor and ethics would wind up hurting the defendant. A case in point was Dr. Edward Blake, who appeared on the defense's original witness list. He had observed all the scientific testing and was in a position to comment on whether it was aboveboard. Since there *was* no conspiracy, of course, by the time the trial began, Dr. Blake not so mysteriously had disappeared from their witness list. (We would have loved to call him ourselves. It was a sure bet, however, that Ito would rule Blake was shielded by the attorney-client and work-product privilege, and therefore off-limits for us.) Instead, the Dream Team put on a string of weak, unconvincing, and irrelevant witnesses. And we had one of our best streaks during the entire trial, batting them down one by one.

Following cameo appearances by Simpson's daughter, sister, and aged mother, the defense presented a series of witnesses whose job it was to push the murders later and later toward the hour of eleven. They started with Ellen Aaronson and Danny Mandel.

This couple had been on a blind date the night of the murders. On the surface, they seemed benign enough. Mandel was a junior executive at Sony Pictures. Aaronson worked in toy licensing. (She apologized to the court for her part in the proliferation of Power Rangers.) They testified that on the way back from dinner at Mezzaluna, they'd passed Nicole's condo around 10:26 P.M. They'd seen nothing. No bodies, no bloody pawprints, no signs of mayhem.

On the stand, I blasted the lights out of Aaronson. The reason wasn't, as pundits later suggested, that her recollection of 10:26 played havoc with my time line. This murder could have occurred as late as

10:40, and O. J. Simpson would still have gotten home in time to be seen skulking in through his front door.

It was simply that, when Ellen and Danny had first been interviewed by the LAPD, Mandel wasn't even sure what time they'd left the restaurant. Aaronson remembered looking at her watch on the way home and seeing that it was eleven o'clock. *Not* 10:26 P.M., as she later testified. During that first interview, they'd described taking an entirely different route to Aaronson's apartment. On the stand I pointed out these inconsistencies with a vigor that was, I have to admit, excessive. Particularly when I asked Aaronson whether she'd been drinking at dinner. (Turns out she hadn't.)

Critics have taken me to task for my aggressive cross of this pair. But try to put yourself in my position. For a year now, I'd been coping with publicity seekers and showboats willing to say just about anything to get themselves on the witness stand. Aaronson and Mandel had given inconsistent statements. If the defense team was not going to give its own witnesses a rigorous screening before throwing them up there, then it fell to Chris and me to expose their flaws.

Maybe I'll go to hell for it. But I had no patience with Hansel and Gretel.

Denise Pilnak's assertions were flat-out comical. She was a Bundy neighbor who professed with certainty that she'd looked at a clock at 10:18, and had heard no barking. She'd glanced out her window. It was quiet on the street.

Denise staked her claim to credibility on the fact that she was a fanatic about time. On the witness stand, she'd rolled up the sleeve of her blazer to show that she wore not one but two watches. She'd spun out this elaborate story about having been with her girlfriend that night and having looked at the clock every ten seconds. She'd even gone so far as to type out a time line of the evening, including where she and her friend had had dinner. When we checked out this document, we found that she'd actually gotten the restaurant wrong.

On cross-examination I asked her, "Do you recall how long you've been here today?"

Denise Pilnak, clockophile, couldn't remember what time she'd arrived at court.

*   *   *

My favorite was Mark Partridge, a lawyer who sat next to Simpson on the airplane home from Chicago.

Partridge, who seemed sympathetic to the defendant, apparently decided that his seating assignment was a potential gold mine. He handwrote eight pages of memories from the flight. On cross, I made a point of putting part of this valuable intellectual property on the overhead projector—specifically the notice he affixed to each page that read "©1994 PARTRIDGE, ALL RIGHTS RESERVED" and had him explain, as an attorney, why he had affixed a copyright notice to each page.

"In an effort to prevent people from distributing them without my consent," he said.

"Doesn't it also mean you have a financial interest in the privacy of that matter you copyright?" I continued.

He professed not to understand. I found this an unusual response, considering he was an attorney specializing in trademark and copyright law. Finally, I managed to wheedle from him the admission that, yes, copyrights are sometimes used by authors to ensure they profit from the work.

With that out of the way, I asked him to describe the nature of the phone calls his seatmate had placed during the flight. Partridge provided a bit of information that somewhat contradicted the image of a distraught mourner headed home to console the children of their dead mother: Simpson was repeatedly calling his lawyer.

By this time the law clerks watching all this on TV upstairs in our offices were rolling on the floor with laughter. And it was all Chris and I could do to keep a straight face.

The next performance was perhaps the weirdest of all. Robert Heidstra, a wizened little Frenchman who lived in a converted garage and earned his living detailing luxury cars, claimed to have been walking his dog near Nicole's condo at 10:30 P.M. when he heard a young man shout, "Hey, hey, hey," followed by the screaming of an older man who sounded black. Heidstra's testimony was fully consistent with our time line. We had, in fact, considered calling him as a prosecution wit-

ness. But after I'd spent about five minutes with him, I decided he was
not credible. People who lived right next door to Nicole heard nothing
but a dog barking, and he heard all that? No way. If I needed further
corroboration for my skepticism, it came when I learned he'd been
boasting to people that he was going to make some money from being
a witness. We declined to put him on. Instead, the defense did.

After testifying that he could have heard the shouts as late as
10:40, Heidstra went on to say that "a white car came out of the darkness into the light." On cross, Chris asked him if he had not told a
friend of his that the vehicle looked like a Ford Bronco.

"Might have said maybe a Bronco . . ." the Frenchman admitted
nervously.

On the other side of the room, the Dream Team had sunk low
into their chairs. The guy couldn't have done a better job for us if *we*
had called him.

But the jewel in the crown was Robert Huizenga, who came at the end
of the defense's first week of testimony. I'm sure the Dream Team
thought he would play splendidly. A former doctor for the NFL,
Huizenga, at forty-two, was one of those archetypal Southern Californians who, even into middle age, retain an unnatural, almost creepy
youthfulness. Shapiro had called him into the case two days after the
murders. He'd examined the defendant at Kardashian's house and was
there, in fact, when Simpson and Cowlings split in the Bronco.

The defense called Huizenga to establish that Simpson didn't have
the physical strength to commit a double murder. Under Shapiro's
friendly questioning, Huizenga started out smiling and confident. His
bias was unbelievable: he compared the suffering of O. J. Simpson to
the biblical trials of Job.

Shapiro called the doctor's attention to a photo of Simpson in his
underwear. "This appears to me as a layperson to be a man in pretty
good shape," Shapiro lobbed. "Would that be your evaluation?"

"Although he looked like Tarzan," Huizenga joked, "he walked
like Tarzan's grandfather."

Brian Kelberg, who took Huizenga on cross, quickly wiped the
smarmy smile off the witness's lips.

For the benefit of the court, Brian ran the raw footage of Simpson's exercise video. It had been shot only two weeks before Nicole's and Ron's deaths, and our man was leaping around like, well, Tarzan. Brian then screened a video of Simpson doing a product endorsement for some elixir that he claimed had ended his arthritis problems and had him "immediately feeling better." It had even added ten yards to his golf drive.

One by one, Brian reduced Huizenga's assertions to rubble. He used him to document extensive cuts on Simpson's hands. Under Brian's pressure, the doctor admitted he'd seen no evidence of a disability that would impede Simpson's movements; that he'd suffered no "acute" episodes of arthritis. Then Brian leveled him with the big one.

"Doctor," he asked, "was there any finding by you . . . which dealt [with] any physical limitation of Mr. Simpson's which, in your opinion, would have prevented him from murdering two human beings using a single-edge knife on June twelfth of 1994?"

"Objection, objection!" Shapiro yelped. But Ito overruled him.

"No, there was not," the witness replied.

It was Huizenga who ended up limping from the witness stand.

At this point, we were beginning to get excited. The defense was making our case for us, tossing us meatball after meatball. The jury *had* to be thinking that an innocent man would have a better case to present.

Next up to bat for the defense, the experts-for-hire.

It is worth noting here that never, during the entire case, did the defense perform one single test on any of the blood found at Bundy, in the Bronco, or at Rockingham. The reason was perfectly clear. *They knew the results would point directly to their client.* Under law, they're allowed to keep those results confidential, but if the word somehow got back to the jury that they'd done the tests and weren't putting their findings into evidence, it could be mighty incriminating.

They elected, instead, to have their own expert, Dr. Edward Blake, observe our testing. But they quickly realized that if he were put under oath, he would have to tell the truth: that the prosecution's blood results were unimpeachable.

As I've said, Dr. Blake disappeared from their witness list. Instead, we got Dr. Fredric Rieders.

Rieders, an Austrian-born toxicologist now working in Philadelphia, was called to support the very essence of the defense's "conspiracy" offensive. He would argue that the blood on certain evidence—like the rear gate at Nicole's condo and the socks found at the foot of Simpson's bed—contained a preservative called EDTA. He would assert that this meant it came from a test tube. Rieders was there to back up the theory that the blood taken from Simpson after his police interview had been subsequently sprinkled on crime-scene evidence. He was basing his claims on his own interpretations of data that had come back to us from the FBI lab.

The challenge sounded serious enough that I wanted to handle this witness myself. That meant getting up to speed very quickly on the science of EDTA. Several weeks before Rieders's scheduled appearance, an FBI toxicologist, Roger Martz, flew in from the East Coast to brief me. Agent Martz gave me a chart with two sets of results. One showed the results from the blood taken from Simpson the morning he'd been brought to Parker Center. That reference blood, of course, had been treated with EDTA to preserve it. The presence of the preservative manifested itself as tall, unmistakable bars. Next to it were the readings from blood on the rear gate and Simpson's socks. Here the EDTA showed up as tiny bars.

The question the defense would ask, of course, was "Why was there any bar at all? Why was *any* trace of EDTA in the blood on the gate and socks?" And that's exactly the question I asked Roger Martz.

Roger explained to me why the low-level readings were meaningless. As a "negative check" against the readings, he'd lifted a bloodstain from Nicole's dress. Now that *had* to be her blood. Right? No one had a reason to plant it; it hadn't come from a test tube. The results on that sample came back with the *same EDTA reading* as the disputed blood from the gate and socks. Agent Martz had gone a step further: he'd drawn blood from his own arm and tested it. Sure enough, there it was again. The same low-level reading of EDTA.

"EDTA is used as a preservative in foods and detergents," he explained to me. "A small amount of EDTA can stay in your system when you eat preserved foods. Or on your clothes after you wash. It's everywhere then. It's the matter of degree that tells the story. You see this huge bar?"

He pointed to the reading from the vial of reference blood taken from Simpson.

"If the blood on the rear gate and the socks had come from the preserved tube, the EDTA indicators would have been just as high. Instead, they're about a hundredth the size."

Wonderfully clear and graphic. But could I get this across to the jury?

Since the defense had done no tests of their own, we knew they would have to call Agent Martz as their own witness—after all, he had performed the case's only EDTA testing. Only he could give the testimony that would get the results into evidence. Had they been interested in getting to the truth of the matter, they would have called him first to explain his testing, then followed up with Rieders offering his own interpretation, obviously one more favorable to the defense.

But of course they weren't interested in the truth. Late in the day on July 17, we got notice that they wanted to call Dr. Rieders first, and only then call Agent Martz. Worse, they waited until that moment to release a dense technical report on Rieders's interpretation of the test—which we'd have to analyze closely before responding to it. It would be very tough, but at that point the defense was listing seven or so witnesses ahead of Rieders.

At nearly eight o'clock on the evening of July 19, however, we got notice that they might be calling Rieders as early as *the next day*. This flew in the face of Ito's rule requiring both sets of counsel to give a few days' notice before they called a witness. We'd complied, but the defense virtually ignored the rule. They knew all they had to do was give some lame excuse, and Lance would shrug his shoulders and let them off the hook.

I was pissed, and made no bones about it.

"I'm really outraged at the way the defense has proceeded," I charged in court the next morning, so angry I was stammering. "It is a trial by ambush." I outlined the history of this issue, noting that Rieders had received the test results in February, giving him months to prepare his report. There was no excuse for springing it on us just before he testified. Furthermore, I explained why it was unacceptable for the defense to put Rieders on before Martz. They had a guy who was going to put his own twisted spin on a set of scientific tests—*before* the tests themselves were presented to the court.

"I think it is scandalous what has occurred here," I said. "I think it is a very deliberate attempt to try to . . . prevent the people from adequately meeting this testimony. . . . I mean, where is the fairness?"

The defense, of course, acted stunned and accused me of trying to manipulate their witness order. They even tried to insinuate that Lisa Kahn had told them that we were ready for Rieders anytime. When I called that "the biggest bald-face lie we have heard yet in this case," Ito warned me about making personal attacks. But Lance knew what was happening. "If the shoe were on the other foot," he said to the defense, "I would be peeling you off the ceiling right now."

Damned straight.

Nevertheless, Ito was loath to give me the prep time I needed. The jury was restless; the case had already dragged on way past its original estimated four months. Bob Blasier had the gall to mock my argument that Martz should go first: "I can't believe that Miss Clark says she's ready for Martz but she's not ready for Rieders."

"Oh come on," I charged. "That's so obvious it doesn't even bear addressing. Agent Martz is going to be an *honest* witness who's going to testify *truthfully* to the results. That's a little easier—" (I had not intended to suggest that Rieders was lying so much as that he was distorting the evidence to such an extent that it would have the same effect.)

Lance cut me off. "Miss Clark, earlier today I cautioned you about personal attacks." I began to apologize but he stepped on me again. "Sanction is two hundred and fifty dollars. Don't leave court without writing a check."

Thanks, Lance.

At the end of the day, he ruled that the defense could put Rieders on first, and they could do it on Monday, July 24. This gave me only three or four days to prepare an incredibly complicated cross. With the witness order inverted, the defense would use Rieders to distort the test results before Martz, an honest and knowledgeable witness, could explain what they meant. Instead, I'd be forced to try and extract simple explanations of scientific evidence from a hostile witness bent on confusion and distortion. At the same time, I'd need to use my now bulging dossier on Rieders's professional history to impeach both his ethics and his expertise.

This task would have been daunting if I'd had three months to prepare, but three days? Even as Ito admitted the situation was unfair, he wouldn't budge. His rationale: "Professional attorneys are paid to work twenty-four hours day when they're in trial."

Which rules out, I guess, single parents, people with sick relatives, or human beings who simply require sleep.

On July 24, Dr. Fredric Rieders took the witness stand. After putting in a very long weekend, I was ready for him.

Rieders was a portly man with wisps of long, wild hair swirling about his head. His thick Austrian accent made him difficult to understand and he had a gruff, abrasive demeanor that turned condescending when he explained technical terms to the jury. With any other jury, I would have leaned back and let him hang himself. But not this one. He was going to give them the excuse they needed to dismiss key blood evidence. I had to hang tough. During his direct testimony, which was every bit as convoluted and misleading as I'd expected, I took careful notes.

When it came time for cross, I promptly introduced a copy of a study conducted by the EPA. It showed that the levels of EDTA found in the environment at large were consistent with those measured on the rear gate and the sock. Further, I noted that these levels were also consistent with the unpreserved blood from Agent Martz's own body. Didn't this, I asked the witness, show that the levels in the untreated evidence were meaningless?

Rieders resisted, calling the EPA study "either a typo or a complete absurdity."

"But isn't it true, Doctor, that [Martz's] unpreserved blood came out very similarly in result to bloodstains found on the gate and the sock? Isn't that true, Doctor?"

"Surprisingly, yes," was his answer.

"Yes," I repeated with exaggerated emphasis.

Ito demanded a sidebar. "Miss Clark . . . I know you're enjoying yourself," he began. "But I'm warning you in no uncertain terms, if I see any more of that commentary, there's going to be severe sanctions. And I underline the word 'severe.' "

I couldn't believe it. Barry Scheck could stand up there and sneer, "Where isss ittttt, Misterrr Fung?" and Ito would shine it on. I emphasize one word for effect and get dragged to sidebar.

I returned to Rieders.

"Doctor," I asked him, "how do you account for the readings that came up from Agent Martz's blood?"

"I don't have to account for it," he sniffed. "I think he would have to account for it because it's absurd to find that much EDTA in normal blood."

Great. You dismiss our tests as "absurd." Not that you have any evidence to the contrary. In fact, you haven't done one single test of your own. What a despicable sham. They claimed the blood was planted—that was their whole defense against all our evidence—and yet they don't even perform *one* test? How could it be more obvious that their claims were fiction?

All that remained, at this point, was to impeach Rieders's competence as a toxicologist—and we believed we had the goods to do it.

Brian Kelberg would present to the court certain details about Rieders's role in a 1985 murder case—a Ventura County man who had allegedly been killed by a fellow named Sconce, one of his competitors in the funeral business. It was suspected that the victim had been poisoned with oleander. Rieders did the original postmortem tests and later appeared in court to say that while he could not be 100 percent certain, he felt that his tests showed, to "a high degree of scientific certainty," the presence of oleander. That testimony led to Sconce's indictment.

But Rieders, as Kelberg would argue, had done only rudimentary tests. Really definitive results would have required a pricey instrument he didn't have. When this weakness was discovered, the district attorney joined the defense and ordered the more sophisticated testing. The results? No oleander. (Rieders argued that the differences between his results and those of the toxicologist who double-checked him is that the latter used a different set of tissue samples, which could have deteriorated with the passage of time.)

That explanation notwithstanding, charges against Sconce were dropped.

The Simpson jury had to hear this.

At the mention of Sconce, Rieders began to fidget and waved his hands at me dismissively. When a witness behaves this way, it is the judge's role to force him to respond to the question. Not only did Ito refuse to do this, but he began to interrupt *my* questions, urging me to move to another topic.

"This is the Simpson case, Ms. Clark. How about getting back to it?"

I couldn't believe it. We'd had to argue the admissibility of the Sconce case at some length before Rieders took the stand. Ito knew perfectly well that this was important impeachment testimony. What was he doing?

I pressed on, determined to show the jury that the witness's interpretation was unreasonable and far-fetched. But after a few more questions, Ito barked, "This inquiry. It is completely irrelevant at this point. Move on to something else."

In that instant this judge had told the jury to disregard a significant point of impeachment and rebuked me as if I were some wayward schoolgirl. I was ready to lock horns with Lance, to keep pursuing Rieders, but Ito's inevitable response would damage my cross even further. I had no choice but to accede.

I could only hope that the jury had troubled to get clear of all the scientific mumbo jumbo to see the truth—which is what Martz himself presented when he took the stand next. The blood on the defendant's sock, Nicole's blood, did *not* come from a test tube containing EDTA. The blood on the rear gate, Simpson's blood, did *not* come from a test tube containing EDTA. Which is to say, in each case the blood came straight from the source.

It should have been a clean win for us—a definitive rebuttal to the defense's lunatic speculations. But I knew that the impact of Martz's testimony was diluted by the circus put on by Rieders and the defense. Any other jury would have seen through it. But by now we had a pretty good idea that this jury liked a circus.

*   *   *

The defense's next witness was Dr. Herbert MacDonell, an expert witness in blood-spatter interpretation. He was the man who would supposedly buttress Johnnie's claims that if Simpson had committed these murders, he would certainly have been drenched in blood. Ironically, MacDonell himself had offered an answer to that question. In a paper entitled "Absence of Evidence Is Not Evidence of Absence," he'd demonstrated how a perpetrator could leave a bloody crime scene without very much blood on him. I couldn't wait to have him discuss it.

We had collected a whole binder of materials to impeach Mac-Donell's testimony with his own writings. But the defense must have seen this coming. To keep us from getting that paper into evidence, they narrowed MacDonell's testimony to a single piece of evidence: the socks found at the foot of Simpson's bed.

The defense had focused upon one sock that had a stain they claimed was a "compression transfer"—meaning that the blood hadn't been spattered onto the sock in the heat of violence, but had been pressed onto it later. The jury was to infer, of course, that the pressing had been done by one of the nameless, faceless conspirators out to frame O. J. Simpson.

MacDonell was harping on certain microscopic spheres of blood found on the inside of the sock that was stained at the ankle with Nicole's blood. I pointed out that these "little balls," as I referred to them pejoratively, could very well have come from the handling the socks received after the crime—but for perfectly innocuous reasons. The socks had been frozen and unfrozen. They had been stretched for microscopic analysis. And in an earlier test, they had been swabbed with water; this alone could easily have caused the blood to rehydrate and leak through to the other side of the sock.

I confronted him with the fact that he had originally referred to the blood pattern as a "swipe," not a "compression." This was important because of the latter term's sinister implications.

"It's a matter of interpretation," he waffled. "It's a distinction that to my mind is totally irrelevant."

But, of course, it wasn't.

I asked the court for permission to question the witness about crime-scene photos. The defense objected frantically, but this time Ito overruled them.

"You saw photographs of the crime scene, have you not?" I asked him.

"Yes," MacDonell answered, "I have."

". . . Let me ask you this, sir," I continued. "If someone wearing the socks that you saw were to step near to the body of the victim, Nicole Brown Simpson, near enough for the ankle bone to come in contact with her bloody hand, could that cause a compression transfer?"

"Certainly," he replied.

I could see Johnnie and Peter Neufeld out of the corner of my eye. Sweating.

"Could it also cause a swipe?" I asked.

"Yes."

I shot it back again, with a cleaner spin. "If Nicole Brown Simpson reached out a bloody hand to touch the ankle of the *murderer* wearing those socks, could *that* cause a compression or a swipe transfer?"

He admitted that it could.

Bingo.

The Dream Team had two big guns left to call: Michael Baden and Henry Lee. Shapiro had called in Baden, a medical examiner for New York State, almost before the bodies were cold. It was Baden, in turn, who'd told him to secure the services of Henry Lee, the forensic scientist who ran Connecticut's state police crime lab. The word of mouth on both men was good. They enjoyed reputations for scientific and personal integrity. Sadly, those stellar reputations would take a beating in the Simpson trial.

Baden was an affable, charming man who always went out of his way to be sweet to me. And I have to admit, he had expert-witnessing down to a science (so to speak). A big man with a winning smile, he sat on the stand as if he owned it. Though Brian is not as physically imposing as Baden, his intensity makes him a formidable courtroom figure. I enjoyed watching their exchanges; to a seasoned legal observer it was like a clash of gods on Mount Olympus. I just hoped the jurors weren't so blown away by the pyrotechnics that they ignored the point: that Brian was able to get Baden to concede that his scenarios were not as watertight as they seemed. Here's how:

Contention: The L.A. County Coroner destroyed evidence when he discarded the food remnants in Nicole's stomach. They might have indicated that she died much later than our time line allowed for.

Refutation: Under pressure from Brian, Baden in effect admitted that even if the contents had been preserved, they wouldn't necessarily have pinpointed the time of death.

Contention: Nine days after the sock was found in Simpson's bedroom, Baden looked at it and saw no blood, the implication being that the blood was planted later.

Refutation: Brian got Baden to admit that he had not inspected the socks carefully. A special high-intensity light is required to see blood on such material, and the defense didn't use it. Thus, Baden couldn't say for certain that there was no blood present.

Contention: The victims' injuries showed that they may have been killed by two people, with two knives.

Refutation: Kelberg got Baden to admit that the evidence was consistent with a single murderer wielding a single knife.

In addition, Baden testified about the cuts on Simpson's hands—and helped us while doing so. He reported that Simpson himself had told him that he'd gotten the cuts while retrieving his cell phone from the Bronco just before he left for Chicago. This line of questioning was important: It allowed us to get in evidence that the cell phone he'd used to call Paula at 10:03 P.M. on June 12 was in the Bronco. Ergo, Simpson had been out driving at 10:03 P.M., just before the murders were committed. Now I didn't even need that snippet from Simpson's statement to Vannatter and Lange. I would put this information to good use in closing arguments. In fact, I would use the Baden "cut" testimony in my summation to show how Simpson's flimsy excuse about the cell phone couldn't possibly account for all the blood in his car and his bathroom.

For his performance, Baden was paid $100,000.

*   *   *

There was even more fanfare for the vaunted superstar of the defense's lineup, Dr. Henry Lee, one of the country's most revered—and charismatic—criminalists. Lee's testimony would focus on evidence collection, the blood on the socks, and the shoe prints—all Hank Goldberg's turf. The job he had ahead of him was the courtroom equivalent of guarding Michael Jordan.

Personally, I thought there was a pretty good chance that Dr. Henry Lee could be helpful to us. He was, for instance, a big proponent of DNA testing in criminal cases. He could also be helpful in answering assertions that the LAPD labs were "cesspools of contamination," as charged by another defense witness, Dr. John Gerdes. Dr. Lee, by his own admission, had at one time done his evidence processing in a men's room! He'd also dried crime-scene clothing in his backyard. (This practice ended when a stray dog took off with a piece of a rape victim's underwear.)

But Hank's work wouldn't end there. Back on June 25, over a year earlier, Lee had gone to Bundy to examine the bloody shoe prints. His notes revealed that he thought he'd found evidence of a second set of prints, different from those made by the Bruno Maglis. Hank pored over the photos Lee had taken, trying to find the supposed shoe prints—to no avail. Finally, by piecing together all the photos, Hank located the exact spot on the tiles where Dr. Lee claimed to have seen that other set of shoe prints. Then he looked at the crime-scene photos taken by LAPD on their first sweep of Bundy. That spot was blank. The lines Dr. Lee found on June 25, two weeks after the murders, had not been there on June 13.

That wasn't surprising. It could easily be explained by the fact that, after the crime-scene tape was removed, cops walked up and down that pathway freely. If, after all the photos were taken and the evidence collected, someone had stepped on some remaining blood and left another imprint, it was no big deal.

But Lee was claiming to have found what he called "parallel lines" that, he said, firmly indicated a second set of shoe prints. Hank located the spot where *those* appeared, and discovered that the parallel lines were actually impressions in the concrete.

Hank sat back while Scheck questioned the affable Dr. Lee for hours on these shoe-print findings. Then, on cross, Hank revealed to the witness the fact that the parallel lines were artifacts in concrete, probably made by a workman years before the crime.

"And now . . ." he asked Lee, "does it appear that the parallel lines are in fact trowel marks or scratches in the surface of the pavement?"

"Could be" was the answer.

"Does that appear to be the most reasonable explanation?"

"Yes, right," Lee conceded.

So much for the two-killer theory.

But the most damaging part of Lee's testimony had nothing to with science and everything to do with theater. I'm referring to a much-hyped remark he offered at the close of the direct testimony. Scheck had asked his opinion of a specific piece of blood collection by the police, and Lee responded, in his broken English, "Only opinion I can giving under the circumstance—something's wrong."

Do you know what Dr. Henry Lee was referring to when he intoned so dramatically that "something's wrong"? A minor, almost insignificant piece of evidence. Eight swatches of blood from one of the Bundy spots had been collected to be stored in a little paper envelope called a bindle. But only four of them left stains on the bindle. The reason, of course, is that four of them were dry and the other four wet at the time they were stored. So what?

"Something's wrong." It was the most unscientific thing I've ever heard a forensic expert say. It was, in fact, Lee's way of helping the defense without saying anything.

"Something's wrong!" Barry Scheck treated it like a message from God, and repeated it like a mantra throughout his summation, suggesting disingenuously that Lee's comment referred to the prosecution's entire case.

In fact, Hank disarmed this insinuation on cross. Wasn't it common, he asked Lee, for a forensic scientist to see something that he couldn't explain? Lee admitted that it was.

"That doesn't mean something is *wrong,* does it?" Hank pressed.

"No," conceded Dr. Lee.

Later, when I learned that our jurors had cited Dr. Lee's testimony as their prime reason for discounting the absolutely definitive physical evidence we had presented over the course of months at trial, I knew the bad vibes I'd been getting from the jury box weren't just figments of my imagination. They were tuning out for the prosecution and tuning in for the defense. Hank might have been asking Dr. Lee about his favorite punk-rock group for all they cared or listened. Once they heard the ominous proclamation "Something's wrong," it became in their minds an emblem for our entire case. It became synonymous with the conditions of society in general. "Something's wrong" in a country where racism flourishes and the law has been known to be dispensed in unequal portions.

We had struck down every single claim made to support a "conspiracy." But our streak of luck was at an end. By the time Lee finished his testimony in August 1995, the focus of the trial no longer bore any relevance to the evidence. Instead, all eyes were fixed on what was "wrong"—wrong with a racist cop, wrong with the legal system, wrong with America.

And all of this—all of what was wrong—was to be symbolized by one man, Mark Fuhrman.

It was early July when I first got a hint of the disaster that would ultimately ruin us. I was feeling a little overwhelmed that day. The case was dragging on far longer than expected. Johnnie had once estimated that he would wrap up his case within the month. I'd hoped to spend more time with my children before school started. But the Glorious Fourth had come and gone, and there was no end in sight.

Bill Hodgman buzzed and asked me to come to his office immediately. He looked ashen.

"Marcia," he told me. "We've heard a rumor that Mark Fuhrman may have been collaborating with some author to write a book. Our source says Mark used racial epithets."

Maybe I was tired, but this sounded to me like just one more of the bullshit rumors we'd had to entertain, investigate, and dismiss in recent months.

"The good news," Bill continued, "is that they were apparently composing a work of fiction where Mark played a racist character."

If this was true, the book would be irrelevant to our case. Still, that wouldn't stop the defense from trying to exploit it. Bill said he was already checking it out.

I returned to my office, where EDTA reports, MacDonell binders, notes for the Rieders cross, and texts illuminating the mysteries of bloodstain patterns blanketed the surface of my desk.

"Maybe," I whispered to myself, "it will just go away."

It didn't. Reports kept filtering in. The project was a movie script and Fuhrman had made tapes in the process. His collaborator was a would-be screenwriter named Laura Hart McKinny, who had retained lawyers in Los Angeles. Lawyers to do what? Shop the screenplay? Sell the tapes?

We had to find out what was in those tapes. Chris wrote a subpoena at warp speed—we were under the impression that the goods were in-state—and Ito approved it. But before we could serve, we learned that the defense had already located McKinny; she had taken some obscure academic post in North Carolina. They were going after her with their own subpoena. The problem was this: a California judge can't demand a witness or a tape from another state unless that state's courts agree to honor the subpoena. So Johnnie himself, with Lee Bailey riding shotgun, headed to the Tar Heel State to make their arguments.

Word got back to us that Johnnie didn't play real well in North Carolina. The judge there barely hid his contempt for the defense's race strategy. I had to smile. Johnnie had gotten a taste of what this trial would have been like if he hadn't been blessed with Lance Ito. The subpoena was denied on the grounds that McKinny's tapes didn't constitute material evidence.

I knew that was not the end of it. The defense was sure to appeal, and they did. In short order, the subpoena was granted and the tapes, along with Ms. McKinny, were on their way to California. Well, we'd expected that.

It would be two weeks before we could get those tapes to make our own transcriptions. In the meantime, I'd gotten some idea of what they contained by reading transcripts of the North Carolina hearing. Fuhrman and McKinny had met periodically over a period of about ten years. During that time he spun out tales for her like Scheherazade. We didn't know all he'd said, but it was clear that the tapes contained at least one thing that was going to be trouble for us. Big, big trouble.

Fuhrman *had* uttered the N-word on those tapes. And Johnnie had made sure to get that on the record.

Oh, God.

The only glimmer of hope here was that Mark had simply been helping McKinny develop a character for a work of fiction. The racial epithets, she insisted, were used "in the context of developing a story. . . . It wasn't a biography of Mr. Fuhrman's life." She went on to say that these sessions gave her "information about ideas and feelings that some people might have about African Americans. I don't know that it reflects his feelings about African Americans."

But I sure knew how it would sound.

On August 11, McKinny's attorneys appeared before Lance to turn over the tapes. They looked as if they'd never set foot in a courtroom. Actually, they looked barely old enough to shave: young, inexperienced guys who thought they'd caught a rocket to fame and fortune. They didn't get it—once the defense got those tapes, it would be only a matter of hours before they were leaked to the press. By then, they would have a commercial value of zero. *Inside Edition* doesn't fork out the big bucks for stuff that's playing free on national television.

I was the one who raised the possibility of leaks, and I saw the lawyers' eyes go wide with panic. They immediately asked Ito for a protective order, which he granted. But I knew it wasn't worth the paper it was printed on. Everyone was shocked—*shocked*, mind you—when, not long after the tapes reached attorneys for both sides, they were leaked to the press.

Our steno pool worked overtime transcribing those fifteen hours of tape. When, at last, a copy reached my desk, I curled up in my chair like a wary cat, lit a Dunhill, took a deep breath, and started to read.

Every racial slur imaginable. "Those niggers, they run like rabbits." Every demeaning stereotype. "Nigger driving a Porsche that doesn't look like he's got a $300 suit on, you always stop him." Every fear that a black man could have about a racist cop, fulfilled. "How do you intellectualize when you punch a nigger? He either deserves it or he doesn't."

Did Mark actually mean these things? Even if he was, as McKinny claimed, spinning out a fictional persona, did he envision this character as a villain or a hero?

If African Americans got rough treatment, women got just as bad. I consider myself fairly well versed in the language of profanity, but Fuhrman had come up with some slurs I'd never even heard.

"Split tail?" I asked Chris, who was slumped dejectedly against my door. He'd just emerged from his own hellish immersion in those transcripts. He shook his head in disgust. "Man," he said, "that motherfucker just lost the whole case for us."

Back in his own neighborhood Chris was going to catch a lot of heat for this. I was glad, for his sake, that I was the one who'd ended up taking Fuhrman on direct.

But at that moment the anger and sadness I felt was not only for the prosecution but for the country, torn by racial hatred. *People v. Orenthal James Simpson* had done nothing but widen the divide. We'd hoped that by carefully presenting the facts, we could convince *all* the people that our charges were justified. Now these horrible epithets were about to infiltrate our courtroom, and they would further strain the uneasy truce between blacks and whites. The release of these tapes, and the prominence they would assume, would mean a step backward for all of us. And a step forward for hate.

Chris left without a word. I returned to the transcripts. The worst racial slur of all, repeated forty-one times. And when I reached the end, I threw the transcript down and cried.

That night I drove home from work in a trance. Got into bed. Stared at the ceiling. On this miserable night, the loneliness of that bedroom was killing me. I wanted to talk to someone who would listen with unconditional sympathy.

I reached for the phone and called my brother, Jon. It was always comforting to talk to him; he could make me laugh, and he shared my sense of outrage about what was happening in Lance's courtroom. When this trial began, he was living nearby, but recently he'd moved north. I missed him.

It took him a moment to recognize my voice. "Marsh. You don't sound too good," he said. I told him about the transcripts.

"I still can't believe it," I said. By now I'd begun to weep. "It's going to be so ugly."

"You've got to pull it together," he told me in his gentle, firm way. "This case is still happening—you've *got* to get through it."

The next morning when I got up, the self-pity was gone. I was just plain angry. *Fuhrman!* Why hadn't he told us about those fucking tapes? It's not like they could have slipped his mind. One illuminating fact to have emerged from the transcripts was that Fuhrman had met with McKinny as recently as July 1994—just a few weeks after the murders—to discuss the "hot property" he'd become. The two of them agreed to lie low until the case was over; then they'd make the sale, and Mark would get a percentage. But apparently McKinny had seen her chance sooner: it was no accident those tapes were surfacing now.

Fuhrman had boasted in that July tape, "I'm the biggest witness in the case of the century—if I go down, they lose the case." No, as a matter of fact, he was not our biggest witness. Just the most vulnerable. And when Johnnie got done with him, this would no longer be the Simpson trial; it would be the Fuhrman trial.

Did I feel betrayed? You bet. We all did. After the tapes came out, I got a lot of criticism for having "embraced" Fuhrman. Bullshit! I never had any choice about calling him as a witness. And it was Mark Fuhrman's job to inform us of anything that might be used against him by the defense. Instead, he took the stand at the preliminary hearing without telling us about his personnel package. Then he testified—as I held my breath and silently screamed, *No, don't do it!*—that he hadn't uttered the N-word in the last ten years. All the while he knew about those tapes.

And now, after all our hard work—DNA, PCR, EDTA—the case came down to this: MF.

Read it any way you like.

Laura Hart McKinny showed up at our eighteenth-floor conference room with her attorneys and her husband. I wasn't surprised when she agreed to talk to us. It was good PR for her to appear not to be taking sides. At first glance she struck me as a flower child gone slightly to seed. She was in her forties, but her hair hung long and free. Her freckled face bore no makeup and she wore the kind of funky, flowing clothing that you'd have seen at a Jefferson Airplane concert.

I wasn't fooled by the packaging. Beneath that hang-loose exterior lay a stratum of steel.

I told her that we routinely taped our interviews, and she balked. Pretty ironic, under the circumstances. She and her team withdrew from the room to confer. I raised an eyebrow at Bill. By the time she returned, several minutes later, she was more compliant. Bill did the questioning while Chris and I sat by.

McKinny told us how one day in 1985 she was sitting at a café table in Westwood, tapping away at her laptop computer, when up sidled Mark Fuhrman. He asked her a question about the computer. (It sounded to me like a come-on line. No way Mark Fuhrman cared about RAM and ROM.) McKinny had something else in mind. Fuhrman, she learned, was a police officer. And, whaddya know, she happened to be writing a screenplay about cops.

They struck a deal: he would give her inside cop skinny, and she would give him credit as her technical adviser and a percentage of whatever. Fuhrman, it turned out, was useful to McKinny not merely because he was an officer with the LAPD. He was also a member of a group called Men Against Women, MAW, which had resisted the advancement of female cops. Talk about an appealing protagonist.

After their decade of interviews on the subject, McKinny turned out a screenplay with the catchy title "Men Against Women." And guess what. It didn't sell.

She recounted this tale with no discernible sense of irony, and I grew increasingly impatient with her. This woman had laughed and giggled with Mark, listened to his chest-thumping accounts of cop life, and accepted without criticism his descriptions of police misconduct against blacks and women, all spiced with the vilest racial and sexual slurs that a human can utter. What was the deal here? Did she believe he was being himself? Or was he playing a role?

I asked her just that.

At the hearing in North Carolina, she'd claimed that what Mark had said was simply theater; now she backed off. Sometimes she knew that he was acting a part, she said. But at times, he seemed to be talking about himself. When he blathered on about police brutality, she didn't bother to distinguish between what might have been true and what imagined. She was working on a piece of fiction. It didn't matter. She was "a writer."

But Laura, I asked her. When you heard him use those epithets, what did you do?

Nothing.

Laura, what did you feel?

Nothing, she replied. I was just listening.

Chris could take no more. "Nothing?" he repeated, incredulous. "You felt nothing when you heard him talk that way?"

At this McKinny got her back up. She was a writer, she insisted. Interjecting her opinion would have made her subject freeze up.

The upshot of Chris's sally, unfortunately, was that McKinny herself froze up, and we got nothing more of substance out of her. As time went on, she would put serious distance between herself and her politically incorrect collaborator.

The leopard had changed her spots. By the time of her court appearance, she would have become mortally offended by this creature who had spewed filth into her tape recorder.

We had to face it—it really didn't matter at this point whether Laura McKinny was going to say that Fuhrman was acting on those tapes. The issue was the tapes themselves. We absolutely had to try to keep them out of evidence. We could argue, with God and Truth firmly on our side, that Fuhrman's boasts had nothing to do with the deaths of Ron Goldman and Nicole Brown. But Lance, through his insupportable error of allowing in the N-word in the first place, had opened the floodgates to travesty.

We worked hard to stop the inevitable. It was a horrible time. I was fighting a low-grade flu that had plagued me for weeks. But hearing those tapes just did me in. After that, I was flat-out sick. During the worst, most feverish part of it, I had to drag myself into the office at 6:30 A.M. one Saturday to work with Bill on our motion. Scott Gordon worked right alongside us, pulling up more cases in which racial epithets had been deemed inadmissible because of their inflammatory impact. I didn't get home until three in the morning.

And if all that weren't enough, by the end of the weekend a new problem had emerged. Cheri Lewis had been going over the transcripts with a fine-tooth comb, filing Fuhrman's utterances under different categories: by racial epithet; by description of misconduct; etc. We realized that there was another issue raised by the tapes.

One that Lance Ito could never rule on.

At one point in the tapes, Fuhrman complained vociferously and pejoratively about a female captain who had supervised him several years earlier in the West L.A. Station. He described her like this:

> Dyed, real white blond hair . . . with one-inch roots. . . . This woman is forty years old. She's got braces on, slumped shoulder. Only marsupial lieutenant on the job. She has a pouch big enough to hide two cats. Under the lower belt it looks like she's hiding a soccer ball. She's not pregnant. And she's never worked the field. Ever. She sued . . . to get the job.

He was talking about Peggy York—Lance Ito's wife.

Mark had described two run-ins with her, including one during which she upbraided the squad for writing "KKK" on the calendar entry for Martin Luther King Day. Mark had snickered, and when she called him on it in private, he claimed, he belittled her to her face. In another dustup, he refused an assignment from her, supposedly saying, "I don't talk to anybody that [sic] isn't a policeman, and you're as far from a policeman as I've seen—and as far as that goes, you're about as far from a woman as I've seen."

This was going to be a source of major grief for Ito, in more ways than one. Earlier the preceding fall, it had come out that York had known Fuhrman as someone under her command. Those of us on the prosecution side felt that Lance had surely looked into this matter privately—at the very least, had asked, "Honey, what do you know about this?"—and had concluded that there was no personal animus between his wife and Detective Fuhrman. Had there been any, Ito should have recused himself right then and there. He didn't. So we all assumed the matter was under control.

In October, I had even met Peggy York. Her lawyer, my old sparring partner–cum–buddy Barry Levin, had introduced us. Captain York struck me as a smart, classy lady. York had given a deposition in which she stated she had no memory of ever having reprimanded Fuhrman. In short, she had no information to offer.

But if you believed what Mark Fuhrman had said about her in the McKinny tapes, it became more difficult to take her assurances at face value. The encounters Mark described were sufficiently hostile that, had they occurred, Captain York would most likely have remembered them. And, if she remembered them, it was hard to believe she wouldn't have told her husband about them—if not at the time, then when his name came up on the short list of judges for the Simpson case.

To state the obvious, if Mark's problems with York were true and Ito knew of them, he should never have taken the case.

But I decided that, although there was certainly a kernel of truth in his stories, Fuhrman was likely distorting whatever had happened between himself and York, just as he had exaggerated other incidents. During the McKinny interviews, Mark described several incidents of racism and brutality, the most graphic being a scene in which he and other officers chased some suspected cop-killers into an apartment.

"We basically tortured them . . ." he reported swaggeringly to his adoring Boswell. "We broke 'em. . . . Their faces were just mush. . . ."

Afterward, he said, he and his colleagues had been so bloody that they had to hose down their uniforms. As he returned to this incident later in the tapes, the brutality became even more intense, and in his final version of the tale the cops actually killed one of the suspects.

This smelled like Fantasyland. Sure enough, when the FBI and other agencies set out to verify Mark's stories, they found no basis in truth. Later on, a former partner of Fuhrman's, Tom Vettraino, would opine that Mark's stories came from old TV cop shows. Fuhrman had been bullshitting, right down to his boast that he was a big bad marine who'd seen all sorts of bloody action in 'Nam—in fact, he never got off some old tub of a ship.

But if the McKinny tapes were admitted, we might have to prove that Fuhrman's stories of police misconduct were unfounded. Our best witness might have been York, who was named on the tapes and might be able to refute Mark Fuhrman's tales. As awkward as it was, we would have to call her to the stand. Quite obviously, Ito could not preside while his wife testified. And there was a broader issue: how could he even make a determination on the admissibility of tapes in which his wife was trashed by a witness?

Ito held a hearing on August 15. He still hadn't heard the tapes, which, he opined, "is a good state of affairs at this point." He framed the issue simply. If his wife was called, he'd disqualify himself from the case. Sounded fair, but it left me trapped: how could I know whether to call York until I knew which parts of the tapes would be admitted as evidence? If Lance allowed in the incidents of police brutality, York's observations of Fuhrman's work would be crucial.

On the other side of the courtroom, they were also in a tactical bind. The defense was pushing like crazy to get the police-brutality stuff into the record, but they didn't want to lose Lance. Who could blame them? A replacement judge might not be so tolerant of their underhanded tricks.

We recessed for a while to research the issue. And when we returned, it was clear that Johnnie had figured out that I had hung a sword over Lance's head: if Ito admitted Mark's nasty statements about police brutality, we'd call York, and Ito would be off the case. Johnnie should have gracefully conceded that someone else should rule on the limited matter of the tapes. I, too, was leaning toward partial recusal, and would have gone with it. But Johnnie was so fixated upon keeping Lance on the bench that he argued against it.

Keep in mind that all of this was going on in open court. The jurors weren't present, but the proceedings were being broadcast, so their families could hear and see it all. I shuddered to think what information they were imparting to their sequestered loved ones during visiting hours at the Inter-Continental. Johnnie took the opportunity to do all he could to convey to the media and the public what was in those tapes. He knew he could get away with it, too—because Lance was almost comatose from the stress of having to deal with his wife's sudden visibility in the case.

I was steaming. Johnnie had found a surefire distraction from all the evidence confirming the guilt of O. J. Simpson. "This is a bomb-shell!" he crowed. "This is perhaps the biggest thing that has happened in any case in this country and they know it." But, Johnnie, there's a more immediate horror at the center of this case, lying all but for-gotten: two young people with their throats cut.

Finally Lance stopped him. "I've heard enough," he said.

He looked shaken. He said that, much as he hated to bring another judge in, for a ruling on these tapes, he would have to.

"I love my wife dearly," he said, "and I am wounded at any criti-cism of her, as any spouse would be, and I think it is reasonable to assume that could have some impact."

That was touching. But then he began speaking of the difficult road that women had to walk in a man's profession, how women take a lot of hits for having to be tough. The irony of it left me breathless. For a year now, I had been browbeaten by this man, suffering the very difficulties that moistened his eyes when he spoke of his wife. Oh, when it suited his Kodak moment, he was Mr. Sensitivity.

Upstairs in the D.A.'s office, anger was building like steam in a pres-sure cooker. By the time I reached the eighteenth floor, brass and deputies alike were gathered in Bill's office. They had reached a con-sensus. We should demand Lance Ito's *full* recusal.

The argument went like this: Even if Lance stepped aside for a ruling on the tapes, he would still be the one to enforce that ruling. But the essential conflict of interest would remain. You'd need two judges on the bench for the rest of the trial. Introducing this unusual set of circumstances would lead the jury to conclude that the Fuhrman tapes were the most important thing in this case.

The pro-recusal faction was insistent. The two-judge scenario would be a disaster. We had to have *one* judge—not Lance—for the rest of the the trial.

My colleagues handed me the draft of a letter, hastily composed, demanding that Lance remove himself from the case for good. I stood for a moment, silent, trying to sort out my thoughts. If Ito recused himself, this case would be over. No trial judge could walk in at this point, pick up, and carry on. Especially considering where things stood—that is, in shambles. We'd probably have to desequester the jury; you couldn't keep them locked up for the weeks it would take a new judge to learn the case. Then the jurors would get an earful of any defense propaganda they hadn't already managed to hear. Probably, during the extension, we'd lose enough jurors to cause a mistrial. Even though I knew in my heart that this case was lost, I believed that at another trial, with another Downtown jury preloaded with tales of Fuhrman, we'd still get the same results. And no one wanted to go through all this again.

But I had another response to this missile we were preparing to hurl. It was a response I could never have predicted. I found myself feeling sorry for Lance Ito. Obviously, I had no reason to love the guy. I had no reason even to like him. But total recusal was going too far. It would destroy him.

"We're not doing this," I said to Gil and the brass. "This letter is not going out over my name. If you don't want to listen to me, then *you* fucking do it."

I stormed to my office and did my best to slam the door, forgetting that those damned county office doors were too heavy to generate a good, old-fashioned, Bette Davis–style slam. I was surprised how the whole incident had shaken me. I was trembling so hard I could barely light a cigarette.

Finally, a knock. It was Chris. He'd been elected to talk me down. But I held firm.

All the way to court, Brian was still ticking off the reasons why Ito should be forced to recuse himself. I knew the rationale, but to me the issue still boiled down to two things: the necessity to finish this trial, and my feeling that Lance's career could be ruined. I had not signed the letter demanding recusal, but as lead prosecutor I was the one who would have to present it. My head was bursting, trying to figure out a way to finesse this.

By now, word of the letter had spread through the courthouse. Johnnie, terrified at the prospect of losing Ito, raced to the podium and began to babble, "The prosecution claims now you're totally recused on this. . . . It's bye-bye forever. We resist that. It's not our understanding."

I explained that the prosecution's decision was only tentative, but that "it would appear, based on consultation with everyone, that the only road to take is"—I faltered—"to proceed with complete recusal from this point forward."

I had become used to my words being greeted at the bench by condescension. Not today. Lance appeared to be holding back tears.

"You sure you want to do this?" he asked with uncharacteristic humility.

The moment was uncomfortably intimate. Lance and I looked at each other for what seemed like a long time. Finally, I spoke.

"I want an opportunity to talk further with [my colleagues] before we adopt this course and it gets set in stone. If we have the time tonight to do it, I would appreciate it and present the court with the final position in writing."

I could tell by his expression that he understood what I was saying. That I was going to fight this. That I would fix it for him.

"All right," he said.

I headed straight to Gil's office, ready for battle. I was amazed by what awaited me. Like a sudden cloudburst, their mood had passed. Now it was as if the skies had been sunny all along. I suspect that was due to the tempering influence of Gil's lieutenant, Frank Sundstedt. But I'll never know.

"Recusal makes no sense," I heard Frank saying. "I think we can leave it with Lance—he'll be at least as fair as any other judge, and he knows the case."

Everyone was nodding. I felt once again like I'd stepped through the looking glass. I was too shocked to feel relief. All I knew was that this trial would continue. For better or worse.

The following morning in court, I withdrew our request for Lance Ito's recusal. And, I added, we wanted him to rule on the admissibility of the tapes in their entirety. Meaning, "Lance, you do it all. We have faith in you." I crossed my fingers and prayed that this gamble would work. A flash of gratitude passed across Lance's face. He looked like a man who'd just been granted a stay of execution.

I was drained. But I had to pull myself together. We still had to finish the motion on the Fuhrman tapes. I tried, but by the end of the day I was shivering with another bout of fever. It was all I could do to make it home. We had Thursday off. I collapsed into bed, shaking with chills. I spent part of that day and the next in bed with a 102-degree fever while Cheri and Bill finished the brief.

I told the kids, "Mommy's sick. Let's watch a movie together, okay?"

We retreated to the "playroom" (which had once called itself a dining room) and for the rest of the day I sat bundled in blankets in a beanbag chair, surrounded by action figures, toy helicopters, two bulldozers, and a cement truck. And we watched *Pete's Dragon*. Over and over again.

What would Ito do about the Fuhrman tapes? We were arguing that not only shouldn't the jurors hear them, but that the tapes shouldn't be aired in court at all. It was an open secret that the jurors learned a lot about what happened outside their presence through phone calls and conjugal visits. One thing was certain. If those tapes were played publicly, the jurors would hear all about them. The reasonable thing for Lance to have done was make his own judgment on the tapes, ruling on what was relevant and keeping the rest of the tapes where they belonged: under seal.

No such luck.

"I am persuaded that this is an issue of national concern, one in which the public has a right to be informed," he proclaimed. "In that light, I will play the tapes as a service to the public."

A matter of national concern? This was a double homicide, not Watergate. There was neither a legal reason nor a logical reason for this. Not only was it doubtful that those tapes would provide an edifying civics lesson to the public in general, but also they sure as hell would prejudice our jury beyond redemption. *Didn't Lance understand that?* Maybe, I thought surly, we *should* have blown him off while we had the chance.

August 29, 1995, was the worst day I ever spent in a court of law. That was the date the Fuhrman tapes were played. I sat mortified as those ugly words washed through the courtroom like a tide of sewage.

"Nigger." God, I despise that word. Every time we heard Fuhrman utter it I felt more and more degraded. Seeing those smug, self-congratulatory expressions at the defense table made it all the worse.

I couldn't breathe. I couldn't move. I felt as though I'd had weights attached to my hands and feet. I looked over at Chris and realized that he was in even more misery than I. I just closed my eyes and prayed for the strength to get through this.

This trial is over, I thought. *We'll never recover.*

But as Fuhrman's clipped, arrogant cadences faded, I felt my back stiffen almost involuntarily with a surge of resolve. *Get off the damned floor, Clark!*

Behind me sat the families of two people murdered by the real defendant in this case. His guilt—that's what we were here to prove.

Yes, Mark Fuhrman had spoken like a racist. But the issue at hand was whether he had planted evidence. He had not.

The defense had proved that Fuhrman was scum—but I could prove that their client was a murderer. Fuhrman could not be allowed to overwhelm Simpson. These two horrible deaths could not go unpunished.

"I am Marcia Clark, the prosecutor," I reminded the court. "And I stand before you today not in defense of Mark Fuhrman but in defense of a case. A case of such overwhelming magnitude in terms of . . . the proof of the defendant's guilt that it would be [a] travesty to allow such a case to be derailed."

As I spoke, I felt detached from the world around me. It was like I'd entered some outside-the-body zone where the only thing I could do was to repeat a silent prayer: *Don't do it, Lance. Don't let the jury hear this.*

"The point that I make [is] that this is a murder trial," I continued. "A murder trial where none of this is relevant. This is not the forum. This is not the forum."

I told the court about a political cartoon I'd seen several days before. It showed a child watching television—the Simpson trial.

"What's the forbidden N-word, Mommy?" asked the little girl.

The mother answered, "Nicole."

The following day, Ito handed down his ruling. It was a victory, I guess. Though he would allow the defense to bring out the number of times Fuhrman said the N-word, he allowed only two brief, relatively innocuous excerpts of Mark actually saying it. Using more, he ruled, would be "overwhelmingly outweighed by the danger of undue prejudice."

This news seemed to leave the defense team in shock. Johnnie hastily called a press conference. With his colleagues on the defense team, he marched outside to the massed media, faced the cameras, and gave his personal verdict on Lance Ito and the system in general. "This inexplicable, indefensible ruling lends credence to all those who say the criminal-justice system is corrupt," he charged. "The cover-up continues."

For weeks now, my own relationship with Johnnie had been icy. His disregard for fairness—his flouting of the law itself—had disgusted me. I guess he knew that, but his mind was focused elsewhere. He still approached the trial with his typical intense energy, but there was no more banter, no willingness to step back and acknowledge the humanity of all those in the courtroom. Now he was carried away with righteous fury. I could almost see the smoke coming out of his ears.

Now, after his shocking press conference, I was less angry than disappointed. Johnnie was once a respected lawyer. Now he was a wild man. Going on national television to call a judge corrupt? That should be grounds for a report to the state bar and a contempt citation. What appalled me even more was how irresponsible and self-centered his actions were. Johnnie's comments seemed deliberately aimed at inciting a goddamned riot. *You don't need to do that, Johnnie,* I told myself. *You're already winning.*

Three whole days passed before Ito responded to the press conference. And even then, he might have ignored it, had Johnnie not forced the issue by resisting an innocuous request from the bench.

"I resent that tone," Johnnie replied petulantly. "I am a man just like you are, Your Honor. I resent that tone. . . ."

The last vestiges of decorum in this courtroom had vanished. I'd hoped that this direct challenge, along with Johnnie's disrespectful public remarks, would force Ito into taking action. No judge worthy of his robes would allow Johnnie's behavior to go unpunished.

Ito ordered us into chambers.

"I have chosen up to this point to ignore your press conference last Thursday and what I consider to be in direct contempt of this court. . . ." he said. "And I want you to know that I have chosen to ignore it thus far and this is because of our long relationship and what I hope will be our continuing friendship."

The penalty? A few of Ito's "deep breaths."

I stared in disbelief. What could he be thinking? Johnnie was not his friend. Never was and never would be. *You've been his patsy through this whole case, Lance—and he's made a fool of you.*

Now that the defense had Fuhrman on the ropes, they went for the final knockout, demanding his reappearance in court. But not before calling Kathleen Bell and a string of other witnesses to attest that Fuhrman had spouted racist remarks in their presence.

Our plan? Dispatch these witnesses with the briefest of questioning. Why bother to impeach these people, with their vague stories of Fuhrman in a marine recruiting office years ago? After the tapes, it was all spilt milk. The one exception to our hurry-up-and-get-'em-out strategy came the day Laura Hart McKinny testified. Chris could not contain himself and went after her with a misplaced vengeance.

Fuhrman's appearance, however, could not be glossed over. Ito had ruled, as we had asked, that he would be called to testify out of the jury's presence. The prospect of Mark's reemergence was generating even more hype than his celebrated cross by Bailey.

By now, we were no longer speaking to him. We remained in suspense until nearly the last minute—would he invoke the Fifth Amendment? I had mixed feelings about this. Part of me wanted him to speak out—to admit he'd lied about the racial slurs, and to reassert the truth that he'd never planted evidence.

The other part of me just wanted him out of my life.

Legally speaking, I didn't think he had to invoke the right against self-incrimination. For Fuhrman to be convicted of perjury, the lie had to be material to the case—and, as I had argued until my voice ran out, all this garbage was utterly *im*material to the matter involving two people murdered in cold blood on Bundy Drive. Still, any lawyer worth his retainer would have advised Fuhrman not to talk, because anything he did say could be used against him if charges were brought. (Eventually, of course, the state attorney general would bring perjury charges, and Mark would plead "No contest.")

For us, however, his taking the Fifth would be a disaster. When you take the Fifth, you can't answer *any* questions. If you do, you've waived your right against self-incrimination. So if you invoke it once, you have to keep invoking it. If he didn't answer questions about his testimony concerning racial epithets, Fuhrman could no longer affirm that the rest of what he'd said under oath was still accurate.

As much as I dreaded Fuhrman's appearance, I knew that Chris dreaded it more. He'd despised Mark from the start, and their hatred for each other had only gotten more personal.

"I don't want to be in the same room with the motherfucker," he told me when I asked if he was coming to the hearing.

Chris and the black law clerks stayed on the eighteenth floor. I went down alone.

I consoled myself with two thoughts. One, the jury wasn't present. Two, I wouldn't have to do anything. Fuhrman was the defense's witness now.

Fuhrman entered with his bodyguards. I sensed, rather than saw, him stride past me to the stand. For reasons still unknown to me, the defense picked Gerald Uelmen to do the questioning. Perhaps they thought assigning a dirty detail like this to an academic would sanitize it.

"Detective Fuhrman, was the testimony that you gave at the preliminary hearing in this case completely truthful?"

There was a deadly pause during which Mark leaned back and whispered something to his lawyer. Then he spoke into the microphone. "I wish to assert my Fifth Amendment privilege," he said.

"Have you ever falsified a police report?"

"I wish to assert my Fifth Amendment privilege."

I forced myself to raise my head and look at him. He was no longer the composed, confident Mark Fuhrman who had parried the thrusts of Lee Bailey. Nor was he the swaggering goon of the McKinny tapes. His face was pained, his features fixed in a tight-lipped grimace that seemed to push everything to a point in the middle of his face. He looked as though he was holding back tears.

Uelmen finally asked him if he intended to assert the Fifth Amendment privilege to every question.

Yes, Mark said. He did.

So far, this was the lawyerly thing to do: ask a couple of questions, show the court that the witness won't answer, and then wrap it up with the catch-all—"Do you intend to invoke as to all the questions?"—to demonstrate that continuing was fruitless. For a moment, I thought Uelmen might stop here. His job done, it appeared that he might be returning to his seat. But just then, Johnnie jumped up and began whispering heatedly to him. I stiffened in my chair. Something nasty was going to happen.

Uelmen turned back toward the podium.

"I only have one more question, Your Honor."

We'd already heard that no more answers would be forthcoming. Ito should have instructed Uelmen to sit down. Instead, Lance asked him what it was. But Uelmen, apparently pumped up by Johnnie, turned directly to Mark.

"Detective Fuhrman," he asked, "did you plant or manufacture any evidence in this case?"

Like an automaton, Fuhrman answered.

"I assert my Fifth Amendment privilege."

Uelmen's gambit was legally wrong, but worse, it was morally reprehensible. He could have asked Mark, "Did you kill Nicole Brown and Ron Goldman, Detective Fuhrman? Did you kill JFK, too?" Fuhrman would have had to answer, "I assert my Fifth Amendment privilege." It was grandstanding—pure and simple. I objected angrily, charging that the question "does nothing but headline," and demanded that the court strike it. But Ito overruled me.

More appalling still was the hero's welcome that the Dream Team gave to Uelmen when he returned to the table. They clapped him on the back. *Great job, guy.* As much as I despised Mark Fuhrman that day, I thought Uelmen brought no distinction upon himself—as a lawyer or a human—by kicking a man at his lowest point.

Later that day, I heard from one of the D.A. investigators guarding Mark. When they were on their way back to the hotel, the radio was on with the story of Fuhrman's day in court. In the backseat, Mark was crying.

All of this occurred outside the jury's presence, but of course that didn't matter. They'd hear about it. Whatever involuntary spasm of pity I'd felt for Fuhrman, I felt a whole lot worse for my team, for the public, and, above all, for the families of the victims. Up in the foyer of the War Room, Kim Goldman was sobbing her heart out. "Why did he do this?" she cried. "I want to tell that son of a bitch off! How could he do this to us?"

Only one more Fuhrman issue was left outstanding: what, if anything, would the jury be allowed to learn officially about his failure to reappear as a witness? Ito correctly ruled that the jury would not be informed that Fuhrman had invoked the Fifth. But the defense was asking that he instruct the jury, when evaluating Fuhrman's integrity, to consider his unavailability for future questioning. And Ito allowed it!

For me, this was the final straw. Ito's ruling was a direct violation of the Constitution, which states you can't sanction anyone for taking the Fifth. If the ruling stood, the jury could reasonably assume that *all* of Mark's testimony was bogus—and more easily accept the conspiracy theory the defense thrust in their faces day after day. I was prepared to fight like an alley cat for this one. I told Ito that I would be taking the matter over his head. I was going to file a writ with the Court of Appeals and try to get him overruled.

Ito was livid with anger. Whatever fragile truce had existed between us after the recusal incident was now broken. But I really didn't care. Seven months earlier, when he issued his disastrous ruling on allowing the N-word in, I'd agonized over whether to try and get him overruled on appeal. I'd decided against it, so as not to prejudice him hopelessly against our side.

I'd been wrong. He'd shafted us anyway. And I'd forgone a shot—admittedly a long shot—at keeping the trial on track. To this day, my personal failure of nerve in not appealing the N-word from the start remains my single biggest regret. I would not compound my error by repeating it.

Ito at first tried to tell me I had only an hour to file my writ, but then backed down and gave me the night. Cheri and our appellate division lawyers worked like crazy to get it done, though I knew it had very little chance of succeeding. In fact, no one in our office could remember the Court of Appeals upholding such a protest in the middle of a trial. The pundits, print and broadcast, thought I'd lost my mind. Even my colleagues thought I was crazy. They all predicted I'd get what's known as a postcard denial—a flat-out no, without the dignity of an opinion. But to me this ruling was so wrong that I had to appeal. Anyway, it was clear that we had nothing to lose in our relationship with Lance Ito.

The next day, I had run an errand during lunch break. About one o'clock or so a TV reporter came tearing up to me.

"Marcia," he cried, "Ito's order was overturned on appeal!"

I was stunned. Within minutes camera crews from NBC and ABC, all of whom had apparently been tracking me, had me surrounded, asking for my reaction.

It was the happiest day I'd had in a very long time. Not only because of the success of the appeal. A few minutes later I was grabbing a bite to eat in a restaurant when my pager went off. It was Judy, my divorce lawyer. I had asked for a gag order. It had been granted, then appealed.

"Marcia," Judy said.

I braced myself for the worst.

"They denied the appeal."

This piece of news gave me even more joy than winning the Ito writ.

It was like winning the lottery.

CAR TAPE. *September 8. Going back to court after the writ, Lance looked like somebody had run him over with a steamroller. It was a Pyrrhic victory. But it just kind of feels good to have him taught a lesson. Man, he hates me. It's a good thing the trial's almost over, because I can see what's going to happen here—he's going to kick the shit out of us on rebuttal, prevent us from getting evidence in any chance he can. He's already thrown the trial to them, so it probably doesn't matter. We'll do our best with what we've got.*

Before prosecution and defense could rest, the defendant, O. J. Simpson, had to waive his right to testify. I do believe that right up until the McKinny tapes surfaced, Simpson had intended to take the stand. But after that windfall of racial obscenity from the mouth of Mark Fuhrman, Simpson had to know that juror sympathy was running so profoundly in his favor, testifying wasn't worth the risk.

The waiver should have been a simple matter. All it required was for Simpson to affirm, with a simple yes, that he understood he was waiving his right. End of story. Instead Johnnie pops up with, "Mr. Simpson would like to make a brief statement regarding that waiver, if the court pleases."

A statement? Since when does the defendant get to make speeches without exposing himself to cross-examination? There wasn't much energy left in me by then, but I was up like a shot, objecting.

"This is a very obvious attempt by the defense to again get material admitted through conjugal visits and phone calls that has not been admitted in court. . . ." I warned. "It is inappropriate and it is done very deliberately by the defense for a clear purpose."

Ito seemed to be considering this possibility for the first time. I was desperate to reach him. And so I said something I'd never thought I'd be brought low enough to say in a court of law.

"Please, don't do this, Your Honor. I beg you. I *beg* you."

All I was asking of Ito was that he make the easiest call he'd ever have to make from the bench. Giving a defendant an opportunity to explain himself—without exposing himself to the rigors of cross-examination—is simply not done. Doing it over the objection of the prosecution is even more outrageous. I doubt that any judge in the history of American jurisprudence has ever made such a gaffe.

But the next thing I knew, without even ruling on my objection, Lance had turned his attention to the defendant.

"Mr. Simpson," he said genially. "Good morning."

Simpson stood.

"As much as I would like to address some of the misrespresentations made [about] myself and my—and Nicole concerning our life together, I am mindful of the mood and stamina of this jury. I have confidence, a lot more, it seems than Miss Clark has of their integrity."

He cast a sideways glance in my direction.

"And that they will find," he continued, "as the record stands now that I did not, could not, and would not have committed that crime."

This was *exactly* the sort of statement that a defendant cannot be allowed to make without having to face cross-examination. At this point Ito realized how serious was the blunder he had just committed. His face fell almost to his laptop computer. I tried to catch his eye in recrimination. But like everyone else in the courtroom, and the country, he was watching Simpson with fascination. Even now, he was somehow loath to interrupt. Only when Simpson began blathering about his children did Ito muster the gumption to try and shut him up. But Simpson rushed in his last words: "I want this trial over." And he sat down.

In the course of that performance, he had not even bothered to mention the fact that he was waiving his right to testify.

I was fairly choking with fury.

"Since he would like to make these statements in court," I raged, "I would like the opportunity to examine him about them. May he take a seat in the blue chair and we will have a discussion."

Lance never responded to my objection. In fact, he ignored me. All he said was "Thank you."

Johnnie held a press conference afterward, shrugging off my objections. "We're not worried about angering Miss Clark," he gloated. He insisted that his client's comments were unscripted and from the heart. He was lying. According to *American Tragedy*, the book published more than a year and a half later by Simpson's *I Want to Tell You* co-author, Larry Schiller, on September 8 Johnnie Cochran, Robert Kardashian, and Robert Shapiro helped Simpson draft the "waiver" speech. Simpson spent the next two weeks refining and rehearsing it.

The fact that they could conceive of a judge letting them get away with that was remarkable. The fact that they succeeded was not remarkable in the least.

Soul Survivor

CAR TAPE. *It's Monday, September 18. We started working on closing argument in earnest this weekend and Chris and I had a huge fight. I think it's primarily because he wants to take a big role in the closing argument, but he's also afraid to because he doesn't know the case that well. . . .*

Originally, I'd intended to do the closing all by myself. I knew this case better than anyone else. On the other hand, I knew the task ahead was awesome. I had to distill the more than 40,000 pages of testimony into a swift, eloquent, compelling argument that would show that the evidence in the case pointed to Orenthal James Simpson, and to him alone. Which, of course, it did. But would this hostile jury ever see that?

The elements of that argument were threefold: opportunity; identity; motive. Opportunity presented no problem. Here was O. J. Simpson, a man whose face was recognized everywhere he went, who had no one to document his whereabouts for what we now computed as seventy-seven minutes, the exact period during which Nicole Brown and Ron Goldman were murdered. Identity was also a lock.

We had identified O. J. Simpson six ways from Sunday as the man whose blood was at the murder scene—*and* in the Bronco *and* on the bloody Rockingham glove, where it was mixed with the blood of his victims.

As I've said, the prosecution never needs to prove that the defendant had motive, only intent. It is usually useful, however, to suggest to a jury why the defendant might have gone so far as to slit another human being's throat. The motive for this particular murder was sexual rage. And I felt that now, in our final moments, we were compelled to pull this jury's nose flat up against the truth. O. J. Simpson was a sadist who'd terrorized his wife for years—until she'd finally stood up to him and paid for it with her life.

Chris wanted to put on the DV. That was understandable—it was his baby. The problem was, he also wanted to argue premeditation. I didn't want him to. Arguing premeditation required a command of both law and the particulars of the coroner's findings. The manner in which someone is killed is one of the primary ways to show premeditation. The more elaborate the attack, the more successfully you can argue it was a premeditated murder. I didn't feel Chris had paid close enough attention to the coroner's testimony to explain how it proved premeditation. I didn't know if he could get up to speed on the law. So he and I went back and forth, back and forth, back and forth.

That's how it was between Chris and me. Always. We were like siblings: close, loyal to the end, but inclined to squabble. Toward the end of the trial we both said and did things we didn't mean, only because we were so strung out on stress. I must say that during these, some of my darkest hours, I felt a gentle hand at my elbow. It was Bill Hodgman come once again to my rescue. Bill knew I hadn't the reserves to waste on infighting. Patiently, tactfully, he drew Chris aside to try and bring him up to speed.

The reports I got back from Bill weren't good. Chris wasn't getting it. There just wasn't enough time. Finally he realized that and gave up the fight.

I was relieved. Chris would argue the domestic violence, but I would take premeditation. Once the program was set, nobody blinked, no one looked back. We charged ahead full-throttle toward closing arguments.

*   *   *

One screwball rumor making its rounds after the trial was that I had thrown my argument together at the last moment. "Crammed like a college kid," I believe, was the expression. Nothing could be further from the truth. In the broadest sense, I had been preparing for my closing for nearly fourteen months. I've had a system that has served me well lo these fourteen years as a prosecutor. From the moment I catch a case, I start an accordion file labeled "Closing Argument Ideas." I stash away clippings in it; also magazine photos and newspaper columns. Sometimes I'll wake up in the middle of the night with an idea, scribble a note, and next day, stick it into the file. When the juror questionnaires come in, I'll look through them to see if there are any expressions, buzzwords, or sentiments they seem fond of. Anything like that goes into the file.

The Simpson case was no exception. My county-issue accordion file had overflowed to a second, then a third.

Everyone was working hard. For several weeks before closing arguments were set to begin, the entire staff had been holding brainstorming sessions in the conference room next to Gil's office. Hank would unroll a scroll of butcher paper on the long granite table and print on it our topics: "Contamination," "Planting," "DNA," and so on. Over the course of a workday, deputies would drift in, add their two cents, then drift out again. By the end, we had over 150 entries pointing to guilt. It was too much for a summation, so we boiled it down to eight key pieces of evidence—each of which had an irrefutable connection to O. J. Simpson:

The knit cap.
Ron Goldman's shirt.
The shoe prints up the Bundy walk.
The droplets of blood leading from Bundy.
The blood in the Bronco.
The Rockingham blood trail.
The Rockingham glove.
The socks found at the foot of Simpson's bed.

We'd originally included the Bundy glove as well, but it had less significant blood, hair, and fibers. Ultimately, we left it out. It didn't add to proof of guilt.

(One episode of the civil trial that gave me a chuckle was when the defense tried to suggest that the Bundy glove had been switched for a ringer. This, like so many other "stunning developments," led to nothing, of course. But I thought to myself, "If you were going to switch a piece of evidence, why not pick one that was incriminating?")

CAR TAPE. *Our genius Judge Ito . . . has preplanned a trip up north for Friday and Monday the twenty-ninth and October second. And he will not cancel for anything or anyone. Instead, he prefers to be going to night sessions after dinner, arguing 7 to 9. . . . That's ridiculous—we argue to a jury that's half asleep? God, you know, Ito would rather inconvenience the whole fucking world than himself for one day.*

I stumbled awake on September 26, the morning of closing arguments. After splashing water in my face, I caught sight of myself in the mirror. I looked skeletal; the circles under my eyes were the color of eggplants. What's more, I had a flaming pain in my lower right jaw. I've had dental problems all my life and this particular discomfort left no doubt as to its cause: an abscessed tooth. A trip to the dentist was out of the question. You do not call in sick when you are scheduled to give the closing argument in the Trial of the Century.

I almost never rehearse my arguments. Sometimes I'll read them aloud to a friend. But I don't memorize them. I don't want them to sound rehearsed, or insincere. Instead, I'll commit the main points to memory and speak from the heart. And that is what I did the morning of my summation in the trial of *People v. Orenthal James Simpson*.

"Good morning, ladies and gentlemen," I greeted them.

"Good morning," they replied in unison. They were looking more cheerful than usual. I'm sure it was because they knew their ordeal was nearing an end.

Straight out of the gate I wanted to make good on my obligation to tell the jury what I thought of Mark Fuhrman. It was part of the pact I'd made with myself the day before I'd interviewed him back in March. If I didn't believe his testimony, I would tell the jury that. And so I did.

"It would be completely understandable," I told them, "if you were to feel angry and disgusted with Mark Fuhrman. As we all are . . . Did he lie when he testified here in this courtroom saying that he did not use racial epithets in the last ten years? Yes. Is he a racist? Yes. Is he the worst [the] LAPD has to offer? Yes . . .

"But the fact that Mark Fuhrman is a racist and lied about it on the witness stand does not mean that we haven't proven the defendant guilty beyond a reasonable doubt."

Then I fulfilled the second part of the pact. I told the jury what Mark Fuhrman had done right. I showed them how impossible it would have been for him to plant evidence—which was, after all, the only thing about Mark Fuhrman that mattered to the case.

Then, for the last time, I walked that jury right through what had happened the night of June 12, 1994.

"The defendant came back from Bundy in a hurry. Ron Goldman upset his plans and things took a little longer than anticipated. He ran back behind the house, that dark, narrow south pathway—you all saw it. You were there in daytime. But imagine how dark it is at night—that dark, narrow south pathway, thinking he could get rid of the glove, the knife, in that dirt area in the back . . .

"But he was in a hurry. He was moving quickly down a dark narrow pathway overhung with trees, strewn with leaves, and in his haste he ran right into that air conditioner. . . . And [that] caused him to fall against the wall, making the wall of Kato's room shake. . . . And it was just as simple as that. Simple common sense tells you that the thumping, the glove and the defendant's appearance on the driveway almost immediately thereafter are all part of one set of events, all connected in time and space. You don't need science to tell you that; you just need reason and logic."

I produced the time line showing the clear connection between the thumps and Simpson's appearance. Johnnie objected, claiming that there had been no testimony to establish that Park had seen Simpson just two minutes after the thumps, but he was promptly and properly overruled. The evidence had shown just that.

"Now, let me ask you this," I continued. "Why didn't the defendant let Allan Park drive into the driveway? Why leave him sitting out there at the gate? Why make him wait outside? Because the defendant was frazzled, ladies and gentlemen, he was hurried, and he needed to buy some time. Time to wash himself up, wash off the blood, change the clothes, and to compose himself to appear normal, to appear business as usual. . . . But there are certain things . . . that tell you that it most certainly was not *business as usual* on the night of June twelfth after he murdered Ron and Nicole. . . ."

There was Simpson's forgetting to set the house alarm after Kato told him about the thumping. Simpson's lying to Allan Park about having overslept. Simpson's leaving blood in the bathroom and in the foyer, leaving his socks on the floor. (We had heard testimony that Simpson was a compulsively tidy man.)

It was definitely not business as usual, I told the jury, when Simpson had complained of being hot and sweaty on a cool night. Unlike the other passengers on the red-eye, he didn't sleep, even though he'd been up at six A.M. for an early golf game. One passenger noticed he wore no socks.

I spent quite a bit of time talking about the cuts on the defendant's left hand. Here, I told the jury, we have the defendant cutting his left hand on the very night of his wife's stabbing. A cut on the *left* hand— which happened to be the hand that the killer cut. "That," I pointed out, was "an alarming coincidence."

If it was true that O. J. Simpson cut his hand on a broken glass in Chicago, why was there no blood on the glass? Why was there no blood in the sink?

"It shows an effort to conceal a wound that he knows will be highly incriminating. This act shows consciousness of guilt. . . ."

I ridiculed the defense's theory that evidence had been contaminated. Remember the compelling testimony of Dr. Robin Cotton, I urged. "When DNA degrades . . . it doesn't turn into someone else's type. You get no result." You don't get a set of results that all point to one suspect. Only one person in 57 *billion* could have left that blood at Bundy. That's about as absolute as you can get.

"The wealth of evidence in this case is simply overwhelming," I said, winding to a close. "If we only had the Bundy blood trail that matched the defendant, it would be enough proof to find him guilty beyond a reasonable doubt. If we only had Nicole Brown's blood on his socks, that would be enough to prove him guilty beyond a reasonable doubt. If we only had Ron Goldman's blood in his Bronco, that would be enough to prove him guilty beyond a reasonable doubt. . . . But we have all that and much more."

I had spoken for six hours. I returned unsteadily to my seat. I was dizzy. My jaw ached.

Chris wrote a note and pushed it over to me. "That was brilliant."

I looked back at him and smiled. It was the most warmth we had shared in weeks.

Ito had decreed that during summations we would go into evening sessions, so it was nearly seven o'clock before Chris rose to speak. If he'd been drained by the strain of waiting, he didn't show it. Very calmly, dramatically, he pointed a finger at the defendant.

"The killing was personal," he told the jury. "You look at the domestic violence, the manner of the killing, the physical evidence, the history of abuse and their relationship, the intimidation, the stalking. You look at it and it all points to him. It all points to him."

Once again, he traced the violence between the Simpsons from 1985 through 1989, and likened it to a burning fuse. "We submit to you that the hand that left [an] imprint [on Nicole's] neck five years ago is the same hand that cut that same throat . . . on June twelfth, 1994. It was the defendant. It was the defendant then. It's the defendant now."

Chris had done good work during hours of closed-door sessions with Scott Gordon and Gavin de Becker. His message and delivery were powerfully sincere. Now, as I watched him, I was reminded of why I'd brought him on board in the first place. Chris Darden was smart; he was tough; and, above all, he was principled. I remembered why I'd been proud to call him my partner.

*   *   *

Over the past nine months, I'd been annoyed repeatedly by the transparent—and, in my opinion, amoral—ploys on the part of the defense to manipulate the jury. Johnnie Cochran had come in for a fair share of my anger. And yet my harsh feelings toward him were always tempered by the realization that for most of his career Johnnie had actually stood for something. He'd seen young black men shaken down and roughed up by cops and he'd felt a righteous outrage. He'd dedicated his career to waking the system up and making it play fair. Crying "racism" in virtually every case where he had a black defendant was his stock-in-trade. It was often disingenuous. But you could argue that it was done in the service of principle.

When on September 27 Johnnie rose to give a summation that would last for parts of two days, he cast principle to the wind.

After complimenting the twelve for being a "truly marvelous jury," he bestowed upon them the blessing in absentia of Abraham Lincoln who'd proclaimed that "service is the highest act of citizenship." He then invoked Frederick Douglass, exalting the ideal of "no white, no black, but common country, common citizenship, equal rights, and a common destiny."

Having intoned those lofty sentiments, Johnnie launched into a harangue of hatred against the "messengers" of the state. He flew at Fuhrman's throat, labeling him a "genocidal racist"—one who had lain in wait nine years for an opportunity to frame O. J. Simpson. Then, through the alchemy of rhetoric, Johnnie fused Fuhrman and Vannatter. They became, progressively, the "Twins of Deception," the "Twin Demons of Evil," and finally the "Twin Devils of Deception."

"There was another man, not too long ago, who had those same views, who wanted to burn people," Johnnie said. "This man, this scourge, became one of the worst people in the history of the world. Adolf Hitler."

Hitler? I was nearly breathless with outrage. When Johnnie took the floor that morning, could he really have intended to say these things?

(I later learned this was no heat-of-the-moment excess. This atrocity had been scripted for Johnnie by a fellow defense attorney who was informally assisting the Dream Team. The ghostwriter, I was appalled to discover, was Jewish.)

To have been driven to this excess, Johnnie had to feel desperate. He and his whole crew, in fact, had to be scared to death that the jury might, just for one moment, come to their senses and listen to the evidence. If they did, of course, they would have no choice but to convict. Instead, Johnnie showed them a face-saving detour around the truth. A shortcut that would leave them with the illusion that they were upholding justice.

"Your verdict," he told that mostly African-American jury, "will go far beyond the walls of [this courtroom]. Your verdict talks about justice in America and it talks about the police and whether they should be above the law. . . . Maybe that's why you were selected. There's [someone] in your background . . . that helps you understand that this is wrong. . . . Maybe you're the right people, at the right time, at the right place to say, 'No more—we're not going to have this.' "

Johnnie was asking for the jury to deliver a big "Screw you." It's called "jury nullification." It's not legal. It's not allowed. But it's not necessarily evil. Jury nullification can sometimes serve a greater good. The example most often given is that of Northern juries who, during the days before the Civil War, refused to sentence fugitive slaves to death. Jurors on these cases often acted with courage, flying in the face of bad law by voting to acquit.

But there was no such exalted legal or social issue at stake here. Johnnie Cochran was exhorting this jury to turn its back on perfectly good laws in order to free his client. And who was his client? Not some fugitive from oppression. His client was a homicidal narcissist, a man who, for the entire span of his overrated career, stood for nothing but his own self-aggrandizement. His client was a man who lived by no creed except to pursue his own infantile impulses. His client was a black man who had done nothing to further the welfare of his black brothers and black sisters and had, in fact, turned his back on them.

This put me in a bind. If I objected, it would look to the jury—at least *this* jury—like the prosecution was trying to stifle a plea for justice. And that impression would only be reinforced if my objection was sustained. (Later, out of the presence of the jury, I did protest the call for nullification.) The fact of the matter, however, is that it's the job of the judge in a situation like this to step in and object on his own motion. His is the only action powerful enough to scotch such a plea. But Ito stood passively by while Johnnie turned that jury into a mob.

And I thought, *Shouldn't your ideals, Johnnie, have brought you to a better place than this?*

I also thought, *My jaw is killing me, and I'm about to pass out.*

Johnnie spoke for two days, followed by Barry Scheck. Upstairs in our office, a platoon of D.A.s and law clerks remained stationed at television sets, taking notes. I'd given orders that I wanted a complete inventory of every distortion, misrepresentation, half-truth, and outright lie that came out of the defense's performance.

I had intended to oversee the business of parceling out the list for rebuttal after we broke for the day. But by the time I got off the elevator on the eighteenth floor, I was beyond coherent thought. The pain radiating through my skull was blinding.

Hank Goldberg pulled me aside.

"Marcia," he said, "maybe we should ask Ito for a continuance. I think the fact that our lead prosecutor needs dental surgery is plenty good cause."

Hank, I knew, was worried about me. I'm also sure he was concerned about what kind of performance I'd put in during rebuttal the next day. But I knew we couldn't hold off. I didn't want the jury back there cogitating on the swill they'd just heard from Cochran and Scheck.

I had to get rid of this problem fast. The mirror in the women's restroom showed an angry, inflamed lump on my lower gum. For a moment I even considered trying to lance it myself with a needle. Cheri was appalled.

"Who do you think you are?" she screeched. "Gordon-fucking-Liddy?"

Cheri quickly found a dentist who'd see me right away. Then she and Scott bundled me into her car and drove me to West Hollywood. The dentist and an anesthesiologist were waiting for us. The dentist, a very sweet young guy in his thirties, looked at me and deadpanned, "Don't you know you can't perform surgery without a license, Ms. Clark?"

"I can't be knocked out," I told him. "I've got to go back to work."

"Don't worry about it," he reassured me. "You'll just feel good."

Last thing I remember as I slipped under the anesthetic was the ridiculous image of Johnnie pulling O. J. Simpson's knit cap down over his ears. I heard myself chuckle. But the laughter got fainter and fainter as I tumbled down a tunnel of darkness.

I was under for less than an hour. When I awoke, the pain was gone. Draining the abscess, the dentist explained, had relieved the pressure on the nerves. All I felt was a little tenderness. He gave me a painkiller. But I didn't even need it.

It was close to ten P.M. when we got back to the CCB. Given what I'd just gone through, I felt amazingly clearheaded. Forty-five minutes under anesthesia, as it turned out, had given me a much-needed rest. Dr. Magic was right. I did feel good. I had shut myself in my office, hoping to work quietly for a few hours, when Chris blew in.

"They're getting nothing done in there," he said, motioning to the conference room. "They need Mama."

I found the troops in disarray. Marching to the front of the room, I began to hand out assignments to deputies, to law clerks, to everyone. My minions scurried off to the transcripts, looking for ammo to return fire.

Until then, I'd intended to do the rebuttal by myself. But Johnnie had changed that. "If you can't trust the messengers, watch out for their message," he'd said. He'd insinuated that Chris and I were both, at best, overzealous; at worst, dishonest. We were both part of a nefarious conspiracy that now seemed to involve all county employees right down to the steno pool. Chris and I *both* had to put in an appearance to defend our honor.

This caught Chris unawares. Not only did he have to compile the legal materials, but he had to prepare himself psychologically. He had done a first-rate job on his summation, but asking him to go another round on a moment's notice was expecting an awful lot. I called him into my office.

"If you don't think you can do this," I told him, "I'll understand. I'll never hold it against you."

He smiled, as he did so rarely.

"I'm in."

Chris pulled together an ad hoc team consisting of his law clerk,

Melissa Decker; Scott; Cheri; David Wooden; and Gavin de Becker. The five of them holed up in a hotel room to work on his rebuttal.

Hank, Woody, Rock, and I convened in my office. My vigilant team kept refilling my coffee mug to keep me awake until we had a draft we could live with. Hank left at two A.M. Woody left at 2:30. Rock left at three. I left at 3:30.

As I went to shut down my computer for the night, something flashed on the main menu. My law clerks had posted a message on the screen. It read, "We Love You, Boss."

You save your good stuff for last. And on the morning of Friday, September 29, Christopher Darden gave them the best he had. Chris and I had decided that we might actually use Johnnie's plea for nullification to our advantage; spin it around to remind the jury what this trial was *not* about. So he hit the issue head-on.

"You can't send a message to Fuhrman," he told the jury. "You can't send a message to the LAPD. You can't eradicate racism within the LAPD or the L.A. community or within the nation as a whole by delivering a verdict of 'not guilty.' In a case like this, the evidence is there. You just have to find your way through the smoke."

His message was so eloquent, he should have reached them.

But my heart sank when I saw what was happening—or not happening—in that jury box. The jurors were shifting in their seats, turning their heads, tapping their feet. And this was really scary: Juror Number 98, a fifty-three-year-old postal clerk, one of the three black women who later went on to write a book about the case, was giving Chris a hateful stare. She was sighing and tapping her feet—as if to say, "Shut up and siddown."

And then it was my turn. I would like to say that my mind was clear and my attention sharp. But the truth, tens of millions of Americans might have noticed, was otherwise. I was struggling to maintain my focus. One commentator later described my demeanor as "subdued." I would have described it as simply worn out.

But as I rose to address the twelve, I drew on the last of my depleted reserves to bring this thing to an honorable finish. I had to make each word count. I had a feeling, even then, that this would be the last argument I would ever make in a court of law.

I spoke from my heart.

"I've been doing this a lot of years," I told the jurors quietly. "I started on that side of counsel table," I said, gesturing to the defense. "I know what the ethical obligations are of a prosecutor. . . . I took a cut in pay to join this office because I believe in this job. I believe in doing it fairly and doing it right. And I like the luxury of being a prosecutor because I have the luxury on any case of going to the judge and saying . . . 'Your Honor, dismiss it' . . . I will never ask for a conviction unless . . . the law says I must, unless [the defendant] is proven guilty beyond a reasonable doubt on credible evidence that you can trust. . . . I can never do it otherwise. That is my obligation."

"Improper!" Barry Scheck barked.

Now, a prosecutor is not normally allowed to tell a jury about the ethical obligations of his office and how superior he is to those scoundrels on the defense side. That's called "personal vouching," and it's strictly disallowed. The exception is when the defense has called a prosecutor's integrity into question. Then all bets are off.

Lance knew this. I believe that by this time he was fed up to the gills with the Dream Team. And so he did what he should have done months before. He took control of the courtroom.

"Overruled." He cut Scheck down with a word. For the next two hours that I would speak, the defense would object over fifty times, trying to break my stride. But Lance Ito ran interference for me, overruling them again and again and again.

Before me I had a green binder, three inches thick with misstatements or inconsistencies in the defense's closing arguments. Most of them had to do with claims of evidence having been "contaminated" or "planted." One of the most amazing things to me was that after all the hours spent ragging Dennis Fung and Andrea Mazzola for their sloppiness in the field, Barry Scheck backed off this line during closing argument. He and the defense had now retreated to the position that the so-called contamination had occurred at the hands of Collin Yamauchi in the Evidence Processing Room of the LAPD.

Once again I reminded this jury what a bogus issue this whole business of contamination really was. As Gary Sims had observed, "DNA cannot fly." Nothing in this case could account for the wholly consistent blood results except Simpson's guilt.

It has really bugged me since the trial to hear the pundits say that I didn't spend enough of my closing on debunking the notion of a police conspiracy. This is absolutely untrue. I brought it up over and over and over again. I brought it up, in fact, every time I attacked the premise of "planted" evidence. In fact I brought it up over fifty-three times.

I wanted this jury to see the lengths to which the defense would go to sell their package of contorted and contradictory "planting" theories. There was no more telling example of this, in my estimation, than their attempts to account for the presence of Ronald Goldman's blood on the console of Simpson's Bronco. Of all the blood evidence against O. J. Simpson, this was probably the most damning. There was simply no explanation for it, other than the obvious: when Simpson got into the Bronco after the murders, he dropped his right glove on the console beside him.

As I've said, Dennis Fung had failed to collect all of those samples when he did his first sweep of the vehicle on July 14; we didn't get the rest until September 1. This now left Scheck an opening to contend that they had been planted on the later date. Problem was, photos taken on both dates showed blood spots in absolutely identical configuration. You would have needed a skilled counterfeiter to pull that one off.

So, I pointed out to the jury, the defense had neatly jettisoned that theory and tried another. In this version of reality, O. J. Simpson had reached over the console and bled on it with his left hand—and *then,* on the same spot, Mark Fuhrman wiped the glove bearing the blood of the two victims. That's why all the blood was mixed.

In order to wrap your mind around this theory, you'd have to believe that Fuhrman had filched a glove from Bundy, hidden it in his pocket until he got to Rockingham, slim-jimmed the door of the Bronco, slipped into it unnoticed, and rubbed the bloody glove on the console.

"If you wanted to sell this story in Hollywood," I told that jury, "they wouldn't buy it because it's so incredible."

I continued ticking off absurdities until I got to the bottom line: You could forget the DNA. Even if you put it aside, the People had amassed such an archive of circumstantial evidence that a reasonable juror could vote to convict even if he or she had slept right through the scientific testimony.

"I have one more exhibit I would like to show you," I told the jury. "This is entitled 'Unrefuted Evidence.' And I think that this will bring home to you the power of the evidence in this case."

The Unrefuted Evidence idea was the brainchild of Bill Hodgman. And it was brilliant. Show the jury, in the aggregate, all the strange occurrences, the bizarre coincidences, for which the defense had no explanation whatsoever. The evidence had been arranged in the shape of a pyramid and mounted on a magnetic board. It was so heavy two men had to carry it to the easel.

"This is evidence," I continued, "which has not been contested by any contradictory evidence."

- First of all, opportunity . . . between 9:36* and 10:53, the defendant's whereabouts are unaccounted for. No dispute about that. Nobody's contradicting that.

- Kato Kaelin saw the defendant wearing a dark sweat suit at 9:36. No contradictory testimony about that.

- The defendant tried to call Paula Barbieri on his cell phone from the Bronco at . . . 10:03. There's no contradictory testimony as to that fact.

- Allan Park buzzed the intercom at Rockingham at 10:40, at 10:43, and at 10:49. There was no answer. No testimony contradicts that.

- Kato Kaelin heard the three thumps on his wall at 10:51 or 10:52. That testimony isn't contradicted.

- Allan Park saw the person in dark clothes, six feet, 200 pounds, walk across the driveway at 10:54, walking into the house, testimony that is uncontradicted. Two minutes after the thumps heard by Kato, uncontradicted testimony.

*Times here are more accurate than those given during previous testimony, as they were verified by our investigators using phone records.

- And at 10:55, when Allan Park got out of his limo to go and buzz the defendant, the defendant finally answered. That testimony, ladies and gentlemen, is uncontradicted.

"What this testimony proves," I argued, "is not only that the defendant was not home, but it proves he was not sleeping. And it proves that he lied about it . . . to create an alibi for himself. You don't need to do that unless you've been doing something . . . that you need to hide."

The coincidences were too blatant to ignore. Defendant wears same shoe size as killer. Defendant wears same brand of glove as killer. Killer drops blood to the left of his shoe prints. Defendant has a fresh cut on his left hand immediately after the murders.

Evidence that *all* remained uncontradicted.

Fibers consistent with the Bronco carpet found on the knit cap and the Rockingham glove. Blue-black cotton fiber (presumably from a sweatsuit worn by Simpson) found on Ron Goldman's shirt, Simpson's socks, and the Rockingham glove. Hair consistent with the defendant's found on the knit cap and Ron Goldman's shirt.

All uncontradicted!

Even now, as I think back on that pyramid—that *mountain*—of evidence, it blows my mind. How could anyone fail to see?

The objections from the defense were flying fast and furious. Ito was slapping them down at every turn. I got to the point where I wouldn't even stop and wait for a ruling. I just talked over them. The jurors seemed absolutely riveted. They didn't budge. They never blinked, sighed, or moved a muscle. For once, I felt that they were actually listening.

By now, I was running on fumes. But the end was in sight. And now, at last, I was about to speak to what this case was really about: the two dead human beings for whom we sought justice. I let them guide me through the rest of my rebuttal.

"Usually," I told the jury, "I feel like I'm the only one left to speak for the victims. But in this case, Ron and Nicole are speaking to you. They're speaking to you and they're telling you who murdered them.

"Nicole started to speak before she even died. Remember, back in

1989, she cried to Detective Edwards, 'He's going to kill me. . . .' The children were there.

"In 1990, she made a safe deposit box, put photographs of her beaten face and her haunted look in a safe deposit box along with a will. She was only thirty years old! How many thirty-year-olds [do] you know who do that? A will? A safe deposit box? It's like writing 'In the event of my death.' She knew. . . .

"Nineteen ninety-three, the 911 tape; the children were there. He was screaming . . . she was frightened.

"I think the thing that perhaps was so chilling about her voice is that sound of resignation . . . inevitability. She knew she was going to die.

"And Ron—he speaks to you. [By] struggling so valiantly, he forced his murderer to leave the evidence behind that you might not ordinarily have found. And they both are telling you who did it—with their hair, their clothes, their bodies, their blood. They tell you he did it. He did it. Mr. Simpson. Orenthal Simpson. He did it.

"They told you the only way they can. Will you hear them or will you ignore their plea for justice? Or, as Nicole said to Detective Edwards, 'You never do anything about him.' "

I looked at the faces of my jury.

"Will you?"

I gestured to Jonathan.

For several weeks now, the team had been pulling together a montage, a sort of visual history of this crime. Over the images, we'd decided that we would play the 911 tapes. Although I'd seen bits and pieces of this opus as it was coming together, I didn't feel the full power of it until this morning, when Jonathan hit the "play" button.

You heard "Emergency 911," then the static confusion on the caller's end. The thumps of blows landing on flesh. Then, the more frantic pleas of the 1993 call. "He's O. J. Simpson. I think you know his record. He's fucking going nuts." All the while, on the large screen, we showed the photo of Nicole taken after the beating of 1989. She was lifting her hair to reveal the full extent of the damage to her face. Her eyes were downcast, as if in shame. Then, the photo of her smeared with mud. Cut to the Bundy trail, the knit cap, a close-up of Ron's shirt. Behind those images, O. J. Simpson's voice rose to a peak of rage. Suddenly, the audio stopped, and all that was left was a picture of Nicole's body curled in a pool of blood. We held on that image for thirty seconds in complete silence.

There was sobbing throughout the courtroom. But all I could think was, *It's over.*

Up in the War Room, there were tears of relief. We'd ended strong and we knew it.

I was numb. After 372 grueling days and nearly 48,000 pages of trial transcript entered into the ages, the thought foremost in my mind was *Please, God. No retrial.*

That afternoon the jury picked a forewoman, Number 230, Armanda Cooley. I was encouraged. I wouldn't say that I'd enjoyed rapport with Cooley, but every so often I had gotten a smile from her. She was the best-educated of the jurors, with two years of college to her credit. I harbored private hopes that she was both intelligent enough and neutral enough to keep an open mind to the evidence. That she'd been picked leader of the pack was good news.

The Goldmans took Chris and me, in fact, the whole team, out to the L.A. Athletic Club. Everybody was feeling upbeat. Our reviews were already coming in, and the pundits were saying terrific things about us. The montage was being hailed as a stroke of brilliance. Kim and I held each other and cried over Ron. The D.A. investigators followed me home that night to make sure I wasn't followed by reporters.

That weekend we went to Santa Barbara to take refuge with Lynn Reed. I felt like a convict savoring her first delirious moments of freedom. I took naps. I did a crossword puzzle for the first time in a year.

At that moment, I thought there was some fighting chance that my life had returned to normal. I realize now that I was in denial. I guess in my heart of hearts I realized that the worst still lay ahead.

On Sunday night we got back to L.A., and on Monday I went out shopping with my friend Kathy. Earlier in the morning I had gotten word that the jury had asked for a read-back of Allan Park's testimony.

Everyone at the D.A.'s office was interpreting that as good news for us. If, in fact, Park's testimony was all the jury wanted to hear, they were focusing on key prosecution evidence. If you believed Park's account of that night, you had to believe Simpson was lying. They had been presented with a hundred file drawers of damning evidence against O. J. Simpson. If Allen Park's words were *all* they needed to hear, how could they fail to convict?

But I wasn't sure what to think. One thing I know is that when juries ask for a read-back, it is seldom for the reason you think it is. So I refused to give in to euphoria. As I was sitting in the parking lot with Kathy, my car phone rang. It was Chris. He sounded both anxious and excited.

"The jury has a decision," he said.

"How can that be?" I asked, incredulous. I'd been looking forward to a week off while they deliberated. We'd presented evidence for the better part of a year. What jury could come to an agreement on a case this complicated in *two fucking hours?*

"Stay put," he told me. "Ito won't accept a verdict from them until tomorrow morning at ten."

I didn't have to be told why. No one had anticipated this quick turnaround. Not the LAPD. Not the Sheriff's Department. They had to ramp up security in case the verdict lit a torch to the city.

That evening Chris, Cheri, and I went out to shoot some pool at a little out-of-the-way hall in Glendale. No frills. I loved the place. The first couple of times we'd gone I'd been mobbed. After that the management put me up in their VIP room, where no one would bug me. Chris was in buoyant spirits. Ito had made some comment to him at sidebar. Something to the effect, "Allan Park? You're a lawyer. You read tea leaves."

I said nothing. I can read tea leaves as well as the next guy, and to me the short deliberation meant trouble. All it said to me was that the jury had made up its mind weeks, probably months, before.

The next morning, October 3, I walked out the door intending to take Matt to school and ran smack into a guy with a TV cam on his shoulder. He was filming us! I was already way tweaked about the media, because I'd spoken to Gil the evening before and he'd told me that he'd allowed the placement of cameras all over the eighteenth floor.

"I don't think that's appropriate," I told him. "What if we get a 'not guilty'?"

No one else seemed to be seriously considering that prospect. The pundits were almost unanimously predicting conviction. But I felt uneasy.

"I think one short, dignified press conference where we stand up and talk to everyone jointly is plenty," I reiterated.

But Gil was jazzed. Finally I said, "You guys want to do it, that's fine. But I'm not gonna take part in it."

And now there's a TV camera blocking my driveway.

"How dare you invade my privacy this way?" I yelled at the cameraman. "Can't you see I just want to take my child to school? Here, film *this*." I flipped him off.

By the time I got into the office, the halls were bristling with cameras. I ran the gauntlet to Gil's office. He'd gathered everyone in the conference room. The main topic of discussion seemed to be what to say about the fact that O. J. Simpson had been convicted. If that isn't just asking God to smack you silly, I don't know what is.

I was frankly worried about security. I didn't know what might happen in court today, but I didn't want to be caught in the crossfire. Four D.A. investigators were assigned to take me down the back way to the ninth floor. We arrived only minutes before Johnnie, accompanied by his four bodyguards from the Nation of Islam, filed in. It felt like springtime in Beirut.

The deputies brought Simpson in from lockup. He was wearing a gray suit and a bold yellow tie. His eyes appeared more sunken than usual. No doubt he had spent a long night.

"Counsel," Ito asked us, "is there anything else we need to take up before we invite the jurors to join us?"

No one said a thing.

From the corner of my eye, I watched the jurors file in. I thought I saw a couple of them smile at the defendant.

Lance asked Deirdre to hand the envelope with the verdict forms to a deputy. He walked it over to Armanda Cooley.

"Madam Foreperson," Ito said. His voice sounded strangely small. "Would you please open the envelope and check the condition of the verdict forms?"

Cooley did as instructed. She assured the court that they were signed and in order.

Deirdre faltered a little as she read the defendant's name. Then she regained her composure.

"We the jury . . . find the defendant, Orenthal James Simpson, not guilty of the crime of murder . . . upon Nicole Brown Simpson, a human being . . ."

I'd prepared myself for the worst, but now that the moment had come, I felt pain spreading through my body like I'd been pierced by a thousand tiny needles.

We'd lost.

Deirdre's sweet, sorrowful voice droned on, reading the verdict of "not guilty" in the death of Ronald Goldman.

"My God," I whispered.

Behind us Kim Goldman let out an unearthly howl. I couldn't turn to face the families.

"The defendant," said Judge Lance Ito, "having been acquitted of both charges . . . is ordered . . . released forthwith."

As the jurors filed out of the courtroom, Lon Cryer turned toward the defense table and raised his fist in a power salute.

You sonofabitch.

I don't remember exactly what happened after that. I know that Bob Shapiro walked over to me, looking stunned and disappointed.

"It's not the verdict I would've thought," he admitted. I'm sure he shook my hand. But I have no recollection of the touch. Once again, I seemed surrounded by a vacuum that no one could penetrate.

How can I explain it? The sense of violation, the confusion, the dislocation. I could remember myself having once waded dreamlike into the surf. This time, as I made my way through a sea of photographers, I found myself walking into waves of grief. The War Room was jammed with warriors in defeat. I remember seeing the young law clerks crying. I wanted to tell them, *This doesn't mean anything about the real world and the way justice is dispensed. Or the way it should be dispensed. It won't always be this way. It may never be this way again.*

Ahead lay that excruciating press conference. There, before all the media he'd gathered in anticipation of victory, Gil had to admit that he was "profoundly disappointed" in the verdict. But he implored the nation not to lose faith in its system of criminal justice.

I hadn't wanted to speak. I didn't know if I could get the words out of my throat. I managed to say something about my sorrow for the families: "Their strength and dignity have been a source of inspiration." It was a poor expression of my feelings. I hadn't prepared more.

Chris was at the mike now. I heard him say, "I'm not bitter. . . .I'm not angry. I am honored to have—"

Then he choked and slumped forward. Several of us reached for him to keep him from falling. I put my hand on Chris's back and followed him through the thrashing strobes into the anteroom next to Gil's office.

"Anything I can do?" I asked him.

"I want to go to my office" was all he said.

As I watched him disappear down the hall, I stood for what seemed like an hour. I'm sure it was only minutes. And gradually, it dawned on me. *"I'm still here."*

Like someone walking out of the wreckage of a 747, I looked around and saw that I'd fallen 30,000 feet and my legs weren't broken. I wanted everyone to witness the fact of my survival. I wanted the law clerks, the brass, the TV crews, the black gals out in that Chicago women's shelter who'd cheered Simpson's acquittal, the jurors who were planning to attend O. J. Simpson's victory party in a few hours . . . I wanted them all to see me now. Bloody, dazed, and reeling. But upright. I wanted them to see that I'd stood for something. I wanted them to see that I'd put myself through hell for the right thing.

I had to believe that suffering was part of something bigger. Justice, like the will of God, doesn't always manifest itself on the spur of the moment. It doesn't always come when you think it should. You just gotta wait it out.

And when it comes, I'll still be standing. Without a doubt.

Postscript

After the verdict I slipped into a malaise. I told myself that this was only post-trial letdown, the kind you always feel after a verdict comes in—even when it's favorable. It takes a while to wean yourself off the adrenaline. But this was different.

For quite a while, five months at least, I couldn't shake the sense of dislocation. And guilt. I felt such guilt. I felt like I'd let everyone down. The Goldmans. The Browns. My team. The country. The fog didn't begin to lift until the spring of 1996, when I finally sat down to write.

Let me be perfectly frank with you. I am not a memoirist by nature. Left to my own inclinations, I might never have done this book. In a perfect world I would have slipped quietly out of the spotlight and tried to get some semblance of my old life back. But my old life was gone.

I could have continued being a D.A. But I knew what would happen. I wouldn't be able to try cases for a long, long time. Either the defense would try to get me removed, for fear the jury would be biased in my favor—or my own office would be afraid to deploy me, because a jury might be biased against me. As I saw it, the Simpson trial had ruined me as a prosecutor.

That caused me more pain than I can tell you. For fourteen years so much of my image of myself had rested upon being a deputy D.A., an advocate of the People, that leaving the office felt like amputating a limb. But I knew there was no place for me there any longer and I had to move on.

Throughout the trial, I would wake up at three in the morning with night sweats, worrying over how I would support two small sons. What kind of work could I get that would allow me to raise and educate them, that would also allow me to spend time with them? I don't mean "quality time." I wanted to be—please don't laugh—a soccer mom. In short, I wanted to do all those things that working mothers manage only with the greatest difficulty.

This book came to my rescue. When I received my contract—bearing a figure I could never have imagined in my wildest dreams—I breathed a sigh of relief, knowing that I could both support my family and do my writing at home.

But this book has done even more than give me financial peace of mind. It's given me an opportunity to set the record straight.

Since the verdict, I feel that my actual accomplishments—and those of my team—have been obscured by revisionism, some of it simpleminded, much of it downright vicious. I have found myself accused of being too arrogant and too meek; of being too flirtatious and too butch; of cozying up to Mark Fuhrman and of distancing myself from Mark Fuhrman; of protecting the LAPD and not being loyal enough to the LAPD; of being too attentive to detail and too inattentive to detail; of being too passionate and too listless; of being too high-minded and too underhanded. There has been no coherent theme to this criticism, which serves to underscore one point: when a verdict assumes the proportions of a national crisis, someone has to take the fall.

I know that to the vast majority of Americans, that verdict came as a gut shot. I've seen photos of the faces of people watching television as it was read back. I'm talking about the look of dumb shock caught on the face of Americans in bars and beauty salons and living rooms all over the country. They *knew* he was guilty. We all did. How could something like this happen in a country where every sixty-minute weekly courtroom drama has conditioned us to expect—in the face of overwhelming evidence of guilt—a triumph of justice?

Was the prosecution perfect? Of course not. No prosecution is perfect. If prosecutions had to be mistake-free, no defendant with a semiconscious lawyer would ever go to jail. But this truth seems to have been lost on the pop chroniclers who, during the months since the criminal verdict, have rewritten history. To a man, they've taken the easy road, pinning the blame for the verdict on me and my colleagues rather than explaining to their readers some very complex and brutal realities. The People lost this case not because we introduced too much evidence or too little evidence. We lost because American justice is distorted by race. We lost because American justice is corrupted by celebrity. Any lawyer willing to exploit those weaknesses can convince a jury predisposed to acquittal of just about anything. In the case of *People v. Orenthal James Simpson,* a handful of clever, expensive attorneys were allowed to manipulate the system by invoking the wholly irrelevant, yet provocative issue of racism.

In recent months I've watched members of Simpson's defense team try in their various ways to distance themselves from the race issue. Tune in to late-night TV talk, and you'll never hear them brag about what a clever move it was steering that kid from *The New Yorker* to the Fuhrman story. They've all been remarkably silent about that—with the exception of Alan Dershowitz, who has made some of the most baldly ill-considered comments I have heard on national airwaves.

Last December, while appearing as a guest commentator on *Rivera Live,* Dershowitz proclaimed that the defense had never really played the "race card," only the "perjury card." In this revisionist reality, we're asked to believe that it was really just Mark Fuhrman's *denial* of using racial epithets the defense was concerned about. Which conveniently ignores the fact that the Dream Team was arguing for the right to introduce the term "nigger" at least two months before Fuhrman even took the witness stand. Dershowitz was hooted off the screen by fellow commentators.

Make no mistake about it, this so-called Dream Team *played the race card.* I'd just like to ask those guys a question: Did it ever occur to you, as you broke your buns getting your spoiled, rich, sadistic jerk of a client acquitted, that you might just be putting public safety at risk? Whole neighborhoods of Los Angeles—and other cities—could have gone down in flames, Johnnie, because of your irresponsible, inflammatory rhetoric. And no amount of revisionist fast talk is going to change the fact that you guys pandered to racial hatred in order to win. You took a jury itching to avenge Rodney King and incited it to nullify the law. The result was a miscarriage of justice, which, in turn, left many whites gunning for payback.

In November 1996, California voters went to the polls and did something unthinkable: they voted to do away with affirmative action programs in this state. Think about that. Twenty years of social reforms blown away like ashes in the wind. I'm not alone in believing that Proposition 209 would never have stood an ice cube's chance in hell if white Californians had not been so infuriated by the Simpson verdict. There's all kinds of ways to riot: in the streets or at the ballot box. That's the problem with payback. It never stops.

As you might imagine, I followed O. J. Simpson's civil trial with bittersweet fascination. I like the idea that O. J. Simpson has been found "liable," as they say in civil law, for the deaths of Ron Goldman and Nicole Brown Simpson. Given the circumstances of those deaths, you can't very well hold him "liable" unless you buy the proposition that he slashed them to death. Bottom line, murder.

A civil trial, I'm sure I don't have to tell you, is a whole different ballgame. You've got a different standard of proof: "preponderance of evidence" instead of "reasonable doubt." In a civil case, you can present the kinds of evidence we could only dream about. I'm thinking of Nicole's diary and the results of O. J. Simpson's failed polygraph.

But the plaintiffs had something even better going the second time around. Public opinion was running against O. J. Simpson. The ramifications of that fact resonated throughout the proceedings. For the duration of the criminal trial, the aura of wealth and public acclaim still clung to defendant Simpson so stubbornly that even as he sat a prisoner in the dock, prospective witnesses pulled their punches, afraid of offending him. If they were sycophants or hangers-on, they didn't want to cut off the flow of his largesse. If they were honest-to-goodness admirers, they didn't want to be "the one" to bring him down.

After the criminal verdict, when public opinion turned abruptly against him, these same witnesses stuck a finger in the air, caught the shift in the wind, and altered their testimony accordingly. I couldn't believe it when I heard Kato Kaelin, who has apparently learned to speak in complete sentences, telling the world how distraught Simpson appeared on the night of the murders. And I regarded with absolute disgust the videotape of Paula Barbieri's deposition. When questioned by our office during the Al Cowlings investigation, she wouldn't even admit that she was Simpson's girlfriend. Now she's gabbing that she'd broken up with him the day of the murders.

Even more upsetting to me was the behavior of the expert witnesses. For the plaintiffs, Dr. Werner Spitz, the former chief medical examiner of Wayne County, Michigan, made himself available. We were never able to get him to do the same for us. And those scientific hotshots who'd renounced integrity to swap spit with the defense team? Dr. Henry Lee did not show his face in Santa Monica. Defense lawyers had to content themselves with introducing his videotaped deposition. And Dr. Michael Baden, who'd postulated during the criminal trial that the assailant had struggled with his victims for ten to fifteen minutes—an absurdly exaggerated estimate that gave credence to the defense time line—conceded during his testimony at the civil trial that the murders could have been committed in half that time.

Then, of course, there's the fact that O. J. Simpson *had* to testify this time around. As I predicted, his ego tripped him up big-time.

But the biggest blessing by far to drop into the plaintiffs' laps was a judge who took the reins tightly in that courtroom. Hiroshi Fujisaki kept cross-examination confined to the scope of the direct, as it should be. So the defense never got to play its case through the plaintiffs' witnesses. Most important, Fujisaki firmly refused to let race or Mark Fuhrman become an issue in this trial. The wild speculation that formed the cornerstone of the defense in the criminal case was now finally deemed inadmissible. Thank God for a judge with backbone.

While I hope the civil judgment has brought some peace to the victims' families, it leaves me with some lingering concerns. What kind of message does this verdict really send? That whenever you have a black defendant whom you simply *must* convict, you gotta be sure he's tried by white people? I felt a little queasy at the public rejoicing when a black juror in Santa Monica was booted for having a purported drinking problem. The ideal worth striving for, it seems to me, is that justice can be done in any venue, with any defendant. And for that to happen, there's going to have to be some serious rethinking of the jury system.

I am not a social theorist, but I do have a few informed suggestions. In order for the jury system to survive, we have to do something to ensure that every jury pool contains a true cross section of the community—not the most underemployed, least-invested segment of it. That means when a lawyer goes to pick a jury, she's looking at a room full of doctors, engineers, full-time moms and dads, teachers, students, secretaries, college chancellors, postal workers, supermarket cashiers. You need that whole range. I wouldn't want a jury of Ph.D.s any more than I'd want a jury of high school drop-outs.

The way it stands now, a lot of thoughtful employed citizens who have an interest in seeing that justice works can't afford to leave their jobs for eight months at a stretch. Somehow, some way, employers, the government, *somebody* is going to have to foot the bill for careful, honest, intelligent jurors to perform unlimited duty. The business lobby will shriek bloody murder at this. But the next time you hear some CEO on a soapbox complaining about how the Simpson jurors couldn't cut it, please remind him that you get the justice you pay for.

At the risk of sounding preachy, let me offer one earnest, and very personal, admonishment. The next time you receive a jury summons, respond and serve. A summons is not some party invitation to which you can RSVP. It is the notification of a legal and moral obligation. Don't complain about the verdicts that juries bring in if you won't answer the call. Enough said.

Other suggestions? Lawyers should be gagged, pure and simple. There'll always be leaks, but a judge with resolve can dream up sufficiently painful sanctions to make an attorney think twice before taking the risk. Next, kick cameras out of the courtroom. I didn't always feel this way. In fact, I started the Simpson trial believing that cameras could actually serve a useful purpose. Can you believe it—I thought they could teach the public what real trials are all about. The performance of the media in this case disabused me totally of that notion. The cameras in the Simpson courtroom not only encouraged lawyers to preen for the lens and prolong the life of every goddamned motion to increase their time on the air, it reduced a criminal trial to the status of a sporting event. Court TV has given rise to a bizarre burlesque of half-time commentary according to which one side or the other has "won" or "lost" on any given day. A criminal case is not won or lost by the motion or by the day. Its outcome is determined by weeks and months of cumulative testimony. Until someone yanks the cameras, the public will continue to be systematically miseducated about the process of justice.

Other small things spring to mind, such as stricter rules of evidence to keep defense attorneys from slipping so much swill into the record. But more regulations, new laws are not the answer. Laws are only as good as the people—the judges—who enforce them. There were ample laws on the books to keep Lance Ito from allowing the N-word into *People v. Orenthal James Simpson.* But he did it anyway. He caved to the bullying of the defense, and in committing that single egregious error, he assured a hung jury, if not acquittal.

I found the process of writing this book cathartic. It was painful at first having to get up every day to relive the stress, anxiety, and exhaustion of that marathon. But it was worth it. The more I wrote, the more my vision cleared. And as that happened, the sense of guilt lifted. In going back through the case day by grueling day, I rediscovered not only the pain but the exhilaration. Being forced to reexamine those months made me appreciate how hard we all fought, against impossible odds, to elicit justice from that jury.

In the future I will want to tell my sons about this case. And when I do, I will be able to hand them this book and say, "This is my story. Your mother was not perfect, but she had conviction. She fought with every ounce of strength for what she thought was right."

It's all we can ever do.

—February 28, 1997

_A_fterword

It's been a year since the initial publication of _Without a Doubt_. While I was writing it I was so completely immersed that I had no time to worry about whether anyone would still be interested in hearing what I had to say by the time the book came out. Which was a good thing, because how much can you worry about at once, anyway?

No sooner had the final draft gone to press though than that particular nightmare caught up with me big time. Of course it was at that exact moment that someone was so kind as to inform me that there had been almost fifty books published on the Simpson case since the verdict. I had an attack of nerves like you wouldn't believe. After all this time and all those books, who would care what anyone had to say about the trial?

When I started the book tour my stomach felt like it was weighted with lead. Sure, the talk show circuit wanted me, but given my under-cover status since the verdict, that was no surprise. The acid test would come with the first book signing and the publication of the bestseller lists. I looked forward to the former with more apprehension than I'd felt since jury selection. What if no one showed up?

On the day of the first book signing, I remember being hustled straight from a TV interview to Barnes & Noble in Manhattan. I kept my head down all the way, mostly so I wouldn't have to see that no one was there.

As I neared the door I finally had to lift my head or I'd walk into a wall. What I saw actually made me light-headed with relief. The line wrapped around the block! Those jaded, world-weary, no doubt Simpson-soaked New Yorkers had shown up in force to see me and have their books signed!

The following week my second fear was similarly laid to rest. With only half a week's sales to go on, the book was number six on the *New York Times* Bestseller List. After another week of sales it went straight to number one. Shortly thereafter, *USA Today* reported that the book topped the charts as number one over all: fiction, nonfiction, hardback, and paperback! It went on to top bestseller lists across the country, from Los Angeles to Washington.

I couldn't have hoped for more, but I got it anyway.

The interminable media interviews that so often repeated the same questions were grueling. The only things that really kept me going were the book signings, where I got to meet the people. I loved every single one of those. I've never seen so many warm, kind-hearted people in one spot in my entire life, and I left every signing with my flagging, interview-drained energy renewed.

And some of those signings were a real hoot.

In L.A., where I thought I'd encounter the greatest ennui of all, I found lines wrapped around the block at both signings I did. Some of the most hilarious and fun people I'd met on tour were there. Like the tall, nice-looking man in casual but conservative dress who shared photographs of himself taken the previous Halloween when he went as—you guessed it—ME! The hair, the serious skirt suit, the whole shooting match. I laughed so hard I couldn't breathe. And he handed me a letter of real warmth and kindness, which I'll treasure forever. In fact, there were so many who came to express their appreciation, I was humbled with gratitude.

At the book signing in Santa Monica the angel of a store manager had the Doors playing on the sound system and actually gave me the CDs at the end. And all over the country I kept hearing from women—and from men too—that I had inspired them to do all kinds of things, like finish school, go into law, get out of a bad relationship. I can't tell you how good that felt. The outpouring of support I received went a long way toward healing the wounds of TFC.

I'd be lying to you if I suggested I've reached some Zen plane of tranquillity. I thrive, as usual, on constant motion. But I do feel more at peace with myself and the world than at any time since that June morning when I first laid eyes on Bundy. I know that some of my critics complained that I didn't take the fall for O. J. Simpson's acquittal. But I am not going to make empty gestures of contrition to placate them.

It's much easier to blame an individual than to understand the far more complex realities that led to that verdict. Those critics, who I can now see are in the minority, were not there with me when I had to stare down the Juice groupies who called themselves prospective jurors. They didn't live through day after grueling day in that pressure cooker of a courtroom and they weren't there to see the endless strategy meetings, debates, and scrutiny that went into nearly every move.

But I did. I did all my second-guessing before the fact; there's none left to do now.

Will I ever return to the criminal justice system? I can't say never. Maybe as a judge? In a few more years, I think I might really enjoy that. I'll take it as it comes.

I do know this: I have no more fuel to burn on outrage. I'd rather spend the years I have left on the positive side of things, finding ways to help, inform, and kindle hope.

There—that's nice and open-ended. Now we'll see what happens.

Acknowledgments

To the Brown and Goldman families: My deepest sympathies and gratitude for your support and understanding. I want to especially thank Fred, Patti, and Kim for their unswerving loyalty and kindness throughout this ordeal. I hope the sun is shining for you now.

To all the people who were so kind and thoughtful as to send letters, faxes, presents, and messages to show their support: You lifted my spirits and helped me get through the long, lonely days and nights. Thank you all.

To the real Dream Team: William Hodgman—you are a true friend, a team player, and a helluva lawyer. Hank Goldberg—the word "trouper" was invented for you. Your soul and brilliance were a constant source of strength and inspiration. Scott Gordon—a dear friend whose dedication and insight were indispensable to the case, and to me. Bless you and your wonderful wife, Lisa. Cheri Lewis—who innocently befriended me before the case and got repaid with a spot on the Simpson team. Your loyalty, talent, and inexhaustible energy cannot be overstated. I will be forever grateful to you. It was a joy to work with you—and we're still having fun, hey girlfriend? Brian Kelberg—my guru. I've been blessed to have had the privilege of your advice and your friendship over the years. Your work was a source of pride and inspiration to us all. I wish you only the best; you deserve nothing less. Lisa Kahn—thank you, Lisa, for teaching me so patiently, for making me laugh till my sides ached, for being a friend, and for your excellent work. Lydia Bodin—for your help on the domestic violence evidence, it's been great working with you. George "Woody" Clarke and Rockne Harmon—I really can't thank you guys enough for your brilliant work. It was an honor to have you as colleagues. Alan Yochelson, Terry White, Pat Dixon, and John Zajec—your work behind the scenes, investigating, advising, and just being supportive, was great. You're terrific guys. Letty Minjares, my former secretary/assistant, and Cathy Ozawa—I was so lucky to get to work with you, both on the case and before. You're both gems. The young lawyers: Dana Escobar, my dragon-slaying assistant—you were dynamite; you're going to tear them up in court. Kenneth Lynch, Diana Martinez, David Wooden, Darrel Mavis, and Michael Runyon—you were real pros who knew how to give heart and soul. The newest lawyers: Tracy Miller—special thanks to you, Tracy, for all your help on this book after that grueling trial. Natalie Agajanian, Melissa Decker, Kathy Behfarin, Susan Dozier, Lisa Fox, Michael Price, Matthew Gibbs, and Tom Ratanavaraha—your energy, optimism, and support were unparalleled. Gavin de Becker—how many times have you come to my rescue? You are a rare and special man.

The L.A. County District Attorney investigators: Michael Stevens, Dana Thompson, Pat McPherson, Steve Oppler, Jack Gonterman, George Mueller, Bill Guidas, Brian Hale, Will Abrams, Ken Godinez, Mike Armstrong—for your outstanding investigative work, but even more for keeping us safe. Thank you from the bottom of my heart. Lieutenant Gary Schram—God bless you, Gary. You were my guardian angel. I don't know what I would have done without you.

To my friends on the LAPD—it's been a real privilege to know you and to work with you. Thank you all.

To Media Relations—Maria Pollerana and Elka Woerner, for your dedication and understanding. Sandi Gibbons—it sure was great working with you, we've had some good times. I miss you. Suzanne Childs—I can't count all the times you ran interference for me, nor can I repay you. Just know that my gratitude is endless.

Chris—for being there when I needed you, for knowing what to say when it counted, for marching through hell with me. Thank you, partner.

To all my friends in the D.A.'s office—I've loved working with you and I'm proud to have known you. Gil Garcetti—there couldn't have been a boss more understanding or supportive. It's been an honor to have worked for you. C.H.—my former colleague, for your wisdom, support, and friendship. Bless you.

Allan Schwartz, my lawyer, and his assistant, Pie Walker—thank you for helping to make this book possible.

Norman Brokaw, chairman and CEO of William Morris, my agent, my friend, and my guide, and his assistants Mary Feinberg, Linda Pollack-Violante, and Dana Schelette; and also Maggie, who kindly turned her house over for this effort. Joni Evans, my tireless literary agent, and her assistant, Sarah Rosen, for all your hard work above and beyond the call of duty. William Novak, who helped out of sheer goodness. Esther Newberg; her assistant, Jack Horner; and Victor Kovner, who cheered us on from the wings.

Viking Penguin: Pamela Dorman and Barbara Grossman, I can never adequately thank you for your vision, support, and unflagging belief in this project. I'd also like to applaud the editorial team who worked overtime and beyond: Susan Hans O'Connor; Victoria Wright, our transcriber; Mervyn Keizer; Dot McMahon, photo researcher; in-house counsel Karen Mayer and Maura Wogan of Frankfurt, Garbus, Klein & Selz; copyeditor Jolanta Benal, and Cynthia Achar, Roni Axelrod, Paul Buckley, Leigh Butler, Hal Fessenden, Kate Griggs, Cathy Hemming, Patti Kelly, Laurie Rippon, Teddy Rosenbaum, and Jaye Zimet. Special thanks to Phyllis Grann and Michael Lynton. I'm so proud of our team, who pulled together to make the vision come true. Thank you.

Judith Forman, my lawyer and dear friend, and her assistant, Ruth Becker—how did you put up with me? My gratitude is boundless. Thank you so much for all you've done. Mark Fleischer and Susan Fleischer—you were balm on an aching soul. You're wonderful. Allen Edwards and Eugenia West—my hair and my face—thank you. Roz Dauber, my "oldest" friend— I mean my only childhood friend. Thank you for being there for me. So who woulda thunk it, Rozzie? Jon, my brother—could there ever be a better brother? Brother, confidant, therapist, you name it, that's what you've been to me, through thick and thin, all my life. I love you, Jonnie. Lynn Reed— my best friend, sister for life. I swear we were separated at birth. You were there through some of my darkest hours. Could I have made it without you? I don't know, and I'm glad I didn't have to find out. I don't think anyone ever owed a friend more. All my love and gratitude to you, Marc, and Matthew.

Mitchell Kashmar—how did I get so lucky to have found you? Your love and support got me through so many rough spots, not to mention the ordeal of writing this book. You've made my whole world brighter. I could write reams about it, but I'll just say it this way: I love you.

Teresa Carpenter, Steven Levy, and Andrew Levy:

Teresa—I couldn't have made a better choice. What you do is magic, nothing less. You are absolutely brilliant. Not to mention a wonderful person. Knowing you, working with you, has enriched me in ways I couldn't have imagined. I want to thank you for all your hard work, but more than that, I want to thank you for coming into my life. I don't have enough superlatives in my vocabulary to express my appreciation and my admiration for what you did, and for who you are. Steven Levy—what a pleasure it's been to work with you and talk to you! I don't know what we would have done without you. You came to our rescue when we needed it most. I can't thank you enough for your help on this project. Man, you are good. And Andrew—thank you for loaning me your mommy. I know it's been tough, but you've been a good sport and I'm going to make it up to you. I think it's time for a trip to Disneyland, what do you say?

Index

FOR THE BEST IN PAPERBACKS, LOOK FOR THE

In every corner of the world, on every subject under the sun, Penguin represents quality and variety—the very best in publishing today.

For complete information about books available from Penguin—including Puffins, Penguin Classics, and Arkana—and how to order them, write to us at the appropriate address below. Please note that for copyright reasons the selection of books varies from country to country.

In the United Kingdom: Please write to *Dept. JC, Penguin Books Ltd, FREEPOST, West Drayton, Middlesex UB7 0BR*.

If you have any difficulty in obtaining a title, please send your order with the correct money, plus ten percent for postage and packaging, to *P.O. Box No. 11, West Drayton, Middlesex UB7 0BR*

In the United States: Please write to *Consumer Sales, Penguin USA, P.O. Box 999, Dept. 17109, Bergenfield, New Jersey 07621-0120.* VISA and MasterCard holders call 1-800-253-6476 to order all Penguin titles

In Canada: Please write to *Penguin Books Canada Ltd, 10 Alcorn Avenue, Suite 300, Toronto, Ontario M4V 3B2*

In Australia: Please write to *Penguin Books Australia Ltd, P.O. Box 257, Ringwood, Victoria 3134*

In New Zealand: Please write to *Penguin Books (NZ) Ltd, Private Bag 102902, North Shore Mail Centre, Auckland 10*

In India: Please write to *Penguin Books India Pvt Ltd, 706 Eros Apartments, 56 Nehru Place, New Delhi 110 019*

In the Netherlands: Please write to *Penguin Books Netherlands bv, Postbus 3507, NL-1001 AH Amsterdam*

In Germany: Please write to *Penguin Books Deutschland GmbH, Metzlerstrasse 26, 60594 Frankfurt am Main*

In Spain: Please write to *Penguin Books S. A., Bravo Murillo 19, 1° B, 28015 Madrid*

In Italy: Please write to *Penguin Italia s.r.l., Via Felice Casati 20, I-20124 Milano*

In France: Please write to *Penguin France S. A., 17 rue Lejeune, F-31000 Toulouse*

In Japan: Please write to *Penguin Books Japan, Ishikiribashi Building, 2-5-4, Suido, Bunkyo-ku, Tokyo 112*

In Greece: Please write to *Penguin Hellas Ltd, Dimocritou 3, GR-106 71 Athens*

In South Africa: Please write to *Longman Penguin Southern Africa (Pty) Ltd, Private Bag X08, Bertsham 2013*